Performance-Based INSTRUCTIONAL DESIGN

David J. Pucel, Ph.D.
Professor, Department of Vocational
and Technical Education
University of Minnesota
St. Paul, Minnesota

Gregg Division
McGraw-Hill Publishing Company

New York Atlanta Dallas St. Louis San Francisco
Auckland Bogotá Caracas Hamburg Lisbon
London Madrid Mexico Milan Montreal New Delhi
Paris San Juan São Paulo Singapore
Sydney Tokyo Toronto

Sponsoring Editor: Mary McGarry
Design and Art Supervisor: Janice Noto
Production Supervisor: Kathryn Porzio

Text Designer: Delgado Design, Inc.
Cover Design: Edward Smith Design, Inc.

Library of Congress Cataloging-in-Publication Data

Pucel, David J.
Performance-based instructional design.

Includes index.
1. Instructional systems—Design. 2. Educational evaluation. I. Title.
LB1028.35.P83 1989 371.3 88-27197
ISBN 0-07-050911-5

Performance-Based Instructional Design

1 2 3 4 5 6 7 8 9 0 EBREBR 8 9 6 5 4 3 2 1 0 9

ISBN 0-07-050911-5

CONTENTS

PREFACE/ viii

CHAPTER 1
Introduction/ 3

CHAPTER OBJECTIVE/ 4

OVERVIEW/ 4
- Instructional Design and the Individual/ 5
- The Need for Instructional Design/ 5

SOCIETY'S EXPECTATIONS OF OCCUPATIONAL EDUCATION/ 5

THE EVOLUTION OF PERFORMANCE-BASED INSTRUCTION/ 7
- The First Generation: Responding to the Industrial Age/ 7
- The Second Generation: Implementing the Systems Approach and Mastery Learning/ 8
- The Next Generation: Adapting to the Information Age/ 11

SUMMARY/ 12

ACTIVITIES AND EVALUATION/ 12

REFERENCES/ 13

CHAPTER 2
The Performance-Based Instructional Design System/ 15

CHAPTER OBJECTIVE/ 16

OVERVIEW/ 16

INTENT OF THE SYSTEM/ 16

COMPONENTS/ 17
- Program Description/ 17
- Content Analysis/ 17
- Content Selection/ 19
- Content Sequencing/ 20
- Lesson Structuring/ 21
- Lesson Delivery Formatting/ 24
- Evaluation and Feedback Procedures/ 25

SUMMARY/ 25

ACTIVITIES AND EVALUATION/ 25

REFERENCES/ 25

CHAPTER 3
Program Description/ 27

CHAPTER OBJECTIVE/ 28

OVERVIEW/ 28

COMPONENTS/ 28
- The Content Area/ 28
- The Context/ 29

VALIDATION/ 31

SUMMARY/ 31

ACTIVITIES AND EVALUATION/ 31

REFERENCES/ 31

CHAPTER 4
Content Analysis: Function Identification and Behavior Analysis/ 33

CHAPTER OBJECTIVE/ 34

OVERVIEW/ 34

STATING BEHAVIORS/ 34

TYPES OF BEHAVIORS/ 35

FUNCTION IDENTIFICATION/ 36

BEHAVIOR ANALYSIS/ 38
- Alternative Methods of Identifying Behaviors/ 38
- Preparing to Conduct a Behavior Analysis/ 39
- Developing the Analysis Chart and Analyzing Psychomotor Behaviors/ 40
- Analyzing Cognitive Behaviors/ 41
- Analyzing Affective Behaviors/ 41

DEVELOPING A BEHAVIOR LISTING/ 42

SUMMARY/ 43

ACTIVITIES AND EVALUATION/ 43

REFERENCES/ 43

CHAPTER 5
Content Selection/ 45

CHAPTER OBJECTIVE/ 45

OVERVIEW/ 46

PROCEDURE FOR SELECTING BEHAVIORS/ 46
Determining the Program Length/ 47
Estimating the Instructional Time to Teach Each Behavior/ 47
Assigning the Priority Rankings/ 47

VALIDATING PRIORITY JUDGMENTS/ 48

DETERMINING PROGRAM PREREQUISITES VERSUS BEHAVIORS TO BE TAUGHT IN THE PROGRAM/ 48

COSTS AND BEHAVIOR SELECTION/ 49

SUMMARY/ 49

ACTIVITIES AND EVALUATION/ 49

CHAPTER 6
Content Sequencing/ 51

CHAPTER OBJECTIVE/ 52

OVERVIEW/ 52
Meaning and Sequencing/ 52
Efficiency and Sequencing/ 52
Sequencing for Meaning/ 53

SEQUENCING PROCEDURES/ 54
Dependent and Independent Behaviors/ 54
Content Dependency/ 56
Proximity Dependency/ 56

DETERMINING THE DEPENDENCY AMONG BEHAVIORS/ 56

SEQUENCING THE BEHAVIORS/ 57

DEVELOPING COURSES/ 57

DEVELOPING SEQUENCE CHARTS/ 58

BRANCHING SEQUENCES/ 58

LINEAR SEQUENCES/ 58

SUMMARY/ 59

ACTIVITIES AND EVALUATION/ 59

REFERENCES/ 59

CHAPTER 7
Content Analysis:
Behavior Detailing/ 61

CHAPTER OBJECTIVE/ 61

OVERVIEW/ 62

PROCESS DETAILING/ 62
Types of Processes/ 62
Stating the Process/ 63
Alternative Process-Detailing Approaches/ 64
Knowledge-Base Identification/ 65

DETERMINING HOW FAR TO BREAK DOWN BEHAVIORS/ 66

SUMMARY/ 67

ACTIVITIES AND EVALUATION/ 67

REFERENCE/ 67

CHAPTER 8
Lesson Structuring:
Behavioral Objectives,
Lesson Flow, and Content/ 69

CHAPTER OBJECTIVE/ 70

OVERVIEW/ 70

LESSON STRUCTURING STEPS/ 71
Developing the Behavioral Objective/ 71
Developing the Lesson Flow/ 73
Specify the Content to Be Taught/ 77

SUMMARY/ 77

ACTIVITIES AND EVALUATION/ 77

REFERENCES/ 77

CHAPTER 9
Lesson Structuring:
Selecting Lesson Delivery Format,
Methods, and Media/ 79

CHAPTER OBJECTIVE/ 80

OVERVIEW/ 80

SELECTING THE LESSON DELIVERY FORMAT/ 80
Lesson Management/ 81
Types of Content/ 82
Types of Learning Resources/ 82
Need for Uniformity of Instruction and Performance Assurance/ 83

SELECTING METHODS AND MEDIA/ 83
Instructional Methods Selection/ 84
Media Selection/ 85

SPECIFYING THE METHODS AND MEDIA/ 88

SUMMARY/ 88

ACTIVITIES AND EVALUATION/ 91

REFERENCES/ 91

CHAPTER 10
Lesson Structuring:
Selecting Evaluation
and Feedback Procedures/ 93

CHAPTER OBJECTIVE/ 94

OVERVIEW/ 94

SELECTING EVALUATION PROCEDURES/ 94

Formality of the Evaluation/ 94
Type of Content to Be Evaluated/ 95
Indicating the Evaluation Procedures Selections/ 97

SELECTING FEEDBACK PROCEDURES/ 98
Forms of Feedback Procedures/ 98
Types of Feedback/ 98
Entering Feedback Selections in the Lesson Structure/ 101

SUMMARY/ 101

ACTIVITIES AND EVALUATION/ 101

REFERENCES/ 101

CHAPTER 11
Formatting Traditional and Modularized Instruction, and Creating Multiple-Lesson Units/ 103

CHAPTER OBJECTIVE/ 104

OVERVIEW/ 104

FORMATS VERSUS LEARNING RESOURCES/ 104

EXPLICIT AND IMPLICIT LESSON PLANS/ 105

FORMATTING TRADITIONAL INSTRUCTION/ 106

FORMATTING MODULARIZED INSTRUCTION/ 106

COMBINING SEPARATE BEHAVIORS INTO LARGER UNITS/ 107
Developing Multiple-Behavior Delivery Units/ 108
Developing Learning Packages/ 108
Teaching Lessons Near One Another/ 109

SUMMARY/ 109

ACTIVITIES AND EVALUATION/ 109

CHAPTER 12
Formatting Programmed and Computer-Assisted Instruction/ 111

CHAPTER OBJECTIVE/ 112

OVERVIEW/ 112

FORMATTING PROGRAMMED INSTRUCTION/ 113

INTRODUCTION TO COMPUTER-ASSISTED INSTRUCTION PROGRAMS/ 116

FORMATTING COMPUTER-ASSISTED INSTRUCTION (CAI)/ 117

SUMMARY/ 122

ACTIVITIES AND EVALUATION/ 122

REFERENCES/ 123

CHAPTER 13
Programming CAI/ 125

CHAPTER OBJECTIVE/ 126

OVERVIEW/ 126

COMMUNICATING WITH THE COMPUTER/ 126

SELECTING HARDWARE FOR INSTRUCTIONAL PROGRAMS/ 126

ALTERNATIVE METHODS OF AUTHORING SOFTWARE/ 127
Programming Languages/ 128
Authoring Systems/ 128

SELECTING THE METHOD OF AUTHORING SOFTWARE/ 129

DEVELOPING SCREENS/ 130
Content Organization/ 130
Text Writing/ 131
Scrolling/ 131
Graphics/ 131
Density/ 131
Highlighting/ 131
Interactive Video Segments/ 132
Conventions/ 132

SUMMARY/ 132

ACTIVITIES AND EVALUATION/ 132

REFERENCES/ 132

CHAPTER 14
Introduction to Evaluation Procedures Development/ 135

CHAPTER OBJECTIVES/ 136

OVERVIEW/ 136

OVERALL GOAL OF EVALUATION/ 136

THE TIMING AND INTENT OF EVALUATION/ 136
Pretesting/ 136
Testing During Instructional Delivery/ 137
Posttesting/ 137

EVALUATING VERSUS MEASURING/ 137

EVALUATION ERROR/ 137
Learner Error/ 138
Instrument Error/ 138
Scorer Error/ 138
Guessing Error/ 138

NEED FOR MULTIPLE EVALUATIONS/ 139

CHARACTERISTICS OF GOOD EVALUATION/ 139
Validity/ 139
Comprehensiveness/ 139
Discrimination/ 139

Objectivity/ 140
Reliability/ 140

SUMMARY/ 140

ACTIVITIES AND EVALUATION/ 141

CHAPTER 15
Developing Knowledge-Base Evaluation Instruments/ 143

CHAPTER OBJECTIVE/ 144

OVERVIEW/ 144

LEVELS OF TEST ITEMS/ 144
Knowledge-Level Items/ 144
Comprehension-Level Items/ 144
Application-Level Items/ 145

TEST-CONSTRUCTION BLUEPRINT/ 146

CONSTRUCTING TEST ITEMS/ 146
Objective Items/ 147
Subjective Items/ 149

ASSEMBLING A TEST/ 152
Item Order/ 152
Test Heading/ 152
Directions/ 152
Item Numbering/ 153
Space For Responses/ 153

SUMMARY/ 153

ACTIVITIES AND EVALUATION/ 153

REFERENCES/ 153

CHAPTER 16
Developing Performance Tests/ 155

CHAPTER OBJECTIVE/ 156

OVERVIEW/ 156

PERFORMANCE TEST DEVELOPMENT PROCEDURES/ 156
Psychomotor Performance Tests/ 157
Cognitive Performance Tests/ 160
Affective Performance Tests/ 160

PERFORMANCE TEST ASSIGNMENTS/ 162
Psychomotor or Cognitive Performance Test Assignment/ 162
Affective Performance Test Assignment/ 163

SUMMARY/ 164

ACTIVITIES AND EVALUATION/ 165

REFERENCE/ 165

CHAPTER 17
Developing Product Tests/ 167

CHAPTER OBJECTIVE/ 168

OVERVIEW/ 168

PRODUCT TEST DEVELOPMENT/ 168
Objective/ 168
Product Characteristics/ 169
Criteria/ 169
Scoring Procedure/ 169
Performance Time/ 169
Minimum Acceptable Score/ 170

PRODUCT TEST ASSIGNMENT/ 170

INSTRUCTOR CHECKPOINTS/ 170

RATING SCALES/ 171

SUMMARY/ 172

ACTIVITIES AND EVALUATION/ 172

REFERENCE/ 172

CHAPTER 18
Informal Evaluation/ 173

CHAPTER OBJECTIVE/ 174

OVERVIEW/ 174

DEVELOPING INFORMAL EVALUATION PROCEDURES/ 174
Self-Checks/ 174
Tutorial Questioning and Observation/ 174

SUMMARY/ 176

ACTIVITIES AND EVALUATION/ 176

CHAPTER 19
Summarizing and Reporting Learner Progress/ 177

OVERVIEW/ 178

ALTERNATIVE TYPES OF REPORTING/ 178
Mastery Approach/ 178
Multiple-Criterion Approach/ 181
Time-Period Approach/ 182

POSTINSTRUCTION PROGRESS/ 183

SUMMARY/ 185

ACTIVITIES AND EVALUATION/ 185

REFERENCES/ 185

APPENDIXES

Appendix A: National College Verb List: The Functional, Forceful Four Hundred Fifty-Five/ 187

Appendix B: Legal Office Procedures PBID Sample Components/ 190

Appendix C: Introduction to (IBM) Microcomputer Systems PBID Sample Components/ 201

Appendix D: Sample Written Test: Apply for a Job/ 213

Appendix E: Sample Written Test: Communicate with Others/ 219

Appendix F: Telemarketing Call Performance Checklist/ 224

Appendix G: Separate from a Child Performance Checklist/ 226

Glossary/ 229

Index/ 233

Preface

Performance and productivity have become essential measurements of knowledge and skills in all occupations in the information age. At the same time, the amount of specific knowledge and skills required for adequate performance and productivity has increased significantly, leading to the need for more formal education and training as well as for effective and efficient methods of planning and evaluating instruction. Further, the instruction must include the psychomotor skills of manipulating tools and objects, the cognitive skills of mentally processing information, and the affective skills of exhibiting occupationally relevant emotional tones toward people, data, and things.

Performance-Based Instructional Design (PBID) presents a system for planning and evaluating instruction which is focused on preparing people to perform effectively and efficiently in all information-age occupations. The PBID system is organized into seven components that parallel the decision-making process for developing and evaluating instruction:

1. Program description
2. Content analysis
3. Content selection
4. Content sequencing
5. Lesson structuring (planning)
6. Lesson delivery formatting
7. Evaluation and feedback procedures development

PBID is a *system.* The output from one component becomes the input for other components, and the sum of all the components results in an integrated plan of instruction. The system focuses on developing the capability of individuals to perform. Therefore, the goal is learning—that is, a change in behavior brought about through instruction. This definition of learning sets the stage for the development of implementation of PBID.

PBID is based on research on learning and instruction. One premise of the system is that meaningful learning will allow people to see interrelationships that facilitate the transferability of what they learn to new situations.

Teachers and instructional designers in many fields of vocational education and training in business and industry have used the PBID system successfully. People who have used the PBID system report reduced time to learn instructional design and increased ability to produce quality curricula in all occupational fields.

PBID is the basis of courses in instructional development and evaluation at the University of Minnesota, State University of New York at Buffalo, Southern Illinois University, Western Michigan University, and others. It is also used as the basis for curriculum development by a number of vocational schools and technical institutes, among them St. Cloud Technical Institute, St. Cloud, Minnesota; Houston Community College, Houston, Texas; Northwest Technical Institute, Green Bay, Wisconsin; and British Columbia Institute of Technology, Burnaby, British Columbia. Further, PBID is used in business and industry—for example, by the *Minneapolis Star and Tribune* in Minneapolis, Minnesota; Minnesota Department of Transportation, St. Paul; and Instructional Systems Design, Buffalo, New York.

David J. Pucel

Performance-Based INSTRUCTIONAL DESIGN

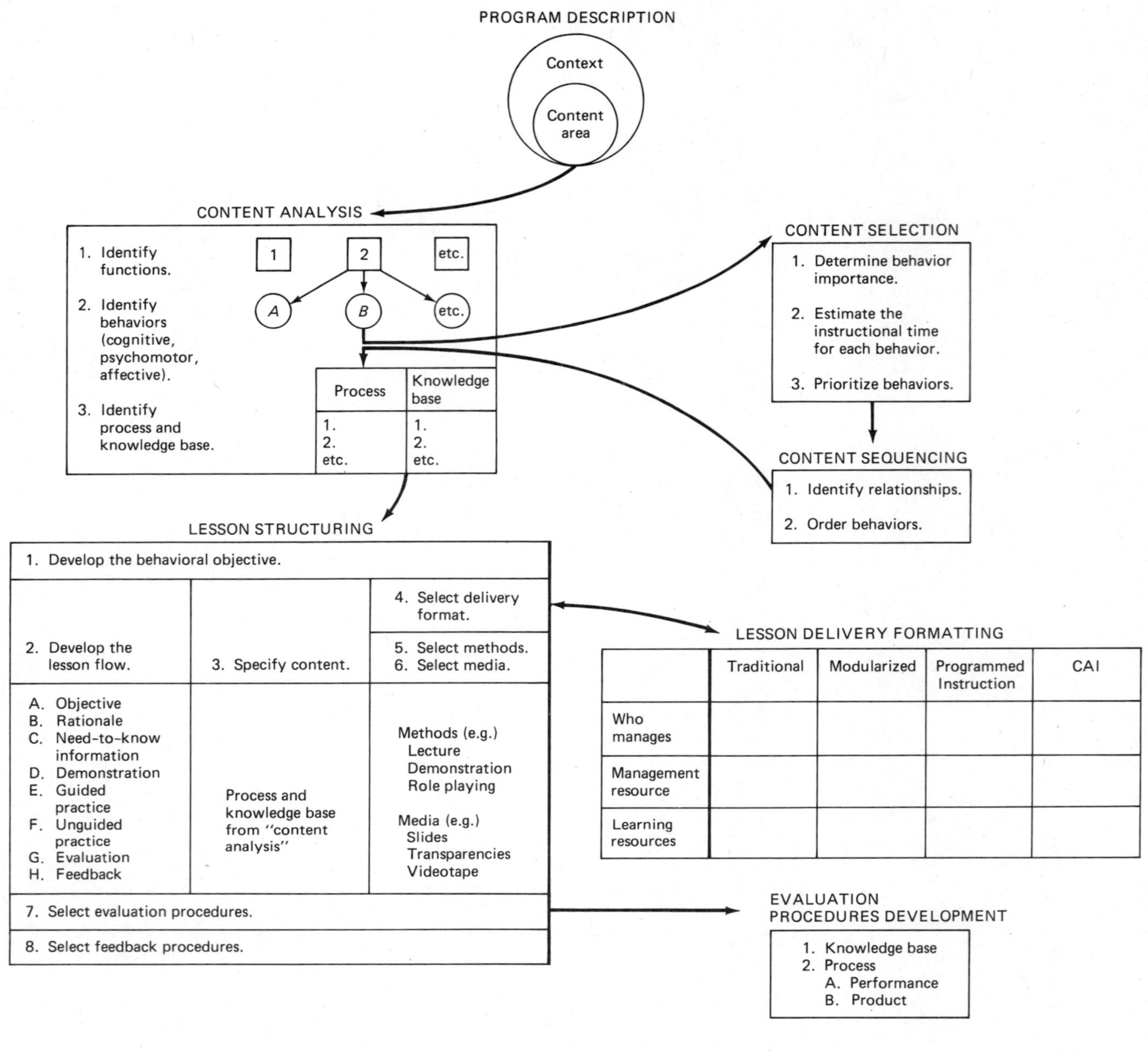
PROGRAM DESCRIPTION
Context
Content area
CONTENT ANALYSIS
1. Identify functions.
2. Identify behaviors (cognitive, psychomotor, affective).
3. Identify process and knowledge base.
1
2
etc.
A
B
etc.
Process
Knowledge base
1.
2.
etc.
1.
2.
etc.
CONTENT SELECTION
1. Determine behavior importance.
2. Estimate the instructional time for each behavior.
3. Prioritize behaviors.
CONTENT SEQUENCING
1. Identify relationships.
2. Order behaviors.
LESSON STRUCTURING
1. Develop the behavioral objective.
2. Develop the lesson flow.
3. Specify content.
4. Select delivery format.
5. Select methods.
6. Select media.
A. Objective
B. Rationale
C. Need-to-know information
D. Demonstration
E. Guided practice
F. Unguided practice
G. Evaluation
H. Feedback
Process and knowledge base from "content analysis"
Methods (e.g.)
Lecture
Demonstration
Role playing
Media (e.g.)
Slides
Transparencies
Videotape
7. Select evaluation procedures.
8. Select feedback procedures.
LESSON DELIVERY FORMATTING
Traditional
Modularized
Programmed Instruction
CAI
Who manages
Management resource
Learning resources
EVALUATION PROCEDURES DEVELOPMENT
1. Knowledge base
2. Process
A. Performance
B. Product

Introduction

▽ CHAPTER OBJECTIVE

Givens

An overview of the history of instructional design for vocational education and training in business and industry and its relationship to a changing society

Behavior

Recall the role of performance-based instructional design (PBID) in meeting the changing educational needs and expectations of society

Standard

Explanations of the evolution and purposes of performance-based instruction will be consistent with its historical development.

OVERVIEW

The *performance-based instructional design (PBID)* system is a set of procedures for assisting educators and trainers in planning and evaluating instruction; its focus is on performance capability. The system was designed for instructors to prepare instruction consistent with a society that has evolved to an information age, and that now emphasizes service. It presents precise techniques for developing and evaluating instruction, and it teaches people to make decisions and to efficiently interact with others in addition to manipulating tools and objects.

The PBID system is compatible with traditional, competency-based, programmed, and computer-assisted instruction (CAI). (See Chapter 2.) It supports the development of each of these types of instruction by using techniques which represent the next generation of instructional design systems. It is based on 20 years of experience with people in vocational education and in training for business and industry. The first generation of this system, published in *Individualizing Vocational and Technical Instruction* (Pucel and Knaak, 1975), was consistent with the evolving concepts of competency-based education during the 1970s and early 1980s. PBID capitalizes on the good things that have been learned about the design of typical competency-based instruction and goes beyond to address issues that have been frustrating instructional developers, such as how to design instruction for roles which require more decision making and interpersonal interaction, and proportionately less physical manipulation of tools and objects.

The PBID system presents step-by-step procedures for designing and evaluating instruction for all three major domains of behavior: psychomotor (e.g., the manipulation of tools and objects), cognitive (e.g., the processing of information, as during decision making), and affective (e.g., the communication of emotional tones such as feelings).

The major concepts of instructional design are presented as a system in the order in which instructional programs are typically developed. All of the major components are additive to a whole concept of the instructional design. The presentation of components starts with the assumption that a needs assessment has already been conducted which has established the need for an instructional program. In other words, someone has already decided that a program—whether it be a machine shop program, a data processing program, a practical nursing program, a remedial math program, a parenting program, or a management development program—needs to be developed or modified. The instructional designer (often the instructor) is then asked to develop the program.

Throughout this book an *instructional program* is defined as the total amount of instruction to be developed regarding a content area (e.g., a role, an occupation, or a type of basic skill). A program typically includes instruction about more than one behavior and is limited to one content area. At times a program might include only a series of lessions regarding a limited set of skills; at other times it might include a course or series of courses, or all of the instruction needed to prepare people for an occupation. Ways of specifying the particular type of instructional program are explained further in Chapter 3.

This book's discussion of the PBID system concludes with a brief discussion of postinstruction evaluation of the impact of the program. The evaluation is based on the extent to which learners have modified their behavior as a means for accomplishing both their goals and the goals of the program. Can they obtain and maintain a job in an occupation? Are they more effective parents? Are they more efficient managers?

The system components presented concentrate primarily on the planning of instruction and the evaluation of instruction. Although in-depth discussions of establishing the need for a program and the evaluation of postinstruction outcomes are beyond the scope of this book, they are recognized as additional components to the total design process.

The major PBID components presented include:

- How to develop program descriptions
- How to analyze content to be taught (including psychomotor, cognitive, and affective behaviors)
- How to select specific content to be taught from that which was analyzed
- How to sequence the content for presentation to learners
- How to structure performance-based lessons (e.g., how to organize lessons, select methods and media, and select evaluation and feedback procedures)

- How to format lessons for delivery to learners using the traditional, modularized, programmed, and computer-assisted instruction formats
- How to evaluate the ability of learners to perform

Instructional Design and the Individual

We assume, as instructional design is presented, that the needs of individual learners must be met as they proceed through instruction. The PBID system is based on diagnostic evaluation, feedback, and instruction which assist individuals in performing desired behaviors. Each learner is unique and requires individual attention and evaluation throughout instruction to attain performance capability. Individual attention includes, when appropriate, the adaptation of instructional methods and media.

In designing instruction one must consider not only effectiveness for individuals but also the efficiency of instruction. There is no doubt that all of us would learn best if every element of instruction were tailored to our individual needs—for example, if individual tutors could design instruction only for us. However, such instruction would be impossible to deliver because of the cost, personnel, and other resources required. Therefore, the instruction to be developed must be based on an anticipated group of learners. Members of the group should take part in the program with a clear understanding that variations to accommodate individuals will have to be made during the delivery of that instruction. These accommodations can be facilitated by understanding individual learning styles and by diagnostic evaluation throughout the instructional process.

The Need for Instructional Design

Changes in society have caused increased concern about the need to effectively and efficiently educate people so that they can occupy constructive roles within society. The amount of content to be communicated is growing rapidly, the amount of highly specialized knowledge is increasing, the numbers of people requiring the same content is increasing, and the cost of errors due to inadequate learning is becoming greater. These concerns have, in turn, raised public questions about how education is planned and delivered: What should be taught? How should it be taught? What assurance is there that people have learned? In response, educators have had to study educational practice in more intensive ways. "Today, in the United States, professional students of education tend increasingly to work as scientists; in the future, this trend surely will not be reversed" (Beck, p. 95). Educators are assembling knowledge about what works best with which types of learners. They are adopting learning theories as a basis for designing educational practice. They are also examining their goals in terms of the society within which the education is to take place.

Education is also being viewed as a lifelong necessity. Our technology and culture are changing so rapidly that people need to continually evolve. A doctor or a carpenter who does not keep up with new technology and techniques is out of date within a short period of time. That is also true for factory workers and farmers.

The remainder of this chapter is focused on showing how the evolution of society eventually brings about a corresponding evolution in the role of education and the methods for preparing people for occupations. Particularly, the chapter focuses on the evolution of PBID as an instructional design system aimed at developing people's capabilities to perform desired skills.

SOCIETY'S EXPECTATIONS OF OCCUPATIONAL EDUCATION

For centuries the basic forms of education remained the same. Some of the earliest records of education describe the educational system of the culture that developed in Mesopotamia between 3000 and 1500 B.C.:

> The culture that took shape in the valley between the Tigris-Euphrates rivers created an educational structure consistent with its fundamental nature and (was) designed to perpetuate and transmit its basic values to the young. . . . Its all-pervading aim was practical, a preparation for the professions in which the elite spent their time. Since most professions were manned by priests or controlled by them, including even the offices of king and the political hierarchy, this education has been called "priestly." . . . Learning was largely a matter of memorizing materials and imitating set patterns. . . . Many technical subjects were taught, including engineering, astronomy, architecture, and medicine. (Frost, p. 16)

Much of the education mentioned in the quote above took place through apprenticeship. Arrangements were made for an apprentice to work alongside a master who was practicing an occupation. This was formal education in the sense that it was focused on a specific goal: to learn to perform in an occupation. The ability to perform an occupation was communicated by an instructor (master), who presented knowledge or performed activities while the learner listened and watched. The learner then imitated the instructor. If the learner did not adequately master the information, the learner watched the instructor again or reviewed the knowledge. This procedure was repeated until the content was mastered.

This form of education had little, if any, structure. The interaction between the instructor and the learner was mostly unplanned. Broad goals were established as to the types of content to be taught: a carpenter's apprentice would learn about being a carpenter; a person studying to be a priest would learn about being a priest; and so on. Details about the methods that would be used to teach, and what exactly would be taught, were not of great concern. Since there was relatively little content to be taught, and because the learner and instructor were together for an extended period of time, it was assumed that all necessary content would be taught at some time during their extended interaction.

Teaching was considered an art; therefore, as long as instructors were expert in their fields (carpentry, religion, rhetoric, philosophy, etc.), there was little need to be concerned about how they taught. It was thought that good teachers were born and that little could be done, or should be done, to improve the skills of those who were not good teachers.

This situation remained the same for centuries. Education was focused on being functional. Religion, rhetoric, and philosophy were important for priests, governmental officers, and other elite persons. Education for workers in skilled occupations involved learning the necessary skills. All members of the community were also provided an education which oriented them to the culture within which they lived.

As society evolved and the roles of people in society changed, the focus and content of education also evolved. For example, early Roman society required the management of lands, slaves, and farmers, and the preparation of soldiers. Since Roman education was essentially utilitarian (Gwynn, 1926), it was focused on preparing people for these roles in addition to preparing them to be good citizens and members of their religion.

During the seventeenth century, education began to receive serious criticism from outspoken leaders. Sir Francis Bacon (1561–1626) of England was one of the leading critics of the schools of the day. He criticized education and "despaired of existing colleges, where knowledge was as it were imprisoned in the writings of certain authors (of the past), from whom if any man dissent, he is (was) straightway arranged as a 'turbulent person or innovator'" (Armytage, 1970, p. 16). Bacon believed man's life could be made better through "kindling a light in nature, through experimentation" (Armytage, 1970, p. 16). He demanded that schools focus on experimentation and that colleges and universities include "a series of conservatories, laboratories, engines, gardens, anatomy theaters, sound houses, and furnaces where, by experiment, man could enlarge the bounds of his empire to the 'effecting of all things possible'" (Armytage, 1970, p. 16). In questioning the relevance of education based solely on the past, Bacon was saying that such education was no longer functionally relevant to the society of the day. He was also questioning the methods that were being used to deliver instruction and suggesting that experimentation rather than memorization become a primary method in education. This concept was revolutionary because if people were taught to experiment, they might also begin to question religious and political doctrine.

It was not until the eighteenth century that major reforms were made in the development and delivery of education as a result of increasing social pressure for relevance to an evolved society. The three major reforms were teaching in the mother language (instead of Latin), including the exact sciences into the curriculum, and questioning and studying methods of teaching.

At about the same time as education was being reformed, the European expansion to the new worlds, including America, took place. The amount of trade increased and the wealth of the European countries created an expanded middle class which also demanded schooling. These changes were taking place at the same time as technological changes such as the invention of the steam engine and the evolution of the factory system, which created the need for mass labor.

With the industrial revolution came a significant increase in the demand for skilled and semiskilled workers. It also created a demand for a generally educated populace that could adapt and work in the evolving industrial society. Industry found it no longer possible to train all skilled workers through apprenticeship, and it was no longer necessary for all workers to be competent in all aspects of a skilled trade or craft within the factory setting. The concept of mass production evolved, which caused the breakdown of the production of products into component manufacturing processes. For example, it was no longer necessary for one machinist to produce an entire rifle. One person could prepare the barrel, one the sights, and so on. Each of the workers producing these parts still had to be skilled, but the range of skills needed by each one in a particular factory setting was limited. Therefore, these workers were considered to be semiskilled.

Society had entered the "industrial age." Since public schools were not addressing the need of industry for skilled and semiskilled workers, industries addressed the need themselves. Besides the apprenticeship programs which were the norm in the past, large industries established schools in separate facilities (vestibules) attached to the factories to train workers for skilled and semiskilled jobs. These "vestibule schools" trained new workers in specific skills.

The industrial schools were expensive and could only be afforded by the larger employers. By 1900, industrial employers insisted that they needed the secondary schools to prepare skilled mechanics. They wanted education (which was later to be termed *vocational education*) focused on the preparation of people for a career in a skill or trade. This pressure on the public schools was reflected in a presentation by Elmer Ellsworth Brown from the University of California: "The recognition of the importance and need of purely vocational schools of secondary grade puts a new aspect on the problem of the school curriculum." . . (Brown, 1900, pp. 41–42).

At the beginning of the twentieth century both educators and industrial trainers found themselves with a challenge to prepare people in skilled and semiskilled occupations in relatively large quantities. Little was known about the process of delivering such instruction, and numerous questions arose. Which skills are needed by each worker? What types of procedures and knowledge do they need in order to perform? How should each type of worker be trained? Who should do the training? These questions, which were informally addressed by the master in an apprenticeship program, needed to be formally addressed in the teaching of large numbers of people.

In an attempt to develop meaningful instructional methods, educators (both trainers in business and industry, and vocational educators) sought effective instructional techniques in order to meet society's needs.

THE EVOLUTION OF PERFORMANCE-BASED INSTRUCTION

It was during the last half of the nineteenth century that pedagogical theory began to formally evolve. It is generally recognized that the development of education as a science began in Germany with Johann Friedrich Herbart (1776–1841) and his attempts at developing a logical, comprehensive, and internally consistent theory about how people learned. Although he did not base his theory on experimental research, he attempted to synthesize what was known about psychology as it might apply to education. His primary writings about education were completed between 1833 and 1836. In 1898, they were translated into English in the book *The Application of Psychology to the Science of Education* (Herbart, 1898).

The First Generation: Responding to the Industrial Age

Herbart was concerned with how people learned and how instruction could be delivered to facilitate that learning. In the past, instruction was based primarily on rote learning, or memorizing. There was little concern for motivating people to learn or that learning be meaningful. It was assumed that people would learn what was taught because it was taught. Learners had to try to integrate and make sense out of all of the separate ideas taught. Because of this, the relevance of what was being learned often escaped the learners and they saw little value in what was being taught. In addition, teaching was considered to be an art, and therefore, there were no established practices for the teaching process.

Herbart believed that learning could be facilitated if the functional value of what was being learned could be established for the learner in terms of the learner's past experience. He believed this would not only make what was to be learned more meaningful, but it would facilitate learning because learners would see value in what was being taught, and therefore, would be motivated.

Herbart believed that the past-accumulated experience of an individual was stored in the brain in an "apperceptive mass." He believed it was the instructor's job to clearly relate what was being taught to what the learner previously knew, and to provide activities for the learner that would allow the new content to be integrated into what was previously known.

The Herbartian Lesson. The basic instructional principles proposed by Herbart were the foundational principles of vocational education methodology, and they have persisted throughout the years in various modifications. "Where instruction is (was) called for, the vocational school has very generally used the standard Herbartian Lesson." . . (Prosser and Quigley, 1957). The steps in what vocational educators referred to as the Herbartian lesson were originally developed by Charles R. Allen (Allen, 1919).

Allen was one of the first writers who specifically addressed the process of teaching vocational skills in business and industry and in the schools. In 1919, he suggested that lessons be prepared to teach units of instruction with very clear purposes. He suggested that

> each complete teaching lesson calls for four steps, or teaching operations known as step 1, **Preparation,** step 2, **Presentation,** step 3, **Application** and step 4, **Testing** (or Inspection). These steps, are always carried out in the order given—The purpose of step 1 is to get the learner ready to be instructed, of step 2 to instruct him (her), of step 3 to check up errors, and of step 4 to give a final inspection of the instruction job. (Allen, 1919, p. 129)

Although Allen outlined these steps, he spent less than one page describing how to carry each of them out. In the case of step 4, he devoted only one sentence.

The steps outlined in Allen's work were based on Herbart's theory, and they became the basic lesson structure followed by vocational educators, but they did not accurately reflect all of Herbart's work. Allen's steps were viewed even by him as a simplification of Herbart's ideas. He stated: "Different authorities on teaching have divided the lesson into different numbers of steps, but the following arrangement (the four steps) is one of the simplest for emergency training instruction" (Allen, 1919, p. 129).

A relatively pure application of Herbart's theory to modern education has been summarized by his followers in the following five steps, which were suggested for presenting new content to learners:

> 1. *Preparation.* In this step . . . subject matter which has been previously learned [and which is related to the subject at hand] is recalled. This involves Herbart's main psychological principle: the law of apperception. He held that the mind is simply one's previous experiences, and that new experiences must be related to past experiences in order to become part of one's self. When new experiences are so related, they can be consciously perceived, or apperceived. Herbart is making this point when he speaks of "apperceptive mass." Hence, the first step in teaching new material is to relate the material to something previously known.

2. *Presentation.* Here the new material is presented (to the learner) for observation.
3. *Association.* The new material is compared with the old, and likenesses and differences are noted.
4. *Generalization.* (Classification) The relationships between the new and old material are given statement in definite form (clearly stated).
5. *Application.* Practical application must be made in order to consummate the process. (Gwynn, 1960)

Content Identification, Delivery, and Testing. Herbart's theory of instruction provided a format for the structuring of how to teach, but it did not answer the question, "What should be taught?" Allen addressed the issue of what to teach in his discussion of "the classification of what must be taught." He suggested that the content must be classified in terms of jobs. He indicated that a job meant anything that someone is paid to do. He gave the following examples of jobs: "Reading a blueprint is a job, running an automatic machine is a job, setting type is a job" (Allen, 1919, p. 47).

Allen focused on the process of performing components of a job but also recognized the need for related knowledge. He called the related knowledge *auxiliary knowledge,* or *information:*

> In general, this auxiliary material, as it may be called, will consist of a knowledge of trade terms, of a few simple scientific facts, mainly connected with the effects of heat on material, a knowledge of the working properties of stock and the ability to pick out one kind or another, a knowledge of the precautions which must be taken to avoid accidents and the ability to take care of tools and equipment. (Allen, 1919, p. 54)

Allen viewed the testing of the learner after instruction as an inspection process. He suggested,

> The instructor must now stop being an instructor and, becoming an inspector, proceed to inspect the results of his teaching by testing, in some suitable way, the ability of the learner to do the entire job alone. (Allen, 1919, p. 142)

The jobs which Allen was preparing instructors to teach were the skilled and semiskilled jobs of the early 1900s. The technology and the amount of information needed to practice in those occupations were relatively uncomplicated. The content to be taught was essentially the procedural aspects of operating machines, using tools, and manipulating objects. The procedures which were outlined in his initial text became the basic premises under which skill training has been done within the United States.

Various sections of the process of developing and delivering instruction have been refined since then, but the thrust has remained the same. The central focus has been on preparing people to perform the psychomotor or physical portions of jobs or occupations.

In 1942, Verne C. Fryklund's book *Trade and Job Analysis* refined and developed more specific procedures for analyzing jobs to determine the content to be taught. He recognized the fact that many times jobs were too complex to be taught without breaking them down further. He indicated that they should be broken down into elements. He defined *job elements* as "operations and information topics." Operations were specified as "skills, processes, and job operations" (Fryklund, 1942, pp. 50–51). Information topics were essentially the same as what Allen called *auxiliary knowledge,* or *information.*

Fryklund spent little time explaining how the lessons should be delivered. He covered the delivery of instruction in less than one page, indicating the following:

> There are certain principles that should guide the teacher in presenting a lesson. The first one . . . is that of understanding the learners. Next, the teacher should know what he is to teach and the learner should know what he is expected to learn. Third, the teacher should know how best to present the particular lesson; that is, he should know what method of presentation to use. Fourth, he must have a thorough knowledge of the various aids and devices that have proved helpful in industrial teaching.
>
> *What to Teach.* The thing to teach is the instructional unit. The instructional unit is an element of the trade or job. The elements consist of operations and information topics. One instructional unit and no more should be taught at one time. (Fryklund, 1942, p. 125)

Fryklund also spent little time on how to evaluate learner progress. In fact, he minimized the need for testing, particularly manipulative performance testing. He indicated the following:

> Any tests used to evaluate results should be constructed according to the aims of the course. If the aims are conceived in terms of ideals, attitudes, appreciations, and skills, then the tests should measure these qualities according to the desired emphasis. However, it hardly seems necessary to measure manipulative skills beyond the appraisal made in the routine of the teacher's observation. Adequate judgment of performance can, for practical purposes, be determined by judgment of the teacher. (Fryklund, 1942, pp. 143–144)

In 1950, William J. Micheels and M. Ray Karnes published the book *Measuring Educational Achievement.* For the first time there was a book that systematically addressed the evaluation of learner progress related to vocational education and training in business and industry. The book provided detailed procedures for developing tests to measure the information possessed by learners. It also presented some general procedures for assessing learners' manipulative performance. These procedures built upon the works of Allen and Fryklund and assumed that the teachable content was the information topics and operations to be performed on the job.

The Second Generation: Implementing the Systems Approach and Mastery Learning

During the early 1960s a new generation of curriculum procedures began to evolve: the *systems approach.* The systems approach had been used in product engineering for some time. A *system* is a regularly interacting or interdependent group of items forming a unified whole. In engineering it is defined as a *process.* The process involves the accurate identification of a problem and its requirements, the setting of specific performance objectives, the application of logic and analysis techniques to the problem, the development of methods for the solution of the problem, and the rigorous measurement of the product designed to solve the problem against the specific performance objectives (Butler, 1972, p. xi).

The Systems Approach. In 1972, F. Coit Butler in his book *Instructional Systems Development for Vocational and Technical Training* argued that a system's engineering concepts could be applied to vocational course development. He indicated that by using the systems approach, it was possible to build a curriculum based on an analysis of learner performance data and to validate the curriculum against the performance data.

At about the same time, July 1973, The U.S. Department of the Air Force published the *Handbook for Designers of Instructional Systems* (U.S. Department of the Air Force, 1973). It contained many of the same elements as those in Butler's book. The handbook was revised and published again in 1978, and the system became known as the Instructional Systems Design (ISD) model.

Both Butler's book and the handbook were developed from a body of literature outside of vocational education. They were based primarily on work being done by people prepared as instructional designers and learning theorists working at the American Institute for Research in Pittsburgh (Altman, 1966; Briggs, 1970; Briggs et al., 1966; Butler, 1968; and Butler and Crozier, 1968) and within the U.S. Air Force (Butler, 1964). These people drew on the work of other learning theorists and educators not associated with vocational education (Baker, 1966; Bloom, 1956; Bruner, 1966; Cook, 1964; Cronbach, 1963; Gage, 1962; Gagné, 1962; and Glaser, 1963).

Behavioral Objectives. Benjamin S. Bloom in 1956 and Robert M. Gagné in 1965 came out with books that dealt with a major step of the systems approach: specifying performance objectives. The major impact of both books was that they presented classifications which could be used to describe human behaviors as, first, performances, and then as performance objectives. Bloom's book, *Taxonomy of Educational Objectives: The Classification of Educational Goals, Handbook I: Cognitive Domain,* presented the classification of human behaviors in terms of cognitive, affective, and psychomotor objectives (Bloom, 1956). Gagné's book entitled *The Conditions of Learning* classified human behaviors as a hierarchy of learned capabilities. He suggested that learning could be focused on developing five different capabilities of humans: (1) intellectual skills, (2) cognitive strategies, (3) verbal information, (4) motor skills, and (5) attitude (Gagné, 1965). Educators now had classification systems to describe human behavior in terms of performance, which could be used to focus instruction.

A major pioneering example of the implementation of behavioral objectives in vocational education was a federally funded project in distributive education, or marketing education, conducted during the mid-1960s (Crawford, 1967). People in the distributive education field felt that stating objectives relative to the cognitive, affective, and psychomotor domains would facilitate their curriculum development efforts. This work is still being used in the field as a basis for curriculum development, although its application has evolved as educational practice has evolved. But as happened with most attempts at implementing new categories of objectives, the psychomotor behaviors, or tasks, were stated as expected behaviors, but the cognitive and affective behaviors were not. The latter types of objectives were stated in terms of supporting information and mental skills (cognitive objectives) and a set of desired beliefs (affective objectives) which supported the tasks. Because of this, cognitive and affective objectives still lacked the necessary precision to develop adequate criterion tests and to develop precise instruction focused on performance.

Criterion Tests. The focus on specifying and categorizing behaviors also caused a concern as to how to measure whether learners had developed the behaviors. This concern was consistent with the systems approach concern for validating whether a prespecified performance, or objective, has been accomplished. A number of writers of the time focused on procedures for developing tests to determine if performance objectives had been attained. These tests became known as criterion tests (Baker, 1966; Cronbach, 1963; Glaser, 1963; and Popham, 1967, 1969, 1971).

The people who wrote about applying the systems approach to education concentrated on defining the problem (educational objectives) and evaluating whether the problem had been solved (criterion measures). However, little was presented as to how to teach students to attain the objectives. Gagné devoted little time in his book to the actual development of instruction to present lessons. Butler devoted about four pages to the subject. This was typical of the textbooks written about teaching at the time.

Vocational educators viewed the developments in education at large and adopted portions of the systems approach to their instruction. For example, *trade analysis* and *job analysis* evolved to *task analysis.* Whereas trade and job analysis broke occupations into jobs performed by people in the occupations and then into operations, task analysis broke occupations into duties, and then duties into tasks. Tasks were then broken down into activities, and activities were broken down into actions or manipulations.

> Actions or manipulations are [were] defined [as] short, simple operations that are frequently common to many different activities and involve using tools, devices, controls, and simple test equipment. (Butler, 1972, p. 74)

In the final analysis, tasks were still perceived to be psychomotor in nature, and knowledge taught was still considered to be knowledge supporting those tasks: "The supporting knowledge structure should include little information that is not specifically required for task performance" (Butler, 1972, p. 83).

The end goal of the process was essentially the same, but the terminology was different. People talked about the cognitive and affective domains of human behavior, but in vocational education these domains were still treated as auxiliary to psychomotor behaviors. The system still analyzed occupations in terms of psychomotor behaviors, which is what Allen had proposed during the early 1900s.

However, the systems approach did further refine the analysis process, introduced the concept of performance objectives, and heightened concern for testing of development of performance capability. Testing became a critical ingredient in the instructional process, and the informality of evaluation procedures proposed by Fryklund and others was no longer accepted.

Mastery Learning. During the same time period as the systems approach was being introduced into education, the concept of *mastery learning* was also being introduced. John B. Carroll wrote an article in 1963 entitled "A Model of School Learning" (Carroll, 1963) in which he suggested that if one wanted all people to master a task, one should vary the amount of time that each individual could study the material. One should also vary the instructional approach used with individuals, depending upon how they learned best. People who learned more slowly would take more time, but most people could master most tasks. The notion of mastery learning emphasized the concept of individualized instruction in education.

Prior to that time, most instruction in schools was presented to groups of learners at a fixed rate of speed, and because people have different abilities to learn what is presented to them, learners would learn different amounts. For example, if 10 people were taught how to operate a computer in two hours, some would be able to operate the computer after instruction, and the others would learn various amounts about how to operate the computer. However, if each person could study the material at his or her own rate, using instructional materials consistent with how he or she learns best, most of the learners could learn to operate the computer.

Mastery learning grew out of the concern that many learners never mastered what was presented to them in schools and then they found that they could not functionally use the material taught after leaving school. This situation was recognized for years, but it was not regarded with concern. Society previously did not need large numbers of highly educated people, and the educational system produced enough well-educated people to fulfill society's needs. However, as society changed, and as the demand for basic skills (reading, writing, and arithmetic) and occupational skills increased, it was recognized that a person would have great difficulty surviving without those skills.

The concept of individualizing the instruction of individuals, which was an essential part of the training of people through apprenticeship, was now being introduced back into formal school programs. The systems approach to education and the concept of mastery learning came together in the modularizing of instruction. If learners were to progress at their own rates of speed, learning materials were needed which allowed them to learn at their own rates of speed. The learning module, or package, became the vehicle which would be used to facilitate individualized learning.

In 1975, Pucel and Knaak published the book *Individualizing Vocational and Technical Instruction* (Pucel and Knaak, 1975), which brought together the concepts of mastery learning, the systems approach, and criterion evaluation. The result was a systematic approach for designing, delivering, and evaluating individualized instruction which was focused on occupational task mastery. The book was based on five years of curriculum model development and experimentation at the 916 Area Vocational-Technical Institute in Minnesota. It provided detailed information on ways to analyze content using task analysis, the logic of mastery learning applied to vocational education, techniques for developing individualized learning materials, and detailed procedures for developing criterion tests (including performance and product evaluations). However, it, as other books of its time, did not spend a great deal of time on how instruction should be designed for actual presentation and delivery to learners.

Over the years, *competency-based education* has evolved as the predominant term to describe this type of education as it has been used in vocational education and training. In 1985, the Division of Vocational, Adult, and Community Education of the State of Florida published a report which defined the major elements of competency-based vocational education:

> Competency-based vocational education (CBVE) focuses on the occupational skills ("competencies") trainees are expected to achieve, and the performances of those competencies. Briefly, the foundation of CBVE is built on two unalterable essentials.

1. The occupational competencies to be achieved by the trainee are derived from a rigorous analysis of the occupation to ensure that they are accurate, complete, and up-to-date.
2. Trainees are assessed on the competencies by observing their performance in conditions similar to that of the occupation. Occupational criteria and standards of performance are used to determine trainees' proficiency.

Competencies are those observable skills incumbent workers use on the job—the things they actually get paid to do. Knowledge and attitudes are considered to be *integral* to the occupational competencies to which they are related, not separate entities, and are taught and learned as such. Progress through the training program is based on mastery of each competency, not on time enrolled or effort expended.

CBVE is concerned little with *how* the competencies are to be learned. It is possible to use many methods of teaching: large group instruction, small group instruction, independent study, projects, textbooks, etc. However, because mastery of competencies is required, and because individuals learn at different rates, CBVE programs tend to move logically toward some form of self-pacing and individualization. Note, however, that these approaches are facilitating, not essential, elements of CBVE. (State of Florida, 1985, pp. 5–6)

It is obvious that CBVE again concentrates on the psychomotor aspects of an occupation as the primary focus of analysis and, therefore, instruction. Little is said about how to deliver the instruction; in fact, instructional design for delivery is considered to be of minimal concern. The teaching of knowledge and attitudes is considered to be auxiliary to the psychomotor activity.

The Next Generation: Adapting to the Information Age

Throughout the evolution of the instructional design systems there has been a common frame of reference which has been a result of society at the time when structured vocational education began. At the turn of the century, when people began to write about instructional development related to vocational education, industry demanded skilled and semiskilled workers.

Those skilled and semiskilled workers essentially manipulated tools and objects in order to practice their occupations. As a result, the focal point for designing instruction to prepare people for occupations was the observable, psychomotor aspects of those occupations. Analytical tools were developed to determine what those psychomotor aspects were (e.g., jobs and tasks). Knowledge was viewed as being needed only to support the psychomotor aspects of the occupation. Attitudes were mentioned in passing as being important, but they were rarely addressed in terms of teachable content or techniques for teaching.

Since the turn of the century the evolution of instructional design procedures has consisted of refinements of techniques for accomplishing the basic premises of how to prepare people for occupations. The primary focus of design has been on doing a better job of analyzing the psychomotor aspects of occupations so that the occupational tasks can be defined more accurately, and on developing procedures for measuring whether learners have developed those psychomotor aspects.

Changing Needs and a New Vision. As occurred at the time of Bacon during the seventeenth century and again at the turn of this century, society has continued to change while the educational system has not changed with it. What vocational educators and trainers in business and industry have done in the past is not wrong, but it is no longer sufficient. Occupations in society have evolved and now require larger and larger amounts of occupationally specific cognitive and affective behaviors. Society is leaving the industrial age, which was the context for the development of past instructional design procedures in vocational education. It is in the information age in which occupations require not only psychomotor skills but also much larger amounts of cognitive and affective skills. Many occupations no longer are involved with the actual production of goods the way most occupations were at the turn of the century. Now many are service occupations requiring significant amounts of affective skills in order for people to interact effectively with the people for whom they provide service.

The U.S. Bureau of Labor Statistics (Kutcher, 1987) projects no change in employment in goods-producing industries between 1986 and the year 2000: "Service-producing industries, therefore, will account for nearly all the projected growth. . . . [T]he service industries will expand by more than 10 million jobs." . . (Kutcher, 1987, p. 5). The five occupational groups projected to experience the most growth are technicians, service workers, professional workers, sales workers, and executive and managerial employees.

The underlying assumptions of what constitutes productivity in industry, which were in place during the industrial age, must be questioned. Those underlying assumptions are well stated by Paul Strassmann as follows:

> The underlying assumptions about what "productivity" is go back to the industrial-age model of what a person, aided by a machine, does. [Such assumptions were that] . . . the handling of complexity requires information which is a manager's, not a worker's, prerogative. A person's superior coordination of eye and hand are what wages will purchase—until improved machines buy it for less. A person's brain is not a valuable asset per se under such assumptions, because the engineer designs into the manufacturing sequence everything which needs to be done. The employee's thinking is only useful insofar as it retains simple procedural instructions. (Strassmann, 1985, pp. 103–104)

Strassmann's position may be a little harsh, but it provides a frame of reference which is compatible with past instructional design procedures in vocational education where the focus almost solely rested on the psychomotor aspects of occupations.

We still need people in society who can operate machines and manipulate objects and tools, and training to do these should still be a major focus of vocational education. However, as was pointed out earlier, that is no longer sufficient. Many of the occupations in society today require cognitive and affective skills in larger quantities than psychomotor skills. Therefore, vocational education and training in business and industry must incorporate the teaching of those skills into instructional programs with the same level of planning, precision, and commitment as they have devoted to psychomotor skills.

A new framework is needed for the development of instructional programs, one that is adapted to the changed needs of society and accepts cognitive and affective behaviors on an equal par with psychomotor behaviors. All three behaviors must still be occupationally related so the instruction is focused and functional, but each must have value in and of itself.

It is also time to recognize that you cannot develop an effective instructional program only by defining the goals of the program (content analysis) and by measuring whether those goals have been accomplished (criterion measures). That is like developing goals for an airplane and evaluation procedures for evaluating if the plane achieved those goals, and leaving out how the plane will actually be produced. If we want people to learn certain behaviors, we must attend to the instructional process that is used to teach people to perform those behaviors.

Performance-Based Instructional Design. The PBID system allows for the development of the equivalent of what has become known as competency-based vocational education for the delivery of psychomotor behaviors; in addition, it also presents techniques for the development of instruction at the same level of precision for occupationally specific cognitive and affective behaviors. The system is based on what learning theory has to say about the way people learn, and on research concerning effective instructional techniques (Pucel, 1986; Pucel, 1987).

The PBID system provides a rationale and detailed procedures for developing each component of an instructional program starting with the assumption that the instructional program is needed. It provides detailed procedures for the identification of role-specific psychomotor, cognitive, and affective behaviors, and it uses analytical techniques which insure role relevancy and focus. It provides a detailed planning procedure for structuring performance-based lessons which are developed to ensure the performance capability of the learner. The lesson structuring procedure is generic, so lessons that are structured can be delivered equally well through a variety of delivery formats (e.g., traditional instruction, modularized instruction, programmed instruction, and computer-assisted instruction (CAI)). The PBID system also provides detailed procedures for developing performance-focused evaluation procedures, or criterion measures, for all three types of behaviors. Chapter 2 gives an overview of the entire PBID system. It is followed by chapters which detail the procedures for implementing the system.

SUMMARY

Throughout history, educational practice has evolved along with the society it has served. In order for education to be viewed as valuable, it must have a functional relationship to the society which supports it. When educational institutions and pedagogical practice no longer are viewed as being responsive to a society, pressures are mounted to change them.

Society has now evolved to an information age in which a large component is service. This evolution has put tension on vocational education and training in business and industry to more functionally address the needs of people preparing for the new age. People are calling for an evolution in procedures and practices related to preparing, evaluating, and delivering instruction. The need for change does not mean that practices of the past are wrong; it suggests that they are no longer sufficient. Practices must evolve to incorporate techniques and ideas that will make them more functionally related to the needs of society. The PBID system builds upon the best of the past and provides ideas and techniques to bring instructional development into a more functional relationship with societal needs.

ACTIVITIES AND EVALUATION

1. Develop a chart, similar to the one presented below, which chronologically presents the historical development of instructional development processes in vocational education. Indicate the approximate date and nature of each innovation.

Date	Innovation
Mid-1800s	Herbart developed his theory of learning which attempted to explain how people learned and could effectively be taught.

2. Describe why vocational education and training curricula of the past focused on the psychomotor aspects of occupations.

3. Describe the past relationship between occupational knowledge and tasks (jobs).

4. Explain why the focus on psychomotor tasks has become questioned.

5. Explain how the performance-based instructional design system relates to the movement of society from the industrial age to the information age.

REFERENCES

Allen, C. R., *The Instructor: The Man and The Job,* J. B. Lippincott Company, Philadelphia, 1919, pp. 47, 54, 129, 142.

Altman, J. W., *Research on General Vocational Capabilities (Skills and Knowledges),* American Institutes for Research, Pittsburgh, 1966.

Armytage, W. H. G., *Four Hundred Years of English Education*, 2d ed., Cambridge University Press, Cambridge, MA, 1970, p. 16.

Baker, E., *Establishing Performance Standards,* Vimcet Associates, Los Angeles, 1966.

Beck, R. H., *A Social History of Education,* Prentice-Hall, Englewood Cliffs, NJ, 1965.

Bloom, B. S., *Taxonomy of Educational Objectives: The Classification of Educational Goals, Handbook I: Cognitive Domain,* David McKay, New York, 1956.

Briggs, L. J., *Handbook of Procedures for the Design of Instruction,* American Institutes for Research, Pittsburgh, 1970.

———, P. L. Campeau, R. M. Gagné, and M. A. May, *Instructional Media: A Procedure for the Design of Multi-media Instruction, a Critical Review of Research, and Suggestions for Future Research,* American Institutes for Research, Pittsburgh, 1966.

Brown, E. E., "Secondary Education," *Monographs on Education in the United States,* vol. 1, Nicholas Murray Butler (ed.), J. B. Lyon Company, Albany, NY, 1900, pp. 41–42.

Bruner, Jerome S., *Toward a Theory of Instruction,* The Belknap Press of Harvard University Press, Cambridge, MA, 1966.

Butler, F. C., *A Programmed Television Course in Basic Typing,* Faculty Research Report, U.S. Air Force Academy, Colorado Springs, CO, 1964.

———, *Objectives for Occupational Education,* American Institutes for Research, Pittsburgh, 1968.

———, *Instructional Systems Development for Vocational and Technical Training,* Educational Technology Publications, Englewood Cliffs, NJ, 1972, pp. xi, 74, 83.

Butler, F. C., and P. W. Crozier, *An Individualized Electronics Curriculum,* American Institutes for Research, Pittsburgh, 1968.

Carroll, J. B., " A Model of School Learning," *Teachers College Record,* vol. 64, 1963.

Cook, Desmond L., *A New Approach to the Planning and Management of Educational Research,* The PERT Project, School of Education, Ohio State University (mimeographed), Columbus, 1964.

Crawford, L. C., *A Competency Pattern Approach to Curriculum Construction in Distributive Teacher Education,* College of Arts and Sciences, Virginia Polytechnic Institute, Blacksburg, 1967.

Cronbach, L. J., "Course Improvement through Evaluation," *Teachers College Record,* vol. 64, 1963, pp. 672–683.

Frost, S. E., Jr., *Historical and Philosophical Foundations of Western Education,* Charles E. Merrill, Columbus, OH, 1966, p. 16.

Fryklund, V. C., *Trade and Job Analysis,* The Bruce Publishing Co., Milwaukee, 1942, pp. 50–51, 125, 143–144.

Gage, N. L., *Handbook of Research on Teaching,* Rand-McNally, Chicago, 1962.

Gagné, R. M. (ed.), *Psychological Principles in Systems Development,* Holt, Rinehart & Winston, New York, 1962.

———, *The Conditions of Learning,* Holt, Rinehart, & Winston, New York, 1965.

Glaser, R. L., "Instructional Technology and the Measurement of Learning Outcomes," *American Psychologist,* vol. 18, 1963, pp. 519–521.

Gwynn, A., *Roman Education from Cicero to Quintilian,* Clarendon Press, Oxford, 1926.

Gwynn, J. M., *Curriculum Principles and Social Trends,* Macmillan, New York, 1960.

Herbart, J. F., *The Application of Psychology to the Science of Education,* Beatrice C. Mulliner (trans.), Charles Scribner's Sons, New York, 1898.

Kutcher, R. E., "Overview and Implications of the Projections to 2000," *Monthly Labor Review,* vol. 110, no. 9, 1987, p. 5.

Micheels, W. J., and M. R. Karnes, *Measuring Educational Achievement,* McGraw-Hill, New York, 1950.

Popham, W. J., *Educational Criterion Measures,* Southwest Regional Laboratory for Educational Research and Development, Inglewood, CA, 1967.

———, *Validation Results: Performance Tests of Teaching Proficiency in Vocational Education,* Paper presented at the American Educational Research Association Meeting, Los Angeles, 1969.

Popham, W. J., et al., *Criterion-Referenced Measurement (An Introduction),* Educational Technology Publications, Englewood Cliffs, NJ, 1971.

Prosser, C. A., and T. H. Quigley, *Vocational Education in a Democracy,* American Technical Society, Chicago, 1957.

Pucel, D. J., *The Minnesota Vocational Follow-up System: Rationale and Methods,* Department of Industrial Education, University of Minnesota, St. Paul, 1972.

Puce, D. J., *Performance Based Instructional Design*, Performance Training Systems, St. Paul, MN, 1986.

Pucel, D. J., "The Performance-based Instructional Design System," *Journal of Industrial Teacher Education*, vol. 24, no. 4, 1987, pp. 27–35.

Pucel, D. J., and W. C. Knaak, *Individualizing Vocational and Technical Instruction,* Charles E. Merrill, Columbus, OH, 1975.

State of Florida, *Barriers to Implementing Competency-Based Vocational Education in Postsecondary Schools,* Division of Vocational, Adult, and Community Education, Tallahassee, April 1985, pp. 5–6.

Strassman, P. A., *Information Payoff,* Free Press, New York, 1985, pp. 103–104.

U.S. Department of the Air Force, *Handbook For Designers of Instructional Systems,* vol. 4, Washington, DC, 1978, AFP 50–58.

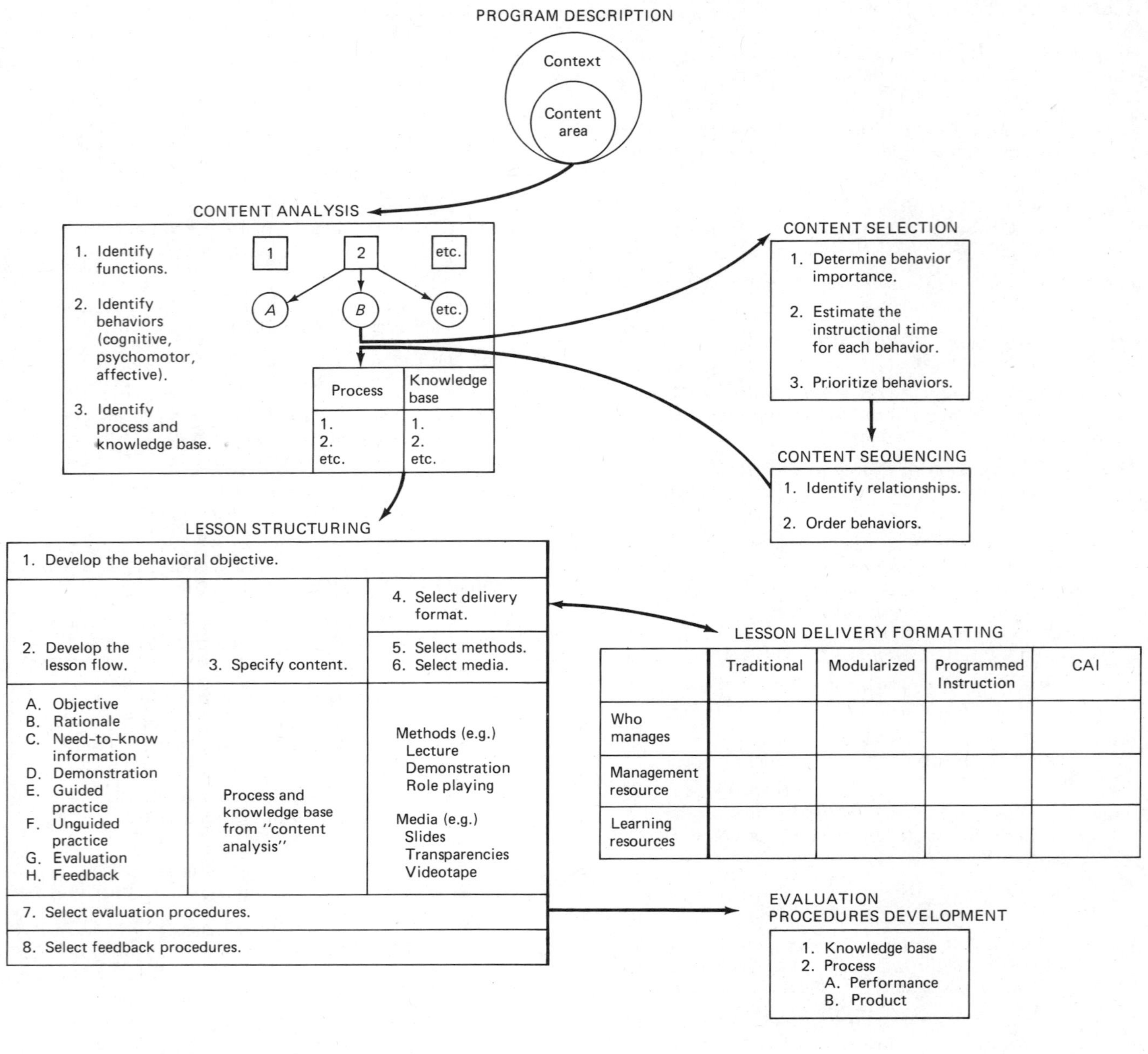
PROGRAM DESCRIPTION
Context
Content area
CONTENT ANALYSIS
1. Identify functions.
2. Identify behaviors (cognitive, psychomotor, affective).
3. Identify process and knowledge base.
1
2
etc.
A
B
etc.
Process
Knowledge base
1.
2.
etc.
1.
2.
etc.
CONTENT SELECTION
1. Determine behavior importance.
2. Estimate the instructional time for each behavior.
3. Prioritize behaviors.
CONTENT SEQUENCING
1. Identify relationships.
2. Order behaviors.
LESSON STRUCTURING
1. Develop the behavioral objective.
2. Develop the lesson flow.
3. Specify content.
4. Select delivery format.
5. Select methods.
6. Select media.
A. Objective
B. Rationale
C. Need-to-know information
D. Demonstration
E. Guided practice
F. Unguided practice
G. Evaluation
H. Feedback
Process and knowledge base from "content analysis"
Methods (e.g.)
Lecture
Demonstration
Role playing
Media (e.g.)
Slides
Transparencies
Videotape
7. Select evaluation procedures.
8. Select feedback procedures.
LESSON DELIVERY FORMATTING
Traditional
Modularized
Programmed Instruction
CAI
Who manages
Management resource
Learning resources
EVALUATION PROCEDURES DEVELOPMENT
1. Knowledge base
2. Process
A. Performance
B. Product

The Performance-Based Instructional Design System

CHAPTER OBJECTIVE

Givens

A diagram of the performance-based instructional design system, a description of each of its components, and a discussion of the interrelationships among the components

Performance

Recall the intent of the performance-based instructional design system, its components, and the interrelationships between components.

Standard

Descriptions of the components and their interrelationships will be consistent with those presented in this chapter.

OVERVIEW

This chapter provides an overview and summary of the PBID system, which is discussed in detail throughout this book. The purpose of this overview is to allow you to become familiar with the system and its components, and with the relationships among the components. You will thus be able to see what the system includes, how the components of the system relate with one another, and what the order is in which each of the components would normally be completed. Understanding of any one component of this system, as with any system, is increased by understanding its relationship to other portions of the system.

Each of the subsequent chapters in this book discusses one of the components of the system and begins with a highlighted diagram which relates the component to the whole system. After mastering each of the chapters pertaining to portions of the system, you may again wish to review this chapter as an overall summary of the system.

INTENT OF THE SYSTEM

PBID is an integrated system for developing and evaluating instruction, and its aim is to ensure the performance capability of learners. It is organized into components that parallel the decision-making process of an instructional designer who wishes to develop and evaluate instruction. The figure at the beginning of the chapter presents the major components of the system as a decision-making flowchart. The boldface arrows indicate the typical flow of decision making.

The PBID system can be used to develop programs of instruction, courses, or instruction pertaining to individual behaviors. For simplicity in describing the system, however, the term *program* will be used throughout the book.

The major components of the system are:

1. Program description
2. Content analysis
3. Content selection
4. Content sequencing
5. Lesson structuring
6. Lesson delivery formatting
7. Evaluation and feedback procedures development

PBID is a system. The output from one component becomes the input for other components, and the sum of all of the components results in an integrated plan of instruction. Because it is a system and each component is directly related to other components, the relationships among the components must be understood for the system to be used effectively.

The design of an instructional program starts with a *program description,* in which the intent of the program to be developed is described in terms of the content area to be taught and the context within which that content will be taught. Next, specific behaviors related to the content area to be taught in the program must be identified through *content analysis* and listed. Since more content is usually identified than can be taught within a given program, the actual content (behaviors) to be included must be selected from that which could be taught through *content selection.* Once the content to be taught has been identified, the order in which the content will be presented to learners must be determined through *content sequencing.*

Next, how the content will be taught must be determined. Content is taught through *lessons.* Each lesson is developed around a behavior that students are expected to learn and perform. Each lesson must be generally planned or organized through *lesson structuring* to bring about effective learning. After the lessons are structured, they must be formatted for delivery to learners through *lesson delivery formatting.* For example, lessons can be formatted and presented as traditional instruction, modularized instruction, computer-assisted instruction (CAI), or programmed instruction. *Evaluation procedures* must be selected to determine whether learning has taken place, and *feedback procedures* must be chosen to inform learners of their progress. These evaluation and feedback procedures must then be developed.

PBID utilizes the process described previously for the development and evaluation of instruction related to psychomotor (doing), cognitive (knowing), and affective (feeling) behaviors. (These terms are defined in more detail in Chapter 4 and can be found in the glossary.) For example, the system can be used to design instruction to teach people to manipulate tools and equipment, to make decisions, and to interact with other people. Instruction is designed to teach people to meaningfully perform each of these types of behaviors in an integrated way.

The concept of meaningful learning as an important underlying principle of performance-based instruction will be expanded throughout the rest of this book. Performance-based instruction is not consistent with training built on the premise that learners merely imitate modeled behavior: "monkey see–monkey do." It is based on the premise that meaningful learning will allow people to see interrelationships which facilitate the transferability of what they learn to new situations.

COMPONENTS

Now that you have been provided with a brief overview of the system, the components of the system will be briefly introduced to give you an understanding of each and how it relates to the others. Subsequent chapters will discuss each component in detail, give specific examples of how each is implemented, and include practice activities.

Program Description

An instructional program is developed only after a need for the program has been established. This book does not address that needs assessment process. It begins with the assumption that the need for the program has been established.

No instructional program can be developed without first determining its overall intent. The *program description* defines the intent of the instructional program. The actual program to be developed may be a series of lessons regarding a limited set of skills, a course or series of courses, or all of the instruction needed to prepare people for an occupation. It must provide the instructional designer, as well as people who will use or review the program, with a clear understanding of both the content area to be taught and its educational context.

The *content* can be specified in a number of different ways. For example, it may be specified in terms of a job (e.g., an instructional designer, a machinist, or a secretary) or a skill area (e.g., math or job-seeking skills).

The *context* provides the designer with a clear description of the environment within which the content will be taught. It includes the following:

1. Level of program (e.g., secondary, postsecondary, adult, or industry training)
2. Expected length of program (e.g., hours, days, or months)
3. Program focus (e.g., upgrading, initial preparation, remediation, retraining, or exploration)
4. Institutional setting (e.g., instructional format used such as a self-paced course; location; resource restrictions; and/or personnel available)
5. Relationships to other programs (e.g., which courses will follow, or which are prerequisites)
6. Special learner characteristics (e.g., handicapped, disadvantaged, or employed)

Table 2.1 presents a sample program description for a program intended to help people develop remedial math skills.

Content Analysis

Once the intent of the program has been described, the exact content to be taught must be determined. *Content analysis* is the process of identifying the specific content to be taught in a program. At times, content analysis is also referred to as *task analysis.* However, the latter term is not used with this system because it is often associated with the analysis of content and the development of instruction that concentrates primarily on psychomotor behavior without adequate consideration of affective and cognitive behaviors. Content analysis is commonly associated with the analysis of any type of content. It is used in association with PBID because the system can be applied to developing instruction with all three types of behavior.

Content analysis is accomplished in three stages:

1. Function identification
2. Behavior analysis
3. Behavior detailing (process and knowledge-base identification)

Figure 2.1 presents each of these stages in relation to one another.

The focus of PBID is on developing performance capability. Therefore, content must be specified in terms of desired performance. It is not sufficient to define topic areas to be taught, such as typing, closing, or electricity. One must specify the performance expected as behaviors: "type a business letter," "close a sale," "decide which portion of the electrical system needs repair," and so on. Those behaviors then become the focus of instruction.

TABLE 2.1 Sample Program Description

CONTENT AREA	
Basic math skills	
CONTEXT	
Program level:	Secondary
Expected length:	One month, 80 hours
Program focus:	Remediation
Institutional setting:	Traditional, school, course
Relationships to other programs:	Basic skills for accounting program
Special learner characteristics:	Tested math skills below seventh-grade level

FIGURE 2.1 Stages of Content Analysis

Content to be taught in a program is analyzed in three stages:

1. *Function identification* Identification of groupings of behaviors called functions
2. *Behavior analysis* Identification of behaviors
3. *Behavior detailing* Identification of the process of performing each behavior and the knowledge base needed to meaningfully apply the behavior

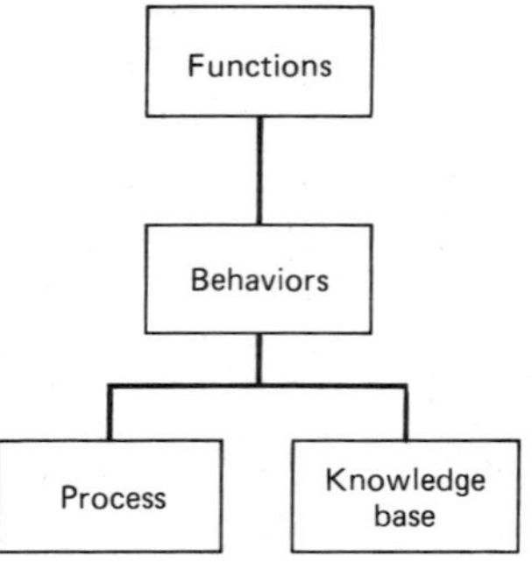

Function Identification. The first stage of content analysis is *function identification.* The content area is broken down into functions performed by individuals who apply that content in the context of the program description. *Functions* are major groupings of behaviors that are usually performed together; they represent major activity subdivisions within the content area. At times they are also called *duties.* Because functions contain groupings of behaviors that are commonly performed together, they usually have a name that describes that grouping of behaviors. For example, "complete a job application" or "repair an electrical system" are functions within the content areas of "job-seeking skills" and "auto mechanics." Each function represents a collection of related behaviors.

Behavior Analysis. As indicated in Figure 2.1, once the functions are identified, the behaviors within each function are identified. Figure 2.2 presents this relationship between functions and behaviors more explicitly. The process of identifying and classifying behaviors is called *behavior analysis.* Behavior analysis is accomplished by breaking functions down into component behaviors and classifying each behavior as primarily psychomotor, cognitive, or affective. Sample behaviors include "close a sale," "replace a spark plug," "solve a problem," "decide which tool to use," "accept another person," and "cooperate with co-workers."

Behaviors are visible actions of an individual. Most require varying amounts of psychomotor, cognitive, and affective activity. *How a behavior is categorized is based upon the predominant activity involved in performing the behavior.* Psychomotor and affective behaviors are relatively easy to classify because the primary process for performing them is visible, observed behavior. For example, the primary process of changing a tire, which is a psychomotor behavior, is the observable changing of a tire. The primary process of cooperating with co-workers, which is an affective behavior, is the observable cooperation among the workers. The identification and classification of cognitive behaviors is less direct. For example, although one must do something visible in order for another person to determine if a problem has been solved, the visible action performed may not adequately reflect the primary process used to arrive at the problem solution. The primary *process* to arrive at the solution may be occurring in a person's mind. Therefore, even though the process may result in an associated, visible psychomotor behavior, if the primary emphasis of the process were cognitive, the behavior would be classified as cognitive.

For example, an auto mechanic is faced with a decision to repair a part or to replace it with a new one. The ultimate psychomotor result will be that the part is repaired or replaced, which can be visibly observed. However, if the behavior to be taught were "decide whether to repair or replace a part," the visible psychomotor result would not be the focus of instruction, nor would it provide a basis for evaluating the quality of the *decision.* The instructional focus would have to be placed on the decision process, and the behavior would be a cognitive behavior even though it has a visible psychomotor result. The challenge to the instructional designer is to somehow make the decision-making process visible so that it can be observed and evaluated. Techniques for doing so are presented in Chapters 16 through 20 on developing evaluation procedures.

Behavior analysis is accomplished through the use of analysis charts such as the one presented in Figure 2.3. The functions of an auto mechanic identified earlier are presented across the top of the chart. Along the left side of the chart space is provided to write in behaviors that are components of each function. In the example for auto mechanics, the functions are: "perform maintenance," "repair the cooling system," and "resolve customer problems." The partial list of behaviors identified include: "check and add oil," "treat tools with care," and "diagnose which systems need maintenance." The "X's" in the chart indicate which behaviors relate to each function. The use of an analysis chart is described in detail in Chapter 4.

The sample analysis chart presents typical psychomotor, affective, and cognitive behaviors associated with auto mechanics. Regardless which type of behavior is being analyzed, it is analyzed in relation to functions. This ensures that all behaviors identified are focused on the content area being analyzed and that they are relevant. Cognitive behaviors concentrate on decision making. Affective behaviors concentrate on communicating emotional tones of individuals through actions such as speech, body language, and inflection. Psycho-

FIGURE 2.2 Relationship between Functions and Behaviors

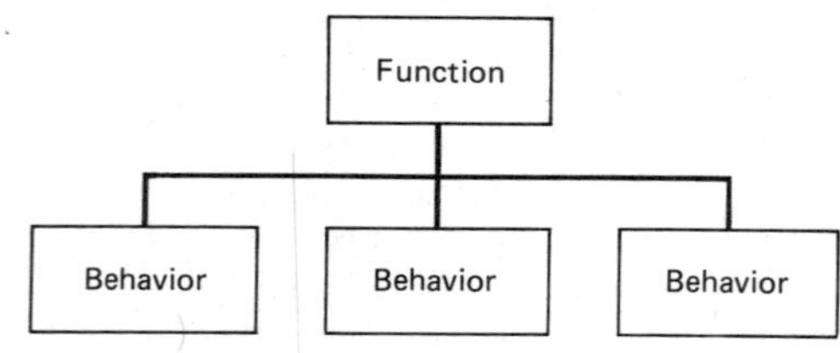

FIGURE 2.3 Sample Analysis Chart

AUTO MECHANICS

PSYCHOMOTOR BEHAVIORS	FUNCTIONS: 1. Perform maintenance.	2. Repair cooling system.	3. Resolve customer problem.
1. Change a tire.	X		
2. Check and add oil.	X		
3. Drain coolant.	X	X	
4. Replace the thermostat.		X	
COGNITIVE BEHAVIORS			
1. Diagnose which systems need maintenance.	X		
2. Decide which tool to use.	X	X	
3. Determine which customer to serve first.			X
AFFECTIVE BEHAVIORS			
1. Treat tools with care.	X	X	
2. Cooperate with co-workers.	X	X	X
3. Accept the customer as an individual.			X

motor behaviors concentrate on the manipulations of tools, materials, and objects.

The result of behavior analysis is a behavior listing. It should contain all of the behaviors that have been identified. Usually the behavior listing includes more behaviors than can be taught within the instructional time allowed for the program, so the designer must select those that *will be* taught from the total list of behaviors possible. Behaviors are selected using *content selection,* which will be discussed later.

Behavior Detailing. The third stage of content analysis is behavior detailing. *Behavior detailing* is the procedure of identifying the process and knowledge base that an instructor must teach and that the learner must master in order for the learner to be able to perform a behavior. Detailing is completed separately for each behavior to be taught. The process and knowledge base become the actual content that an instructor will teach in order for learners to master the behavior. The process is the central focus of the instruction because it is how the behavior is performed. However, the knowledge base is also essential because it provides "need to know" information that allows a person to perform the behavior meaningfully and with understanding. Notice that *knowledge base* is not called *cognitive content.* Within this system, the word *cognitive* refers to a type of behavior which becomes a goal of instruction. Information required by the learner is referred to as the *knowledge base.*

Each behavior, whether it is psychomotor, cognitive, or affective, can be analyzed into both the process of applying the behavior and the knowledge base needed to meaningfully apply the behavior. This is portrayed in Figure 2.4.

At times, the process may be a step-by-step procedure, for example, the procedure for changing a tire. At other times, the process may be a set of actions which might be applied in different orders, depending upon circumstance. An example would be the actions which depict cooperative behavior.

Tables 2.2, 2.3, and 2.4 are examples of processes and knowledge bases for each of the three types of behaviors. Notice that each portion of the process and the knowledge base for each behavior is stated as a performance. Each begins with a verb. This maintains the focus on performance.

In summary, content analysis is conducted in three stages. These stages are: function identification, behavior analysis, and behavior detailing (process and knowledge-base identification). The stages are conducted within the context of performance-based instruction, which focuses on the behavior expected of the learner. A completed content analysis yields the content the designer must teach a learner so that the learner is able to perform a behavior. It becomes the content around which lessons are structured for delivery to learners. Reexamine the diagram at the opening of this chapter to see this relationship.

Content Selection

As indicated earlier, content selection typically would be done prior to the behavior-detailing stage of content analysis. Selection is done at that time so energy is not expended on identifying processes and knowledge bases for behaviors that will not be selected for inclu-

FIGURE 2.4 Relationships between Functions, Behaviors, and Process and Knowledge Base

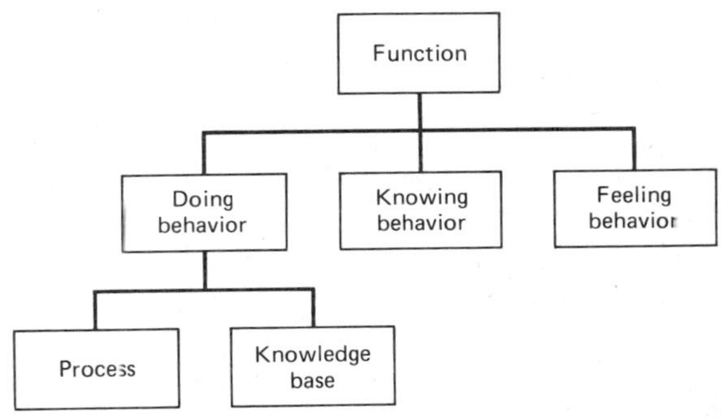

TABLE 2.2 Psychomotor Behavior Example

BEHAVIOR: CHANGE A TIRE	
Process (procedure)	Knowledge Base
1. Block the tires. 2. Position the jack. 3. Remove the hubcap. 4. Loosen the lug nuts. 5. Jack the car. 6. Remove the lug nuts. (etc.)	1. Recall safety precautions. 2. Recall procedures for lifting heavy objects. 3. Explain the procedure for changing a tire.

TABLE 2.3 Cognitive Behavior Example

BEHAVIOR: DECIDE WHICH WRENCH TO USE	
Process (procedure)	Knowledge Base
1. Identify the location of the object. 2. Determine the type of object (e.g., a bolt or a stud). 3. Determine the size of the object. 4. Match the functions of types of wrenches with the object. (etc.)	1. Recall types of wrenches and their functions. 2. Differentiate between objects manipulated with wrenches. (etc.)

TABLE 2.4 Affective Behavior Example

BEHAVIOR: COOPERATE WITH CO-WORKERS	
Process (actions)	Knowledge Base
1. Listen to co-workers. 2. Communicate with co-workers. 3. Assist others when asked. 4. Compromise. (etc.)	1. Explain the benefits of cooperation. 2. Differentiate between assisting and taking over. (etc.)

sion in the program. *Content selection* is the process of selecting the behaviors to be taught within a program from a total set of possible behaviors. The total set of behaviors is identified during the first two stages of content analysis.

Content selection is accomplished using a five-step procedure:

1. Determine the importance of each behavior.
2. Estimate the instructional time required to teach each behavior.
3. Determine the instructional time that can be devoted to the program.
4. Prioritize the behaviors based on importance and time.
5. Select high-priority behaviors that can be taught within the time available.

A chart similar to Figure 2.5 is used to determine the priority of each behavior. The importance of each behavior is determined by considering criteria such as how often the behavior is used, how much it provides a foundation for learning other behaviors, and how often it may be needed in the future. Next, the amount of instructional time it will take to teach each behavior is estimated. Importance and instructional time, along with other relevant criteria, are considered in determining the priority of each behavior. The priority is assigned to behaviors in the form of ranks (i.e., the behavior with a rank of 1 would have the highest priority, the behavior with a rank of 2 would have the second highest, and so on). Once the priority for each behavior is established, the highest-priority behaviors are selected that can be taught within the instructional time allocated to the program. This procedure will be discussed in more detail in Chapter 5.

Content Sequencing

After the content to be taught in a program has been identified and selected, it must be sequenced. *Content sequencing* is the process of arranging the behaviors to be taught into the order in which they will be taught. Before behaviors can be sequenced, they must be characterized as dependent or independent. *Dependent behaviors* are those that must be taught in a certain order because they build upon one another, or because they are usually performed together. For example, one must be able to "operate a microcomputer" before being able to "maintain a database with a microcomputer." Therefore, "maintain a database with a microcomputer" is dependent upon "operate a microcomputer."

Independent behaviors are those that can be taught at any time during the program because they are not

FIGURE 2.5 Sample Priority Chart

JOB-SEEKING			
BEHAVIOR LIST	Importance rating*	Estimated time**	Priority†
1. Summarize work experience.	5	4	2
2. List education.	5	2	1
3. List references.	4	1.5	3

* From 1 to 5 (5 = high)
** In hours
† In rank order (1 = highest priority)

the basis for learning other behaviors in the program, or because they are not performed together with other behaviors. For example, the behavior "purchase a microcomputer" could be taught at any time during a program focused on how to use a microcomputer. You can use a microcomputer without purchasing one.

Figure 2.6 presents a graphic example of dependent and independent behaviors. Notice that independent behaviors *A* and *B* could be taught at any time. They are not related to any of the other behaviors. Dependent behaviors 1, 2, 3, and 4 are connected. Reading the chart from the bottom to the top, behavior 4 must be taught after behaviors 1, 2, or 3. However, behavior 4 could be taught after either behavior 1, 2, or 3. Chapter 6 presents the process of behavior sequencing in detail.

Sequencing is one of the most important steps in providing meaningful learning experiences for learners, but it is often neglected. Learning theorists such as Herbart (1898) have told us that people learn best and retain what they learn longer when what they learn is meaningful to them. Part of the process of meaningful learning is for the learner to clearly see relationships among the things being learned so that they add up to a meaningful whole. Sequencing of behaviors for instruction is a key to bringing about meaningful learning. Teaching isolated behaviors without attempting to integrate them leads to fragmented learning and reduced ability on the part of learners to relate what they have learned in a meaningful way. Therefore, it is not only necessary to determine which behaviors are necessary as a basis for learning a new behavior, it is also important to relate behaviors that logically occur together so that learners can see interrelationships.

Because some behaviors are dependent and learning should be meaningful, it sometimes makes good instructional sense not to teach the lessons developed for each behavior separately, even though they may be taught in a proper sequence. If dependent behaviors always occur together, or if they have meaning only in reference to one another, they should be taught in one lesson delivery unit. A *lesson delivery unit* is a combination of lessons for one or more behaviors that are taught together. During the process of developing lessons to deliver instruction, a separate lesson should be planned for each behavior to be taught. However, highly related lessons might be taught together, at the same time, in one lesson delivery unit. For example, you would not pick up a heavy object without needing to put it down. Therefore, it would not make sense to teach the behavior "pick up a heavy object" and the behavior "put down a heavy object" separately. They should be taught together as one delivery unit.

FIGURE 2.6 Dependent and Independent Behaviors

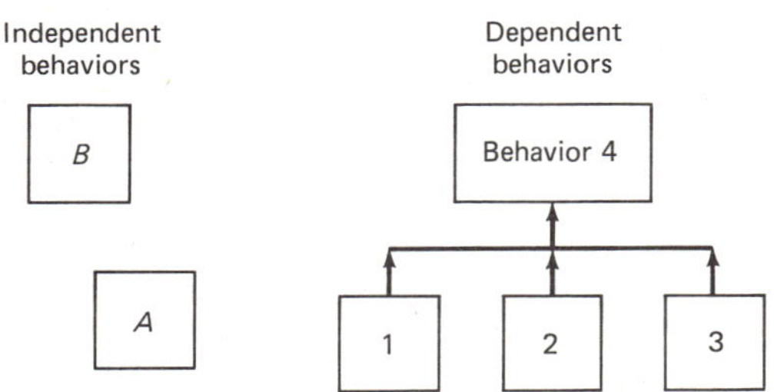

Content sequencing is also used to break down large instructional programs into component courses. For example, assume that an auto mechanics program is going to be taught within a community college which has its curriculum organized into three quarter-credit courses. Further assume that completion of the entire auto mechanics program requires nine months of full-time study. Given these circumstances, the nine-month program would need to be broken down into a number of three-credit courses. Content sequencing, as presented in Chapter 6, can be used to accomplish this by grouping dependent behaviors.

Core courses are also developed through content sequencing. A *core course* is a course designed to serve people preparing for a number of different roles which require the development of a common set of behaviors. For example, an introductory electronics course may be a core course for advanced electonics, robotics, and television repair programs.

Lesson Structuring

After the behaviors have been identified and the content relative to each behavior has been determined, the designer must determine how each behavior's content will be taught and evaluated. This determination must be made for each behavior even though the behaviors may be taught as one lesson delivery unit.

Lessons are planned for delivery to learners in two separate but related stages: lesson structuring and lesson delivery formatting. *Lesson structuring* is the process of developing a general plan for how the content will be pedagogically organized, presented to learners, and evaluated. It addresses each of the major stages of the lesson and what will be taught or evaluated at each stage. It also involves the tentative selection of the *type* of lesson delivery format that will be used to implement the lesson as well as the *types* of methods, media, evaluation tools, and feedback procedures that will be used. These decisions are tentative at this point; they become finalized during the lesson delivery formatting process when the actual selection or development decisions are made.

For example, the designer might decide that the lesson should be delivered with the traditional instructional format: an instructor presenting lectures and demonstrations to learners. Or, the designer might decide to use computer-assisted instruction (CAI), modularized instruction, or programmed instruction. These different delivery formats may require different types of instructional methods, media, evaluation tools, and feedback procedures. However, regardless which of these formats is used, the lesson first must be structured, or what will be delivered through the format may be meaningless.

Lesson structuring includes the following eight steps.

1. Develop the behavioral objective.
2. Develop the lesson flow.
3. Specify the content to be taught or evaluated at each lesson-flow stage.
4. Select the lesson delivery format.
5. Select instructional methods for each stage.
6. Select instructional media for each stage.
7. Select evaluation procedures.
8. Select feedback procedures.

These steps are presented in Figure 2.7. Each of the steps will be briefly reviewed here and will be discussed in detail in Chapters 8, 9, and 10.

Developing the Behavioral Objective. During the content identification process, behaviors are identified. In order for a lesson to be planned, the identified behaviors must be converted to behavioral objectives, or learning objectives. Besides the expected behavior, a behavioral objective indicates what the learner will be expected to have available to perform the behavior, and the standard to which the learner will be expected to perform. Therefore, a behavioral objective includes the following three parts:

1. *Givens:* the conditions under which the behavior is expected to be performed (this may include the environment, tools, materials, and other people needed to perform the behavior)
2. *Behavior:* the behavior to be performed
3. *Standard:* the standard against which performance of the behavior will be judged

The behavioral objective becomes the target for the instructor as well as the goal for the learner. Listed below are sample behavioral objectives for the behaviors presented in Tables 2.2, 2.3, and 2.4.

PSYCHOMOTOR OBJECTIVE

Givens: A car with a flat tire, tools, and a replacement tire
Behavior: Change a tire.
Standard: The replacement tire is mounted on the car, the lugs are tight, and the tools and replaced tire are stored.

COGNITIVE OBJECTIVE

Givens: A part requiring a wrench for removal
Behavior: Decide which wrench to use.
Standard: A verbal description of the decision process is consistent with that specified on the instructor checklist.

AFFECTIVE OBJECTIVE

Givens: Co-workers and a situation requiring cooperation
Behavior: Cooperate with co-workers.
Standard: Actions depicting cooperative activity are consistent with those specified on the instructor checklist (*Note:* Learners would have already been taught this content.)

Developing the Lesson Flow. Just as the designer must sequence the teaching of behaviors within a program, he or she must also sequence the stages within a lesson. The sequence of stages within a lesson is called

FIGURE 2.7 Lesson Structuring

<table>
<tr><td colspan="3">1. Develop the behavioral objective.</td></tr>
<tr><td>2. Develop the lesson flow.</td><td>3. Specify the content.</td><td>4. Select the delivery format.
5. Select methods.
6. Select media.</td></tr>
<tr><td>A. Objective
B. Rationale
C. Need-to-know information
D. Demonstration
E. Guided practice
F. Unguided practice
G. Evaluation
H. Feedback</td><td>Process and knowledge base from content analysis</td><td>Methods (e.g.)
Lecture
Demonstration
Role playing

Media (e.g.)
Slides
Transparencies
Videotapes</td></tr>
<tr><td colspan="3">7. Select evaluation procedures.</td></tr>
<tr><td colspan="3">8. Select feedback procedures.</td></tr>
</table>

the *lesson flow.* The PBID system uses a lesson flow called the *performance-based lesson flow.* As with other components of the system, it is designed to help the learner achieve performance capability.

The performance-based lesson flow contains eight stages:

A. State the objective.

B. Present the rationale for why it is important to learn the behavior.

C. Provide the learner with need-to-know information.

D. Demonstrate how to perform the behavior.

E. Let the learner practice the behavior with guidance.

F. Allow the learner to practice without guidance to perfect the behavior.

G. Evaluate learner performance of the behavior and understanding of the related knowledge base.

H. Provide the learner with feedback and direction about what to do next.

Specifying the Content to Be Taught. The actual content presented to learners, practiced, and evaluated at various stages throughout this lesson flow is identified through behavior detailing during content analysis. The knowledge base identified becomes the need-to-know information, and the process becomes the basis for teaching learners how to perform the behavior. A detailed discussion of which types of content to present and evaluate at each of the stages will be presented in Chapter 7.

Selecting the Lesson Delivery Format. A *lesson delivery format* is an instructional management system used to manage the interaction of learners and resources to bring about and evaluate learning. As indicated earlier, in order to complete the lesson structuring process, a tentative selection decision must be made about the type of lesson delivery format that will be used with a lesson. The types of methods, media, evaluation tools, and feedback procedures that will be used will depend in part upon which are compatible with the format selected. For example, live instructor–delivered lectures are most compatible with traditional instruction, while videotape demonstrations are very compatible with modularized instruction. The actual process of formatting lessons involves planning the orchestration, selection, and development of the methods, media, evaluation tools, and feedback procedures of a lesson.

The selection of a delivery format is tentative at this point because the designer may change her or his mind after attempting to actually format the lesson. Once the formatting and instructional materials development processes begin, it may be more efficient to use a different type of format than the one originally selected. (Lesson delivery formatting is reviewed in a later section of this chapter.)

Selecting Methods and Media. Once the content of each stage of a lesson has been determined and a tentative decision has been made about the delivery format to use, the methods and media that will be used to present the content must be selected. Instructional *methods* are procedures or processes for presenting learning materials and activities (e.g., a demonstration or a lecture). Instructional *media* are modes of communication used in presenting the learning materials and information (e.g., a videotape recorder, a live instructor, or a computer) (U.S. Department of the Air Force, 1973). Instructional media have also been defined as "printed and audiovisual forms of communication and their accompanying technology" (American Library Association, 1969). Both of these definitions consider media to be a form or mode of communication, in contrast to methods, which are instructional procedures.

Making the distinction between *methods* and *media* is important for the instructional designer. It provides for a much more flexible approach to determining how to deliver content to learners. Each method, or procedure, should be thought of as being communicable through a variety of forms of media. Such thinking is in contrast to the idea that method and media decisions are one, as was the case when media alternatives were limited and most instruction was delivered using the traditional format. For example, one common viewpoint was that a lecture was given by a live person. Therefore, when a person made the decision to use a lecture, he or she assumed that it would require a live person to be present to deliver it. Consequently, when individualized instruction and computer-assisted instruction (CAI) became more widely accepted alternative delivery formats to traditional instruction, people automatically thought lectures could not be used with those formats. However, if the decisions concerning methods and media are viewed separately, it becomes apparent that lectures can be used with these other formats. The key is to use other forms of appropriate media such as videotapes and audio tapes in place of a live lecturer as the basis for communicating the lectures. Chapter 9 will show in detail how these decisions are made.

At this point, a plan has been structured which includes the behavioral objective, the content that will be taught at various stages of the lesson flow, and the instructional methods and media that will be used to present the content. The next stage is to determine how the learner's progress will be evaluated.

Selecting Evaluation Procedures. *Evaluation procedures* are used for determining the learner's learning progress. As was indicated in the discussion of content analysis, the content to teach each behavior is broken down into the *process* of performing the behavior and the *knowledge base* needed to meaningfully apply the behavior. Therefore, evaluation procedures focus on both process evaluations and knowledge-base evaluations.

Process evaluations are used to determine if a person can perform a desired behavior. The ability of a person to perform a behavior is usually determined by observing the person performing the process, or by examining the product which results from performing the process. Therefore, there are two major focuses to process evaluation: performance (the process of performing) and product (the product of performing). Performance is evaluated with a performance test, and products are evaluated with product tests. Process can also be evaluated through learner self-checks and observation.

Knowledge-base evaluations are used to determine the information possessed by the learner. They usually take the form of written tests, oral tests, learner self-checks, or oral questioning.

Regardless of which type of behavior is to be taught (cognitive, psychomotor, or affective), both knowledge-base and process evaluations should be conducted. The focus of performance-based instruction on meaningful performance requires that people not only be able to do, but be able to understand what they are doing and why. Chapter 10 will present in more detail how to select evaluation procedures.

Selecting Feedback Procedures. After selecting evaluation procedures, the instructional designer must determine how learners will be informed about their progress. Because the PBID system is focused on helping learners develop the capability to perform, the interpretation of the evaluation results and the presentation of those results to learners should be considered to be diagnostic. In other words, the information should be used to inform learners of their progress and ways in which they might improve, if improvement is needed.

The information provided to learners about their learning progress is called *feedback*. Chapter 10 will provide more detail on feedback procedures and how to select them.

Summary. In summary, lesson structuring is the process of developing a plan for how the instructional content will be pedagogically organized, presented to learners, and evaluated. This component is crucial to the process of instructional design. Lesson structuring performs the same function as a blueprint for an architect. It is a plan for the logic of a lesson and indicates how the designer plans to bring the learner to performance capability relative to a behavior.

Lesson Delivery Formatting

Lessons are planned for delivery in two separate but related stages: lesson structuring and lesson delivery formatting. Although during lesson structuring the designer must tentatively make a decision about the type of delivery format that will be used to deliver the lesson, the actual formatting of the lesson takes place after the lesson is structured. *Lesson delivery formatting* is the process of planning how a structured lesson will be implemented as it is presented to learners and evaluated. The format developed includes the orchestration and selection of, or the decision to develop, *specific* methods, media, evaluation tools, and feedback procedures that will be used to implement the lesson. A *lesson delivery format* is an instructional management system used to manage the interaction of learners and resources to bring about and evaluate learning. Examples of lesson delivery formats are the traditional instructional format of an instructor presenting lectures and demonstrations to learners, CAI, modularized instruction, and programmed instruction.

Table 2.5 presents sample lesson delivery formats. Notice that each format addresses who will manage the lesson, what management resource will be used, and what learning resources will be utilized. The traditional format is managed by the instructor; he or she uses a lesson plan which outlines instructor actions; and she or he uses resources delivered through instructor-intensive instructional methods. Modularized instruction is managed by the learner; he or she uses a learning guide which is a lesson plan in the form of directions to

TABLE 2.5 Management and Typical Learning Resources Associated With Delivery Formats

	LESSON DELIVERY FORMATS			
	TRADITIONAL	MODULARIZED	PROGRAMMED INSTRUCTION	COMPUTER-ASSISTED INSTRUCTION (CAI)
WHO MANAGES	Instructor	Learner	Learner	Learner
MANAGEMENT RESOURCE	Lesson plan	Learning guide	Programmed text	Computer program
TYPICAL LEARNING RESOURCES	Instructor as the primary resource with support materials	Independent study material with the instructor and other people as resources	Programmed "text"	Computer "program" and computer-controlled devices

the learner; and the directions lead the learner though learning resources using highly individualized learning methods. Programmed instruction is managed by the learner using a programmed text; the text leads the learner through the instruction by using individualized learning methods. CAI is managed by the learner who uses a computer; the computer program leads the learner through learning resources controlled by the computer using highly individualized methods.

Although the management vehicle and resources take different forms, depending upon the lesson delivery format selected, the instruction being managed should always be structured as performance-based instruction.

Regardless of which delivery format is selected, the designer and instructor will still be in control of the learning environment. They will develop the lesson structure, select and develop the management vehicle, select or develop the learning resources, and act as resources during the learning process. Lesson delivery formatting will be discussed in detail in Chapters 11 through 13. The development of each of the four formats mentioned above will be presented along with examples.

Evaluation and Feedback Procedures Development

Once the lesson has been structured and the delivery format selected, resource materials actually need to be selected and developed. This book does not include detailed techniques for the selection and development of specific learning resources. However, it does present procedures for the development of evaluation and feedback procedures once they are selected. Those procedures are presented in Chapters 14 through 18.

SUMMARY

This chapter has presented an introduction to the PBID system. PBID is an integrated system for developing and evaluating instruction aimed at ensuring the performance capability of learners. It is organized into components that parallel the decision-making process of an instructional designer who wishes to develop and evaluate instruction.

The seven major components of the system are:

1. Program description
2. Content analysis
3. Content selection
4. Content sequencing
5. Lesson structuring
6. Lesson delivery formatting
7. Evaluation and feedback procedures development

At this point, you should refer to the diagram at the opening of this chapter to review the relationships among each of the major components of the system.

PBID utilizes the process described above for the teaching of content related to psychomotor (doing), cognitive (knowing), and affective (feeling) behaviors. It can be applied to teaching each of these types of behaviors. The system teaches people to meaningfully perform each of these behaviors in an integrated way.

ACTIVITIES AND EVALUATION

Directions: Complete each of the activities listed below to reinforce your learning and to determine your learning progress.

1. Describe the intent of the PBID system. Compare your responses with the statement of intent in this chapter.
2. List each of the major components of the PBID system. Check your list with the diagram at the opening of the chapter.
3. Write the definition of each of the seven major components of the PBID system. Check your definitions with the glossary.
4. Draw a diagram of the PBID system, including the arrows that indicate the flow of the system. Check your diagram with the PBID chart at the beginning of this chapter.
5. Explain the relationship between content analysis and lesson structuring. Compare your response with the description of the relationship in the section of this chapter on lesson structuring.
6. Explain the relationship between lesson structuring and lesson delivery formatting. Compare your response with the description of the relationship in the section of this chapter on lesson structuring.

REFERENCES

American Library Association, *Purchasing Library Materials in Public and School Libraries,* Doralyn J. Hickey (ed.), American Library Association, Chicago, 1969.

U.S. Department of the Air Force, *Handbook For Designers of Instructional Systems,* vol. 4, Washington, DC, 1973.

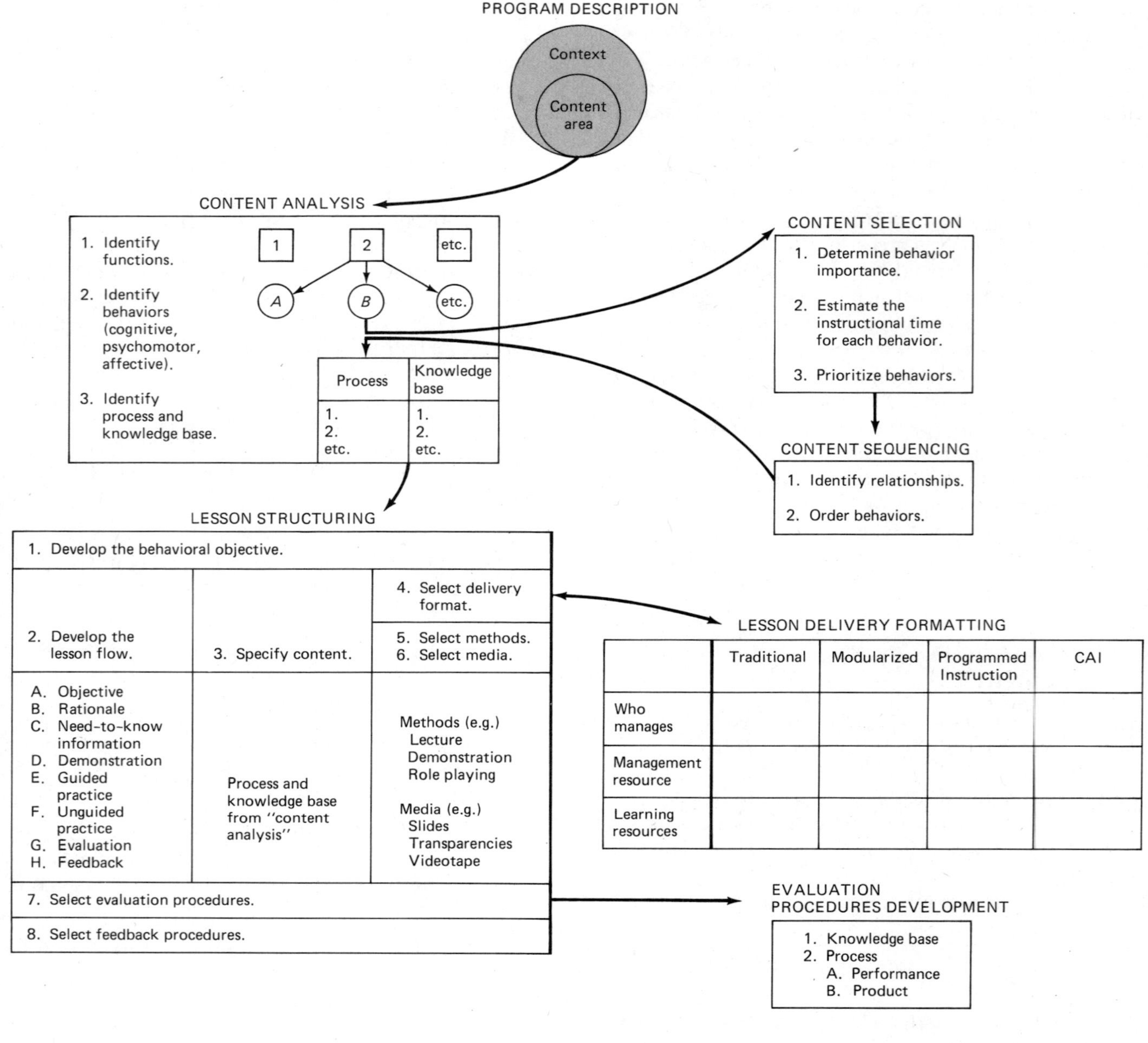
PROGRAM DESCRIPTION
Context
Content area
CONTENT ANALYSIS
1. Identify functions.
2. Identify behaviors (cognitive, psychomotor, affective).
3. Identify process and knowledge base.
1
2
etc.
A
B
etc.
Process
Knowledge base
1.
2.
etc.
1.
2.
etc.
CONTENT SELECTION
1. Determine behavior importance.
2. Estimate the instructional time for each behavior.
3. Prioritize behaviors.
CONTENT SEQUENCING
1. Identify relationships.
2. Order behaviors.
LESSON STRUCTURING
1. Develop the behavioral objective.
2. Develop the lesson flow.
3. Specify content.
4. Select delivery format.
5. Select methods.
6. Select media.
A. Objective
B. Rationale
C. Need-to-know information
D. Demonstration
E. Guided practice
F. Unguided practice
G. Evaluation
H. Feedback
Process and knowledge base from "content analysis"
Methods (e.g.)
Lecture
Demonstration
Role playing
Media (e.g.)
Slides
Transparencies
Videotape
7. Select evaluation procedures.
8. Select feedback procedures.
LESSON DELIVERY FORMATTING
Traditional
Modularized
Programmed Instruction
CAI
Who manages
Management resource
Learning resources
EVALUATION PROCEDURES DEVELOPMENT
1. Knowledge base
2. Process
A. Performance
B. Product

Chapter 3

Program Description

CHAPTER OBJECTIVE

Givens

A needs assessment

Behavior

Develop a program description.

Standard

All of the components of a program description are clearly stated and meet the criteria presented in this chapter.

TABLE 3.1 Same Program Description

CONTENT AREA

Computer programming

CONTEXT

Program level:	Adult training
Expected length:	40 hours
Program focus:	Updating
Institutional setting:	Industry, traditional instructional format
Relationship to other programs:	Standalone program
Special learner characteristics:	Journeyman machinists

OVERVIEW

A program desciption defines the intent of an instructional program. It indicates the content area(s) to be taught and the context within which that content is to be taught. It becomes the instructional designer's development target. Therefore, its creation is the first step in the design of an instructional program. The actual instructional program to be developed may include only a series of lessons regarding a limited set of skills, a course or series of courses, or all of the instruction needed to prepare people for an occupation.

The program description is developed in light of an established program need. The process of establishing that need is called *needs assessment.* Program needs assessment takes different forms, depending upon the nature of the organization for which the program is to be developed. In vocational and technical education the need for programs is judged relative to factors such as occupational demand, student demand, cost of operating the program, economic development potential, and other sources of trained people. In business and industry the need is judged on factors such as potential increased productivity, cost of developing versus buying training services, availability of training services, and morale of employees. The procedures for actually conducting needs assessments are beyond the scope of this book.

Because the need for a program is often established by people other than the instructional designer, the designer must closely communicate with those people during the development of the program description. The formulation of the program description provides a vehicle for clarifying expectations.

Program descriptions do not have to be lengthy documents. They can be presented precisely and clearly in an outline format. Tables 3.1 and 3.2 provide examples of program descriptions for computer programming and general auto mechanics programs. Notice that the outline style provides all of the information needed to understand the intent of these instructional programs. Each of the components of a program description will be discussed later.

COMPONENTS

A program description contains two major components: the content area(s) to be taught in the program (e.g., occupation, job, or type of skills or behaviors); and the context within which the program will be delivered.

The Content Area

In vocational and technical education and training the content area is generally specified in terms of roles for which people are to be prepared, or types of skills that are to be developed. Sample roles would be a machinist, a practical nurse, a data processing assistant, a secretary, an instructional designer, or a parent. Sample types of skills are basic skills (reading, writing, and arithmetic) or job-seeking skills.

During the development of a program description, the content area need only be described globally (e.g., by occupation or job title or by type of behaviors). Later, during content analysis, the content area is broken down to determine the exact behaviors to be taught. At this point, the goal is to define the content area that will later undergo further analysis.

At times, people differentiate between an occupation and a job as a way of specifying roles, and at other times

TABLE 3.2 Sample Program Description

CONTENT AREA

Basic math skills

CONTEXT

Program level:	Postsecondary
Expected length:	12 months, 1060 hours
Program focus:	Initial preparation
Institutional setting:	Modularized, self-paced, three quarter-credit courses, school
Relationship to other programs:	First in the auto mechanics series
Special learner characteristics:	High school graduate or equivalent

they are considered to be the same. In developing a program description, the differentiation is useful. Occupations are considered to be more inclusive and represent a type of role that is common to many different settings such as firms or companies. A job is usually considered to be how that occupation is defined within a specific firm or company.

An example of an occupation is a machinist, a secretary, or a computer programmer. These are readily identifiable occupations, or professions, that people perform in society. Standard occupational titles and descriptions of occupations can be found in the *Dictionary of Occupational Titles* (U.S. Department of Labor, 1977). Another useful document which identifies titles of content areas and instructional programs is published by the National Center for Educational Statistics; it is entitled *A Classification of Instructional Programs* (National Center for Educational Statistics, 1981). It was developed by the U.S. Department of Education as a tool to establish uniform titles for educational programs.

Within a occupation it is possible to identify specific jobs. For example, a number of firms may have machinists (a machinist is an occupation), but their machinists may perform different subsets of the role of a machinist, depending upon the nature of the firm. The job of the machinists in one firm might be operating lathes; in another firm, operating milling machines. Or, within one firm some machinists might be operating lathes and others might be operating milling machines. Even though both would be in the occupation of machinist, one would have to identify the specific job to further focus the nature of the behaviors that would have to be mastered to reach performance capability. Therefore, in describing the content area, designers should be as specific as possible in listing an occupation, a job, or a type of skill to be learned. This specificity will later provide a clearer focus for development.

The Context

Once the content area or areas are specified, the instructional context for teaching that content must be clearly defined. The context influences many of the program design decisions. For example: How long will the program be? Will it be taught in industry, a secondary school, or a postsecondary institution? What type of learners are expected?

The context should include six major elements:

1. The level of the program
2. The expected length of the program
3. The program focus
4. The instructional setting
5. The relationships with other programs
6. Special learner characteristics

Level of the Program. The level of the program indicates whether the program will be offered at the elementary, secondary, postsecondary, or adult level. The first three terms are most often associated with formal schooling. The adult level is often associated with adult extension programs offered through schools or with training programs in business and industry.

Expected Length of the Program. The expected length of the program indicates the amount of time that will be devoted to the program. Length can be specified in terms of years, months, weeks, or hours. The expected length of the program provides the designer with boundaries as to how much instruction can actually be presented. It is an important element in prioritizing and selecting behaviors. The expected length might have to be adjusted as the program continues to be developed.

Program Focus. The focus of an instructional program is defined using terms which communicate the expected skill levels with which learners will come to and leave the program. The PBID system is particularly well-suited for programs with the purpose of leading people to performance mastery. This includes mastery of selected behaviors in exploration or work sampling programs as well as programs developed to prepare people to functionally perform the behaviors associated with selected roles (e.g., jobs, occupations, or specific skills).

Within this broad goal of assisting learners to develop performance capability, it is important to define the expected purpose more precisely. A program can be focused on assisting learners with:

1. Initial preparation
2. Retraining
3. Exploration
4. Remediation
5. Updating

Initial preparation takes place when the content is new to the learners and they have had little prior experience related to it. For example, if the people who will be enrolling in an Introduction to Microcomputers course are not expected to have prior experience related to microcomputers, the course will be considered to be initial preparation.

Retraining takes place when a person has already been prepared for one role and it is possible to develop training for a new role based upon the skills of the first. For example, a person may have been prepared to work as a machinist in a steel mill, but the steel mill has shut down. Therefore, the person is to be retrained as a mechanic in an automated factory where jobs are available; the new training can be built upon the person's machinist background. If this person had been working as a machinist and is to be prepared for another occupation to which none of the skills of the first occupation can be transferred, this would be considered to be new initial training, not retraining.

Programs are designed for *exploration* when the intent is for learners to experience a wide range of activities so that they are better informed, or so they can select roles which they would like to pursue in-depth in the future. Such programs are often used with special-needs learners or with other individuals who are having difficulty selecting what they would like to do and can do as work. For example, a person may be uncertain about preparing to become a medical receptionist; he or she can be provided with an opportunity to perform some of the behaviors of a medical receptionist to explore his or her interest and ability relative to being a receptionist.

Another program focus is *remediation.* Remediation takes place when a person already has some level of skill with a behavior but that level is not sufficient for adequate performance. Remediation is the process of bringing a person's skill level up to that which is required. For example, a person wishing to become a practical nurse may have developed writing skills sufficient for communicating during everyday life; however, those writing skills will not be sufficient to communicate the condition of patients to doctors. Therefore, the learner would need remediation in the area of writing skills to bring those behaviors up to the proficiency needed to perform as a practical nurse.

Another program focus is *updating.* Updating occurs when a person is actually performing in a role but needs to develop a new set of behaviors to continue to be effective. For example, a sales clerk in a major department store may have been employed in that job and used a standard cash register for 10 years. However, the employer has installed computerized cash registers, and therefore, there is a need for updating for the sales clerk to be able to continue to perform that job. The person must now be updated and taught how to operate a computerized cash register.

It is important that one clearly identify which of these program focuses underlies the intent of an instructional program. The focus is critical in determining a program's intent and, therefore, the perspective that one has when developing a program.

Instructional Setting. *Instructional setting* refers to the type of institutional environment within which the program is expected to take place. Will the program be offered in a school, a business, or an industry? Will the program use modularized instruction, traditional instruction, or CAI? Will it include components of in-class training or on-the-job training? What is the training philosophy of the institution (a school, a business, or an industry) in which the program will be offered? Will the program be delivered as a total program, or will it be broken down into courses?

Each institution has its own unique settings within which it provides instructional programs. These settings came to be as a result of many prior decisions made by the institution as it historically evolved. Each institution has its own organizational structure within which it conducts business, a commitment to a curriculum format into which it tries to fit instructional programs, limitations on resources that are available for an instructional program, and staff with varying talents to actually develop and conduct instructional programs. An understanding of these institutional factors is crucial during the development of an instructional program. If such factors are not adequately considered during the design process, the program eventually developed will not function effectively within the institution.

Relationships with Other Programs. No instructional program stands completely alone. It is not possible for any one program to teach learners everything. Therefore, one must consider the types of behaviors that a learner will be assumed to bring to the program. For example, when designing a beginning course in accounting, the designer must make some assumptions about the math skills that learners will bring with them. These assumptions will determine the point at which the program will begin to develop new math behaviors. If it is assumed that the learners will come to the program with fifth-grade math skills, the accounting program must start developing further math behaviors from the fifth-grade level.

Behaviors which a learner is expected to have obtained prior to entering an instructional program are called *prerequisite behaviors.* It is important to make these prerequisites explicit in order to have a clear perspective of where to begin the instructional process.

Another consideration in designing a program is whether it will be part of a sequence of programs. If it will be, other programs that are to be taken prior to the program being developed should be examined to determine the behaviors that will have already been developed. Also, programs expected to be taken after the new program must be considered to ensure that behaviors necessary for a smooth transition into those programs are developed.

Special Learner Characteristics. Special learner characteristics must also be considered when developing a program description. Each instructional program is developed with a certain population of learners in mind. Understanding the characteristics of the anticipated learner population gives the instructional designer information on the skill-level range that one would assume learners will bring with them to the instructional program. For example, if all of the learners are machinists working in exactly the same job in the same firm, and if the program is focused on updating those machinists, the group would be very uniform in terms of their past skills. Therefore, the program could be built on the skills which the machinists already have. If, on the other hand, the machinist program were being developed as an adult extension program and learners were expected to come from a range of industries and might include people who would like to take up machining as a hobby, the designer would be faced with a much more complicated problem: how to identify where the program should begin.

Besides considering differences in past experiences of learners, a designer must also consider differences in their actual learning ability. For example, a program designed for educable mentally retarded (EMR) learners would be substantially different from one designed for average high school graduates.

A designer needs to identify any special learner characteristics of the group for whom the program is being designed. Without doing so, the designer may develop a program for a group of people that does not really exist; therefore, the program will not work with the group of learners for which it was really intended. This phenomenon occurs more often than people are willing to acknowledge. It occurs quite often in highly technical fields such as electronics and health occupations. Instructional designers of such programs, and the members of their program development advisory committees, tend not to have evolved from groups for which training is to be developed. This is understandable, particularly when the jobs for which training is to be provided are at relatively low levels. Actual job incumbents may not have the ability or preparation in the actual design of programs. Because the developers tend to be much more highly educated than the people for whom the program is to be designed, there is a natural tendency to "inflate" the skill levels expected of learners. This inflated expectation can then cause a program to be developed to prepare people who do not "fit" the actual role requirements. A clear definition of the types of people who are to perform in the roles for which the program is to be developed helps keep this phenomenon under control.

VALIDATION

Once a program description has been initially developed, it should be validated to make sure that the instructional designer's perception of the intent of the program is accurate. Validation should begin by presenting the program description to the people that commissioned the program. In many cases this will be the people who conducted the initial needs assessment. They should be asked whether the program description adequately conveys the intent of the program.

In addition, the people who will utilize the talents of the learners after they complete the program should be consulted. In vocational and technical education, the consultation is usually done through an advisory committee. In business and industry, it is done through an advisory committee or with the people within the company who are most knowledgeable about the training problem which the program is to address. Early on, it is desirable to establish an advisory committee or to identify the people who best understand the training problem. If the program is designed to prepare computer programmers, then people who are knowledgeable about the expectations for computer programmers should be identified. If the intent of the program is to teach basic math skills to people in the accounting department, then people who are knowledgeable about the math skills required of people in the accounting department should be identified.

It is important to establish the validity of the program description to ensure that the program to be designed will be focused on an agreed-upon intent. A well-designed program focused on the wrong intent is useless.

See Appendices B and C for additional examples of a program description.

SUMMARY

The development of a program description is the first step of instructional design. That description defines the intent of an instructional program. It describes the content area or areas to be taught and the context within which that content will be taught. The description globally defines the goal of an instructional designer.

ACTIVITIES AND EVALUATION

Directions: Complete each of the activities below to reinforce your learning and to determine your learning progress.

1. Indicate the two major subdivisions of a program description and explain the function of each.

2. List the six components of the context of a program. Indicate the types of information included in a description of each of these components.

3. Develop a program description for a program that you would like to design. Use an outline format such as that presented in Tables 3.1 and 3.2. Refer to other examples in Appendix A.

REFERENCES

National Center for Educational Statistics, *A Classification of Instructional Programs,* National Center for Educational Statistics, Washington, DC, 1981.

U.S. Department of Labor, *Dictionary of Occupational Titles,* Washington, DC, 1977.

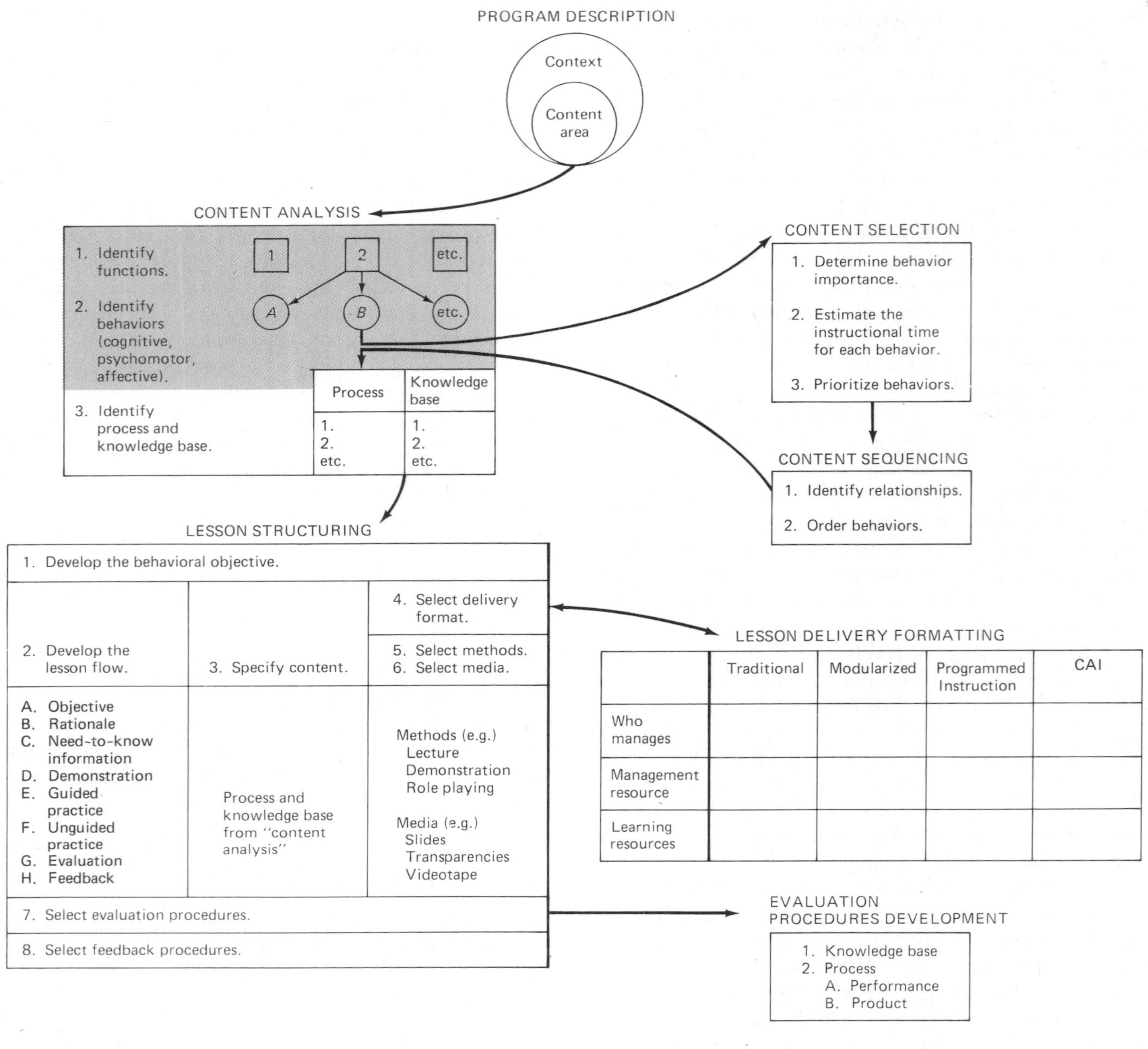
PROGRAM DESCRIPTION
Context
Content area
CONTENT ANALYSIS
1. Identify functions.
2. Identify behaviors (cognitive, psychomotor, affective).
3. Identify process and knowledge base.
1
2
etc.
A
B
etc.
Process
Knowledge base
1.
2.
etc.
1.
2.
etc.
CONTENT SELECTION
1. Determine behavior importance.
2. Estimate the instructional time for each behavior.
3. Prioritize behaviors.
CONTENT SEQUENCING
1. Identify relationships.
2. Order behaviors.
LESSON STRUCTURING
1. Develop the behavioral objective.
2. Develop the lesson flow.
3. Specify content.
4. Select delivery format.
5. Select methods.
6. Select media.
A. Objective
B. Rationale
C. Need-to-know information
D. Demonstration
E. Guided practice
F. Unguided practice
G. Evaluation
H. Feedback
Process and knowledge base from "content analysis"
Methods (e.g.)
Lecture
Demonstration
Role playing
Media (e.g.)
Slides
Transparencies
Videotape
7. Select evaluation procedures.
8. Select feedback procedures.
LESSON DELIVERY FORMATTING
Traditional
Modularized
Programmed Instruction
CAI
Who manages
Management resource
Learning resources
EVALUATION PROCEDURES DEVELOPMENT
1. Knowledge base
2. Process
A. Performance
B. Product

Content Analysis: Function Identification and Behavior Analysis

CHAPTER OBJECTIVE

Givens

A program description which includes the content area or areas and context of the program to be developed

Behavior

Identify the functions and behaviors to be taught.

Standard

Content area will be analyzed into functions and behaviors.

OVERVIEW

The process of identifying the specific content to be taught in a program is called *content analysis.* It is accomplished within the parameters of an already-defined program description. As shown in Figure 4.1, content analysis is conducted in three stages. Each of the three stages is briefly described in Chapter 2. It is recommended that you review the content analysis section of Chapter 2 before proceeding with this chapter.

This chapter presents an overview of content analysis and a detailed discussion of its first two stages: function identification and behavior analysis. The purpose of these first two stages is to identify what people will be expected to be able to do after they complete the instructional program. What people will be expected to be able to do is first specified as functions, which are major subdivisions of the roles people will be expected to perform, and then as component behaviors, which allow people to perform those functions. The third stage, behavior detailing, will be discussed in Chapter 7. The purpose of that stage is to identify the content that will need to be taught in order for people to be able to perform the behaviors and, therefore, the functions.

Before continuing with the discussion, it is important to relate content analysis to the widely used practice of task analysis. Task analysis follows the same three basic stages as content analysis, but it has been used in the past primarily for the analysis of psychomotor behavior. Therefore, the terminology used to describe the three stages of task analysis is consistent with descriptions of psychomotor behaviors. The common term used in task analysis equivalent to *functions* is *duties.* Duties are then analyzed into *tasks,* which are equivalent to *behaviors.* Finally, tasks are broken down into the procedure for performing the task and the related knowledge that is needed to perform the task through *task detailing,* which is equivalent to *behavior detailing* (Butler, 1972; Pucel and Knaak, 1975; and State of Florida, 1985).

When content analysis, as it is described here, is applied to the psychomotor aspects of a content area,

FIGURE 4.1 Stages of Content Analysis

Content to be taught in a program is analyzed in three stages:

1. *Function identification*
   Identification of groupings of behaviors called functions
2. *Behavior analysis*
   Identification of behaviors
3. *Behavior detailing*
   Identification of the process of performing each behavior and the knowledge base needed to meaningfully apply the behavior

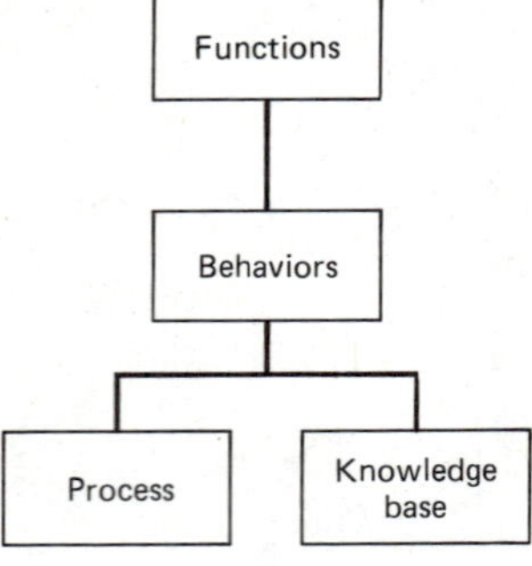

the procedure is the same as task analysis and the results are the same. *Functions* may be defined as *duties* have been in the past; *behaviors* may be specified as *tasks*; and *behavior details* may be specified as *task details.*

The terminology of content analysis generalizes the processes of task analysis to all three behavioral domains. Thus, performance-based instructional design methods may be applied to cognitive and affective behaviors as well as to those in the psychomotor realm. (The three domains of behavior are described in detail later.)

STATING BEHAVIORS

A behavior is a visible action of an individual, for example, replacing a light bulb, solving a problem, blinking an eye, accepting another person, or cooperating with others.

Behaviors are stated with three parts:

1. An action verb
2. What is acted upon
3. Modifying information

Table 4.1 presents some sample behaviors. It is important not to confuse stating the behavior with stating an instructional objective, which will be discussed in Chapter 8. Although a behavior is part of an instructional objective, it does not contain all the elements of an objective.

Notice that each behavior statement must contain at least the first two parts: an action verb and what is acted upon. However, only some of the behavior statements require the addition of modifying information. Modifying information is added to the statement of a behavior when the behavior could be performed differently under different circumstances. Modifying information clarifies the particular circumstance. For example, one might collect data for many purposes, and the behavior "collect data" would be performed differently, depending upon the specific purpose. Therefore, the purpose for which the data will be collected (e.g., for analysis or for reporting) must also be stated. The example in Table 4.1 indicates "collect data for analysis."

TABLE 4.1 Sample Behaviors

Action Verb	What Is Acted Upon	Modifying Information
Collect	data	for analysis
Evaluate	a job application	for completeness
Measure	diameter	with a micrometer
Cooperate	with co-workers	
Treat	tools	with care
Decide	which staff member	will be promoted

On the other hand, the example "cooperate with co-workers" does not contain modifying information. That is because it is assumed that one would cooperate with co-workers using the same process in essentially all situations related to the particular program being developed. Modifying information is not considered necessary to further clarify the behavior to be taught. If cooperation with co-workers could be done in two different ways, and if both ways were to be taught in the same program, then there would be two stated behaviors (e.g., "cooperate with co-workers in quality circles"; "cooperate with co-workers when assembling equipment").

When stating a behavior, care must be taken in selecting the verb. The verb specifies the type of action that will be expected of the learner and becomes the focus for the development of instruction to teach the behavior. For example, it is not sufficient to use verbs such as *understand, know,* or *learn.* These verbs do not focus the learner, the instructional designer, or the instructor. Why should the learner understand, know, or learn? What will the learner be expected to do? If a person needs to understand in order to select, then the verb should be *select.* If the person is to learn to cooperate, then the verb should be *cooperate.* Appendix A presents a list of suggested verbs that might be used in stating behaviors (Claus, 1968). It is a useful tool for selecting the most appropriate verb.

TYPES OF BEHAVIORS

Behaviors can be grouped into three major domains which were presented by Benjamin Bloom (Bloom, 1956). Bloom's definitions have been modified slightly for use here with performance-based instructional design. However, the definitions presented contain the essence of Bloom's original definitions. Table 4.2 indicates the three major domains of behaviors and the definitions of each.

Each of the three behavior domains will be presented from the perspective of what a person would observe while a learner performs such behaviors; however, it is important to realize that one need not be present to observe such performance. Behaviors can be recorded on audio- and videotape and observed later. It is also possible to judge performance by observing the physical products that are the result of a performance. When and how to evaluate performance through direct observation, products, or both, are discussed in detail in Chapter 18.

TABLE 4.2 Three Major Domains of Behavior

1. *Psychomotor* (doing) behaviors, which involve visible physical manipulations
2. *Cognitive* (knowing) behaviors, which involve the manipulation of information and result in a visible action
3. *Affective* (feeling) behaviors, which involve visible actions that communicate emotional tones

Psychomotor behaviors involve visible physical manipulations, for example, making a table, changing a tire, baking a cake, changing a diaper, or placing a disk into a computer. They are usually performed by completing a procedure, which results in a completed behavior. For example, if one follows the steps indicated in a recipe for baking a cake, a cake should result. If one follows the procedural steps for changing a tire, a tire will be changed. During the procedure for baking a cake or changing a tire, each procedural step is visible; each step is also a psychomotor activity.

Cognitive behaviors involve the manipulation of information, which results in visible action; however, the visible action is not the primary focus. The primary focus is on the mental manipulation of information which results in the visible action.

The process of performing a cognitive behavior is also usually procedural. For example, if one asks an individual to add three numbers (2, 4, and 6), the visible, physical action of writing the number 12 on a piece of paper is not the primary concern. The primary concern is how the person arrived at the number 12, in other words, the procedure the person used to manipulate information to arrive at the answer. Each step of such a procedure is usually not a visible psychomotor activity. The steps are performed in a person's mind.

Another cognitive behavior example is "determine margins for a business letter." The visible action would be a person actually setting the margins on a printer or typewriter for a business letter. However, the process which is of interest is not the actual setting of the margins, but the mental manipulation of information that was undertaken to determine where the margins should be set. Methods of making cognitive procedures visible will be discussed later during the discussion of evaluation procedures presented in Chapter 18.

Affective behaviors involve visible actions that communicate emotional tones. The visible actions usually occur in three different forms:

1. Body language
2. The actual words expressed
3. The way in which the words are expressed

These are observed by people and are often interpreted as being a person's attitude. Although they are usually observed as someone performs them, they can also be recorded and observed later. The actions can be recorded by writing or printing words, or through sound and/or video recordings.

Body language involves actions which communicate emotional tone without words, for example, a smile, a frown, the way a person positions his or her body in relation to another person, a person's physical appearance (dress), or how a person positions himself or herself in a chair during a discussion.

Words also communicate emotional tone, both in which ones are selected and in how they are expressed. For example, someone can say to another individual that he is *pleased* or *angry.* These two words communicate very different emotional tones.

The way in which words are expressed also communicates emotional tone. One could say the word *hello* in a pleasant voice, which would tend to indicate the acceptance of the individual to whom the word was spoken, or in a very gruff or angry voice, which would communicate the nonacceptance of the individual. The context within which words are presented also communicates emotional tones. The word *hello* can be presented within an argument or within a warm greeting. The single word does not communicate the entire emotional message.

We all communicate emotional tones continually as we conduct other activities. Affective behaviors are usually performed while performing some other psychomotor or cognitive behavior. Let us look at the affective behavior "cooperate with co-workers." Cooperation usually takes place among individuals who are performing another behavior. For example, two people might cooperate while carrying a table from one room to another. An evaluator could observe the carrying of the table from a psychomotor perspective or from an affective perspective. If she viewed it from a psychomotor perspective, she would observe the actual process of carrying the table from one room to the other (e.g., where the movers grabbed it; how they hit or avoided the walls as they moved it). If she viewed the activity from an affective perspective, she would observe the cooperation and interaction between the co-workers during the process of carrying the table: the way they spoke to each other, whether the words spoken by one communicated acceptance of the other's point of view, whether they listened to each other, and whether they were willing to compromise with each other.

All three domains of behavior (psychomotor, cognitive, and affective) are extremely important in the education and training of individuals who are expected to develop performance capability relative to roles in society. As the performance of individuals becomes more complex, they must not only develop performance capability relative to psychomotor behaviors, they must also develop performance capability relative to cognitive and affective behaviors. For example, it is just as important for an auto mechanic to decide what needs to be repaired, and be able to relate to customers, as it is to be able to actually repair a defective part. Therefore, the instructional designer must develop programs which prepare people in all three domains of behavior.

As will be seen as we progress, often a learner must develop all three types of behaviors in order to perform a function. In other words, if one is going to move furniture, it is important to decide which furniture to move, to be able to move it properly, and to cooperate with the other individuals who will be moving it. All three behaviors (cognitive, psychomotor, and affective) must be performed to a minimal standard if the correct furniture is to be moved to the correct location. Therefore, at times related psychomotor, cognitive, and affective behaviors might be taught together in a lesson delivery unit containing one or more of each type of behavior. The concept of a lesson delivery unit will be discussed later during lesson structuring.

How does one determine if a behavior is psychomotor, cognitive, or affective? It is obvious that every behavior requires more than one type of activity. How a behavior is categorized is based on the predominant process involved in performing the behavior. As indicated in the example of adding the three numbers, which was presented earlier, there is a psychomotor behavior of writing the number 12. However, that is not the process of primary interest. The predominant process, and the one of primary interest, is the cognitive process of actually assembling the numbers together to arrive at the number 12.

FUNCTION IDENTIFICATION

As indicated in Figure 4.1, the first stage of analyzing a content area is identification of functions one expects people to be able to perform. Most content areas contain far more potential functions than the designer would want to include in a particular program. Therefore, the designer must identify the particular ones to be included in the program. For example, people who have the occupational title of machinist operate a large number of different machines in all industries. If the designer were developing a machinist program, it would be important to determine the particular machines which people would be expected to operate after completing the program. The same would be true if one were developing a management training program. The designer must decide which major types of management activities will be included in the particular program.

Functions are major groupings of behaviors that are performed together and which result in a more complex performance (e.g., "supervise employees" and "operate a milling machine"). They typically represent the major performance subdivisions of a job, occupation, or role. Because they are readily identifiable subdivisions, they usually are precise statements (e.g., "perform routine maintenance," "communicate orally," and "supervise employees"). Functions involve fewer behaviors than a content area, but they usually contain more than one. In other words, functions typically involve multiple behaviors. In order to perform a function, one must be able to perform the component behaviors.

Functions within different content areas may be organized around different dimensions. Table 4.3 presents some of those dimensions. The various dimensions presented are not totally independent, and at times it would be possible to analyze a given content area using more than one dimension.

Some functions are organized around job *duties* performed by a person in an occupation (e.g., "operate a lathe," "tune up a car," and "type a letter"). This has been the typical way of deriving functions in the past, as indicated in the discussion of task analysis.

Functions may also be organized around *problems* a person is expected to solve. For example, in developing a course in advanced television maintenance, the content may be organized around typical diagnostic problems such as "diagnose video failure," "diagnose audio failure," or "diagnose lack of power." Then during the teaching of television maintenance, examples from many different electronic circuits would be used to make the content relevant, but the course would not be organized around any one television circuit. The functions would be organized around types of problems needing to be solved, regardless of the specific electronic circuits being diagnosed.

Functions may also be organized around *products* a person is expected to be able to produce. For example, a company may produce photocopiers. Therefore, the content in the company's training programs could be organized around the company's processes to produce photocopiers. The process of producing the photocopiers could be outlined. Each major process for producing a component could be considered a function. Instruction, therefore, would be organized around these functions, or processes, for producing the product.

Some functions are organized around *types of decisions* that need to be made. This is particularly true for people in supervisory or management positions. A manager may need to hire people, fire people, or supervise people. These are all decision-based; therefore, it may make more sense to determine the types of decisions that managers are expected to make rather than analyze the result of what managers do as the basis for deriving their functions.

Other functions are organized around *systems* that an individual is expected to develop or maintain. This is particularly true in a high-technology industry. Many applications of high-technology are planned and implemented in terms of systems. For example, a company may be producing automobiles using robots. The robots have electrical, mechanical, and hydraulic systems. Repair manuals tend to be organized around these systems. Therefore, it would be reasonable to analyze the role of a maintenance mechanic trained to maintain these systems in terms of the systems.

At times it is not reasonable to organize a course around typical functions that are based on subdivisions of the role a person is expected to perform after training. Such organization would be unreasonable in the case of a program intended to prepare people in a set of generic skills that are not specific to a given role. For example, a program may be designed to prepare people in basic math, reading, or writing skills. In this case, the program is typically organized according to the *component skills* of math, reading, or writing. However, the level of component skill development that is expected of learners after completing the program must be consistent with the roles they will be expected to enter. For example, a designer may be asked to develop a basic math program for welders and machinists. The course may be organized around basic math skills such as addition, subtraction, division, and multiplication. However, the nature of the math problems to be solved must be placed in the perspective of the roles of welders and machinists.

Table 4.4 presents some sample functions for the content area "secretarial occupation" organized around job duties. Table 4.5 indicates some sample functions from the content area "job-seeking skills" organized around component skills.

Functions can be identified by, first, examining the content area and, then, asking the following six questions:

1. What job duties will a person be expected to perform?
2. What problems will a person be expected to solve?
3. What products will a person be expected to produce?
4. What major types of decisions will a person be expected to make?
5. What systems will the person be expected to maintain?
6. What are the component skills?

TABLE 4.3 Dimensions for Organizing Functions

- Job duties
- Problems to be solved
- Products to be produced
- Types of decisions to be made
- Systems to be maintained
- Component skills

TABLE 4.4 Sample Functions

CONTENT AREA

Secretarial occupation

FUNCTIONS

1. Operate office equipment.
2. Communicate orally.
3. Communicate in writing.
4. Manage clerical staff.
5. Keep records.

TABLE 4.5 Sample Functions

CONTENT AREA

Job-seeking skills

FUNCTIONS

1. Write a resume.
2. Complete a job application.
3. Interview an employer.

Based on answers to these questions, a designer can determine which dimension should be used to organize the functions within a given analysis. The analysis should use the dimension which is most consistent with the content area to be analyzed. Usually, the one which is most consistent will allow one to most easily envision the content area. In other words, if a content area does not lend itself to analysis using one of these dimensions, one will find oneself having to force the content area into that dimension. If the dimension fits the content area, it will be relatively easy to envision the content area in terms of that dimension.

The functions identified should consist of logical groupings of behaviors. If the activities consist of single behaviors, they are probably not functions, but behaviors. Rarely does a function contain only one behavior. Remember, functions are groups of behaviors that are typically performed together.

BEHAVIOR ANALYSIS

In order for people to perform a function, they must be able to perform the component behaviors of that function. Figure 4.1 shows the relationship between functions and behaviors. The process of identifying and classifying behaviors is called *behavior analysis.* The goal of this process is to identify the behaviors expected of the learner after completing instruction.

Alternative Methods of Identifying Behaviors

There are a number of common methods that are used to identify behaviors. Table 4.6 lists the five that will be discussed in this text.

TABLE 4.6 Alternative Methods of Identifying Behaviors

1. Directly observing people performing the behavior
2. Analyzing existing documents (e.g. behavior listings, texts, and/or manuals)
3. Analyzing job descriptions
4. Consulting advisory committees
5. Interviewing successful performers

Directly Observing Behaviors. One method of identifying behaviors is to directly observe people performing the behaviors. For example, if one wished to analyze the behaviors performed by a computer operator, one would observe computer operators as they performed their jobs. If one wished to identify the mathematical behaviors needed by a machinist, one would observe machinists performing types of mathematical calculations at their jobs. If one wished to determine the types of affective behaviors needed by a salesperson, one would observe salespeople as they performed their jobs.

Analyzing Existing Documents. A second method of identifying behaviors is to analyze existing documents such as existing behavior listings (task listings), texts, and manuals. Behavior listings are the simplest to analyze because the behaviors are already explicitly stated. Typically, a behavior listing is reviewed to determine which behaviors on the list would be appropriate for a given instructional program.

The analysis of texts and manuals is more complicated than the analysis of behavior listings. The designer must read through the texts and manuals and infer the behaviors which need to be performed. In some cases, the texts or manuals may have been developed using competency-based or performance-based instructional design techniques. In those cases, the behaviors will be stated explicitly. However, most texts and manuals are not written in one of those formats. Therefore, it is necessary to infer the actual behaviors that individuals will need to exhibit in order to apply the content area.

Analyzing Job Descriptions. Although job descriptions are existing documents, they are discussed separately from other existing documents because their analysis is somewhat unique. A *job description* is a written document which describes the expectations an employer has for a person in a particular job. There is wide variation in how employers actually write job descriptions. As with texts and manuals, some job descriptions are written in terms of the behaviors expected of the individual. In many other cases, they are written as narratives, with expected activities of a person performing the job stated throughout the narrative. The activities are usually not stated as behaviors; therefore, as with analyzing texts and manuals, the designer must at times infer the behaviors. In most cases, it is easier to analyze job descriptions into behaviors than it is to analyze texts and manuals.

Consulting Advisory Committees. Another commonly used method of identifying behaviors is to consult an advisory committee. An *advisory committee* is a group of individuals that is assembled to advise people who are developing or operating an instructional program. An advisory committee can have a variety of titles such as advisory committee, craft committee, steering committee, or planning committee. Different titles have different meanings in different organizations. An advisory committee is usually composed of people who have knowledge about the content area that is to be included in the instructional program. In the case of the development of a training program to prepare people for a job, the advisory committee usually would include people employed by different employers who either perform the job or who supervise people who perform the job. When the advisory committee is assembled, the opinions of members are sought concerning the behaviors to be included in the program. The opinions are recorded, which results in a list of behaviors to be included in the program.

Interviewing Successful Performers. Another method of identifying behaviors is to interview individuals who actually perform the behaviors successfully. Rather than observing the people while they are performing the behaviors, one can ask individuals to provide information about the behaviors they perform. For example, if one were developing a program to prepare people to become computer operators, a number of computer operators would be identified. Each of the computer operators would be interviewed and asked to indicate the behaviors that she or he performs as a computer operator.

Selecting Methods for Identifying Behaviors. Of the five alternative methods of identifying behaviors presented, the most precise is direct observation. Each of the other procedures requires the use of existing documents or the opinions of individuals as to what is needed to perform a given role. When an instructional designer utilizes one of these other approaches, he or she is relying on the ability of others to capably analyze the role of the individual who is to be prepared. For example, if an instructional designer goes to an existing behavioral listing, the assumption is made that the individuals who created the original list did so correctly. When a designer analyzes texts, manuals, and job descriptions, he or she is again assuming that the writers of those documents did adequate analyses. When a designer consults an advisory committee or interviews people, the assumption is made that the individuals on the advisory committee or the individuals interviewed are capable of analyzing the occupation or role.

The assumption that others can objectively analyze roles into component behaviors needs to be questioned each time it is done. Few people are trained in methods of identifying behaviors; therefore, even though they may be competent in the content area, they may not have the ability to analyze that content area.

Although direct observation is the most precise method of identifying behaviors, it also has limitations. The most obvious limitation is that it is very time-consuming and expensive. It is also limited by the fact that identifying some behaviors through direct observation is difficult. Some behaviors may be very important but rarely performed. They may not be performed at all during the time that observation takes place; however, they are essential and should be included in the program. For example, emergency safety procedures are only needed in case of an emergency. If an emergency does not occur during the observation period, the safety procedures would not be identified.

It is also difficult to identify cognitive behaviors through direct observation. What is occurring in a person's mind is not directly apparent by observation.

Because of these limitations, it is best to use a combination of approaches when identifying behaviors. For example, one might develop a list from existing sources and then verify the list through direct observation and interviewing. Such combinations of methods generally result in more efficient and effective behavior analyses.

Preparing to Conduct a Behavior Analysis

Table 4.7 presents some items to consider before conducting a behavior analysis. First, the content area or areas to be analyzed must be identified. They should be listed in the program description. If more than one content area has been identified, each should be analyzed separately. It is not recommended that the analyses of multiple content areas be conducted simultaneously. It is extremely difficult for people to focus their attention on multiple content areas at the same time. For example, if machinists' performance on machines and mathematical skills needed by machinists are to be analyzed, one should first analyze the behaviors needed to operate the machines, and then conduct an analysis of mathematical skills. If someone tries to do the two simultaneously, the analyses will usually not be as complete as if they were done separately.

Second, the functions that a person is expected to perform within a content area must be identified using the procedures described previously. These functions

TABLE 4.7 Items to Consider before Conducting a Behavior Analysis

1. The content area to be included in the analysis
2. The functions people will be expected to perform
3. The intended use for the analysis (e.g., for designing a training program or for compensation plans)
4. Sources of information about the behaviors (e.g., experts or existing documents)
5. How the decision will be made to include some behaviors but to exclude others
6. How the behaviors will be validated (e.g., by experts' ratings)

will provide the framework within which the behavior analysis will be conducted.

Third, the intended use of the analysis should be clear. In this book, behavior analysis is discussed as the basis for designing a training program. It is also possible to use behavior analysis for other purposes such as for developing job descriptions or compensation plans. Often, when job descriptions and compensation plans are being precisely developed, the behavior analysis is not conducted to the same level of precision.

Fourth, the sources from which the information about the behaviors will be gathered should be considered. This decision relates to the prior discussion about alternative methods for identifying behaviors. The method selected will require specific types of sources of the information. For example, if someone is going to observe people performing a job or is going to be interviewing people performing the job, then the source of information will be people performing the job. If someone intends to analyze existing documents, that person must identify which existing documents will be analyzed.

Fifth, when planning to conduct a behavior analysis someone must consider how the decision will be made to include behaviors on the list. When conducting an analysis, many behaviors may be identified that are not relevant to the particular training program under development. Usually the decision as to which behaviors to include is based on the particular content area being analyzed at the time. In other words, if someone were conducting an analysis of the mathematics skills needed by a machinist, the analysis would focus solely on mathematics. Even though the machinist would be operating machinery, the process of operating machinery would not be included in the behavior analysis. Therefore, all behaviors that do not relate to the mathematical skills needed by a machinist would be eliminated. Behaviors may also be excluded because they are considered to be prerequisite to the instruction under design, or because they will be taught in subsequent training programs. These behaviors should have been identified in the program description.

Sixth, one should consider how the behaviors will be validated. It is possible to include in a behavioral listing behaviors that should not be included in an instructional program. How will they be eliminated after the list is developed? For example, most instructional programs are aimed at developing performance capability behaviors that are typically needed by people in order to perform a role. When observing individuals, one will obtain information not only as to what is typically needed to perform a given role, but also as to what behaviors are unique to a given individual. One may also discover individual uniquenesses when analyzing existing documents, depending upon the individuals being analyzed or upon who wrote the documents. The instructional designer must, therefore, develop procedures to ensure that the behaviors to be included in the instructional program are not unique to a given individual, but are required by most of the people who are expected to perform in a particular role. For example, one machinist may use a microcomputer to calculate the speed at which a drill press should be set to drill a piece of steel. Does that mean that all machinists must be trained to operate a microcomputer? One way to make that decision would be to interview or to observe a number of different machinists and to identify the most common practice for calculating the drill speed. Another way to validate the list of behaviors is to have a group of experts review it and include behaviors based on the extent of their agreement.

Once the factors indicated in Table 4.7 have been considered, a format for the behavior analysis can be developed.

Developing the Analysis Chart and Analyzing Psychomotor Behaviors

An analysis chart gives direction to the analysis process and to the recording of data once it is obtained. A separate analysis chart is developed for each of the different content areas to be analyzed. Figures 4.2 and 4.3 present two partial sample analysis charts. Only the analysis of psychomotor behaviors is presented; the analysis of cognitive and affective behaviors will be presented later.

Notice that in the charts the functions are presented as columns and the behaviors are presented as rows. If a behavior pertains to a given function, an *X* is entered where the column for that function intersects with the row for the particular behavior. For example, in Figure 4.3 the behavior "connect hoses" pertains to the function "maintain the hydraulic system." Therefore, an *X* is entered where the row for the behavior "connect hoses" and the column for the function "maintain the hydraulic system" intersect. "Connect hoses" is one of a number of behaviors required to "maintain the hy-

FIGURE 4.2 Sample Auto Mechanics Analysis Chart

	FUNCTIONS		
PSYCHOMOTOR BEHAVIORS	1. Perform maintenance.	2. Repair cooling system.	3. Resolve customer problem.
1. Change a tire.	X		
2. Check and add oil.	X		
3. Drain coolant.	X	X	
4. Replace the thermostat.		X	

FIGURE 4.3 Sample Robotics Maintenance Analysis Chart

	FUNCTIONS		
	Maintain the:		
PSYCHOMOTOR BEHAVIORS	1. Hydraulic system.	2. Electrical system.	3. Mechanical system.
1. Connect hoses.	X		
2. Install pump.	X	X	X
3. Install a circuit breaker.		X	
4. Replace a solenoid.		X	
5. Replace a gear.		X	

draulic system." Notice that the behavior "install pump" pertains to all three of the functions indicated. It is considered to be part of all three of the systems. Therefore, there is an *X* at the intersection of the row for that behavior and the columns for each of the three functions.

A behavior analysis is conducted as follows. A blank analysis chart is obtained and the functions are entered across the top of the chart. The analysis is then conducted function by function: the first function is analyzed, then the second, and so on. Each new behavior that is identified is listed along the left side of the chart. If a behavior that was identified when analyzing function 1 is also needed to carry out function 2, that behavior is not re-entered. An *X* is entered at the intersection of that behavior and the new function, indicating that the behavior pertains to both functions. If a behavior that is identified during the analysis of function 1 does not pertain to the analysis of function 2, an *X* is not entered under function 2. In Figure 4.2, the first two behaviors needed for function 1, "perform maintenance," are not needed to perform function 2, and therefore, there is no *X* indicated after those behaviors in the column for function 2. However, the third behavior, "drain coolant," is needed for functions 1 and 2 and an *X* is placed in both columns. The fourth behavior, "replace the thermostat," is a new behavior needed for only function 2. Therefore, it is entered into the list of behaviors along the left side, and an *X* is placed after that behavior in the column pertaining to function 2.

Analyzing Cognitive Behaviors

Just as psychomotor behaviors are analyzed in relation to the functions a person is expected to perform, cognitive behaviors are also analyzed in relation to those same functions. Figure 4.4 presents a sample analysis of cognitive behaviors for the auto mechanics example. Notice that the same functions presented in Figure 4.2 are presented in Figure 4.4. This again reinforces the basic premise that the analysis of any type of behaviors is done in relation to the functions a person is expected to perform. This ensures the relevance of those behaviors to the role a person will be expected to perform.

With performance-based instruction, the cognitive behaviors are processes for manipulating information needed for a person to be able to perform. The role of the instructional designer is to identify those processes and then to teach learners how to perform them. The ability to "know" something is to be able to apply the correct procedures to alternative situations when they are presented. It is just as important to be able to decide, or choose, among alternatives as it is to be able to repair something. For example, a fluid power technician must be able to decide which type of hydraulic pump to install based on the characteristics of different pumps. That decision is just as important as the ability to repair a pump. If the wrong pump is installed, the costs could be great in terms of safety as well as future repairs. People who are to subtract 2 from 5 are expected to arrive at the answer 3. If they do not, they do not understand the rules governing the subtraction of numbers.

Three sample cognitive behaviors are presented in Figure 4.4. The first behavior, "diagnose which system needs maintenance," relates to the first function, "perform maintenance." The second behavior, "decide which tool to use," pertains to the first two functions, and the third, "determine which customer to serve first," pertains to the third function.

Analyzing Affective Behaviors

Affective behaviors are also analyzed in reference to the functions. Just as it would not be reasonable to analyze psychomotor behaviors relative to a role without identifying the role to be analyzed, it would not be reasonable to attempt to identify affective behaviors without identifying the role. What are role-related affective behaviors for one role are not necessarily role-related behaviors for another role.

Before continuing, it is important to define a role-related affective behavior. Affective behaviors are *role-related* if their absence inhibits a person from entering that role or from continuing in that role. In other words, role-related affective behaviors must be defined in relation to a particular role and should become a concern of the instructional designer if they are critical to entering or continuing in that role. Affective behaviors which are not role-related should not be included in an instructional program without a clear rationale justifying their inclusion.

The technique of analyzing affective behaviors in re-

FIGURE 4.4 Sample Analysis of Cognitive Behaviors for Auto Mechanics

COGNITIVE BEHAVIORS	FUNCTIONS: 1. Perform maintenance.	2. Repair cooling system.	3. Resolve customer problem.
1. Diagnose which system needs maintenance.	X		
2. Decide which tool to use.	X	X	
3. Determine which customer to serve first.			X

FIGURE 4.5 Sample Analysis of Affective Behaviors for Auto Mechanics

AFFECTIVE BEHAVIORS	FUNCTIONS: 1. Perform maintenance.	2. Repair cooling system.	3. Resolve customer problem.
1. Treat tools with care.	X	X	
2. Cooperate with co-workers.	X	X	X
3. Accept the customer as an individual.			X

lation to functions verifies that the affective behaviors identified are role-related. If an affective behavior cannot be related to one of the functions, it is not role-related. Figure 4.5 presents a sample analysis of affective behaviors for auto mechanics.

Notice that the functions presented in Figure 4.5 are the same as those presented in Figure 4.2. The first affective behavior, "treat tools with care," pertains to the functions "perform maintenance" and "repair cooling system." The second, "cooperate with co-workers," pertains to all three functions. The third, "accept the customer as an individual," pertains to function 3. Thus, each of the affective behaviors presented is role-related to auto mechanics.

DEVELOPING A BEHAVIOR LISTING

Once the behavior analysis is completed and the behaviors have been identified, they are summarized into a behavior listing. The *behavior listing* includes all of the behaviors identified during the analysis that might be taught within the instructional program. Often a behavior listing is presented in alphabetical form. Such a form has been popular because most behavior listings include only psychomotor behaviors.

However, if one uses a simple alphabetical listing of all behaviors identified during an analysis of psychomotor behaviors, cognitive behaviors, and affective behaviors, the types of behaviors get mixed together and it becomes difficult to make design decisions. Therefore, it is suggested that the alphabetical listings present each of the three types of behaviors separately. Table 4.8 presents a sample of such a listing. It presents the behaviors alphabetically within each of the three major types of behaviors.

Another alternative form of behavior listing is presented in Figure 4.6. The listing not only presents the behaviors alphabetically within each of the three types of behaviors, but it also indicates the functions to which each behavior pertains. It is a summary analysis chart with all types of behaviors indicated.

It is recommended that the behavior listing be created in the form presented in Figure 4.6, if possible. This format presents the behaviors in relation to functions and retains information from the behavior analysis that will be useful to the instructional designer later in the design process when he or she sequences the behaviors for teaching. For example, if psychomotor, cognitive, and affective behaviors pertain to the same function, it may be reasonable to teach those behaviors together or near one another.

The behavior listing usually includes more behaviors than can be taught within the program being designed. Therefore, the actual behaviors to be included in the instructional program must be selected from the total

TABLE 4.8 Sample Behavior Listing (Arranged Alphabetically by Type of Behavior)

CONTENT AREA: AUTO MECHANICS

Psychomotor behaviors
- Change a tire.
- Check and add oil.
- Drain coolant.
- Replace the thermostat.

Cognitive behaviors
- Diagnose which system needs maintenance.
- Decide which tool to use.
- Determine which customer to serve first.

Affective behaviors
- Treat tools with care.
- Cooperate with co-workers.
- Accept the customer as an individual.

FIGURE 4.6 Sample Behavior Listing (Organized Alphabetically by Type of Behavior with Behaviors Related to Functions)

	FUNCTIONS		
PSYCHOMOTOR BEHAVIORS	1. Perform maintenance.	2. Repair cooling system.	3. Resolve customer problem.
1. Change a tire.	X		
2. Check and add oil.	X		
3. Drain coolant.	X	X	
4. Replace the thermostat.		X	
COGNITIVE BEHAVIORS			
1. Diagnose which systems need maintenance.	X		
2. Decide which tool to use.	X	X	
3. Determine which customer to serve first.			X
AFFECTIVE BEHAVIORS			
1. Treat tools with care.	X	X	
2. Cooperate with co-workers.	X	X	X
3. Accept the customer as an individual.			X

list of behaviors. Procedures for selecting the actual behaviors are presented in Chapter 5. See Appendices B and C for additional examples of a program description.

SUMMARY

This chapter has presented an overview of content analysis and a detailed presentation of its first two stages. During these stages, what people will be expected to do after they complete the instructional program will be identified. What people will be expected to be able to do is specified first as *functions,* which are major subdivisions of the roles people will be expected to perform, and then as *behaviors,* which will allow people to perform those functions. The third stage of content analysis, behavior detailing, is presented in Chapter 7. It usually takes place after the specific behaviors to be included in the program have been selected from the list of potential behaviors, and after the behaviors are sequenced into the order in which they will be taught. The behavior-detailing stage is delayed until that point for efficiency. It is inefficient to detail behaviors that will not be included in the program or that will have to be taught with a behavior sequenced earlier in the program.

ACTIVITIES AND EVALUATION

1. Select a content area to analyze (e.g., an occupation or a type of skills).
2. Within the content area selected in activity 1, identify the functions you expect people to be able to perform. (List at least three functions.)
3. Draw an analysis chart, and list the functions identified across the top.
4. Identify at least three psychomotor behaviors and list them down the left side of the analysis chart. Indicate which behaviors pertain to each function.
5. Identify at least three cognitive behaviors and list them down the left side of the analysis chart. Indicate which behaviors pertain to each function.
6. Identify at least three affective behaviors and list them down the left side of the analysis chart. Indicate which behaviors pertain to each function.

REFERENCES

Bloom, B. S., *Taxonomy of Educational Objectives: The Classification of Educational Goals, Handbook I: Cognitive Domain,* David McKay, New York, 1956.

Butler, F. C., *Instructional Systems Development for Vocational and Technical Training,* Educational Technology Publications, Englewood Cliffs, NJ, 1972, pp. xi, 74, 83.

Claus, Calvin K., *National College Verb List,* paper presented at a meeting of the National Council on Measurement in Education, Chicago, February 1968.

Pucel, D. J., and W. C. Knaak, *Individualizing Vocational and Technical Instruction,* Charles E. Merrill, Columbus, OH, 1975.

State of Florida, *Barriers to Implementing Competency-Based Vocational Education in Postsecondary Schools,* Division of Vocational, Adult, and Community Education, Tallahassee, April 1985.

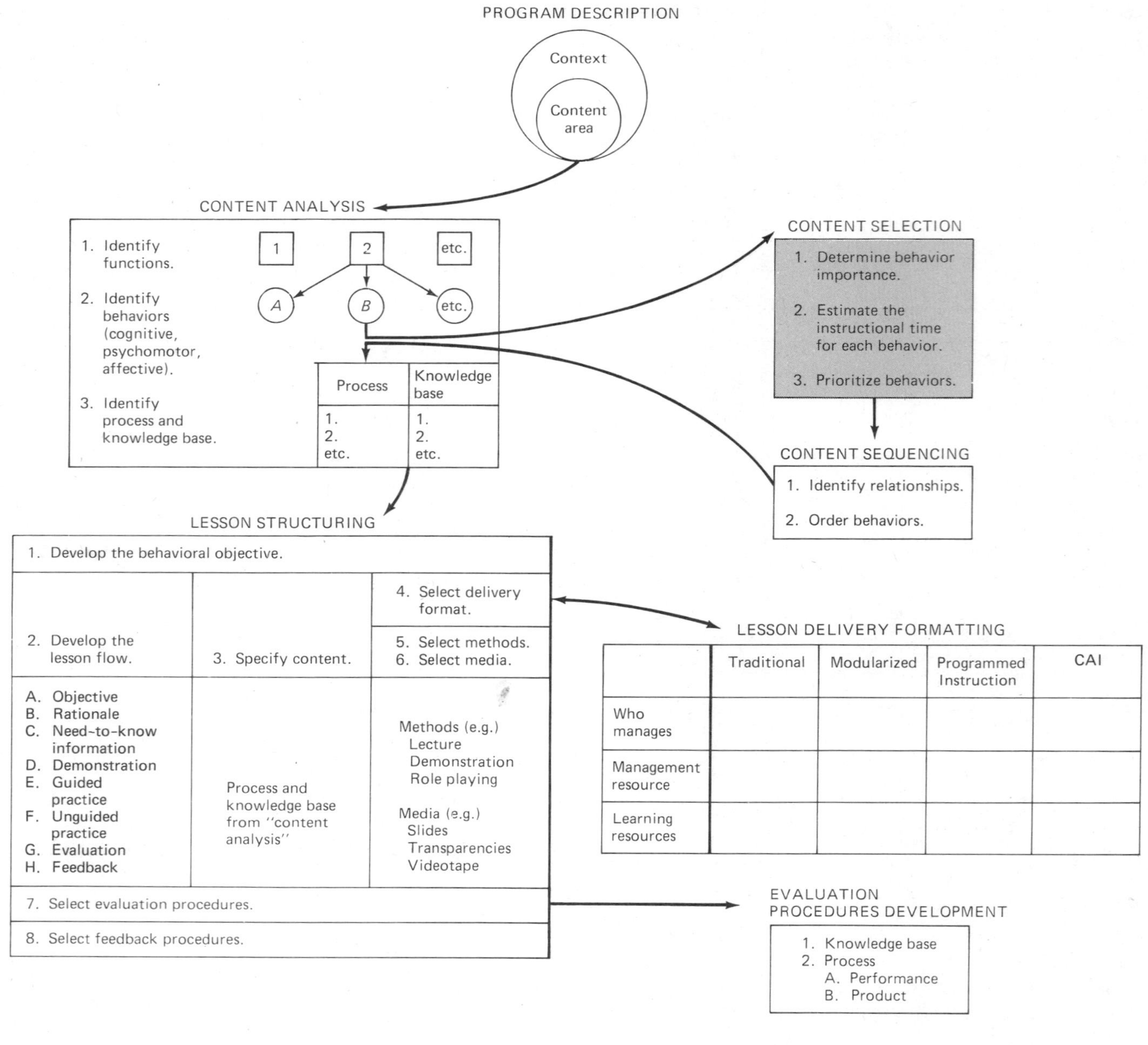

PROGRAM DESCRIPTION
Context
Content area
CONTENT ANALYSIS
1. Identify functions.
2. Identify behaviors (cognitive, psychomotor, affective).
3. Identify process and knowledge base.
1
2
etc.
A
B
etc.
Process
Knowledge base
1.
2.
etc.
1.
2.
etc.
CONTENT SELECTION
1. Determine behavior importance.
2. Estimate the instructional time for each behavior.
3. Prioritize behaviors.
CONTENT SEQUENCING
1. Identify relationships.
2. Order behaviors.
LESSON STRUCTURING
1. Develop the behavioral objective.
2. Develop the lesson flow.
3. Specify content.
4. Select delivery format.
5. Select methods.
6. Select media.
A. Objective
B. Rationale
C. Need-to-know information
D. Demonstration
E. Guided practice
F. Unguided practice
G. Evaluation
H. Feedback
Process and knowledge base from "content analysis"
Methods (e.g.)
Lecture
Demonstration
Role playing
Media (e.g.)
Slides
Transparencies
Videotape
7. Select evaluation procedures.
8. Select feedback procedures.
LESSON DELIVERY FORMATTING
Traditional
Modularized
Programmed Instruction
CAI
Who manages
Management resource
Learning resources
EVALUATION PROCEDURES DEVELOPMENT
1. Knowledge base
2. Process
A. Performance
B. Product

Content Selection

CHAPTER OBJECTIVE

Givens

A list of behaviors that might be included within an instructional program

Behavior

Select those behaviors which will actually be included in the program.

Standard

The behaviors selected are those of highest priority and meet the criteria specified in this chapter.

OVERVIEW

Content analysis usually identifies more behaviors than can be taught within one instructional program. Therefore, the behaviors which actually will be taught must be selected from the behavior listing generated through the content analysis procedures presented in Chapter 4. *Content selection* is the process of selecting the behaviors to be taught within a program from a total set of possible behaviors. The behaviors that are eventually selected are the highest priority behaviors.

PROCEDURE FOR SELECTING BEHAVIORS

Table 5.1 presents a five-step procedure for selecting behaviors to be included in an instructional program. The first step is to determine how important each behavior is in terms of a person's performance in the role for which the program is being developed. Importance can be defined using a number of different criteria. Typically one or more of these criteria are considered together. One criterion is how frequently the behavior is used by the people who perform in a particular role. The more often a behavior is used, the greater the need for a person performing in that role to learn it. For example, if a microcomputer operator must be able to format a disk each time she or he starts a new project, then "format a disk" would be an important behavior for a microcomputer operator. If, on the other hand, "clean the floppy disk drive heads" is done once every six months, that might be considered to be a less important behavior. This does not mean that both behaviors do not have to be performed by a microcomputer operator. It only means that one occurs more frequently and, therefore, should be considered to be more important for inclusion in the instructional program.

A second criterion for determining the importance of behaviors is how necessary it is to learn a behavior as a prerequisite for learning other behaviors. The term *prerequisite* generically means "something that is necessary for something else to occur." In instructional design, the term is used to define both behaviors a person is expected to bring to the instructional program, as discussed in Chapter 4, and behaviors that must be developed in the program before people can learn other behaviors. In this context, the second definition is used. For example, an administrator may need to be able to "compose a letter." That behavior may be identified during the analysis of a written communication function. In order to correctly compose a letter, a person needs to be able to "punctuate a sentence." Therefore, in order for an administrator to be taught to compose a letter, he or she will first need to develop competency in the punctuation of sentences. In this case, "punctuate a sentence" is a prerequisite to being able to compose a letter. The key point underlying the concept of a prerequisite as presented here is that not only the behaviors which people will be expected to perform frequently need to be included in a program, but other behaviors may also need to be included which develop foundational skills for the performance of those behaviors.

TABLE 5.1 Procedure for Selecting Behaviors

1. Determine the importance of each behavior.
2. Determine the estimated program length.
3. Estimate the instructional time required to teach each behavior.
4. Prioritize the behaviors.
5. Select the high-priority behaviors that can be taught within the time available.

A third criterion in determining the relative importance of behaviors is potential future need. *Potential future need* is the likelihood that a behavior will become critical in the future because of the evolution of the field. For example, there is a rapidly expanding use of microcomputers in occupations requiring the storage, retrieval, or transmission of information. Therefore, most programs designed to prepare people for such occupations include components on the use of microcomputers. Microcomputer instruction is being given even though microcomputers have not actually been introduced into the daily work lives of people currently performing in many of these occupations, particularly in small businesses. If a content analysis of what is being done on the job at the present time were conducted, one might find very few microcomputers being used by people performing a particular role. However, looking at our society in general, it is apparent that if a job requires the storage, retrieval, or transmission of information, eventually microcomputers will be introduced. Therefore, preparation for that type of job should include behaviors related to microcomputer usage.

A fourth criterion for determining the relative importance of behaviors is ratings from advisory committees. Advisory committees are used to gather the collective wisdom of individuals who are knowledgeable about the purposes of a particular program and/or the roles for which the program is to prepare people. Committee members usually include one or more of the following: potential employers, school board members, management teams, potential customers, and employees. Usually, the list of potential behaviors to be included within an instructional program is provided to each advisory committee member and she or he is asked to rate the importance of each behavior. The ratings of the members are then averaged and the averages are used in decision making. It is important to make sure the members know about the potential program and the roles for which people will be prepared.

A fifth criterion is how critical a behavior is to job performance. Obvious critical behaviors relate to safety and emergency procedures. Even though they are performed seldom, when they are needed, performance capability is essential—for example, when responding to an acid spill in a medical laboratory.

As was pointed out earlier, all of these criteria for determining the importance of behaviors are usually considered together. Depending upon the circumstance and the program, the influence of each criterion may vary. For example, if an instructional program is to be short-term to prepare people to enter a relatively low-skilled job, the criterion of "frequency of use" might carry much more weight than the criterion of "future need" for a behavior; but if a program is to prepare people for a long-term career in an occupation, then "future need" will take on greater importance.

Determining the Program Length

A second major factor in prioritizing behaviors for inclusion in a program is to determine the instructional time that can be allocated to the program. Most programs must be presented within a defined period of time because of the organizational structure of the institution within which it is being presented. For example, schools tend to offer one- or two-year programs, semester or quarter programs, or month-long programs. Industrial training programs are often broken down into units of similar length within a given institution so that people can more easily schedule their time.

Some institutions are performance- or competency-based and allow different learners to complete their programs in varying amounts of time. They may also allow learners to elect to study different behaviors so the program length for individual learners may vary. Even though it may be expected that individual learners may vary in the amount of time it takes them to complete the program, as the program is being designed, an ideal program length should be established as a basis for program development.

Therefore, when developing a program, one usually starts out thinking in terms of an expected length for the program based on the institutional constraints and past history. The length may be adjusted later as it becomes clear how much time will actually be needed to adequately prepare people.

Estimating the Instructional Time to Teach Each Behavior

After determining the expected program length, the instructional time required to teach each behavior listed is estimated. The estimates are made in terms of the average amount of time learners, as defined in the program description, would take to complete instruction on a behavior. If the behavior listing is long, and if it is unlikely that all of the behaviors can seriously be considered for inclusion in the program, then only those behaviors with high importance ratings should initially receive time estimates.

The instructional time required to teach each behavior should be estimated after considering the factors presented in Table 5.2.

Assigning the Priority Rankings

The importance rating and the estimated instructional time for each behavior are the two main considerations in assigning priority ranks to the behaviors. The behavior considered to be highest priority for inclusion in the program is assigned a rank of 1, the next highest priority a rank of 2, and so on. In assigning priority rankings, the importance rating and estimated time are considered along with the person's knowledge of the role who is assigning the rankings. There is no direct mathematical relationship between the assignment of the priority rankings and the importance rating and time estimates. However, the information is usually used as follows: First, one examines the importance rating. The behaviors with the highest importance ratings are identified. Second, the estimated instructional time for each of the behaviors is examined. Most designers would agree that if a number of behaviors are judged to be of equally high importance, it would be better to teach people a larger number of important behaviors than it would be to spend an extremely long period of time teaching only one behavior. Therefore, those behaviors which are of equal importance but take less time to teach would receive a higher priority than those which take an unusually long time to teach. However, if one behavior requiring a large amount of time is considered to be more essential than those behaviors requiring less time, then it should be taught first. In other words, at this point a certain amount of judgment is required.

TABLE 5.2 Factors to Consider When Estimating Instructional Time

1. The amount of new material that will need to be introduced in the lesson to teach each behavior
2. The amount of practice that will be needed to develop performance capability
3. The amount of instructor time it will take to monitor the learning so that it can be done safely and without damage to equipment and material

Figure 5.1 presents a portion of a sample priority chart for an auto mechanics program with an expected program length of one academic year, or 960 hours. The chart is created by first entering the behaviors which have been identified during content analysis down the left side. The next step is to rate the importance of each of these behaviors and to record those ratings. Those behaviors rated the highest based on the importance criteria discussed earlier are assigned a rating of 5. Those that are judged to be least important receive an importance rating of 1. Next, the estimated instructional time it would take to teach each behavior is determined and entered for each behavior. The estimated amount of time is entered in hours. Next the priority for including each behavior within the instructional program is indicated in the form of a rank. The behavior with the highest priority is assigned a rank of 1, the next highest priority a rank of 2, and so on.

After the priority chart has been completed, the estimated program length should be reexamined in terms of the total amount of instructional time it would take to teach all of the high-priority behaviors. The estimated program length may need to be adjusted to be shorter or longer. If it cannot be adjusted, low-priority behaviors should be included to make it longer, or some of the lower priority behaviors should be eliminated to make it shorter. If some high-priority behaviors cannot be included, they could be considered as prerequisites.

FIGURE 5.1 Partial Sample Auto Mechanics Priority Chart

Expected program length = 960 hours PSYCHOMOTOR BEHAVIORS	1. Importance rating*	2. Estimated instructional time**	3. Priority†
1. Change a tire.	5	4	6
2. Check and add oil.	5	2	5
3. Drain coolant.	4	1.5	7
4. Replace the thermostat.	4	2	8
COGNITIVE BEHAVIORS			
1. Diagnose which systems need maintenance.	5	6	1
2. Decide which tool to use.	5	7	2
3. Determine which customer to serve first.	3	1	9
AFFECTIVE BEHAVIORS			
1. Treat tools with care.	5	4	3
2. Cooperate with co-workers.	5	5	4
3. Accept the customer as an individual.	3	5	10

* From 1 to 5 (5 = high)
** In seconds
† In rank order (1 = highest priority)

VALIDATING PRIORITY JUDGMENTS

The procedure for assigning priority rankings assumes that one individual, the instructional designer, will select the behaviors to be included in the program. However, often it is important to obtain the collective judgment of a larger group to verify that the judgments of the instructional designer are accurate. The process of verifying the judgments of the instructional designer is called *validation*. The following procedure can be used to validate both the priority assigned to each behavior and the behavioral listing itself. The validation procedure includes the six steps presented in Table 5.3.

DETERMINING PROGRAM PREREQUISITES VERSUS BEHAVIORS TO BE TAUGHT IN THE PROGRAM

Few programs can teach all of the behaviors required for people to perform adequately in a given role. How-

TABLE 5.3 Steps in Behavior and Priority Validation

1. Identify an advisory committee of people knowledgeable about the behaviors performed in the role for which the program is being prepared.
2. Develop a behavior priority chart similar to the one presented in Figure 5.1. List the behaviors identified during content analysis down the left side. Allow a number of empty spaces within the behavior listing for advisory committee members to enter additional behaviors which they feel should be included in the listing.
3. Ask each member to rate the importance of each behavior and to estimate the amount of instructional time she or he feels it would take to teach the behavior.
4. Based on the importance rating assigned, the estimated amount of instructional time, and members' personal knowledge of the role for which people are being prepared, have members assign priority rankings to each behavior.
5. Summarize the information from all committee members and calculate the average importance rating, the average amount of estimated instructional time, and the average priority ranking for each behavior. This is done by adding the rating of a particular behavior for all of the members and dividing by the number of members. These averages then can be used as a basis for considering the collective judgment of a group of knowledgeable people concerning the content to be included within a given program.

ever, if people who complete the program will be expected to perform in that role, then the program must either teach all of the necessary behaviors or people must be required to have mastered some of the behaviors prior to entering the program. For example, an electronics technician must be able to "transpose mathematical formulas." However, should that content be taught within the electronics technician program or should it be assumed that people entering the program will already have developed that skill? In other words, some high-priority behaviors may not need to be taught within the program if prerequisites are established for people entering the program.

In this case, prerequisite behaviors are defined as those which a learner is expected to bring to an instructional program. They are important to success in the program, but they are not taught in the program. The combination of prerequisite behaviors and behaviors developed in the program should be adequate to prepare people for the expected role.

COSTS AND BEHAVIOR SELECTION

Although the cost of teaching a behavior should theoretically not enter into a decision to teach one behavior versus another, in practice it does. Some behaviors require large amounts of materials, instructional time, and/or expensive equipment to teach. If a person needs to develop such behaviors to become productive on a job, the designer is faced with three choices. First, establish them as prerequisite behaviors which learners will be expected to bring to the instructional program. Second, send learners to other institutions to learn the behaviors. Third, despite the costs, include the behaviors as part of the program.

See Appendices B and C for additional examples of content selection.

SUMMARY

The process of selecting behaviors to be taught within a program is conducted after the behavioral listing has been developed through content analysis. Behavior selection is usually done before behavior detailing so that only those behaviors selected for inclusion in the program will have to be detailed. This conserves time and energy on the part of the instructional designers.

The process of selecting behaviors is one of assigning priorities to those behaviors which might be included in the program. Factors considered are the importance of each behavior in the occupation or role, the instructional time it would take to teach each behavior, and the possibility of considering each behavior as a prerequisite rather than teaching it in the program. The process can be used with advisory committees to not only select behaviors, but to validate the behavioral listing.

ACTIVITIES AND EVALUATION

1. Identify at least 10 behaviors which could be included in a program.
2. Enter those behaviors in a table similar to Figure 5.1.
3. Assign an importance rating to each of the behaviors.
4. Assign an estimated instructional time to each of the behaviors.
5. Assign a priority rank to each behavior.
6. Based on the priority rankings, assume that you do not have enough time to teach all of the behaviors and select one that you might require as a prerequisite. Explain why that one behavior might be considered to be a prerequisite.

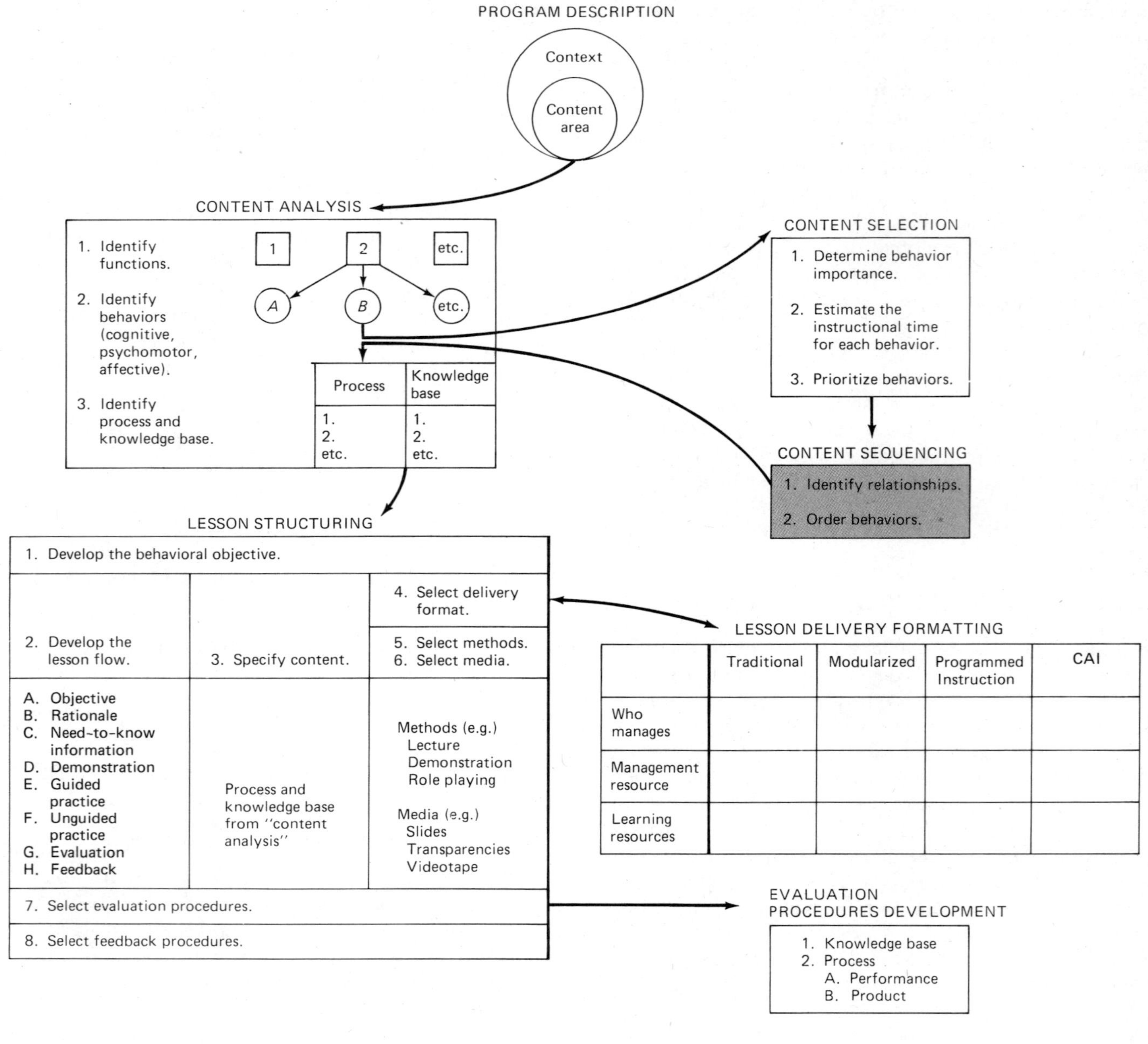
PROGRAM DESCRIPTION
Context
Content area
CONTENT ANALYSIS
1. Identify functions.
2. Identify behaviors (cognitive, psychomotor, affective).
3. Identify process and knowledge base.
1
2
etc.
A
B
etc.
Process
Knowledge base
1.
2.
etc.
1.
2.
etc.
CONTENT SELECTION
1. Determine behavior importance.
2. Estimate the instructional time for each behavior.
3. Prioritize behaviors.
CONTENT SEQUENCING
1. Identify relationships.
2. Order behaviors.
LESSON STRUCTURING
1. Develop the behavioral objective.
2. Develop the lesson flow.
3. Specify content.
4. Select delivery format.
5. Select methods.
6. Select media.
A. Objective
B. Rationale
C. Need-to-know information
D. Demonstration
E. Guided practice
F. Unguided practice
G. Evaluation
H. Feedback
Process and knowledge base from "content analysis"
Methods (e.g.)
Lecture
Demonstration
Role playing
Media (e.g.)
Slides
Transparencies
Videotape
7. Select evaluation procedures.
8. Select feedback procedures.
LESSON DELIVERY FORMATTING
Traditional
Modularized
Programmed Instruction
CAI
Who manages
Management resource
Learning resources
EVALUATION PROCEDURES DEVELOPMENT
1. Knowledge base
2. Process
A. Performance
B. Product

Content Sequencing

CHAPTER OBJECTIVE

Givens

A list of behaviors to be included in an instructional program

Behavior

Develop a content sequence.

Standard

The order in which the behaviors to be included in the program are to be taught is clearly specified.

OVERVIEW

Content sequencing is the process of arranging the behaviors to be taught in an instructional program into the order in which they will be taught. It can be used as the basis for breaking down large programs into courses or for developing "core courses." The designer has two major concerns when developing a content sequence. The first is ensuring that the sequence is meaningful to learners, and the second is that the sequence is instructionally efficient. The primary goal of sequencing is to arrange the behaviors into an order which has a meaning apparent to the learners. Meaning is achieved when people can see the relationships between the various behaviors taught and how they add up to a logical whole. This is the opposite of *rote learning,* in which people are taught things at random without any connections among the things learned. If the behaviors are sequenced into an order that has meaning, what is learned can be internalized more readily, it will tend to be retained longer, and people will be better able to functionally use what they learn.

Meaning and Sequencing

One of the first people to write about sequencing and its effect on learning was Herbart (1898). He argued that a person brings meaning to new learning by relating it to past experience. In other words, meaning is achieved when a person can see how the new thing being learned fits with what she or he already knows. Therefore, Herbart suggested building instructional sequences around what people have already experienced.

Ausubel (1962) developed another approach. He suggested that before each separate behavior is taught, learners should be presented with an overall logic within which the separate behaviors will fit and to which the separate behaviors will add up. For example, before teaching the behaviors needed to maintain the electrical system of a car, one should explain the function of the electrical system as a whole and the ways in which all of the components work together to make an engine operate. This would allow learners to see how the components fit together and would make the learning of individual behaviors more meaningful.

People need a meaningful "road map" through the content to be taught. That road map presents a structure in which new learning can be applied and later recalled if needed. For Herbart that road map was past experience, and for Ausubel it was a logic presented to learners before the learning of separate component behaviors begins.

Other learning theorists and educators such as Rugg (1930), Tyler (1950), Bruner (1960), Taba (1962), Suppes (1966), Gagné (1970), Popham and Baker (1970), Posner (1974), and Posner and Strike (1976) have also argued for alternative procedures and logics for sequencing. However, they all agree that people learn best and retain what they learn longer when content is presented to them in an organized fashion. They also agree that the teaching of isolated behaviors without attempts at integrating them leads to fragmented learning and reduced ability to use what has been learned in an integrated and meaningful way. It also reduces retention of what is learned, because things learned cannot be anchored to other learning and experience which provide increased meaning.

Efficiency and Sequencing

The second major consideration when sequencing is instructional efficiency. Efficiency relates to cost in terms of time and resources needed to bring about effective learning. It is usually more efficient to teach all of one type of content together than to teach separate portions of that content at different times. For example, it may be more efficient to teach all of the basic algebraic equations related to machine shop at the same time in a math class. Teaching the separate equations at different times would require a great deal of additional review to put each new equation into context and to be sure people have not forgotten some of the basics. However, even though such a related math class might be more efficient to teach, it may not result in effective learning. Learners may lack an understanding of how the equations fit into the machine shop occupation for which they are preparing. They may lack motivation to learn, the ability to transfer what is learned to the actual problems faced by machinists, or both. Therefore, the designer is faced with the decision as to whether the algebraic equations should be taught in a separate class for efficiency, or whether they should be taught when they would normally be needed by a machinist (e.g., along with a behavior which requires each equation).

Sequencing for instructional efficiency is often based on an examination of the common content behavioral elements that need to be taught in order for learners to learn the various behaviors. Behaviors requiring the largest number of common content elements tend to be taught together. Those with the least overlap of content elements are taught with other behaviors which overlap more. A problem commonly faced by the designer is that these two major considerations (meaning and efficiency) often lead to different sequencing solutions. Thus, the designer must make compromises between the most meaningful learning and the most efficient instructional sequence.

Sequencing for Meaning

Posner and Strike (1976) present a model for thinking about alternative ways of organizing content that relates primarily to the issue of meaning. They suggest that when sequencing content, one should attempt to answer one or more of the following five questions:

1. What are the empirically verifiable relationships between the phenomena (people, things, or events) in the world about which the pupil is to learn, and in what ways can content be sequenced so that the organization is consistent with the way the world is? Subcategories include relationships based on space, time, and physical attributes.
2. What are the conceptual properties of the knowledge that the pupil is to learn, and in what ways can content be sequenced so that it is logically consistent in organization to that of the concepts? Subcategories include relationships based on class relations, propositional relations, sophistication level, and logical prerequisites.
3. How do propositions and concepts come about, and in what ways can content be sequenced so that it is consistent with the process of inquiry (problem solving)? Subcategories include relationships based on the logic and the empirics of inquiry.
4. How does the pupil learn, and in what ways can the content be sequenced so that it is consistent with the learning process? Subcategories include relationships based on empirical prerequisite, familiarity, difficulty, interest, internalization, and development.
5. How will the pupil utilize the content after he or she has learned it, and in what ways can the content be sequenced so that it is consistent with the utilization process? Subcategories include relationships based on procedure and anticipated frequency of utilization.

Based on answers to these questions, two major systems for conceptualizing sequencing emerge: conceptual systems and empirical systems (how phenomena occur in the real world).

Conceptual Systems. If the content is thought of in terms of a conceptual system, it is examined in terms of how that content can be logically broken down, not of how that content relates to the real world. Such a system would be used to answer question 2 presented by Posner and Strike. For example, geometry is broken down in terms of theorems, postulates, and axioms which relate to one another in the creation of more complex geometric principles and figures. This logical conceptual structure provides a schema for organizing the field of geometry. Because this organization has made logical sense to people, it has become widely accepted and has been found to be functional as a way of sequencing that content for presentation to learners. Using such a conceptual system of sequencing, the focus is on the logical organization of the subject matter to be taught. The sequencing shows little concern, if any, for how the content is used in the real world.

Empirical Systems. An empirical system organizes content around how the content area is applied in the real world. This type of content structure reflects empirical relationships among events, people, and things (Anderson, 1971). Empirical systems can be organized around empirical relationships and utilization. Such systems are used if the designer is primarily interested in questions 1 and 5 in Posner and Strike's list. Using the content analysis procedure for cognitive behaviors presented in this book, the designer can also use an empirical system as a basis for addressing question 3, since problem solving is reduced primarily to an empirical process. With an empirical system content can be sequenced on the basis of empirical relationships or on the basis of the utilization of the content.

Let us first look at content sequencing based on empirical relationships but not on utilization. Such a system categorizes objects based on common physical properties. For example, when designing a veterinary assistant program it would be important for learners to understand differences among the animals to be treated. The differences could be presented by having learners rotely memorize the anatomical characteristics of each animal. However, learning would be inefficient because what they learned about the various animals would not systematically fit together. Therefore, a structure is needed to which learners can meaningfully relate the different animals. Zoology provides such a structure. Animals are categorized based on the types of physical characteristics which are meaningful to a person treating those animals. Placing the various animals within categories as they are being discussed can assist with meaningful learning.

The second empirical approach to sequencing is based on how content is utilized in the real world. This approach is the one most often used by designers in vocational education and in training in business and industry. It is consistent with the primary focus of content analysis presented earlier and with performance-based instruction. The emphasis is on preparing people to be able to perform in a functional role (e.g., a job or an occupation). People entering such programs have expectations that they will be prepared for roles. Showing them how what is being taught relates to those roles presents a concrete framework around which to sequence the instruction, which is motivating to learners. They can actually observe their own progress toward achieving their goals. This approach, along with examples, will be presented in detail later in this chapter.

The Learning Process. Question 4 presented by Posner and Strike raises some issues about how people learn, which should be considered during sequencing. It is not sufficient to merely consider the best conceptual or empirical structure of the content. Relationships among the behaviors to be sequenced should be considered based on the characteristics of the learners. One consideration is the extent to which learners have the necessary prerequisite skills. How advanced are they in the content area? At what level does one need to start to build the skills? For example, one would start at one place to teach experienced typists to operate a word processor and at another place to teach people who have never typed before.

A second consideration is the students' familiarity with what is being taught. If it is new and they have no previous knowledge or experience with what is to be learned, the instruction would have to be especially well-organized around a meaningful framework. Otherwise, learners might perceive what is being learned as isolated behaviors with no logical relationships.

A third set of factors to consider is the complexity or difficulty of the behaviors and how that may affect a learner's ability to internalize the content, interest in the various behaviors, and level of development. If the content regarding a behavior is very complex or difficult, much more instruction may be needed for learners to internalize it. The designer may wish to sequence behaviors in such a way that teaching less-complicated behaviors first may reduce the instructional time needed to teach the more complex behaviors. If learners have shown a strong interest in learning one of the behaviors, that behavior might be taught first to capitalize on that interest, which may carry over to other behaviors.

The developmental level of a learner refers to the ability of the learner to effectively deal with concrete experiences versus abstract experiences. Piaget and others have suggested that learners arrive at different developmental stages of learning at different times in their lives (Wadsworth, 1971). In general, if the learners are not sophisticated with a great deal of prior education, it is best to organize the content from the most concrete experiences (e.g., hands-on) to the more abstract content (e.g., theory).

In summary, there are alternative perceptions about how sequencing should be done and there are different techniques which may be used, depending upon the type of content to be sequenced. Most often, vocational educators and trainers in business and industry are interested in sequencing content to prepare people for roles in the real world. Therefore, they tend to use techniques consistent with the logic underlying the empirical techniques discussed in the previous paragraphs. The remaining discussion presented in this chapter will concentrate on how to use such techniques to sequence.

SEQUENCING PROCEDURES

Butler (1972) suggests that the place to start sequencing is with content analysis. Content analysis is a functional breakdown of the behaviors that are to be performed as part of a role. That functional breakdown provides an empirical base for the relationships among the behaviors. For example, behaviors associated with one function have an empirical relationship because they would be performed together in order to accomplish that function. Butler suggests that content analysis should also serve as a general guide to the development of the final sequence. A sample content analysis is presented in Figure 6.1.

Although content analysis presents a place to start sequencing and provides a general guideline, the designer must still have additional information in order to develop an appropriate sequence. The procedure developed by the U.S. Air Force and published in the *Handbook for Designers of Instructional Systems,* volume 4 (U.S. Department of the Air Force, 1973), is very useful. It concurs with the basic ideas of Posner and Strike, even though it was developed prior to their article. The handbook provides procedures which allow the designer to sequence behaviors based on common content elements and on how the behaviors are related to one another in real-world performances. Its concepts are adapted and presented below in a modified version. The primary modifications are that some terminology has been changed to make the procedure consistent with the rest of this book, and another basis for relating behaviors has been added: the extent to which behaviors are performed together or in proximity to one another in the real world. It is useful to sequence near one another those behaviors that occur together or near one another in the real world in order to capitalize on the context and realism of actual situations.

Dependent and Independent Behaviors

This first step in sequencing is to classify behaviors as dependent or independent. *Dependent behaviors* are related in some way. They are usually taught after one has considered the relationships among them. They may be related because the content needed to learn them is related, because the output of one behavior is needed as the input for another behavior, or because they are usually performed together or in proximity to one an-

FIGURE 6.1 Sample Behavior Listing (Organized Alphabetically by Type of Behavior with Behaviors Related to Functions)

	FUNCTIONS		
PSYCHOMOTOR BEHAVIORS	1. Perform maintenance.	2. Repair cooling system.	3. Resolve customer problem.
1. Change a tire.	X		
2. Check and add oil.	X		
3. Drain coolant.	X	X	
4. Replace the thermostat.		X	
COGNITIVE BEHAVIORS			
1. Diagnose which systems need maintenance.	X		
2. Decide which tool to use.	X	X	
3. Determine which customer to serve first.			X
AFFECTIVE BEHAVIORS			
1. Treat tools with care.	X	X	
2. Cooperate with co-workers.	X	X	X
3. Accept the customer as an individual.			X

TABLE 6.1 Differences Between Dependent and Independent Behaviors

Independent	Dependent
1. Process and knowledge base of the behaviors are unrelated to one another; the behaviors are not performed together.	Process and knowledge base of the behaviors are related to one another; or the behaviors are performed together or in proximity to one another.
Difference may be based on *2a* and/or *2b*.	
2a. Learning of one behavior does not make the learning of another one easier.	To be able to learn one behavior, it is first necessary to learn one or more other behaviors. The learning of one behavior transfers to another, making the learning of the other easier. Thus, a hierarchy of skills and knowledges exists.
2b. Behaviors are not typically performed together with or in proximity to one another.	Behaviors are typically performed together or in proximity to one another.
3. The behaviors can be arranged in any arbitrary or random sequence without any detriment to learning.	Arranging behaviors in a sequence based on the hierarchy of skills and knowledges, or proximity of performance, will increase learning.

other. For example, the behaviors "calculate resistance," "calculate voltage," and "calculate amperage" might be sequenced together because they all use the same formula, Ohm's law. In this case, they all relate to the same content. The next example shows relatedness based on learning one behavior as a prerequisite for another. For example, one must be able to "use a file" before one can "sharpen a saw using a file." Therefore, the behavior "sharpen a saw using a file" is dependent upon the behavior "use a file." The next example shows dependency among the behaviors based on the fact that they usually occur together or in proximity to one another in the real world, and not because of similar content or because the output from one behavior is needed as input to another. For example, even though the behaviors "make a sale" and "accept customers as individuals" may not build directly upon each other's content, they are directly related in the real world and might be taught together. This may be preferable to teaching them in separate units of instruction such as "selling procedures" and "selling attitudes."

Independent behaviors are those which are totally unrelated. They can be taught at any time during the program because they are not the basis for learning other behaviors in the program, because they are not usually performed with any other behavior included in the program, or both. For example, the behavior "purchase a car" could be taught at any time during a program focused on driving a car. You can drive a car without purchasing one. Also, the content needed in learning to drive a car is not built upon the content needed in purchasing a car.

Table 6.1 presents the basic differences between independent and dependent behaviors and how they affect sequencing. The table is adapted from one presented on page 2-2 of the U.S. Air Force *Handbook* (U.S. Department of the Air Force, 1973).

Dependent behaviors should be taught together. These behaviors can depend on one another in the following ways:

1. Content dependency
   a. Common-element dependency CC
   b. Prerequisite dependency CP

2. Proximity dependency
   a. Contingent dependency PC
   b. Proximate dependency PP

Content Dependency

Some behaviors are related because they share parts of a common process or knowledge base, and they are said to be *content dependent.* There are two types of content dependency: common-element dependency and prerequisite dependency.

Common-Element Dependency. *Common-element dependency* occurs when two behaviors have common content as a basis for learning them. In other words, the process and/or knowledge base associated with the behaviors are the same. For example, "measure resistance," "measure voltage," and "measure amperage" are common-element behaviors because they are all measured with an ohmmeter and because Ohm's law is part of a common knowledge base for each of the behaviors.

Prerequisite Dependency. *Prerequisite dependency* occurs when the skills or knowledges learned to perform one behavior are needed to learn another behavior. For example, before a person can multiply, she or he must be able to add. Learning how to add is a prerequisite for multiplying.

Proximity Dependency

If behaviors are related because they occur together or near one another in the real world, they have *proximity dependency.* There are two types of proximity dependency: contingent dependency and proximate dependency.

Contingent Dependency. *Contingent dependency* occurs when the output from performing one behavior becomes the input for performing another behavior. For example, one must "boot a microcomputer" before any program can be run. Therefore, "boot a microcomputer" would be contingent to "run a word processing program."

Proximate Dependency. *Proximate dependency* occurs when behaviors occur in the real world together or in proximity to one another but they are not related as common-element, prerequisite, or contingent behaviors. Although contingent behaviors are also proximate behaviors, all proximate behaviors are not contingent behaviors.

Proximate relationships can be identified by examining the content analysis chart for behaviors that are performed within the same function. Behaviors that occur concurrently, but are otherwise unrelated, should be taught together; otherwise, meaning will be lost. For example, in a welding program the behavior "turn on the exhaust system" should be taught along with the first type of welding, i.e, "weld horizontally." This is true even though turning on the exhaust system is not a prerequisite to learning welding, the output from turning on the system does not provide an input to welding, and the process and knowledge base for turning on the exhaust system and welding do not share anything in common. However, there is no need to turn on the exhaust system unless welding is to take place and the exhausting of fumes is necessary to weld safely. Therefore, they are proximate behaviors.

Another example of proximate behaviors would be "close a sale" and "accept the customer as an individual." Accepting the customer and closing a sale would tend to occur together in the real world, although one is a cognitive behavior and the other is an affective behavior. They do not have common processes or knowledge bases, they do not have to occur in a particular order, and one is not a prerequisite to the other. However, in order for a person to effectively sell, the behaviors should occur together.

DETERMINING THE DEPENDENCY AMONG BEHAVIORS

As indicated, the dependency among behaviors can be organized around content dependency (common-element or prerequisite behaviors) and proximity dependency (contingent or proximate behaviors). Therefore, content dependency and proximity dependency form the two bases for judging whether behaviors are dependent and should be sequenced near one another. If behaviors do not have either of these types of dependency, they are independent. These two factors can be effectively judged relative to each behavior using the matrix presented in Figure 6.2. The table is created as follows.

1. A square matrix is drawn with as many rows and columns as behaviors to be sequenced. Each row and column is assigned a behavior number beginning in the right corner. The cells formed by the matrix are used to analyze the dependency relationship between every pair of behaviors.

2. The cells along the diagonal are also labeled with behavior numbers, dividing the matrix into two halves.

3. The left axis shows that the cells below the diagonal will be used to identify proximity dependency.

4. The top axis shows that the cells above the diagonal will be used to identify content dependency.

The matrix forces the designer to consider each type of dependency for each combination of behaviors. Such detailed consideration is necessary if the eventual sequence is to be most meaningful and efficient. After considering the nature and extent of the dependency among the behaviors, the designer sequences behaviors using the card-sorting and charting procedures presented at the end of this chapter.

The type of dependency to be considered first depends upon the content area to be taught. If the content area contains a predominance of cognitive behaviors, it probably makes sense to begin by analyzing content dependency. If the content area contains a predominance of psychomotor behaviors, one might start by analyzing proximity dependency.

Figure 6.2 shows a sample dependency matrix. Blank cells indicate independence between behaviors. As the key indicates, content common-element dependency is marked "CC"; content prerequisite dependency is marked "CP"; proximity contingent dependency is marked "PC"; and proximity proximate dependency is marked "PP."

Thus, we see that behaviors 1 and 3 are content-dependent by virtue of their common elements. Behaviors 2 and 3 are related through prerequisite dependency. Behaviors 7 and 8 are content-related through both common-element and prerequisite dependency.

In the lower part of the matrix, we see that behaviors 2 and 4 are contingent-dependent, and behaviors 3 and 6 are proximate-dependent.

A dependency matrix is a useful tool not only for sequencing, but also for arriving at a common understanding within an instructional design team as to the logic around which a program will be organized.

SEQUENCING THE BEHAVIORS

As can be seen within the previous discussions of sequencing, the designer must consider many factors before actually arranging the behaviors into a sequence.

FIGURE 6.2 Sample Dependency Matrix

PROXIMITY DEPENDENCY Behavior Number	CONTENT DEPENDENCY Behavior Number 1	2	3	4	5	6	7	8
1	1		CC					
2		2	CP					
3			3					
4		PC		4				
5					5			
6			PP			6		
7							7	CC CP
8								8

Content dependence: common elements CC
prerequisite CP

Proximity dependence: contingent PC
proximate PP

FIGURE 6.3 Sample Sequencing Card

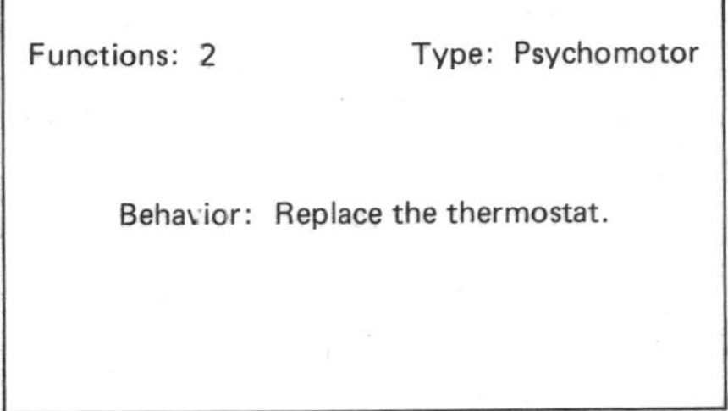

In addition, he or she must consider the program intent as specified in the program description. Once these factors have been considered, the simplest way to actually arrange the behaviors is with a card file. Each of the behaviors is written onto a notecard. The functions to which a behavior relates and the type of behavior are also entered. (See the example of a card presented in Figure 6.3.)

Once the file cards are written, the dependency matrix is consulted and the cards are arranged on a flat surface or bulletin board into a sequence which makes the most instructional sense in terms of the factors previously discussed. The card file has great utility because it allows for quickly changing and testing alternative sequences.

Developing Courses

For a large program that is to be broken down into courses, the dependency matrix provides a basis for doing so. The following procedure is typically used:

1. Determine the amount of instructional time that has been allocated to the total program by consulting the program description. (See Chapter 3.)
2. Determine how much instructional time is allowed for each course within the institution.
3. Develop the notecards described above. Also include the estimated instructional time it will take to teach a behavior on each card. That time is obtained from the priority chart. (See Chapter 5.)
4. Sort the behaviors into the same number of piles as courses to be developed based on type and extent of dependency, and on the total amount of instructional time.

Core courses can be developed from the dependency matrices of two or more programs. A *core course* is a course designed to serve people preparing for a number of different roles which require the development of a common set of behaviors. The dependency matrices of the various programs are examined for content overlap. When content overlap occurs, the behaviors involved are considered for inclusion in a core course.

Core courses are typically developed around content dependency, particularly common-element dependency. That is because although the content may be equally applicable in more than one program, the specific applications of the content vary from one program to another, making other types of dependency less likely to be similar among the different programs.

Core courses are often developed for instructional efficiency. For example, it is more efficient to have one core introductory electronics course serve people entering advanced electronics, robotics, and television repair programs than it is to have a separate introductory course serve each program. However, when this is done, care must be taken to maintain the performance-based focus of instruction by clearly indicating how the content applies to each of the program areas. Otherwise, the inherent meaningfulness of content in performance-based instruction is diminished.

DEVELOPING SEQUENCE CHARTS

Once a sequence is established which has been based on the independence or dependence of the behaviors to be taught, the behaviors are graphically charted to record the sequence order and to make it clearly visible. Figure 6.4 presents a sequence chart of six behaviors. Some of the behaviors are dependent behaviors and others are independent behaviors. Notice that behaviors 5 and 6 are independent behaviors since they are not directly related to any of the other behaviors. (No line connects those behaviors to any other behavior.) Notice that behaviors 1, 2, 3, and 4 are dependent behaviors. (They are connected together with lines.) Either behavior 1, 2, or 3 could be taught prior to behavior 4, because those behaviors are below behavior 4 and the chart is read from the bottom to the top.

Branching Sequences

The two major types of sequences for dependent behaviors are branching sequences and linear sequences. The relationship between behaviors 1, 2, 3, and 4 presented in Figure 6.4 is an example of a branching sequence. In a *branching sequence* there is more than one way to arrive at a particular point or you can go to a number of different points from one point. The concept of branching comes from thinking about a tree. You can arrive at the trunk of the tree by following a number of different branches. Also, you can arrive at a number of different branches by following the trunk of the tree. In the example presented in Figure 6.4, you can arrive at behavior 4 by following the branch from behavior 1, 2, or 3.

FIGURE 6.4 Charting Dependent and Independent Behaviors

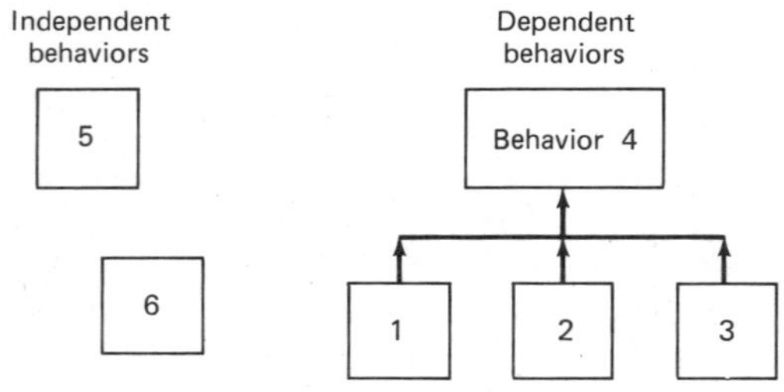

FIGURE 6.5 Linear Sequencing of Dependent Behaviors

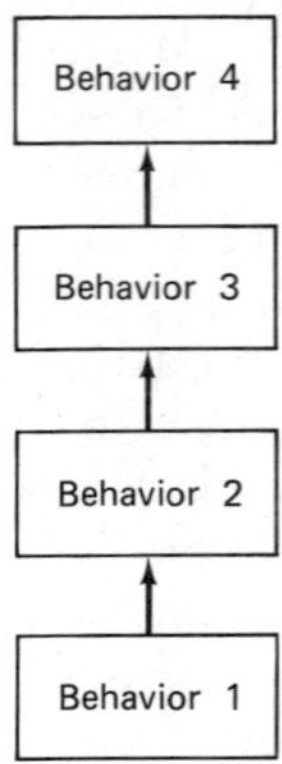

Linear Sequences

The second major type of sequencing is linear sequencing. *Linear sequencing* occurs when you can arrive only at one point from only one other point and you can only go to one other point from that point. Figure 6.5 presents an example of linear sequencing. Reading the chart from the bottom, one can proceed to behavior 2 only from behavior 1, and to behavior 3 only from behavior 2.

The most typical type of sequencing is linear sequencing because it is the easiest to implement during the instructional process. All learners must follow the same sequence. The learning materials do not have to accommodate the ability of learners to arrive at the learning of a behavior after completing instruction on a number of different, alternative behaviors. Linear sequencing is often used with traditional instruction. Instructors teach one behavior to the entire group of learners, then move on to the next behavior, then to the next, and so on. However, linear sequencing offers fewer learning options to learners and tends to make the program very inflexible. Often learners must start at the beginning of a program and continue through the entire program. Branching sequences usually are associated with more flexible programs that provide learning options to learners and allow learners to take part in portions of the program.

In developing the sequencing of behaviors for a program, one may use both types of sequencing. The independent behaviors could just be listed on a separate sheet, since they do not have to be taught in any particular order and since placing them on the chart in graphic form provides little additional information.

Figure 6.6 presents both linear and branching sequences. This chart would be interpreted as follows. Behavior 1 would need to be taught before behaviors 2 and 3, which is a linear sequence. Both behaviors 2

FIGURE 6.6 Branching and Linear Sequences Combined

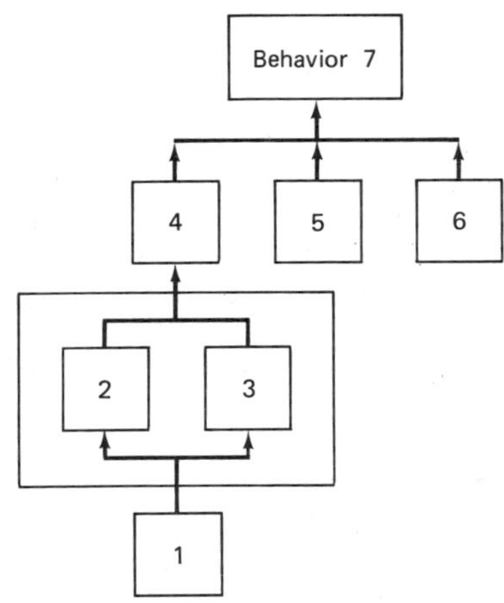

and 3 would have to be taught before behavior 4 (a linear sequence), although 2 and 3 could be taught in any order (a branching sequence). The fact that behaviors 2 and 3 are contained in the same box and that the box is connected to behavior 4 indicates that they both must be taught before behavior 4. Behavior 7 would be taught after behavior 4, 5, or 6 (a branching sequence).

See Appendix B for an additional example of content sequencing.

SUMMARY

Content sequencing is the process of arranging the behaviors to be taught in an instructional program into the order in which they will be taught. The designer has two major concerns when developing a content sequence. They are ensuring that the sequence is meaningful to learners, and ensuring that the sequence is instructionally efficient.

The first step in the process is to determine which behaviors are independent, or not related, and which are dependent, or related. Then, the type of dependency among the dependent behaviors is determined. The dependency among behaviors and factors which might affect learning is considered during the development of the actual sequence. Useful aids in developing the sequence are a dependency matrix and a card file which allow for visual observation of the sequence and experimenting with alternative sequences. Once a suitable sequence is arrived at, it is recorded on a sequencing chart, which graphically presents the behaviors in the order in which they will be taught using branching and/or linear sequencing.

ACTIVITIES AND EVALUATION

1. Obtain a copy of a content analysis which contains the behaviors associated with various functions.
2. Select at least 10 behaviors.
3. Develop a dependency matrix like the one presented in Figure 6.2 showing the interdependence among the behaviors. Indicate the content and proximity dependency of the behaviors.
4. Place the behaviors onto notecards and arrange them into a sequence using the dependency matrix and your knowledge of the types of learners who will take part in the program.
5. Develop a sequencing chart for the behaviors.

REFERENCES

Anderson, O. R., *The Quantitative Analysis of Structure in Teaching*, Teachers College Press, New York, 1971.

Ausubel, D. P., "A Subsumption Theory of Meaningful Verbal Learning and Retention," *Journal of General Psychology*, vol. 66, 1962, pp. 213–214.

Bruner, J. S., *The Process of Education*, Harvard University Press, Cambridge, MA, 1960.

Butler, F. C., *Instructional Systems Development for Vocational and Technical Training*, Educational Technology Publications, Englewood Cliffs, NJ, 1972, pp. xi, 74, 83.

Gagné, R. M., *The Conditions of Learning*, 2d ed., Holt, Rinehart & Winston, New York, 1970.

Herbart, J. F., *The Application of Psychology to the Science of Education*, Beatrice C. Mulliner (trans.), Charles Scribner's Sons, New York, 1898.

Popham, W. J., and E. L. Baker, *Systematic Instruction*, Prentice-Hall, Englewood Cliffs, NJ, 1970.

Posner, G. J., "The Extensiveness of Curriculum Structure: A Conceptual Scheme," *Review of Educational Research*, vol. 44, 1974, pp. 401–407.

Posner, G. J., and K. A. Strike, "A Categorization Scheme for Principles of Sequencing Content," *Review of Educational Research*, vol. 46, no. 4, American Education Research Association, Washington, DC, 1976.

Rugg, H., "The Foundations of Curriculum Making," *The Twenty-Sixth Yearbook: Part II*, The National Society for the Study of Education: Public School Publishing Co., 1930, pp. 11–28.

Suppes, P., "Mathematical Concept Formation in Children," *American Psychologist*, vol. 21, 1966, pp. 139–150.

Taba, H., *Curriculum Development: Theory and Practice*, Harcourt, Brace & World, New York, 1962.

Tyler, R., *Basic Principles of Curriculum and Instruction*, University of Chicago Press, Chicago, 1950.

U.S. Department of the Air Force, *Handbook For Designers of Instructional Systems*, vol. 4, Washington, DC, 1973.

Wadsworth, B. J., *Piaget's Theory of Cognitive Development*, David McKay, New York, 1971.

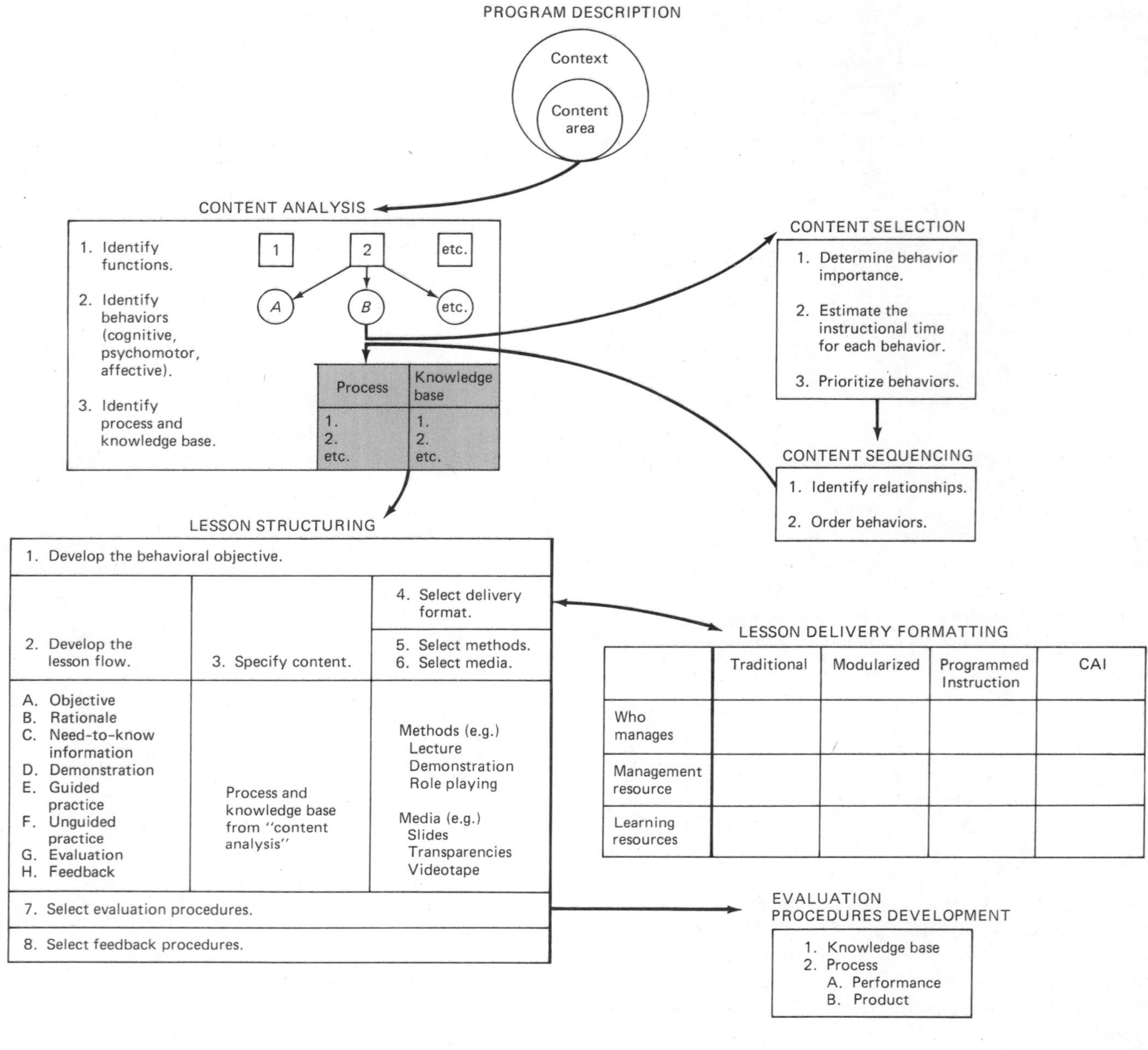
PROGRAM DESCRIPTION
Context
Content area
CONTENT ANALYSIS
1. Identify functions.
2. Identify behaviors (cognitive, psychomotor, affective).
3. Identify process and knowledge base.
1
2
etc.
A
B
etc.
Process
Knowledge base
1.
2.
etc.
1.
2.
etc.
CONTENT SELECTION
1. Determine behavior importance.
2. Estimate the instructional time for each behavior.
3. Prioritize behaviors.
CONTENT SEQUENCING
1. Identify relationships.
2. Order behaviors.
LESSON STRUCTURING
1. Develop the behavioral objective.
2. Develop the lesson flow.
3. Specify content.
4. Select delivery format.
5. Select methods.
6. Select media.
A. Objective
B. Rationale
C. Need-to-know information
D. Demonstration
E. Guided practice
F. Unguided practice
G. Evaluation
H. Feedback
Process and knowledge base from "content analysis"
Methods (e.g.)
Lecture
Demonstration
Role playing
Media (e.g.)
Slides
Transparencies
Videotape
7. Select evaluation procedures.
8. Select feedback procedures.
LESSON DELIVERY FORMATTING
Traditional
Modularized
Programmed Instruction
CAI
Who manages
Management resource
Learning resources
EVALUATION PROCEDURES DEVELOPMENT
1. Knowledge base
2. Process
A. Performance
B. Product

Content Analysis: Behavior Detailing

CHAPTER OBJECTIVE

Givens

A program description, selected functions and behaviors, and a behavior sequencing chart

Behavior

Detail the behaviors to identify content needed to teach the behaviors.

Standard

Behaviors are each analyzed into the process of performing the behavior and the related knowledge base.

OVERVIEW

Once the behaviors and the order in which those behaviors will be taught have been identified, the content which must be taught in order for people to learn to perform each behavior must be identified. This is done through stage 3 of content analysis: behavior detailing. Behavior detailing identifies both the process of performing each behavior and the knowledge base needed to meaningfully apply the behavior. These two components become the content of the instructional lessons that are presented to learners. At this point, it is suggested that you review Figure 4.1 (p. 34), which presents the relationships between the three stages of content analysis.

Both components of behavior detailing are critical to ensuring that people will be able to perform after instruction. The PBID system is founded on the belief that if learners are to perform after instruction, they should be told what behavior they are to learn and how it is done, shown how to do it, allowed to practice, and then be diagnostically evaluated. In order to accomplish this, the designer and the instructor must clearly understand the process of performing the behavior to be taught. However, just teaching the process is not sufficient. People must also develop a knowledge base related to each behavior which will allow them to meaningfully apply that behavior. If only the process is taught, people will not be able to see how that behavior fits in terms of the role for which they are preparing, nor will they be able to adapt the process if new situations arise.

It is equally important not to identify and teach just the knowledge base surrounding a behavior with the belief that people will be able to do it if they understand it. "Telling" people about a behavior and providing extensive related information will not assure performance. Therefore, in determining the content required to teach a behavior, it is essential to identify both the process and the knowledge base.

Behavior detailing should be done within the context of how the behaviors will be sequenced. For efficiency, the behaviors that are sequenced first should be detailed first. There is no point in totally detailing content for a behavior that will be taught later in the sequence if part of that content has already been detailed for a behavior to be taught earlier in the sequence. There should be no need to teach that content again. For example, in a commercial foods program many of the behaviors require people to "dice vegetables." One must dice vegetables in order to make different soups, salads, omelets, and so on. Even though this is true, there is no need to teach dicing vegetables over and over again. If the first behavior in the sequence that requires dicing vegetables is "prepare a table salad," dicing should be detailed and taught at that time. From then on it would be possible to just indicate that the learner must dice vegetables without going into detail. If the learner forgets how to "dice vegetables," he or she can be referred back to the lesson on "prepare a table salad" for review.

TABLE 7.1 Sample Psychomotor Behavior Detailing

BEHAVIOR: CHANGE A TIRE	
Process (Procedure)	Knowledge Base
1. Block the tires. 2. Position the jack. 3. Remove the hubcap. 4. Loosen the lug nuts. 5. Jack the car. 6. Remove the lug nuts. (etc.)	

PROCESS DETAILING

Types of Processes

Process detailing outlines the steps or action of performing a behavior. At times the process may be a step-by-step procedure. At other times it may be a set of

TABLE 7.2 Sample Cognitive Behavior Detailing

BEHAVIOR: DECIDE WHICH WRENCH TO USE	
Process (Procedure)	Knowledge Base
1. Identify the location of the object. 2. Determine the type of object (e.g., a bolt or a stud). 3. Determine the size of the object. 4. Match the functions of types of wrenches with the object. (etc.)	

TABLE 7.3 Sample Affective Behavior Detailing

BEHAVIOR: COOPERATE WITH CO-WORKERS	
Process (Actions)	Knowledge Base
1. Listen to co-workers. 2. Communicate with co-workers. 3. Assist others when asked. 4. Compromise. (etc.)	

actions which can be applied in different orders, depending upon the specific circumstances.

The process associated with both psychomotor behaviors and cognitive behaviors is usually a step-by-step procedure. In both cases, the behaviors are performed by first doing one thing, then doing another, and so on. The process associated with affective behaviors is usually a set of actions. The actions communicate the affective behavior, but they need not take place in any prescribed order.

For example, in order to change a tire (a psychomotor behavior), one would follow the procedure indicated in Table 7.1; in order to decide which wrench to use (a cognitive behavior), one would follow the procedure indicated in Table 7.2. However, if one wished to "cooperate with co-workers" or "accept the customer as an individual" (affective behaviors), one would not follow a specified step-by-step procedure but would exhibit the actions presented in Tables 7.3 and 7.4. The actions that depict cooperation or acceptance are part of processes, but those processes need not always take place in the same order.

Stating the Process

Three rules should be observed when stating the process.

1. Begin each procedural step, or action, with a verb.
2. List all major procedural steps, or actions.

TABLE 7.4 Sample Affective Behavior Detailing

BEHAVIOR: ACCEPT THE CUSTOMER AS AN INDIVIDUAL	
Process (Actions)	Knowledge Base
1. Smile. 2. Control voice volume. 3. Select words. 4. Compromise. 5. Position body. 6. Maintain eye contact.	

3. Include only one major activity in each procedural step, or action.

Each of these rules will be discussed in terms of its implications for identifying the process during behavior detailing.

Notice in the examples presented above that each procedural step or action began with a verb. The selection of these verbs is very important because they are used to direct learning. For example, in Table 7.1, the verb *block* and the verb *position* explicitly indicate the procedure that is expected. In Table 7.3, the verbs *listen* and *communicate* explicitly indicate the type of action that is expected.

One method of determining whether or not a process step is stated correctly is to think of the stereotype of an army sergeant. The army sergeant usually is perceived as giving directive orders such as "Pick that up," "Put that down," "Lift that up," or "Place that here." Each statement begins with a directive verb. Process steps should also be stated as directives and, therefore, should begin with a directive verb.

A sergeant would not give an order by saying "Placing that here" or "Placed that here." Process steps should also not be stated that way. They are intended to direct a learner through the set of desired actions. Therefore, they must be stated as directives.

In specifying each procedural step, or action, one should have each statement include only one major action. For example, assume that you want to teach a person to prepare a pot of coffee with an electric percolator. If the learner is to fill the percolator with cold water, it would be important to separate the actions of "fill the percolator" and "select cold water." Separating actions in this way assures that the instruction will cover each separate action and that each one will be taught in the correct order, if order is important.

Specifying one major action per process step is also important during the design of the evaluation and feedback stages of a lesson, which will be discussed in later chapters. The process identified during behavior detailing becomes the basis upon which performance and product tests are developed to determine if a person can actually perform the process. For example, during evaluation it would be difficult to determine whether a person had a problem with filling the percolator with water or whether he or she filled it with the wrong temperature water if these actions were not separated. When major actions are taught together or evaluated together, it becomes difficult to focus instruction and evaluation. Therefore, each major action should be specified in a separate step.

Finally, all major steps or actions should be presented. If they are not, the instruction and evaluation will also not be complete. Learners will be taught incomplete processes and, therefore, most likely will not reach performance capability. This leads to frustration on the part of the instructor and the learners. For example, if an instructor is teaching a group of people to prepare a pot of coffee and if she or he forgets to include the step of adding coffee to the pot, learners who follow the procedure presented will certainly not end up preparing a pot of coffee. They will fail to reach the performance goal.

Alternative Process-Detailing Approaches

During the identification of the process of performing a behavior it is important to put oneself into the proper perspective for detailing each of the different types of behaviors. For example, the frame of reference that one uses to analyze psychomotor behaviors should be different from the frame of reference used to analyze affective behaviors.

Detailing psychomotor processes should be undertaken with the goal of answering the question, "What process would I need to follow to complete the behavior?" Three approaches to identifying the process of performing a psychomotor behavior are suggested.

1. Complete the behavior yourself.
2. Observe someone else complete the behavior.
3. Mentally complete the behavior.

The best approach is for the person doing the detailing to actually perform the behavior and to write down each process step after completing it. The next-best approach is to observe someone else performing the behavior and to record each process step as it is performed. If neither of these approaches is possible (e.g., if the equipment is expensive and/or unavailable for conducting such an analysis), the designer should at least mentally complete the behavior and record the steps.

For example, if a goal is to teach people how to "prepare a pot of coffee with an electric percolator," the best procedure for identifying the process would be to actually assemble materials and prepare a pot of coffee. Upon completion of each step, that step should be recorded. This procedure is suggested to ensure that all steps are recorded. It is very easy for a person competent in performing a behavior to overlook steps that must be taught to novices. For example, many people perceive the first step of preparing a pot of coffee with an electric percolator to be "fill the percolator with water." In fact, the first step is to disassemble the percolator (take the cover off, take the basket and stem out, etc.). The reason most people perceive the first step to be "fill the percolator with water" is that they are so familiar with the process of making coffee that they do not even think about the fact that they disassemble the percolator before filling it with water.

If the designer cannot actually perform the behavior, the same basic procedure of recording each step should be used during the observation of someone else performing the behavior or while the designer mentally performs the behavior. Table 7.1 presents the result of detailing the process of changing a tire.

Detailing cognitive processes is less direct than detailing psychomotor behaviors. The process steps of psychomotor behaviors are visible. However, most of the process steps for completing a cognitive behavior are not visible. They take place within one's mind as information is being processed. Even though these differences exist, the designer should adopt essentially the same frame of reference to detail the process of performing a cognitive behavior as that used to detail a psychomotor behavior.

When detailing a cognitive process, the designer should again ask the question, "What process would I need to follow to complete the behavior?" The three approaches suggested for identifying a psychomotor process are also suggested for identifying a cognitive process.

The designer should record the process steps while each of these approaches is being used. Again, the best approach is to complete the behavior yourself. The next best is to observe someone else completing the behavior. The approach of observing someone else complete a behavior poses some unique problems when detailing a cognitive process. Since the process is primarily a mental process of manipulating information, little visible action takes place. Therefore, the designer must obtain information from the person completing the behavior in order to record the process. This is done by asking the person to describe the process as he or she is completing it, by asking questions for clarification, and/or by observing the products of the procedure (e.g., numbers as they are written on paper as a mathematical problem is being solved, or items that are being checked off on an evaluation form as a person is evaluating another person). Typical questions which a designer might ask are: "How did you decide to do that?" "Are there standard rules that you use?" "How did you arrive at that solution?" "What did you do first, second, and so on?"

The third approach of mentally completing the process would be least desirable. One would just review the process of performing the behavior mentally without actually performing it. Table 7.2 presents the results of such an analysis for the behavior "decide which wrench to use."

Detailing affective behaviors requires a substantially different frame of reference. Affective behaviors are detailed from the perspective of the recipient of the affective behavior rather than from the perspective of the person performing the behavior. The analysis is done in terms of "What would I observe if a person created the emotional tone desired (e.g., cooperation, warmth or acceptance)?" To develop the affective detailing examples presented in Tables 7.3 and 7.4, the designer must put himself or herself into the perspective of the recipient of actions of another individual. The designer would then list the actions observed as the individual was either cooperating with co-workers or accepting customers as individuals. Those actions would include actual body language, words, or the way in which words were presented. In the case of the cooperation example, one would observe a person performing cooperative action from the perspective of the person receiving cooperation. In the case of the acceptance example, the designer would put herself or himself in the role of the customer and determine which actions convey "acceptance."

In both of these previous situations, the designer would be directly observing a person performing. In the case of written communications behaviors, the actions which convey emotional tones could take the form of the way in which: (1) letters to individuals are structured, (2) words are selected, and (3) adjectives are used. In the latter case, the designer must put himself or herself into the perspective of the recipient of the written communication. The designer must always answer the question, "What would I observe if the desired emotional tone were being communicated to me?"

In many ways, the behavior detailing of affective behaviors is very similar to the behavior detailing of psychomotor behaviors. In both cases, the primary similarity is that one is observing visible actions of an individual. This is in contrast with the behavior detailing of cognitive behaviors, where one is detailing processes that are going on primarily within the mind of an individual.

Two approaches to identifying the process of performing an affective behavior are suggested: actually be the recipient of the behavior, and mentally envision yourself as the recipient of the behavior.

KNOWLEDGE-BASE IDENTIFICATION

After the process of performing a behavior has been detailed, the knowledge base must be identified. *Knowledge-base identification* is the process of determining the information a person "needs to know" in order to meaningfully perform and/or apply a behavior. Such knowledge might take the form of technical information, theory, or background information.

Although the knowledge base contains what many people think of as cognitive information, it is important not to confuse the concepts *knowledge base* and *cognitive behaviors*. Therefore, the term *cognitive* is not used to describe the knowledge base within the PBID system. A knowledge base must be identified for any behavior that is to be taught, regardless of whether it is psychomotor, cognitive, or affective. The knowledge base is the related information needed to perform a given behavior, regardless of type. Therefore, throughout this book it is important to make a clear distinction between *cognitive behaviors* and *knowledge base*. Without this distinction, the ability to clearly perceive cognitive behaviors as being separate from psychomotor and affective behaviors becomes blurred.

Later, during the discussion of the development of performance objectives, the importance of this distinction will again be emphasized. The terms *cognitive, affective,* and *psychomotor* will be used in the same way as Benjamin Bloom (Bloom, 1956) presented them in his book on educational objectives. That book, as well as this one, treats a cognitive behavior as an instructional goal and not as the information needed to accomplish that goal.

The knowledge base should be identified after the process has been specified. This ensures that the items included in the knowledge base are required for performance. It is identified from the perspective of "What does a person need to know in order to meaningfully perform this behavior?" When detailing a behavior, keep in mind the behaviors that were sequenced before as well as the information that will be taught in lessons later. There is no point in detailing the same information again.

In the examples presented in Tables 7.5, 7.6, 7.7, and 7.8, notice that each of the statements of the knowledge base also begins with a verb. This is done so the designer can explicitly communicate the depth of understanding the learner is expected to develop. In Table 7.5, learners would be expected to recall safety procedures, but they would not be expected to be able to explain the procedure for making the decision.

TABLE 7.5 Sample Psychomotor Behavior Detailing

BEHAVIOR: CHANGE A TIRE	
Process (Procedure)	Knowledge Base
1. Block the tires. 2. Position the jack. 3. Remove the hubcap. 4. Loosen the lug nuts. 5. Jack the car. 6. Remove the lug nuts. (etc.)	1. Recall safety precautions. 2. Recall procedures for lifting heavy objects. 3. Explain the procedure for changing a tire.

TABLE 7.6 Sample Cognitive Behavior Detailing

BEHAVIOR: DECIDE WHICH WRENCH TO USE	
Process (Procedure)	Knowledge Base
1. Identify the location of the object. 2. Determine the type of object (e.g., a bolt or a stud). 3. Determine the size of the object. 4. Match the functions of types of wrenches with the object. (etc.)	1. Recall types of wrenches and their functions. 2. Differentiate between objects manipulated with wrenches. 3. Explain the procedure for deciding which wrench to use. (etc.)

TABLE 7.7 Sample Affective Behavior Detailing

BEHAVIOR: COOPERATE WITH CO-WORKERS	
Process (Actions)	Knowledge Base
1. Listen to co-workers. 2. Communicate with co-workers. 3. Assist others when asked. 4. Compromise. (etc.)	1. Explain the benefits of cooperation. 2. Differentiate between assisting and taking over. 3. Explain the process for cooperating with co-workers. (etc.)

TABLE 7.8 Sample Affective Behavior Detailing

BEHAVIOR: ACCEPT THE CUSTOMER AS AN INDIVIDUAL	
Process (Actions)	Knowledge Base
1. Smile. 2. Control voice volume. 3. Select words. 4. Compromise. 5. Position body. 6. Maintain eye contact.	1. Recall the importance of customer comfort. 2. Differentiate meanings conveyed by types of smiles. 3. Recall rules for eye contact. 4. Differentiate body positions and their meanings. (etc.)

The knowledge base specified in this fashion constitutes a set of knowledge-base objectives for each behavior. Later, during the discussion of the construction of evaluation instruments, these knowledge-base objectives will form the basis for knowledge-base evaluations. During the discussion of lesson structuring, they will form the basis for the presentation of information related to the process being taught.

The knowledge base should only contain need-to-know information. *Need-to-know information* is defined as that information which is essential to the meaningful completion of the process for performing a behavior. Unless knowledge-base identification is highly focused, it is possible for the instructional designer to drift into the specification of knowledge beyond that needed to meaningfully perform the behavior. For example, one of the items listed in the knowledge base for the behavior "change a tire" is "recall procedures for lifting heavy objects." The focus is on the procedures for lifting heavy objects. If that focus is lost, it would be possible to drift off into teaching the weights of different types of tires or the reasons for them weighing different amounts. This could lead to the various types of construction that are used to make tires. In other words, it is possible to construct a logical knowledge chain from any behavior to "nice to know" information, which is not directly needed to meaningfully apply behavior. The designer must continually ask the question, "Is this information actually needed?"

The knowledge base should always contain an entry referring to the process of completing the behavior. In order for people to perform a behavior with meaning, they should understand it.

After detailing the process and knowledge base needed for a particular behavior, the designer should have a clear understanding of the content to be taught relative to that behavior. In other words, if one wanted to teach people to "accept the customer as an individual," the actions and knowledge base identified and presented in Table 7.8 would be the content that one would teach. The specific items of information that would have to be taught to accomplish these knowledge-base objectives are selected and specified later, during the development of instructional materials. For example, if the rules regarding eye contact are to be taught so that people can recall them, they must be specified. If a person decided to teach those rules in a lecture, they would be specified during the development of that lecture.

DETERMINING HOW FAR TO BREAK DOWN BEHAVIORS

It is possible to continue breaking a behavior down into finer and finer subdivisions. A major problem facing the designer is to determine how fine to break down a behavior in order for it to be effectively taught. A number of factors affect how far a behavior should be broken down within a given program. Many of those factors should be identifiable within the program description. For example, the program description should provide a description of the type of people expected to take part in the program, and the assumed prerequisite skills those people will be expected to bring with them. The prior experiences of that group would affect how far behaviors would need to be broken down. If the group was already knowledgeable about the content area, one would not have to break the behaviors down as fine as if this were the first time the people encountered it.

The program description should also indicate special learner characteristics. If the group of people to be taught is assumed to include special-needs learners with certain learning difficulties, then the behaviors might need to be broken down very fine in order for those people to be able to learn the behaviors. For example, if the learning difficulties relate to their psychomotor abilities, the psychomotor processes might need to be broken down very fine in order for these learners to master the skills. On the other hand, if the individuals are expected to be retarded, it may be necessary to break down the knowledge base as well as the process very fine for those people to learn a given behavior.

Another factor that affects how fine the designer wishes to break down behaviors is how confident he or she wants to be about the learners' performance capabilities. If it is assumed that *all* learners must be proficient after completing instruction, the detailing and the instruction will need to be more intense than if *most* learners will be expected to be capable of performing.

Two rules can be used when trying to determine how fine to break down behaviors. When identifying the process and knowledge base to teach a behavior:

1. If more than one process requiring instruction is identified within the behavior, then the behavior should be broken down finer into separate behaviors which each represent a separate process.
2. If you do not feel it is reasonable to identify a separate process and knowledge base for a behavior, then you have broken down the behaviors too fine and you should combine that behavior into a more inclusive behavior.

For example, if the behavior specified is "change a tire," one can determine if that behavior is at the correct level of specificity as follows. If the population of learners for which the program is designed needs and can be expected to learn the process steps and knowledge base presented in Table 7.5, then the behavior is specified at the correct level. If one perceives that the people could not perform that behavior without first being taught the separate processes for blocking a tire, jacking the car, removing the lug nuts, and so on, then the behavior "change a tire" must be broken down further and each of these would be treated as behaviors. Each would then be detailed separately. In this case, "jack the car" would become a behavior and the process for jacking the car would be the procedural steps.

On the other hand, if it was determined that the population of people entering the course need not be taught the specific process and knowledge base for changing a tire because they already possess skills at that behavior level, the behavior "change a tire" could be combined with other behaviors into a more inclusive behavior such as "perform tire maintenance." That inclusive behavior could include changing a tire, mounting tires on rims, inflating tires, and so on. In this case, the behavior that would be taught would be "perform tire maintenance," and "change a tire" would be one process step within that behavior.

With experience, the instructional designer develops a "feel" for what is reasonable in terms of breaking down behaviors. In the final analysis, the goal to be achieved is teaching learners a sufficient amount of detail for them to be able to perform without teaching them irrelevant detail which is not needed for their expected level of performance. See Appendices B and C for additional examples of behavior detailing.

SUMMARY

In summary, content analysis is performed in three stages: function identification, behavior analysis, and behavior detailing (process and knowledge-base identification). The result of content analysis is a list of behaviors to be included within an instructional program along with the content that needs to be taught in order for learners to master each behavior.

ACTIVITIES AND EVALUATION

1. Select one psychomotor, one cognitive, and one affective behavior to detail.
2. Identify the process and knowledge base associated with each.
3. Describe the perspective with which you analyzed each behavior. How did your perspectives differ?
4. Describe the difference between a cognitive behavior and a knowledge base.

REFERENCE

Bloom, B. S., *Taxonomy of Educational Objectives: The Classification of Educational Goals, Handbook I: Cognitive Domain,* David McKay, New York, 1956.

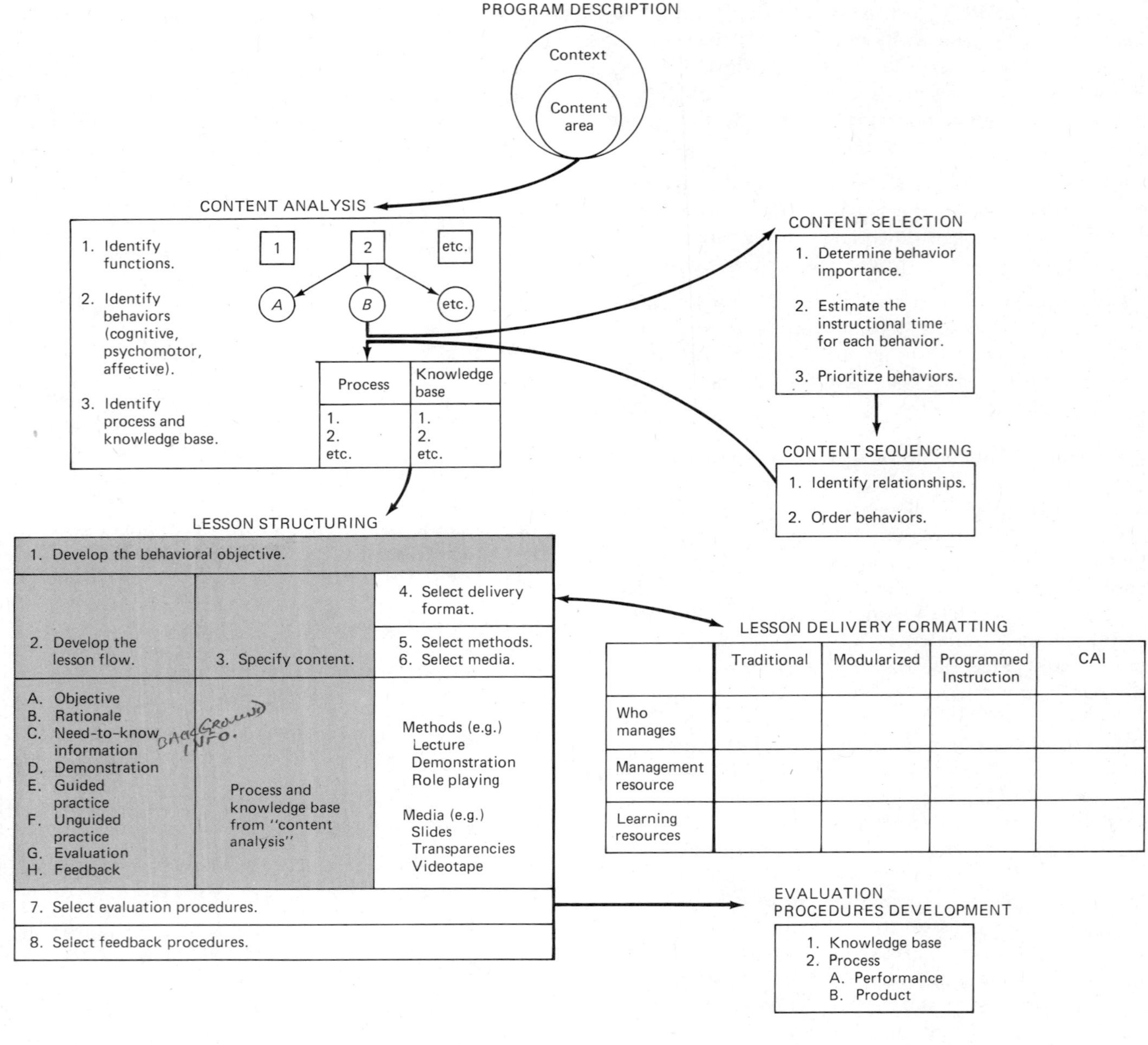

PROGRAM DESCRIPTION
Context
Content area
CONTENT ANALYSIS
1. Identify functions.
2. Identify behaviors (cognitive, psychomotor, affective).
3. Identify process and knowledge base.
1
2
etc.
A
B
etc.
Process
Knowledge base
1.
2.
etc.
1.
2.
etc.
CONTENT SELECTION
1. Determine behavior importance.
2. Estimate the instructional time for each behavior.
3. Prioritize behaviors.
CONTENT SEQUENCING
1. Identify relationships.
2. Order behaviors.
LESSON STRUCTURING
1. Develop the behavioral objective.
2. Develop the lesson flow.
3. Specify content.
4. Select delivery format.
5. Select methods.
6. Select media.
A. Objective
B. Rationale
C. Need-to-know information
D. Demonstration
E. Guided practice
F. Unguided practice
G. Evaluation
H. Feedback
Process and knowledge base from "content analysis"
Methods (e.g.)
Lecture
Demonstration
Role playing
Media (e.g.)
Slides
Transparencies
Videotape
7. Select evaluation procedures.
8. Select feedback procedures.
LESSON DELIVERY FORMATTING
Traditional
Modularized
Programmed Instruction
CAI
Who manages
Management resource
Learning resources
EVALUATION PROCEDURES DEVELOPMENT
1. Knowledge base
2. Process
A. Performance
B. Product

Lesson Structuring: Behavioral Objectives, Lesson Flow, and Content

CHAPTER OBJECTIVE

Givens

A behavior, and the process and knowledge base for teaching that behavior

Behavior

State the lesson objective, determine the lesson flow, and specify content for each lesson-flow stage.

Standard

The lesson objective should be stated as a behavioral objective; the lesson should be organized according to the performance-based lesson flow; and the content for each lesson-flow stage should be indicated.

OVERVIEW

The discussion of lesson structuring has been divided into three chapters. Chapter 8 includes stating the lesson objective, determining the lesson flow, and specifying the content for each lesson-flow stage. Chapter 9 describes the selection of the lesson delivery format, instructional methods, and media, and Chapter 10 describes the selection of evaluation and feedback procedures.

After the behaviors to be taught in a program have been identified and the content to be taught relative to each behavior has been determined, lessons must be developed to teach each behavior. A lesson is a unit of instruction which contains all of the instruction and evaluation necessary to teach a behavior and to verify performance capability. With the PBID system, a complete lesson is defined as one which includes each of the eight lesson-flow stages presented on page 73. These stages lead a learner to performance capability. Even though two or more dependent behaviors may eventually be taught together in one lesson delivery unit, lessons should still be developed separately for each behavior before they are combined. This is done to ensure that all of the components of a total lesson are included for each behavior. Experience has shown that when multiple behaviors are *initially* structured into one lesson delivery unit without first developing a total lesson for each behavior, there is a tendency to not have complete lessons for the individual behaviors in that delivery unit. The process of developing lesson delivery units with multiple behaviors will be discussed in Chapter 11.

A lesson for each behavior is planned for delivery to learners in two separate but related stages: lesson structuring and lesson delivery formatting. *Lesson structuring* is the process of developing a general plan for how the content will be pedagogically organized, presented to learners, and evaluated. It addresses each of the major stages of the lesson and what will be taught or evaluated at each stage. It also involves the tentative selection of the type of lesson delivery format that will be used to implement the lesson as well as tentative decisions regarding which *types* of methods, media, evaluation tools, and feedback procedures will be used. These decisions are tentative during lesson structuring and become finalized during lesson delivery formatting.

A lesson structure performs the same function for an instructional designer as an initial sketch does for an architect or a dress designer. In each case, the goal is to determine the major components and the interrelationships among those components before beginning to develop the project in detail.

Lesson delivery formatting is the process of planning how a structured lesson will actually be implemented with learners and evaluated. It provides answers to questions such as: Who will manage the instruction during delivery? What form will the management vehicle take (e.g., a lesson plan or a learning guide)? What specific learning resources will be used?

A *lesson delivery format* is an instructional management system used to manage the interaction of learners and resources to bring about and evaluate learning. It is the detailed plan for how the structured lesson will be implemented. Typical formats are traditional, modularized, computer-assisted, and programmed instruction.

The separation of lesson structuring and lesson delivery formatting to increase the precision of planning is relatively unique to the PBID system. In the past, the need for their separation had been considered minimal because most lessons were assumed to be planned for traditional instruction. Also, instructors were taught to compensate "on their feet" as classes were taught.

It is still recommended that instructors respond to the needs and progress of learners as instruction is being delivered. Many of the alternative delivery formats (e.g., modularized, CAI, or programmed instruction), however, are not as instructor-intensive; therefore, they cannot be readily adjusted "on the spot," and the negative consequences of a lack of planning become more costly.

In the past there was little formal concern for how lessons were conceptually arranged for delivery to learners. Much instruction was planned around learner activities, with relatively little concern for how those activities were structured and how they related to meaningful learning. Such concepts as making sure that learners are ready to learn and that they clearly understand what they are to learn, and the interplay between practice, evaluation, and feedback were often discussed. However, planning procedures which guaranteed their inclusions in planned lessons were not presented.

The PBID system, on the other hand, is a generic system for planning instruction for any delivery format and does not presume that one type of delivery will be used and not another. In fact, it is possible to present a particular structured lesson through more than one for-

FIGURE 8.1 Lesson Structuring

1. Develop the behavioral objective.		
2. Develop the lesson flow.	3. Specify the content.	4. Select the delivery format. 5. Select methods. 6. Select media.
A. Objective B. Rationale C. Need-to-know information D. Demonstration E. Guided practice F. Unguided practice G. Evaluation H. Feedback	Process and knowledge base from "content analysis"	Methods (e.g.) Lecture Demonstration Role playing Media (e.g.) Slides Transparencies Videotapes
7. Select evaluation procedures.		
8. Select feedback procedures.		

mat. Also, PBID presents procedures which ensure that the designer *consciously* addresses critical considerations about how people learn best.

LESSON STRUCTURING STEPS

Lesson structuring includes the following eight steps:

1. Develop the behavioral objective.
2. Develop the lesson flow.
3. Specify the content to be taught or evaluated at each lesson-flow stage.
4. Select the lesson delivery format.
5. Select instructional methods for each stage.
6. Select instructional media for each stage.
7. Select evaluation procedures.
8. Select feedback procedures.

These steps were presented in Figure 2.7 and are presented again as Figure 8.1 for ready reference.

Developing the Behavioral Objective

In order for a lesson to be planned, behaviors identified during content identification must be converted to behavioral objectives (learning objectives). A behavioral objective becomes the instructor's instructional target and the learner's goal. It states the terminal performance goal of the learner. A behavioral objective includes the following three parts:

1. Givens: the conditions under which the behavior is expected to be performed (this may include the environment, people, data, or things needed to perform the behavior)
2. Behavior: the behavior to be performed
3. Standard: the standard against which performance of the behavior will be judged

Three sample behaviors have been converted to behavioral objectives (see Tables 8.1 to 8.3).

Givens. The givens state what will be needed to perform a behavior in the role for which learners are being prepared. They should *not* include materials that will be used to teach the behavior unless those same materials will be present once the learner assumes the role for which he or she is being prepared. For example, learning materials such as "worksheet 1," "the text-

TABLE 8.1 Psychomotor Objective

Givens
A car with a flat tire, tools, and a replacement tire

Behavior
Change a tire.

Standard
The replacement tire is mounted on the car, the lugs are tight, and the tools and replaced tire are stored.

TABLE 8.2 Cognitive Objective

Givens
A part requiring a wrench for removal and a variety of wrenches

Behavior
Decide which wrench to use.

Standard
A verbal description of the decision process is consistent with that specified on the instructor checklist.

TABLE 8.3 Affective Objective

Givens
Co-workers and a situation requiring cooperation

Behavior
Cooperate with co-workers.

Standard
Actions depicting cooperative activity are consistent with those specified on the instructor checklist.

book," or "learning sample 3" should not be included. These are learning materials and would not be present outside the instructional setting. However, it would be proper to include materials such as "the *Machinist Handbook,*" "the *LOTUS Manual,*" "the *FORD Repair Manual,*" or "the rough draft of a manuscript" because these would actually be used after learners leave instruction and assume desired roles.

Behavior. The behavior is stated in the same form as in content analysis.

Standard. The standard for a behavioral objective presents the basis for judging whether the behavior has been performed correctly. It focuses on the process of performing a behavior versus the knowledge base which supports the learning of the behavior. The end goal of instruction should be mastery of the process. The knowledge base is a necessary ingredient in the instructional process, but it is not the end goal. Chapter 16 presents a detailed discussion of the development of instruments to assess whether learners have attained the standard.

Process evaluation can be conducted either by observing the *product* of the process or by observing a person *performing* the process. The standard should be stated in terms of one or the other. For example, the process of changing a tire can be evaluated in two ways: (1) by observing a tire which has already been changed to determine if the *product of the process,* or the changed tire, is adequate, or (2) by observing a person changing a tire to determine if the *performance of the process* is adequate. In the psychomotor example presented previously, "change a tire," the product would be judged. Therefore, the standard is stated as characteristics of a changed tire. If the actual performance of changing a tire were the primary focus of the objective, the standard would need to be rewritten. For example, it would be rewritten as "the tire will be changed using the process outlined in the owners' manual." At times, another person may be the recipient of the performance process. In these situations, performance can also be judged based on recipient reaction to the process. For example, the performance of the process associated with the behavior "accept the customer as an individual" could be evaluated by observing the person performing the process or by assessing whether the customer feels accepted during the process.

The decision to evaluate either the product of a process or the performance of a process should be based upon the ultimate goal of the objective. In some cases, learning a generalized process is more important than learning to produce a particular product. In the case of the cognitive example shown previously, the goal is for a person to learn how to select a wrench for a given circumstance; the goal is not only to select a particular wrench. Therefore, the generalized process becomes the focus of teaching and learning, and the standard reflects that focus. This standard directs the evaluation toward the performance of the process rather than the product of the process.

Many behaviors can be evaluated in terms of both product and performance. In some cases, however, it is not possible to evaluate a behavior through both. Any process can be evaluated through a performance evaluation requiring the observation of the performance of the process. That is because every behavior has a process. Only some processes, however, can be evaluated by observing the quality of the product of the process. Some do not yield a product. For example, it is not possible to evaluate the affective example shown previously, "cooperate with co-workers," by evaluating a product. There is no product. Once the performance of the process is completed, there is no physical change that remains.

The distinction between evaluating the product of the process and evaluating the performance of the process is important because it is a key to being able to apply performance-based techniques to cognitive and affective behaviors.

Stating the standard for a cognitive objective possesses some unique challenges. That is because when teaching cognitive processes, the instructor usually is not primarily concerned with the particular product produced during the learning exercises. The primary concern is usually for the process that is being used in developing that product. Yet, the process is often not visible as it is being performed. It occurs within a person's mind. Such is the case with the cognitive objective shown previously: "decide which wrench to use." Making the decision involves the invisible processing of information in the person's mind. Although the selection of the correct wrench will result in a product, or the selected wrench, that is not the primary goal of instruction. The primary goal is to ensure that the correct process is being used so the process can be applied to other selections in the future.

In order to evaluate such processes, the designer must create evaluation procedures that make key elements of such processes visible or at least able to be evaluated. For example, it is possible to make a process visible by asking a person to report on it as it is being performed. The reporting can either be written or oral. In the cognitive wrench-selection objective, the standard indicates that the person is to provide a verbal description of the decision-making process. Techniques for making such processes visible and evaluatable are discussed further in Chapter 16.

The standard of an objective should also indicate, or reference, the components of the product or process that will be observed (the product characteristics). At times, the components are few and easily defined. Therefore, they can be included in the standard of the objective directly. At other times, the components are many and/or are not easily defined, so the standard makes reference to other sources where the components are listed and defined, such as reference manuals. It is not adequate to state the standard with statements such as "the behavior will be performed correctly" or "the behavior will be performed to industry standards." What constitutes *correctly* or *industry standards*? Such terms are too vague and need definition in order for the objective to serve as the target of instruction and as the goal for learners. The standard must explicitly state the components that will be used as the basis for evaluating whether a behavior is being done correctly or meets industry standards.

In the previous psychomotor objective, the characteristics of the product of a changed tire are few and easily defined. They are therefore specified in the standard of that objective. In the case of the cognitive and affective objectives, the processes are complex and not easily defined, and reference is made to where they are defined. In both of these examples, if the actual procedural steps or actions to be evaluated were listed in the standard, it would become so large that it would lose its ability to convey the goal of the lesson quickly and concisely. However, in all three objectives the standard is published and the instructor and the learners know what is expected. In the psychomotor objective, the standard is totally published in the objective itself. In the cognitive and affective objectives, the source of the detailed standard is referenced, and the standard is published elsewhere. It is possible to reference many different types of sources as a basis for defining and publishing the standard. For example, manuals, textbooks, articles, and instructor-developed materials can be used. A published standard is important to a clear understanding of the behavioral objective.

Developing the Lesson Flow

Just as the behaviors within an instructional program must be sequenced, the stages of a lesson must also be sequenced. The sequence of stages within a lesson is called the *lesson flow*. The PBID system uses a lesson flow called the *performance-based lesson flow*. As with other components of the system, it is designed to lead the learner to performance capability. The lesson flow is based on how people learn to perform and how they want to learn.

Chase and Chi (1980), after a review of literature concerning problem-solving skills, concluded that "it appears that a large, long-term knowledge base underlies skilled performance." They also concluded: "The most obvious answer [to the development of expertise] is practice, thousands of hours of practice.... There may be some as yet undiscovered basic abilities that underlie the attainment of truly exceptional performance,... but for the most part practice is by far the best predictor of performance."

These findings and the theoretical models by Herbart (1898) and Ausubel (1962) which describe how people learn provide part of the rationale for the lesson flow presented. The PBID lesson flow also reflects how people want to learn to perform. The author has repeatedly asked college classes and people in industry how they would like to be taught a behavior if their lives depended on it. Surprisingly, most groups have responded similarly. First, they want to know what they will be expected to learn and why they should learn it. Then they want to be provided with some background information so they can better understand what they are to learn. Then they want someone to show them how to perform the behavior. Then they want to practice the behavior with guidance so they can be corrected if they are doing it wrong. Then they want to be allowed to practice alone, with the opportunity to have help only if necessary. Then they want to be evaluated and provided with feedback to determine if they can perform the behavior correctly or if they need to correct their performance.

Based on learning theory and experience asking people how they would like to perform, the following eight stages of a lesson flow have evolved:

1. State the objective.
2. State the rationale.
3. Provide need-to-know information.
4. Demonstrate the behavior.
5. Guide practice.
6. Allow for unguided practice.
7. Evaluate the learner's performance and knowledge base.
8. Provide feedback and direction.

Each of these stages and its purpose and rationale are presented in the following sections. Understanding the purposes and rationales is important because they provide meaning to the process of structuring lessons.

State the Objective and Rationale. Stating the objective and rationale are the first two stages of a lesson flow. They are designed to establish a readiness on the part of the learner to learn. Learning requires the attention and commitment of the learner. If the learner is not ready to learn, what is taught will be ignored. Using the PBID system, one can establish readiness first by stating the behavioral objective. It tells the learner what is to be learned (the behavior), what the learner will need to have available to demonstrate the behavior (the givens), and the basis upon which performance will be judged (the standard).

The next step in establishing readiness is to tell the learner why what is to be learned is important. This establishes motivation and relates what is to be learned to past or future learning. In most vocational education and training programs, people are motivated by their desire to achieve their final goal (e.g., being prepared for a role which they would like to occupy); however, that is not enough. Learners should also be told how each behavior "fits" in relation to other behaviors.

People try to attach meaning to whatever they invest time in learning. If they are not presented with a vehicle for developing accurate meanings, they will develop other meanings. This is similar to the story of the blind man trying to describe an elephant. The first thing he touched was the elephant's trunk; that reminded him of a fire hose. The next thing he touched was the tusks; that reminded him of spears. The next thing he touched was the mouth; that reminded him of a hole in a water bag with water dripping out. The next thing he touched was the skin, which reminded him of a leather bag. He concluded that the elephant was a large leather bag which provided water to a fire hose and that someone had thrown spears into it and it was leaking. His perception might have been quite different if he had been provided one piece of information in advance: that the elephant was an animal.

Readiness in terms of where new material fits can be established by using an "advanced organizer," as was discussed by Ausubel (1962), or by relating what is to be learned to the past experience of the learner, as advocated by Herbart (1898). In the case of the blind man, his being told that the elephant was an animal would be an advanced organizer drawn from past experience. Herbart and Ausubel both suggest that instructors relate new content to a larger framework. That framework can actually be presented by the instructor, or it can be part of the learner's past experience. New content should be related to such a framework in terms of the similarities, dissimilarities, or other types of relationships between what is to be learned and what is already known. If learners cannot clearly see how the thing they are learning relates to other things, they may relate it incorrectly or memorize it, both of which reduce motivation and meaning. It is the responsibility of the designer and the instructor to ensure that learners integrate new content meaningfully.

Provide Need-to-Know Information. Providing need-to-know information is the third stage of the lesson flow. The need-to-know information to be taught during a lesson is the knowledge base identified during content analysis. It is information needed by the learner to meaningfully *apply* the behavior. For example, in order to decide which wrench to use, a person needs to know which types of wrenches are available. In order to place a disk into a computer, one must be familiar with disks. Before lifting heavy tires, people should understand the need for caution when lifting heavy objects so that they do not hurt themselves.

Obviously, it is possible to teach people to perform behaviors without telling them what they are to learn or why they are to learn it, or without providing them with a related knowledge base that provides an understanding of the process. However, such teaching produces "monkey see–monkey do" learning, which is ineffective in the long run. If the expectation is for learners to be able to apply behaviors flexibly, then what they learn must be meaningful so that they can apply it to new situations.

Demonstrate the Behavior. Demonstrating the behavior is the fourth stage of a lesson. Learners should be shown how to perform the behavior in the role for which they are preparing. Usually, the more realistic the demonstration, the better. Also, usually the more senses that can be involved within the demonstration, the better. For example, while demonstrating a behavior it is better to allow someone to taste something than to just show him or her the thing and describe the taste. If the object being demonstrated also makes a sound, the sound should be present.

However, there are times when realism detracts from the instruction. In some situations, the setting within which a behavior occurs is so complex that it is difficult for learners to separate a particular behavior from others performed with it. In these cases, it may be necessary to demonstrate the behaviors in settings that allow them to be seen more clearly.

Practice. Guided practice and unguided practice are the fifth and sixth stages of a lesson. After learners have been shown how to perform a behavior, they should be allowed to practice. Practice is the opportunity for them to perform the behavior. In order for a person to become capable of performing, she or he must have opportunities to perform. In teaching, the practice component of lessons is often left out or forgotten. Often, instructors talk about a behavior, show learners how to perform it, evaluate the learner's understanding, and then move on to new content. That approach makes little sense if the goal is to ensure performance capability. As with demonstrations, practice should take place in situations as similar as possible to those within which the behavior will later be performed.

Practice should occur in two stages. First, when a person first tries to do something, someone or some device should be available to guide the practice and to correct processes and procedures. It has been estimated that if a person learns something incorrectly, it will take as much as 10 times longer to relearn it correctly than it would to have learned it correctly at the beginning. That is because the incorrect behavior must be extinguished before it can be learned correctly.

The second stage of practice aims at perfecting the behavior. After guided practice, people need opportunities for continued practice to perfect their skills, with guidance only when necessary. Although different people require different amounts of practice, most behaviors cannot be learned sufficiently without additional practice which will allow learners to perform on their own. It is important for people to practice on their own without reliance upon someone (or something) in order to develop self-assurance and the competence required when they leave the learning environment.

Evaluate and Provide Feedback. Evaluation of learner performance and knowledge base and provision of feedback and direction are the seventh and eighth stages of a lesson. Evaluation and feedback should be thought of together when using the PBID system. *Evaluation* is the process of obtaining information about performance. *Feedback* is information regarding learners' progress which is based on evaluation results; it is provided to learners so that they can verify that learning has taken place or so that they can adjust their learning. The primary purpose of evaluation and feedback is learning diagnosis and correction. Just as a rocket requires a guidance system to redirect it after it is launched because of changes in the wind, changes in thrust, and so on, a person who tries to do something for the first time needs a "guidance system." For the rocket, information concerning its direction is sensed and evaluated through various sensors and computers, and it is redirected based on feedback through a guidance system. For a person, information concerning his or her learning progress should be sensed and evaluated through another person or through devices developed by the instructional designer (e.g., computer programs that monitor progress, self-checks of learning progress, or instructor evaluations); that information should then be interpreted and fed back to the learner to verify that learning has taken place or to redirect learning.

Effective monitoring of learner progress and redirecting of learning can greatly increase the efficiency

TABLE 8.4 Lesson Structure

PSYCHOMOTOR OBJECTIVE

Givens
A car with a flat tire, tools, and a replacement tire

Behavior
Change a tire.

Standard
The replacement tire is mounted on the car, the lugs are tight, and the tools and replacement tire are stored.

LESSON STAGE	CONTENT TO BE TAUGHT, PRACTICED, OR EVALUATED	METHODS/MEDIA (CONSISTENT WITH DELIVERY FORMAT)
RATIONALE	*a.* Consequences of trying to drive on a flat tire *b.* Consequences of being stranded *c.* Money savings	SEE CHAPTER 9 for methods and media selection.
NEED-TO-KNOW INFORMATION	*a.* The step-by-step procedure for changing a tire *b.* Safety precautions *c.* Lifting heavy objects	
DEMONSTRATION	Procedure for changing a tire	
GUIDED PRACTICE	Procedure for changing a tire	
UNGUIDED PRACTICE	Procedure for changing a tire	
EVALUATION	*a.* Knowledge base presented above *b.* Procedure for changing a tire	SEE CHAPTER 10 for evaluation and feedback procedures selection.
FEEDBACK	*a.* Knowledge base presented above *b.* Procedure for changing a tire	

TABLE 8.5 Lesson Structure

COGNITIVE OBJECTIVE

Givens
A part requiring a wrench for removal and a variety of wrenches

Behavior
Decide which wrench to use.

Standard
A verbal description of the decision process is consistent with that specified on the instructor checklist.

LESSON STAGE	CONTENT TO BE TAUGHT, PRACTICED, OR EVALUATED	METHODS/MEDIA (CONSISTENT WITH DELIVERY FORMAT)
RATIONALE	*a.* Consequences of using the wrong wrench *b.* Time savings	SEE CHAPTER 9 for methods and media selection.
NEED-TO-KNOW INFORMATION	*a.* Types of wrenches and their functions *b.* Procedure for making the decision	
DEMONSTRATION	Procedure for making the decision	
GUIDED PRACTICE	Procedure for making the decision	
UNGUIDED PRACTICE	Procedure for making the decision	
EVALUATION	*a.* Knowledge base presented above *b.* Procedure for making the decision	SEE CHAPTER 10 for evaluation and feedback procedures selection.
FEEDBACK	*a.* Knowledge base presented above *b.* Procedure for making the decision	

TABLE 8.6 Lesson Structure

AFFECTIVE OBJECTIVE

Givens
A co-worker and a situation requiring cooperation

Behavior
Cooperate with co-workers.

Standard
Actions depicting cooperative activity are consistent with those specified on the instructor checklist.

LESSON STAGE	CONTENT TO BE TAUGHT, PRACTICED, OR EVALUATED	METHODS/MEDIA (CONSISTENT WITH DELIVERY FORMAT)
RATIONALE	The benefits of cooperation	SEE CHAPTER 9 for methods and media selection.
NEED-TO-KNOW INFORMATION	*a.* Types of actions that convey cooperation versus types of actions that convey noncooperation *b.* Differences between assisting and taking over	
DEMONSTRATION	Cooperative actions	
GUIDED PRACTICE	Cooperative actions	
UNGUIDED PRACTICE	Cooperative actions	
EVALUATION	*a.* Knowledge base presented above *b.* Cooperative actions	SEE CHAPTER 10 for evaluation and feedback procedures selection.
FEEDBACK	*a.* Knowledge base presented above *b.* Cooperative actions	

and effectiveness of learning. They reduce the chances of incorrect learning, breakage of equipment, and waste of materials, as well as waste of instructor and learner time needed to bring people to performance capability. There are a variety of ways to effectively provide feedback, which are discussed in detail in Chapter 10.

Specify the Content to Be Taught

The actual content to be presented, practiced, and evaluated throughout the lesson flow is identified through the behavior-detailing procedures discussed in Chapter 7. Those procedures yield the process for performing a behavior and the supporting knowledge base. As discussed previously, portions of that content are presented, practiced, and evaluated at various stages throughout the lesson. The content for the rationale, which indicates why a person should learn the behavior, is derived from the logic that was used to include the behavior in the program and to sequence the behavior. For example, how are other behaviors dependent upon learning this behavior, and why? What are the consequences of performing the behavior well or poorly?

The content for the need-to-know information stage of the lesson, including an explanation of the process of performing the behavior, is derived from the knowledge base. The content for the demonstration stage and the practice stages is derived from the process of performing the behavior. The content for the evaluation and feedback stages are derived from both the knowledge base and the process.

Tables 8.4, 8.5, and 8.6 present sample lesson structures for a psychomotor, a cognitive, and an affective behavior; they include the objective, the lesson flow, and the content to be presented, practiced, or evaluated at each stage of the lesson flow. Chapters 9 and 10 will present ways to select the delivery format, methods and media, and evaluation and feedback procedures.

The reader should take the time to review the behavior detailings for these sample behaviors which are presented in Chapter 7; the discussions of developing behavior objectives, developing the lesson flow, and specifying the content, presented above; and Tables 8.4, 8.5, and 8.6 to see how they fit together. See Appendices B and C for additional examples of behavioral objectives, lesson flows, and the content to be taught at each stage of the lesson flow.

SUMMARY

In summary, lesson structuring is the process of developing a general plan for how the content will be pedagogically organized, presented to learners, and evaluated. It is crucial to the process of instructional design. The goal is to identify the major components of the lesson and the interrelationships among those components before developing the lesson in detail. It indicates how the designer plans to bring the learner to performance capability relative to a behavior.

ACTIVITIES AND EVALUATION

1. Write a brief explanation of the rationale for each stage of a lesson flow in terms of its impact on the learner. Check your answer against the description of the lesson flow presented in this chapter.
2. *a.* Select a behavior for which a lesson is to be structured.
   b. Convert the behavior into a behavioral objective with the givens, behavior, and standard.
   c. Either select an already existing detailing of that behavior or detail it to arrive at the process of performing the behavior and the supporting knowledge base. (Review Chapter 7, if necessary.)
   d. Develop a partial lesson structure such as those presented in Tables 8.4 through 8.6. Enter the objective at the top of the worksheet. List down the sheet the lesson stages and the content to be taught at each stage.

REFERENCES

Ausubel, D. P., "A Subsumption Theory of Meaningful Verbal Learning and Retention," *Journal of General Psychology,* vol. 66, 1962, pp. 213–224.

Chase, W. G., and M. T. H. Chi, "Cognitive Skill: Implications for Spatial Skill in Large-Scale Environments," in J. Harvey (ed.), *Cognition, Social Behavior, and the Environment,* Erlbaum, Potomac, MD, 1980, pp. 189–195.

Herbart, J. F., *The Application of Psychology to the Science of Education,* Beatrice C. Mulliner (trans.), Charles Scribner's Sons, New York, 1898.

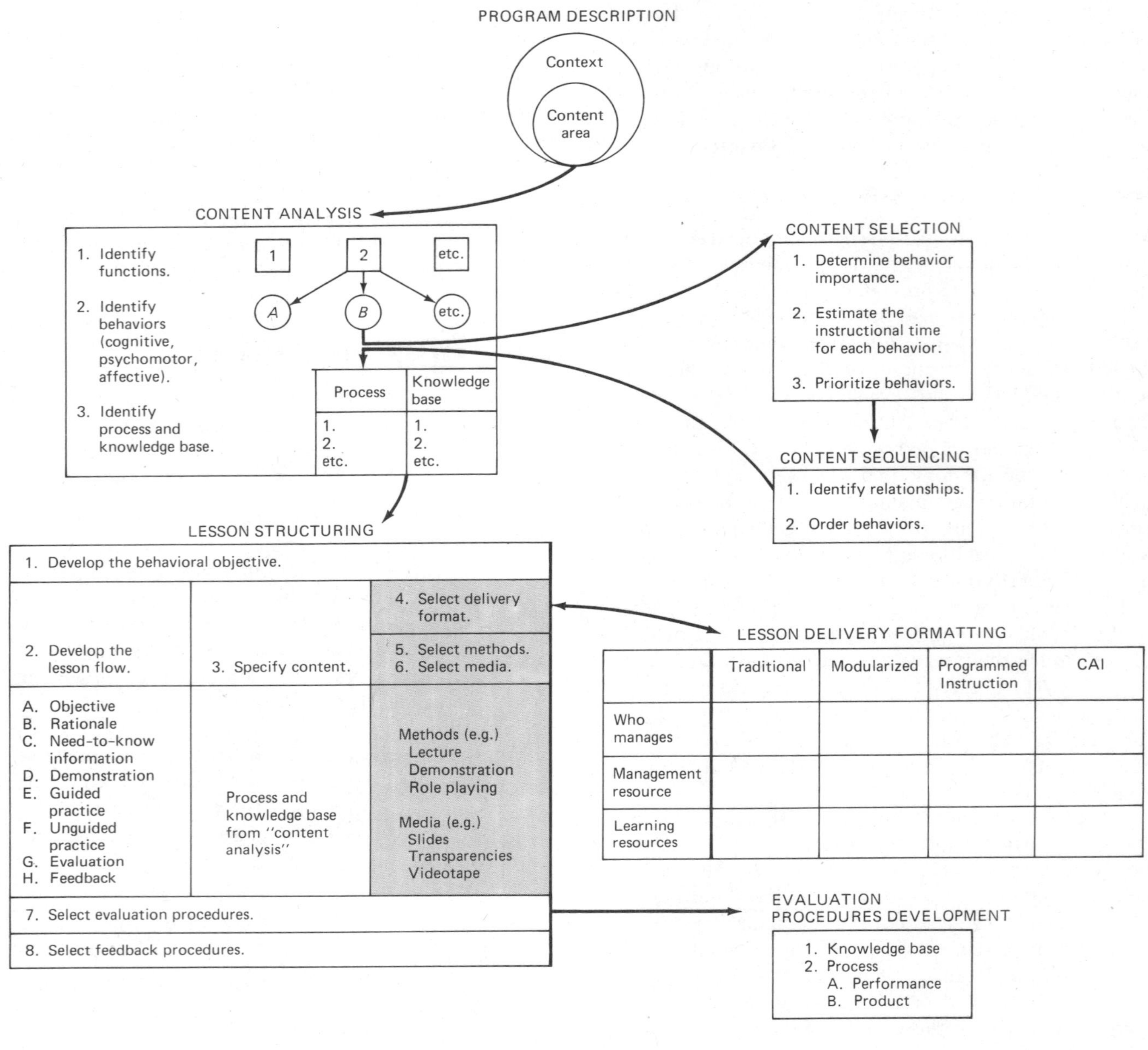

PROGRAM DESCRIPTION
Context
Content area
CONTENT ANALYSIS
1. Identify functions.
2. Identify behaviors (cognitive, psychomotor, affective).
3. Identify process and knowledge base.
1
2
etc.
A
B
etc.
Process
Knowledge base
1.
2.
etc.
1.
2.
etc.
CONTENT SELECTION
1. Determine behavior importance.
2. Estimate the instructional time for each behavior.
3. Prioritize behaviors.
CONTENT SEQUENCING
1. Identify relationships.
2. Order behaviors.
LESSON STRUCTURING
1. Develop the behavioral objective.
2. Develop the lesson flow.
3. Specify content.
4. Select delivery format.
5. Select methods.
6. Select media.
A. Objective
B. Rationale
C. Need-to-know information
D. Demonstration
E. Guided practice
F. Unguided practice
G. Evaluation
H. Feedback
Process and knowledge base from "content analysis"
Methods (e.g.)
Lecture
Demonstration
Role playing
Media (e.g.)
Slides
Transparencies
Videotape
7. Select evaluation procedures.
8. Select feedback procedures.
LESSON DELIVERY FORMATTING
Traditional
Modularized
Programmed Instruction
CAI
Who manages
Management resource
Learning resources
EVALUATION PROCEDURES DEVELOPMENT
1. Knowledge base
2. Process
A. Performance
B. Product

Lesson Structuring: Selecting Delivery Format, Methods, and Media

CHAPTER OBJECTIVE

Givens

A lesson with the objective, lesson flow, and content to be taught at each stage of the lesson flow stated

Behavior

Select the lesson delivery format, methods, and media to present the content to learners.

Standard

The methods and media to be selected must be consistent with the goals of each of the stages of a lesson, the types of content to be taught, and the type of lesson delivery format selected.

OVERVIEW

The lesson delivery format, instructional methods, and instructional media are selected after the objective of a lesson, the lesson flow, and the content to be taught at each stage of the lesson flow have been defined. In Chapter 8 a lesson delivery format was defined as an instructional system used to manage the interaction of learners and resources throughout a lesson; its goal is to bring about and evaluate learning. It will be contrasted with instructional methods and media later in this chapter. *Instructional methods* are instructional procedures or processes used to present content to learners (e.g., demonstrations or lectures). *Instructional media* are the software, hardware, and personnel which serve as modes of communication to convey content to learners (e.g., videotape recorders, live instructors, and computers). Notice that this definition includes personnel as a form of media.

Distinguishing between *methods* and *media* is important when designing lessons. Each method, or procedure, should be thought of as being communicable through a variety of media. This is in contrast to thinking of methods and media decisions as one, as was the case when alternative media were limited and most instruction was delivered using the traditional format. For example, the common view was that a lecture was given by a live person. Therefore, when a designer or instructor made the decision to use a lecture, it was assumed that a live person would deliver it. Consequently, when individualized instruction and computer-assisted instruction (CAI) became more widely accepted as alternative delivery formats, people automatically thought lectures could not be used with those formats. However, if the decisions concerning methods and media are considered separately, it becomes apparent that lectures can be used with these other formats. The key is to use other forms of appropriate media (such as video- or audiotapes) in place of a live lecturer as the basis for communicating the lectures.

The methods and media that are selected in a given circumstance are influenced by three primary factors:

1. The lesson delivery format that will be used to present the lesson
2. The type of content to be taught
3. The stage of the lesson flow

Some methods and media are more compatible with some lesson delivery formats than others. That is because some delivery formats rely primarily on an instructor to deliver content, and others rely on computers, programmed texts, or independent study materials. The mix of methods and media used with each format is different. For example, live demonstrations by instructors are often used with the traditional delivery format. However, they are not used with the CAI format because that instruction is presented through a computer and devices controlled by the computer. Demonstrations using the CAI format would be presented through computer simulations or computer-controlled video devices, not live instructors.

At this point, it is important to clearly differentiate between a lesson delivery format and instructional media. A *lesson delivery format* is an instructional management system used to manage the interaction of learners and resources throughout a lesson to bring about and evaluate learning. It is a format for developing a detailed plan for how the structured lesson will be implemented. Remember, a *lesson* is a unit of instruction which contains all of the instruction and evaluation necessary to teach a behavior and to verify performance capability. *Instructional media* are the means for communicating a specific portion of the content of a lesson through a method. *Formats* and *media* are sometimes confused, since formats are often differentiated on the basis of the dominant medium (hardware and software) used to present them. For example, a computer is a medium. It can be used as a form of instructional media to present a specific portion of the content of a lesson. Computer-assisted instruction is a lesson delivery format. In CAI, the computer is used as the vehicle for directing and managing learners through the stages of a lesson.

SELECTING THE LESSON DELIVERY FORMAT

Usually selection of the lesson delivery format is based on the type of instructional media that will be used to present the majority of the content of the lesson. In other words, it makes sense to manage a lesson through the CAI format when a computer, or computer-controlled devices, will be the primary form of instructional media used to deliver the content of a lesson. It makes sense to use a traditional delivery format if the instructor, or the instructor-controlled devices, will be the primary form of instructional media used to present the content of the lesson.

The four delivery formats most often used with performance-based instruction are presented briefly below. The actual process of developing instruction using each format will be presented in Chapters 11 and 12.

1. *The traditional instruction format.* The instructor manages the delivery of the lesson by following a lesson plan, which is written as directions to the instructor. A variety of learning resources (e.g., transparencies and charts) are used directly by the instructor. The instructor may also direct learners to resources for self-study.
2. *Modularized instruction format.* The learner manages the delivery of the lesson by following a learning guide written as directions to the learner. A variety of learning resources, including the instructor, are used directly by the learner.
3. *Programmed instruction format.* The learner manages the delivery of the lesson by completing a printed, programmed text. The programmed text is the sole learning resource that is used directly by the learner. It contains the information to be learned and directions as to how to proceed through the information.
4. *Computer-assisted instruction (CAI) format.* The learner manages the delivery of the lesson by completing a computer program. The computer, including computer-controlled devices, is the primary learning resource. At time, learners can be referred to additional resources external to the computer (e.g., manuals and an instructor). The computer program contains the information to be learned and directions as to how to proceed through the information.

Regardless as to which of these delivery formats is selected, it is important to remember that the instructional designer, as well as the instructor, are still in control of the instruction. The instructional designer develops the sequence of events through which the learner proceeds during the implementation of the lesson. The instructor, if he or she is not the instructional designer, can review the materials to be presented to learners and judge whether they meet his or her expectations. If they do not, they can be rejected in favor of other materials. The key point is that the instructor is always in control, regardless of the format selected.

Table 9.1 presents a summary of the four major instructional formats. When selecting the type of lesson delivery format to use with a particular instructional program or lesson, the designer must consider a number of factors:

1. Lesson management
2. Types of content to be taught
3. Types of learning resources to be used
4. Need for uniformity of instruction and performance assurance

Lesson Management

First, let us consider how the lesson will be managed. Three questions should be asked.

1. Who will manage the lesson during delivery?
2. What management resource will that person be using?
3. Will learners be managed as a group or as individuals?

TABLE 9.1 Management and Typical Learning Resources Associated With Delivery Formats

	LESSON DELIVERY FORMATS			
	TRADITIONAL (instructor directed)	MODULARIZED (learner-directed)	PROGRAMMED INSTRUCTION	COMPUTER-ASSISTED INSTRUCTION (CAI)
WHO MANAGES	Instructor	Learner	Learner	Learner
MANAGEMENT RESOURCE	Lesson plan	Learning guide	Programmed text	Computer program
TYPICAL LEARNING RESOURCES	Instructor as the primary resource with support materials	Independent study material with the instructor and other people as resources	Programmed "text"	Computer "program" and computer-controlled devices

Instruction can be managed during delivery by an instructor or by a learner. If it is managed by the instructor or by someone other than the learner, directions are given to the learner by the instructor. These directions can be verbal or presented through written assignments. If the lesson is managed by the learner, directions are presented directly to the learner without the need for the instructor to be present. Typically, these directions are presented in writing (e.g., in printed material or on a computer screen), but they can be presented verbally through learner-controlled media (e.g., a videotape). Traditional instruction is most often instructor-managed; modularized, programmed, and computer-assisted instruction are most often learner-managed.

The management resource which presents the directions can take the form of: (1) an instructor lesson plan that indicates actions to be taken by the instructor during the delivery of a lesson, (2) a learning guide that indicates learning steps to be followed by learners, (3) a programmed text that includes directions to the learner, or (4) a computer program that includes directions to the learner. Traditional instruction uses an instructor lesson plan; modularized instruction uses a learning guide; programmed instruction uses a programmed text; and CAI uses a computer program. In each case, the management resource presents a set of directions regarding how to proceed through the learning resources associated with a lesson.

Learners can proceed through a lesson as a group or as individuals. Group instruction is most often presented to a group in which individuals proceed at a fixed pace; the pace is that of the group. Individualized instruction usually allows learners to proceed at their own pace. It is important to recognize the word *usually,* because at times group instruction has individual assignments and at times individualized instruction calls for two or more individuals to work together. There are many factors which enter into the decision to manage lessons based on groups or based on individuals. However, the primary factor is whether the needs of individuals can be served through group instruction. Group instruction makes sense when the members of the group can be assembled at one time and are all ready for the same instruction at the same time. Individualized instruction makes sense when the individuals cannot be assembled as a group or if the instructional needs of various individuals vary substantially. The traditional format is most often used with group instruction, while modularized, programmed, and CAI instruction are used with individualized instruction.

Types of Content

The type of content to be taught should also be considered when selecting a lesson delivery format. Lessons are designed to teach psychomotor, cognitive, and/or affective behaviors and their associated knowledge bases. Some lessons are designed to teach the manipulation of physical objects (psychomotor behaviors). Some require the development of emotional tones through the manipulation of the body or through other directly observable actions (e.g., use of words or the voice) (affective behaviors). In both of these cases, the development and evaluation of physiological skills are required. This usually requires instructional methods such as demonstration, practice, and physical performance evaluation. Therefore, the format selected must allow people to observe and practice, and to be evaluated on their ability to perform these physical actions. For example, to teach a person to remove the dents from a car fender in an auto body shop would require demonstration and practice with tools and equipment in order for him or her to develop the psychomotor skills required. Psychomotor and affective behaviors are most effectively taught through traditional or modularized instruction because they allow for the use of a variety of methods and resources which can be used in the development of physical skills.

Other behaviors require the manipulation of information (cognitive behaviors). The teaching of these behaviors requires the demonstration, practice, and evaluation of information processing. The teaching process for these behaviors does not focus on the development of physical skills, with the exception of those skills needed to make the processing of the information visible so it can be demonstrated, practiced, and evaluated. For example, a person would need physical skills to be able to write numbers in order to record the process used to add 2 + 2 to arrive at 4. Or she would need to be able to verbally communicate the process. In addition, if CAI were being used, the person would need to be able to use a computer. However, the physical actions necessary to use the computer would only be prerequisite skills to being able to proceed through the learning of other content (2 + 2 = 4). They would not be the primary focus of the cognitive lesson. The primary focus would be the information processing.

If the content of a lesson is primarily cognitive and requires the teaching of information processing, then the programmed instruction approach would be appropriate. If the content to be taught is primarily cognitive, and if the capabilities of the computer can increase teaching and learning effectiveness, then CAI would be appropriate.

Types of Learning Resources

In addition to lesson management and the types of content to be taught, the types of learning resources to be used is also an important consideration in selecting a lesson delivery format. Certain lesson delivery formats are more compatible with certain types of learning resources than are others. For example, if CAI is to be used, one must have a computer. Also, it would be appropriate for substantial portions of the instruction to be deliverable through a computer. Transparencies would not be highly appropriate visual media, but computer-controlled videotape presentations would be. On the other hand, if programmed instruction is to be used, the designer is limited to one type of resource: a text.

Some simple considerations in making decisions among lesson delivery formats based on resource availability are:

1. Select the traditional format if most of the resources will require the involvement of the instructor during the delivery of instruction.
2. Select the modularized format if a variety of types of resources will be used and if much of the instruction will be self-paced.
3. Select programmed instruction if the material can be broken down into small bits of information and if it can be presented through a text.
4. Select CAI if the computer provides advantages over a text, such as the ability to use computer graphics or interactive video.

Access to the different types of resources and/or the availability of expertise and equipment to develop the resources are also important considerations in selecting delivery formats. Resources to support traditional instruction are usually readily available. Resources to support modularized instruction which learners can use individually are more difficult to locate and develop. Programmed texts that have already been developed are relatively inexpensive, but such texts require substantial expertise and resources to develop. CAI is the most expensive to purchase and develop.

Need for Uniformity of Instruction and Performance Assurance

Uniformity of instruction and assurance of performance capability after instruction are also important considerations in format selection. If the traditional form of instruction is presented, the variability in the instruction received by learners will depend upon the expertise of the instructor and upon his or her ability to meet the needs of individuals. In some instructional settings, it is critical that learners receive identical instruction; there can be no doubt that they can perform at the expected level. In other instructional settings, there is some room for variation in instruction for individuals and there is a substantial tolerance surrounding the expected performance. For example, when filling spray-paint cans with liquid propellant, there can be no room for error; a major explosion might occur. In this case, there must be assurance that all people receive the same instruction and that evaluation instruments are developed to assure performance capability. On the other hand, if a person is being taught to fix a car fender, the instruction might vary somewhat from person to person, and the quality of the product produced could also vary within certain limits and still be acceptable.

When instruction must be uniform for all learners, the human element in the delivery of instruction must be controlled so that all people receive the required education. Also, instruction must be presented in relatively small increments, with enough repetition and evaluation to assure that all people learn the material. In such cases, the amount of instructor-delivered material is limited through the use of prepackaged material. These include materials such as videotapes, textbooks, programmed texts, or CAI. Also, directions to learners as they use these materials are standardized through modularized instruction, programmed instruction, or CAI. The primary role of instructors is to serve as tutors and to aid learners as they progress through the learning activities; it is not to be the primary deliverers of instruction.

SELECTING METHODS AND MEDIA

The previous discussion of selecting lesson delivery formats has indicated the relationship between the type of lesson delivery format selected and the appropriate methods and media to use. The two additional factors which influence the selection of methods and media are the types of content to be taught, and the stage of the lesson flow in which they will be used.

Methods and media selected to present a knowledge base should focus on the presentation of information. Methods and media used to present the process of performing a behavior should focus on showing people how to perform. For example, lectures and readings are often used to present information. They may or may not use media that depict motion. Demonstrations and simulations are often used to present the processes of performing behaviors. They usually require a medium that shows motion.

The stage of the lesson flow for which methods and media are to be selected is also an important selection factor because each stage has a different purpose. For example, even though the demonstration stage and the guided practice stage focus on the process of performing a behavior, one is designed to show the learner the process and the other is designed to allow the learner to try it out. In the first case, the method used would be a demonstration and in the second case it would be practice.

When selecting methods and media, the designer must balance a number of factors. For example, typically the more senses that can be activated in learning something, the more complete will be the learning. The more similar the learning situation is to the real world, the better. The more efficient learning is in terms of instructional time and cost, the better. The shorter the instructional time to bring a learner to performance capability, the better. Although these factors appear to be simple, they are often competing within a given instructional setting. A real-world setting within which learners may be expected to perform may not be available in the classroom, and it may take too much time and money to bring learners to the setting. The real-world setting may be too complex, and therefore, a more simplified setting might lead to more effective learning. The best solution may be obvious, but it may be too expensive. Therefore, the designer is constantly faced with decisions among various alternatives and must attempt to balance these, and other factors, when making methods and media selections.

Instructional Methods Selection

Table 9.2 presents a list of often-used instructional methods. Each of these instructional methods will be briefly presented. The goal will be to provide the instructional designer with information needed to make a meaningful selection among alternative methods using the three factors described above: delivery format, type of content, and stage of lesson flow. The goal is not to teach how to actually present content using each method. The reader should consult other resources on methods of teaching for such detailed information.

The following definitions of each of the methods have been adapted from those presented in the *Handbook for Designers of Instructional System* (U.S. Department of the Air Force, 1973).

Demonstration. A *demonstration* is an accurate showing of the precise actions necessary to perform skills or processes. It is used during the demonstration stage of a lesson when learners are being shown how to perform a behavior. The content presented during a demonstration is derived from the process of performing the behavior; it was identified during content analysis. A demonstration is used with all types of delivery formats. At least one occurs within every lesson. Demonstrations should be presented in an environment as similar as possible to that found in the role for which the learner is being prepared; if possible, the same tools and equipment should be used.

Lecture. A *lecture* is a verbal presentation of information. It is used primarily during the first two lesson stages: state the rationale, and provide need-to-know information. The content for lectures is derived from the knowledge base which supports a behavior. A lecture can be used with any delivery format that allows for sound presentations.

Discussion. A *discussion* is an instructor-controlled process of people interacting and sharing information and experiences related to an objective. For example, after presenting a number of different approaches for doing something, learners could be asked to discuss the pros and cons of each approach. The content is derived from the knowledge base. Because a discussion is a process of people interacting and sharing information, it assumes that learners have a sufficient background to be able to meaningfully interact. Therefore, a discussion is usually used when learners are practicing and applying content. It can be used with any delivery format which allows for bringing groups of people together for interactions.

TABLE 9.2 Sample Instructional Methods

• Demonstration	• Reading
• Lecture	• Role playing — TYP. USE WITH AFFECTIVE
• Discussion	• Field trip
• Questioning	• Case study
• Simulation	• Practice

Questioning. *Questioning* is the process of presenting learners with questions about what has been taught and having them provide answers. It is used to determine if learners possess a desired knowledge base. It is used throughout the lesson flow as an informal diagnostic tool to determine learner progress.

At times, questioning is also used to establish a readiness to learn. Questions which learners are not expected to be able to answer but which they should be able to answer after completing instruction are sometimes asked at the beginning of a lesson.

Questioning can be used with any of the delivery formats. It is different from testing, which has the purpose of formally judging the learning of individuals.

Simulation. *Simulation* is a realistic showing of a real-world situation in a learning environment such as a classroom or laboratory. It differs from a demonstration in that the goal is not primarily to show the detailed process of a behavior. Simulation is often used to establish a context within which other methods are presented. For example, a demonstration can be presented within a simulation to give the demonstration more realism. Simulation can be used during any stage of a lesson, although its purpose changes, depending upon the lesson stage within which it is being used. For example, during the stages of stating the rationale and providing need-to-know information, it is often used to show learners the context within which a behavior is performed. During the demonstration stage, it is used to create a real-world environment for demonstrating a behavior in detail. Learners can also practice and be evaluated during simulations.

Reading. *Reading* is the presentation of written material directed at an instructional objective, which learners are to read. As with a lecture, reading is used to present the knowledge base associated with a behavior. It can be used at any stage of a lesson, but it is used primarily during the first two stages. Reading can be used with any of the instructional formats.

Role Playing. *Role playing* is the showing of real-life interactions among people or between people and things through simulation. It has the same characteristics as simulation, except it focuses on the interactions between people and other people or things rather than on interactions among processes and events. It is used to demonstrate, practice, and/or evaluate the ability of learners to interact.

Field Trip. A *field trip* is a visit to a real-world location where learners can observe the application of processes. It can be used during the early stages of a lesson as a basis for establishing learner readiness and the context for the behaviors to be learned. It is typically used with the traditional delivery format, but it can also be used as an individualized assignment with other formats.

Case Study. A *case study* is a presentation to learners of a real-life situation that has occurred in the past. It can be used throughout a lesson as a basis for establishing a context within which the content is taught, practiced, and/or evaluated. During the early stages of a lesson, case studies can be used to provide meaningful real-life examples of where a behavior has been used and why it is important. During the demonstration stage, a case study can be used to establish a context for a demonstration. During practice, it can be used to present a real-life situation to which a person is to respond. During evaluation, it can be used to compare the response of the learner with that of the person who actually experienced the circumstance presented in the case study.

Practice. *Practice* is the planned application by the learner of what has been taught. It is used during the practice stages of a lesson to allow learners to apply the processes which they have been taught and to refine their performance. Practice is sometimes mistakenly referred to as *drill and practice.* However, there is a difference between *practice* and *drill. Drill* is usually associated with rote memorization by the learner of a set of important facts for later use, or the development of physical skills which require precise timing. Drill as a basis for memorization can be used as a method for learning facts associated with the knowledge base that supports a behavior. An example is the use of "flash cards" to memorize multiplication tables in mathematics, or vocabulary lists to learn the definitions of words. Drill as a basis for developing physical skills which require precise timing can be used in the "practice for perfection" stage of a lesson. The development of typing speed and accuracy is an example of where drill might be used. During the earlier stages of the lesson, people would meaningfully be taught a typing skill, but they would need extensive drill to develop their physical, or muscle, coordination to reach proficiency.

Practice, on the other hand, is the meaningful application of a process with the intent of learning how to perform. Using the PBID system, which is based on meaningful learning, one should not confuse *practice* and *drill.* People should not be taught to perform a process through drill; they should be presented with opportunities to meaningfully practice and understand it. Practice is used with all types of delivery formats. As with a demonstration, practice should occur in an environment which is as realistic as possible. Practice should occur in every lesson.

Media Selection

Media should be selected after the instructional methods are chosen or in conjunction with the selection of methods. As was pointed out earlier, instructional methods can be delivered through different forms of media. For example, a lecture can be presented through a live instructor or a videotape. In both cases, the method, the lecture, is the same but the form of media used to deliver that lecture is different. Table 9.3 presents the major types of media that are used to present instruction, with examples of each.

The actual selection of media is done in two stages: determine media purpose, and select the hardware and software. *Hardware* refers to the physical devices that are used during instruction (e.g., different types of projectors or a computer) and *software* refers to the materials that are chosen or developed for use with the devices (e.g., transparencies, films, videotapes, or computer programs).

Determining Media Purpose. The need for the following elements should be considered when selecting media based on the purpose to be served:

1. Words
2. Objects or visual images
3. Sound
4. Combined sound and visual images
5. Motion

Each of these five elements will be discussed independently. However, it is important to realize that they must often be considered together when selecting a medium based on instructional purpose, and that different designers may arrive at different media solutions to a particular situation based on their own perceptions of how best to achieve a given purpose. For example, most designers would agree that it would be desirable to have motion during the presentation of the demonstration of how to change a tire. It is important to see how each process step is performed relative to the others, and what the actual timing of the actions in performing those steps should be. However, some designers might feel that sound is also necessary, and some might not. Therefore, some might feel that a silent film or a narrated videotape would be appropriate, while others might feel that a videotape with the actual sounds of changing a tire would be best. Such judgment calls are always necessary.

"INSTRUCTIONAL AID"

TABLE 9.3 Forms of Instructional Media and Examples

PRINT MEDIA	AUDIO MEDIA	VISUAL AIDS: 3-D OBJECTS	LIVE PERSONNEL
Books Microfilm Worksheets Manuals	Radio Tapes Records	Cutaways Mockups Actual objects Models	Instructor Consultant Aide Learner
VISUAL AIDS: GRAPHICS AND PHOTOGRAPHS	**VISUAL AIDS: PROJECTED (WITH OR WITHOUT SOUND)**	**MOTION MEDIA (WITH OR WITHOUT SOUND)**	
Charts Diagrams Graphs Photographs	Slides Overhead transparencies Opaque projections Filmstrips Computers	Live instructor Movies Videotapes Computers with video and/or audio devices	

WORDS. Throughout a lesson, there are various places where information and explanations are required. Such information can be presented through either the printed or the spoken word. Although the printed and spoken word can often be used interchangeably, the printed word is most often used when the learner may need to repeatedly refer to the information and/or when other media to present the spoken word (e.g., a live instructor or a videotape) cannot be made readily available.

Words are used to present all or part of the knowledge base and/or directions. If they are presented in print form, the content should be capable of being understood through reading. The advantages of printed media are that they are relatively inexpensive, they can be studied independently, and they are available for ready reference. Spoken words require live personnel or devices to reproduce recorded sound. Advantages of spoken words are the additional meanings that can be communicated through voice tones and inflections.

OBJECTS OR VISUAL IMAGES. Visual images are necessary if the learner is to be able to visualize an object, an environment, a representation of an object, or the structure of information. That is why three-dimensional objects, graphics, photographs, and/or projected images are included in the presentation of many instructional methods.

Three-dimensional objects include both actual objects and objects which represent actual objects. Actual objects are used when it is important for learners to be able to recognize the objects. For example, actual objects are often used in demonstrations. This provides learners with a sense of realism and acquaints them directly with the objects they must use to perform a behavior.

Although the use of actual objects is recommended, there are situations in which they do not lead to the most effective and efficient learning. For example, a large newspaper printing press would not be available in a classroom for a demonstration on how it works. Therefore, if it is important to show learners the operating parts of the press and how they work together, a small-scale *model* of the press would be appropriate. A model is a miniature representation of something.

Sometimes real objects or models are too complex, or they do not allow the learner to see all of the important components. In such a case, cutaways or mockups are useful. A *cutaway* shows a real object with part of it removed so a person can see inside the object. A *mockup* is a three-dimensional representation of an object which may or may not look like the object.

A cutaway is useful when the goal is to show learners how parts within a device operate in relation to one another. For example, if a goal were to show how a fan motor works, the real motor would be enclosed in a case. If the motor were disassembled to see the parts, it could not be used to demonstrate how the parts work together. However, if a portion of the outer case and a portion of the windings were cut away, it would be possible to see inside the motor and see its moving parts.

A mockup is useful when the real object is too complex to allow one to show the components of interest. For example, if the goal is to show how portions of the electrical system of a car are related to one another, the real electrical system in a car would not be effective. It would be hidden within the car so it could not be seen. One solution would be to try to develop a cutaway. The electrical system, however, is throughout the entire car, and it would not be possible to cut away all of the material necessary without destroying the electrical system itself. Another solution would be to remove the electrical system from the car and have it available for inspection. The problem with this solution is that once the system is removed from the car, it loses its form. It becomes a tangle of wires and components. A mockup would be a solution. A mockup of the electrical system could take the form of the entire electrical system from a car mounted on a flat surface in an orderly fashion. The mockup would allow people to see all of the real components in relation to one another without the interference of the other parts of the car.

Simplified models are three-dimensional objects which do not present all of the components of the real object. They are used when the actual objects are too complex for learners to clearly see the components. For example, a person studying computers could observe the action of a disk drive by viewing the actual disk drive within a microcomputer. However, the disk drive is a mass of printed circuits, solder joints, and other components. Also, its actions occur very rapidly. The many pieces of an actual disk drive are distracting and can confuse observations. A simplified model of the disk drive might be much more effective as an instructional medium than the real thing. The particular components of interest can be highlighted for easy review.

Two-dimensional visual images are another effective way to help learners visualize an object, an environment, a representation of an object, or the structure of information. Two-dimensional visualizations include graphics and photos. A graphic is a two-dimensional representation of something (data or things) on a flat surface such as paper, a computer screen, or a projected image. Graphics are usually used when the content is complex and a visual image would facilitate learning. The following are four examples of graphics:

1. A flowchart of the decision-making process used to decide which wrench to use
2. A schematic drawing of an electronic circuit showing the components and the connections to those components
3. A chart portraying the circulatory system within a human body
4. A pie chart showing the amount of each tax dollar that goes to education

Each of these examples is an attempt to provide a visual image that simplifies a very complex set of events or data. Once graphics are produced, they can be presented through other forms of media such as photographs, slides, or transparencies.

When graphics are used as the basis for presenting complex information or data, they take on different roles and meaning throughout the instructional process for both the instructor and learners. The chart of the PBID system is an example. The chart first serves as an instructional aid for the instructor to present an overview of the system. Using Ausubel's terms, it serves as an advanced organizer for what is to be learned. It then becomes a useful reference for keeping track of where the instructor is in the presentation of the system as each component is presented. Learners can use it initially to visualize how the major components of the system fit together without understanding the detail of each component. As learners develop functional knowledge of each component, the chart takes on additional meaning. Finally, when they have learned the entire system, learners can use it as a reference and as an aid in remembering the detail of the system. The sequencing chart described in Chapter 6 should serve the same functions for programs produced by you.

SOUND. Sound is necessary in those situations in which the ear is being trained to perceive differences, and/or in which it can be used as a basis for providing a context. For example, in diagnosing whether a water pump in an automobile is defective, an auto mechanic would listen to the water pump to determine if the bearing were making noise. A high-pitched squeal would mean that the pump was defective because the bearing was worn. Therefore, in teaching people to diagnose the adequacy of a water pump, it would be important to have sound available. In the same situation, it might be important to teach people to listen to a water pump within the context of the other noises of the engine. That would allow them, when diagnosing the water pump, to learn to differentiate its sounds from other sounds.

Sound is also important as part of media through which verbal presentations are made (e.g., lectures given through videotape require sound).

COMBINED SOUND AND VISUAL IMAGES. Audiovisual media are those that present sound as well as visual images. The sound can accompany either still images or images in motion. Audiovisual media are used when verbal presentations can be simplified by visual images, or when visual images can be best understood when accompanied by verbal explanations or other sounds that would occur within a real-world environment. For example, a verbal presentation of the PBID system can be facilitated by the use of the system chart. Without a visual aid, the verbal explanation would become extremely complex and it would be difficult to systematically keep track of where everything fits. In the case of a photograph of a newspaper printing press, the photograph would be very complex. Without a verbal explanation, learners would not be able to differentiate the various parts of the press.

MOTION. Media which portray motion are used to present real objects moving in relation to one another, or to present the integration of ideas. For example, in demonstrating how to change a tire, motion is important for people to see both how the tools and equipment are used in relation to one another and what timing that takes place.

When using motion to depict the integration of ideas, graphics are created which show ideas flowing together into a composite whole. Such graphics assist in providing meaningful mental images of how the information comes together. For example, when deciding the salaries of employees, a number of types of information must be integrated. The instructional designer might decide that a graphic with motion would be a good way to show how a person making the decision must integrate information about past performance, current salary, and level of responsibility.

Selecting Specific Hardware, Software, and Personnel. Once the decision regarding the purpose of the media has been made, the next decision involves the form of hardware and software, or the type of personnel, that will be used. Decisions such as who or what will actually communicate the content to the learner must be made. For example, if words need to be presented to learners as part of an explanation of the knowledge base for a behavior, should they be presented in print, orally by a live instructor, through an audio recording, or through a videotape of a lecture? If a print medium is to be used, will it take the form of a book, a manual, or worksheets? Will audio media take the form of radio, tapes, or records? Will three-dimensional objects take the form of actual objects, mockups, or models? If a graphic is to be used, what form will it take? Will it be a chart, a graph, a diagram, or a photograph? Will it be presented on paper or on a chalkboard, or will it be projected? If the decision is to project the graphic, which projection system will be used? Still images can be projected in a variety of ways, such as slides, transparencies, opaque projectors, or computers. If the graphics or other visual images are to have motion, will they be projected with motion-picture film, videotape, or computers?

In order to make such decisions wisely, the reader should acquire additional information about the advantages and disadvantages of the various forms of media which is beyond the scope of this book. In general, the basic rule in media selection is to select the simplest form of media that will communicate the content. This not only minimizes costs, but it presents the least confusing message to the learner. Unnecessary motion, words, or complexity confuse learners. If a transparency of a graphic can present a decision-making process effectively, there is no point in developing a videotape that presents graphics in motion, such as a cartoon. Learning will not be increased, yet costs will increase dramatically. If learners are being trained to tune a piano and the goal of the particular lesson is to differentiate sounds, it may be better to train them using high-quality sound equipment than to train them using a film or videotape which also presents motion. The motion may actually detract from a person's concentration on the sound.

The key word in selecting media is "why." One should always ask the question, "Why am I using this particular form of media and not another?" The five elements presented as considerations in determining the need for media should be used as the basis for answering this question.

SPECIFYING THE METHODS AND MEDIA

Tables 9.4 to 9.7 are duplicates of Tables 8.4 to 8.6 presented in Chapter 8, with method and media selections added to the sample lesson structures. Table 9.4 assumes that the modularized lesson delivery format was selected, and Tables 9.5, 9.6, and 9.7 each assume a traditional lesson delivery format. Tables 9.4 and 9.5 each present a structured lesson for the behavior "change a tire." Notice that different resources were selected for the same lesson, depending upon the format selected. Table 9.4 presents selections based on a modularized format, and Table. 9.5 presents selections based on a traditional format. Selections for other formats are discussed in Chapters 12 and 13. Each lesson structure includes the objective; what content is to be presented, practiced, or evaluated at each stage of the lesson flow; and the methods and media tentatively selected to present and practice that content. The decisions are finalized during lesson delivery formatting presented in Chapter 11. The methods and media are presented on the samples, with the method presented first, and then the form of media that will be used to communicate the content through that method. They are separated by a slash (/). For example, in Table 9.4, the method that would be used to present the content for the rationale is a lecture. The medium that would be used to present the content through that method is a videotape. See Appendices B and C for additional examples of delivery format, methods, and media selection.

SUMMARY

This chapter dealt with selecting a lesson delivery format, instructional methods, and instructional media for delivering instruction. Selecting procedures for evaluating learners and providing feedback is presented in Chapter 10.

Methods and media are the means through which content is actually delivered to learners. They are selected after the objective of the lesson, the content to be taught, and the lesson structure have been determined. The selection of methods is done within the context of the lesson delivery format (e.g., traditional or CAI) selected to deliver the lesson. Instructional methods are procedures or processes used to present content to learners (e.g., a demonstration or a lecture).

TABLE 9.4 Lesson Structure

PSYCHOMOTOR OBJECTIVE

Givens
A car with a flat tire, tools, and a replacement tire

Behavior
Change a tire.

Standard
The replacement tire is mounted on the car, the lugs are tight, and the tools and replacement tire are stored.

LESSON STAGE	CONTENT TO BE TAUGHT, PRACTICED, OR EVALUATED	METHODS/MEDIA (CONSISTENT WITH MODULARIZED FORMAT)
RATIONALE	*a.* Consequences of trying to drive on a flat tire *b.* Consequences of being stranded *c.* Money savings	Lecture/videotape
NEED-TO-KNOW INFORMATION	*a.* The step-by-step procedure for changing a tire *b.* Safety precautions *c.* Lifting heavy objects	Reading/information sheet, textbook
DEMONSTRATION	Procedure for changing a tire	Demonstration/videotape, procedure sheet
GUIDED PRACTICE	Procedure for changing a tire	Practice/assignment sheet
UNGUIDED PRACTICE	Procedure for changing a tire	Practice/procedure sheet
EVALUATION	*a.* Knowledge basc presented above *b.* Procedure for changing a tire	SEE CHAPTER 10 for evaluation and feedback procedures selection.
FEEDBACK	*a.* Knowledge base presented above *b.* Procedure for changing a tire	

TABLE 9.5 Lesson Structure

PSYCHOMOTOR OBJECTIVE

Givens
A car with a flat tire, tools, and a replacement tire

Behavior
Change a tire.

Standard
The replacement tire is mounted on the car, the lugs are tight, and the tools and replacement tire are stored.

LESSON STAGE	CONTENT TO BE TAUGHT, PRACTICED, OR EVALUATED	METHODS/MEDIA (CONSISTENT WITH TRADITIONAL FORMAT)
RATIONALE	*a.* Consequences of trying to drive on a flat tire *b.* Consequences of being stranded *c.* Money savings	Lecture/instructor, transparencies
NEED-TO-KNOW INFORMATION	*a.* The step-by-step procedure for changing a tire *b.* Safety precautions *c.* Lifting heavy objects	Reading/textbook, information sheet
DEMONSTRATION	Procedure for changing a tire	Demonstration/instructor, procedure sheet, tools and equipment
GUIDED PRACTICE	Procedure for changing a tire	Practice/assignment sheet
UNGUIDED PRACTICE	Procedure for changing a tire	Practice/procedure sheet
EVALUATION	*a.* Knowledge base presented above *b.* Procedure for changing a tire	SEE CHAPTER 10 for evaluation and feedback procedures selection.
FEEDBACK	*a.* Knowledge base presented above *b.* Procedure for changing a tire	

TABLE 9.6 Lesson Structure

COGNITIVE OBJECTIVE

Givens
A part requiring a wrench for removal and a variety of wrenches

Behavior
Decide which wrench to use.

Standard
A verbal description of the decision process is consistent with that specified on the instructor checklist.

LESSON STAGE	CONTENT TO BE TAUGHT, PRACTICED, OR EVALUATED	METHODS/MEDIA (CONSISTENT WITH TRADITIONAL FORMAT)
RATIONALE	*a.* Consequences of using the wrong wrench *b.* Time savings	Lecture/instructor, transparencies
NEED-TO-KNOW INFORMATION	*a.* Types of wrenches and their functions *b.* Procedure for making the decision	*a.* Reading/textbook *b.* Discussion/instructor
DEMONSTRATION	Procedure for making the decision	Demonstration/film
GUIDED PRACTICE	Procedure for making the decision	Practice/assignment sheet
UNGUIDED PRACTICE	Procedure for making the decision	Practice/procedure sheet
EVALUATION	*a.* Knowledge base presented above *b.* Procedure for making the decision	SEE CHAPTER 10 for evaluation and feedback procedures selection.
FEEDBACK	*a.* Knowledge base presented above *b.* Procedure for making the decision	

TABLE 9.7 Lesson Structure

AFFECTIVE OBJECTIVE

Givens
A co-worker and a situation requiring cooperation

Behavior
Cooperate with co-workers.

Standard
Actions depicting cooperative activity are consistent with those specified on the instructor checklist.

LESSON STAGE	CONTENT TO BE TAUGHT, PRACTICED, OR EVALUATED	METHODS/MEDIA (CONSISTENT WITH TRADITIONAL FORMAT)
RATIONALE	The benefits of cooperation	Lecture/instructor
NEED-TO-KNOW INFORMATION	*a.* Types of actions that convey cooperation versus noncooperation *b.* Differences between assisting and taking over	Reading/textbook
DEMONSTRATION	Cooperative actions	Demonstration/videotape
GUIDED PRACTICE	Cooperative actions	Role playing/script
UNGUIDED PRACTICE	Cooperative actions	Role playing/script; observation/another student
EVALUATION	*a.* Knowledge base presented above *b.* Cooperative actions	SEE CHAPTER 10 for evaluation and feedback procedures selection.
FEEDBACK	*a.* Knowledge base presented above *b.* Cooperative actions	

Instructional media are the software, hardware, and personnel which serve as modes of communication to convey content to learners (e.g., a videotape recorder, a live instructor, or a computer).

ACTIVITIES AND EVALUATION

1. Develop or obtain a lesson structure with the following specified: the objective for the lesson, and the content to be taught at each lesson stage.
2. Select either a modularized or a traditional lesson delivery format, and explain why one was selected and not the other.
3. Select the instructional methods to be used at each stage of the lesson. Explain why each method has been selected.
4. Select the media that will be used to communicate the content through each of the methods identified. Explain why each medium was selected.

REFERENCE

U.S. Department of the Air Force, *Handbook For Designers of Instructional Systems,* vol. 4, Washington, DC, 1973.

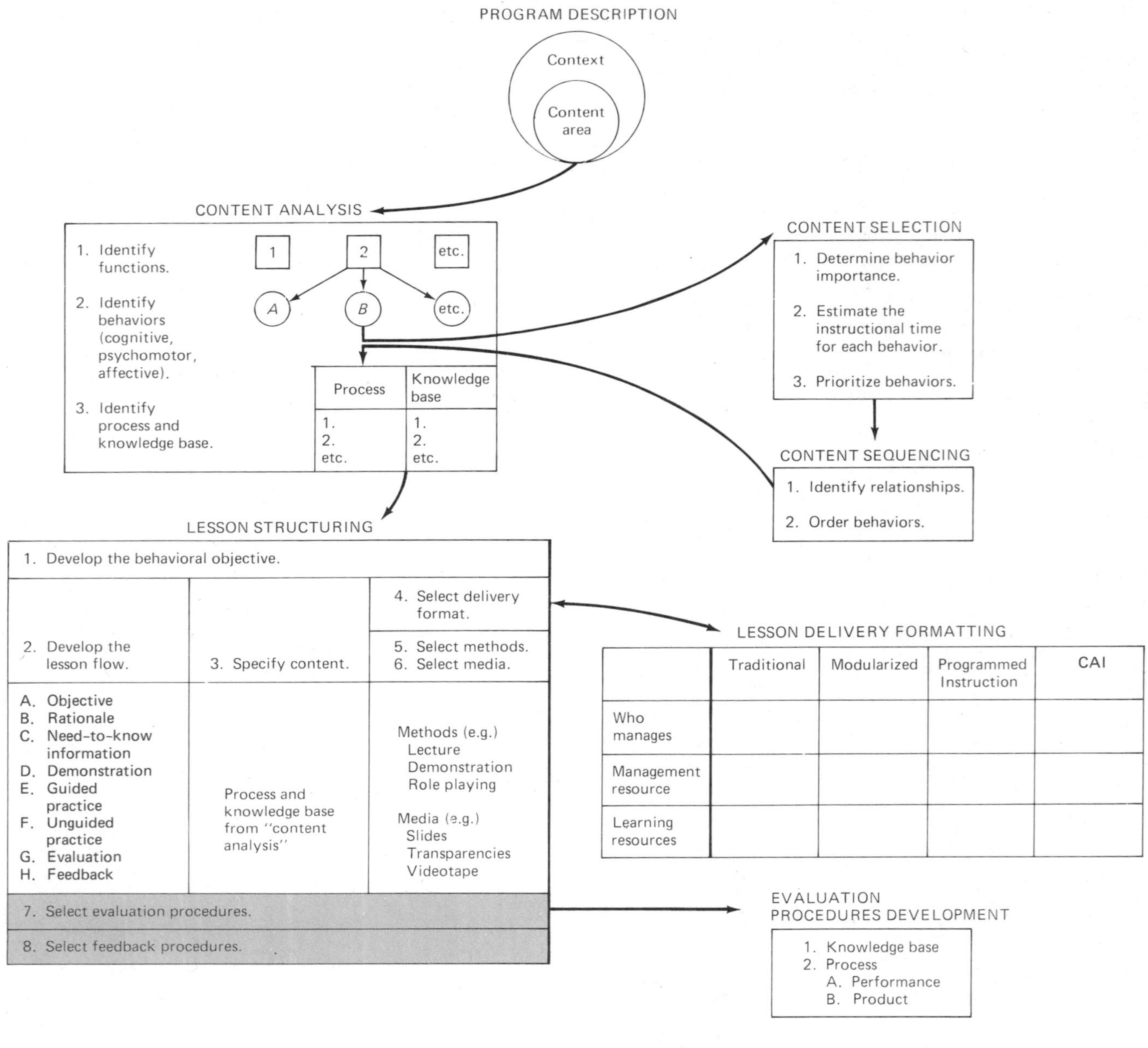
PROGRAM DESCRIPTION
Context
Content area
CONTENT ANALYSIS
1. Identify functions.
2. Identify behaviors (cognitive, psychomotor, affective).
3. Identify process and knowledge base.
1
2
etc.
A
B
etc.
Process
Knowledge base
1.
2.
etc.
1.
2.
etc.
CONTENT SELECTION
1. Determine behavior importance.
2. Estimate the instructional time for each behavior.
3. Prioritize behaviors.
CONTENT SEQUENCING
1. Identify relationships.
2. Order behaviors.
LESSON STRUCTURING
1. Develop the behavioral objective.
2. Develop the lesson flow.
3. Specify content.
4. Select delivery format.
5. Select methods.
6. Select media.
A. Objective
B. Rationale
C. Need-to-know information
D. Demonstration
E. Guided practice
F. Unguided practice
G. Evaluation
H. Feedback
Process and knowledge base from "content analysis"
Methods (e.g.)
Lecture
Demonstration
Role playing
Media (e.g.)
Slides
Transparencies
Videotape
7. Select evaluation procedures.
8. Select feedback procedures.
LESSON DELIVERY FORMATTING
Traditional
Modularized
Programmed Instruction
CAI
Who manages
Management resource
Learning resources
EVALUATION PROCEDURES DEVELOPMENT
1. Knowledge base
2. Process
A. Performance
B. Product

Lesson Structuring: Selecting Evaluation and Feedback Procedures

CHAPTER OBJECTIVE

Givens

A lesson objective, lesson flow, and specific content to be taught in the lesson

Behavior

Select evaluation and feedback procedures.

Standard

The selected evaluation procedures must be consistent with the desired formality and the type of content. Feedback procedures must be selected based on who will provide the feedback and whether it will be natural or artificial.

OVERVIEW

Evaluation and feedback perform related functions. Evaluation is used to obtain information on the learning progress of the learner and the quality of instruction. Feedback is used to communicate interpreted evaluation results and encouragement to learners and information about the quality of instruction to instructors. This chapter focuses on selecting evaluation and feedback procedures used with learners. The same procedures can be used with cognitive, affective, and psychomotor behaviors.

With performance-based instruction, the primary purpose of applying these procedures is diagnostic: to determine the progress of the learner and to provide her or him with feedback so learning can be adjusted, if necessary. This purpose can be compared with the monitoring systems on a rocket. Many forces act upon the rocket as it attempts to complete its mission from launch to expected destination. Some of these forces include changing wind direction and speed, air density, and thrust of the rocket. In order to ensure that the direction of the rocket is correct in this changing environment, one needs to install evaluation or monitoring systems. Those monitoring systems gather information about the direction of the rocket. Once that information is gathered, it must be interpreted to determine whether the rocket is actually going in the correct direction. If it is not, that information must be "fed back" to controlling devices so that the rocket can be redirected.

Learners are similar to rockets. They begin toward a learning objective. As they proceed, many factors affect the direction and accuracy of their progress, such as their ability to understand the learning materials, their past experiences which might facilitate or inhibit learning, or their motivation. Therefore, if an instructor is to guide a learner toward an objective, she or he must monitor whether the learner is on course. If the learner is not on course, the instructor must provide feedback so that the learning process is adjusted.

In order to ensure that the appropriate evaluation and feedback procedures are used with a given lesson and individual, one must select them carefully. Just as there are many sensors that could be placed on a rocket, with some being appropriate and some not, there are many evaluation and feedback procedures that might be used in a given situation, with some being appropriate and some not. The purpose of this chapter is to provide methods of selecting the appropriate evaluation and feedback procedures for a given learning situation. The actual process of developing evaluation is discussed in Chapters 14 through 18. Feedback procedures will be discussed more in Chapter 19.

SELECTING EVALUATION PROCEDURES

An effective first step in selecting evaluation procedures is to determine the desired formality of the evaluation and the type of content to be evaluated. Table 10.1 provides a two-dimensional matrix showing the formality of and the type of content in evaluation. Once a decision is made as to formality and content, it is possible to make further selections among alternative evaluation procedures for each level of formality and for each type of content. The alternative evaluation procedures are presented within the four cells of the matrix in Table 10.1. The selection of each of these procedures will be discussed later.

Formality of the Evaluation

The formality with which an evaluation is conducted is dependent upon its intended use. Evaluations should be formal if one wishes to determine and record the learner's progress toward an educational objective. Formal evaluations are also used if the information on many learners is to be combined for instructor decision-making purposes, such as in determining the extent to which learning materials have been effective.

Formal evaluation is planned evaluation designed to determine progress of a learner toward an instructional objective. It is usually conducted by an instructor or by a person other than the learner. It should be done in such a way that it could be duplicated with different learners. It should also provide information in a recordable form that indicates the extent of progress toward an objective. The information obtained from formal evaluations is used to report the learning progress in the form of behaviors mastered or grades. An example of formal evaluation is a test given to record progress after a learner completes a lesson.

Data obtained from formal evaluations may be interpreted using norm-referenced or criterion-referenced procedures. *Norm-referenced evaluations* are used to compare the learning progress of an individual with that of a larger group. In education and training, this type

TABLE 10.1 Evaluation Procedure Selection

TYPE OF CONTENT	FORMALITY: Formal	FORMALITY: Informal
Knowledge Base	Written tests Oral tests	Self-checks Tutorial questioning
Process	Performance tests Product tests	Self-checks Tutorial observations

of evaluation is associated with "grading on the curve." The progress of an individual is judged relative to other learners and not in terms of a predetermined standard.

Criterion-referenced evaluations are used to determine if a learner has achieved a predetermined standard, or criterion. In vocational education and in training in business and industry that standard is generally set at the minimal level of proficiency needed to perform a role. Criterion-referenced evaluation is often associated with "mastery learning." The PBID system is primarily concerned with criterion-referenced evaluation, since it focuses on the performances and standards set in relation to objectives. Throughout this book, it should be assumed that discussions of formal evaluation refer to criterion-referenced evaluation.

Informal evaluation is designed to provide direct feedback to the learner and instructor about progress toward an educational objective during the learning process. Evaluations are informal if the purpose is only to obtain information to redirect the learner during the learning process or to modify instruction to meet the immediate needs of that learner. An example of informal evaluation would be spontaneous tutorial questions asked by an instructor while a learner is studying a lesson in order to direct the learner to the next step.

Once it is decided whether the evaluation will be formal or informal, the type of content to be evaluated must be determined. The content would have been identified during content analysis and further specified while selecting the content to be taught at each stage of the lesson flow. Content identification and selection techniques were presented in the chapters on content analysis and lesson structuring.

Type of Content to Be Evaluated

The two major types of content to be taught and evaluated are the process and knowledge base. As was indicated in Chapter 7, the content to teach each behavior is analyzed and categorized into the process of performing the behavior and the knowledge base needed to meaningfully apply the behavior. The reader should refer to Tables 7.5 through 7.8 to review process and knowledge-base identification.

Knowledge Base. Knowledge-base evaluations are used to determine the information possessed by the learner. Table 10.1 indicates that typical formal knowledge-base evaluations include written tests and oral tests. A *test* is a procedure used to prove or disprove that something has met a standard. In the case of knowledge-base evaluations, tests are used to prove or disprove that a person has learned the information specified in the knowledge base for a given behavior.

Formal knowledge-base evaluations, or tests, contain a series of items that are used to determine if an individual possesses the information necessary to meaningfully perform a behavior. The test items can be presented in either written or oral form. In either case, test items must be prepared prior to administering the test and must meet the characteristics of good evaluation (e.g., validity, reliability, and objectivity) that will be discussed in Chapter 14. The only difference between a written test and an oral test is the means used to present items to the learner. In both tests, items must be presented in the same way to the learners so that the proof of learning for the learners is the same.

Formal written or oral tests are administered at predetermined times when the instructor wants to determine if the learners have mastered the information. For example, after a lesson has been completed on the behavior "take an oral temperature," a nursing instructor would want to determine whether or not learners have mastered the knowledge base necessary to meaningfully take an oral temperature. Therefore, when learners ended a lesson, they would be administered a test and the results of that test would be used to judge whether each of them had mastered the content.

Informal knowledge-base evaluations take the form of self-checks or tutorial questioning. *Self-checks* are evaluations designed to be used by individual learners to determine their progress. They can be used with both knowledge-base and process evaluation. However, their structure changes, depending upon the type of content being evaluated. Self-checks are prepared by the instructional designer in the same way as tests. The primary difference between a test and a self-check is in who administers the evaluation and who determines whether or not a person has met the evaluation standard. A test is administered by an individual other than the learner; judgment as to whether the learner has met the standard is made by another individual. A self-check is administered by the learner, and the learner judges whether or not the standard has been met. When designed to evaluate a knowledge base, a self-check is developed as a written test.

The word *tutorial* refers to actions focused on instructing an individual learner. *Tutorial questioning* is the process of an instructor or another individual asking a learner questions in order to determine the extent to which that learner has mastered the required information. Tutorial questioning differs from oral testing in formality and uniformity. Oral testing requires that the same questions be asked of all learners in a formal, prepared fashion in order to gather the same information from all learners. Tutorial questioning is a vehicle for asking learners unique questions during the learning process based on the instructor's judgment regarding content they may or may not have mastered.

For example, if an instructor asked individuals in the class different questions to determine their individual learning progress on a lesson, that would be tutorial questioning. If learners administered a test to themselves during the learning process and judged their own progress, that would be self-questioning using a self-check. Both tutorial questioning and self-checks are informal forms of evaluation.

Process. *Process evaluations* are used to determine if one can perform a desired behavior. Table 10.1 indicates formal and informal process evaluations that are typically used. The ability to perform a behavior can be determined by observing a person performing the process or by examining the product of performing the process. Therefore, there are two major types of process evaluation: performance tests and product tests.

Formal process evaluations are tests, whether they are in the form of performance tests or product tests. They are used to gather information to prove or disprove that a person has mastered the process of performing a behavior. Performance tests can be constructed for use by a person observing the process and/or by the recipient of the process. For example, if a learner were exhibiting the process of accepting a customer as an individual, the instructor could observe and evaluate the process, or the customer could be asked to evaluate the extent to which he or she felt accepted.

The actual instruments used for formal process evaluation usually take the form of checklists and rating scales. They are used to record observations of the quality of a performance or a product. The procedures for the development of these instruments are presented in Chapter 16. Table 10.2 presents a sample performance checklist for the behavior "change a tire" (Pucel, 1986).

The key components of a performance checklist are the objective, the procedure that is to be evaluated, and the criteria that will be used to determine whether or not each step is completed correctly. The sample performance checklist would be used to evaluate the process of performing. If one were interested in evaluating the product of performing, the checklist would concentrate on the characteristics of the product and the criteria for judging its quality.

In order to formally evaluate the process of performing a behavior, the designer must prepare formal instruments just as in the evaluation of the knowledge base. The goal of formal process evaluation is to determine if an individual has mastered the process of performing a behavior; determination is made by comparing the performance of the learner with a standard (a criterion-referenced evaluation) or by comparing the individual's performance with that of a group (a norm-referenced evaluation).

The primary difference between a checklist, as presented in Table 10.2, and a rating scale is in how fine one wishes to make judgments concerning each step of the procedure. In other words, in the checklist presented in Table 10.2, the performance would be judged in terms of satisfactory versus unsatisfactory. In that case, the evaluator would have to decide between just two levels of performance: satisfactory and unsatisfactory. If one wished to make finer judgments, such as between below-average performance, average performance, and above-average performance, one would develop a rating scale. Checklist and rating-scale development will be discussed in Chapter 16. As with formal knowledge-base evaluation, formal process evaluation is administered by an individual other than the learner, and the results are judged by an individual other than the learner.

Informal process evaluation takes the form of self-observations or tutorial observations. Self-observations are administered by the learner, and the results are judged by the learner. Instructors can guide self-observations through the use of self-checks in much the same way as individuals conduct self-questioning with self-checks during knowledge-based evaluation. Tutorial observations are conducted by an instructor as individuals progress through the learning process. These are used to judge whether an individual is performing correctly and to provide corrective feedback, if needed.

For example, if an instructor were teaching learners how to change a tire, formal process evaluation would take place after the learners completed the learning process. The instructor would observe either a person performing the process (changing the tire) or the product of the performance (the changed tire). Informal process evaluation would be conducted during the time the learner was learning how to change a tire. It could be accomplished by learners judging their performance by completing a checklist or a rating scale, or by the instructor informally evaluating learners' performance through tutorial observations made during the time they were practicing how to change a tire.

Performance and product evaluations each have advantages and disadvantages which must be considered when one is selecting between them. These advantages and disadvantages are summarized in Table 10.3

The primary advantage of a performance test is that the learners can be observed as they perform the process. Therefore, the instructor can observe safety pro-

TABLE 10.2 Sample Performance Checklist

OBJECTIVE

Givens
A car with a flat tire, tools, and a replacement tire

Behavior
Change a tire.

Standard
Satisfactory score on the procedure checklist

PROCEDURAL STEPS	SAT.	UNSAT.	CRITERIA
1. Block the tires.	1	0	Blocks placed in front and back of tires not to be raised
2. Position the jack.	1	0	Under jack-point as in manual
3. Remove the hubcap.	1	0	Hubcap pried off
4. Loosen the lug nuts.	1	0	Lug nuts loosened by one-quarter turn
5. Etc.			

Total score: ________

Minimum acceptable score = 12

cedures, whether or not the process has been performed in the correct order, whether or not the timing of the actions has been correct, and whether or not the equipment has been used properly.

The following are disadvantages of a performance test: It takes a great deal of time to observe each learner complete the process. Also, if one observes only the process of performing the behavior, the process may be correct but the product may be unacceptable. An additional concern is for the possible interference by the evaluator with the learner's ability to perform. The learner may not do as well with a person observing.

The advantages of a product evaluation are that it typically takes less time to evaluate a product than to evaluate the performance, the entire product can be judged for quality, and there is no evaluator present during the performance to interfere with the learner.

The disadvantages of a product evaluation are the opposite of the advantages of a performance evaluation: one cannot monitor safety procedure, view process sequence, determine the "timing" of actions, or view equipment usage.

TABLE 10.3 Advantages of Performance and Product Evaluations

Performance Evaluations	Product Evaluations
1. Can monitor safety procedures 2. Can view process sequence 3. Can verify who is performing 4. Can determine the "timing" of actions 5. Can view equipment usage	1. Can save time 2. Can review the completed product 3. Instructor does not interfere with the performance

In other words, the advantages of a performance evaluation are the disadvantages of a product evaluation, and the advantages of a product evaluation are the disadvantages of a performance evaluation. The designer must base his decision as to whether to select performance or product evaluation on which advantages are the most important in a given situation. At times, it might be necessary to select both types of evaluation to be used in a particular circumstance.

Indicating the Evaluation Procedures Selections

Throughout the chapters pertaining to lesson structuring, we have been developing lessons for the behaviors "change a tire," "decide which wrench to use," and "cooperate with co-workers." Tables 10.4 through 10.6, near the end of this chapter, add the selection of evaluation procedures and the form of those procedures to those sample lesson structures. Feedback procedure methods and media have also been added to these tables and will be discussed later in this chapter.

The evaluation procedures should be considered as methods, and the vehicle used to present them as media. Therefore, evaluation decisions are listed in the column labeled "Methods/Media." Evaluation procedures are not indicated only for the evaluation stage of a lesson. They must be considered for each lesson stage that the designer feels requires evaluation.

For example, Table 10.4 indicates that during the presentation of the rationale, tutorial questioning will be conducted by the instructor. During the presentation of the need-to-know information, self-questioning will be conducted with a self-check. During guided practice, tutorial observation will be conducted by the instructor. In the "evaluation" stage of the lesson, a knowledge-base test will be given in written form, and a product test will be given using a checklist. This method of indicating the evaluation procedure and the form of media that will be used clearly specifies the types of evaluation instruments that need to be produced for a given lesson.

SELECTING FEEDBACK PROCEDURES

The next step in the development of a performance-based lesson structure is to determine the procedures that will be used to provide feedback about learning progress. *Feedback* is the process of communicating interpreted results and encouragement to learners.

Forms of Feedback Procedures

Two major forms of feedback procedures are conferences and self-determined feedback.

A *conference procedure* is a meeting of the learner and one or more other individuals which is designed to provide feedback. *Self-determined feedback* allows the learner to directly interpret learning progress without the aid of another individual.

Both conferences and self-determined feedback have advantages. Conferencing is useful as a vehicle to provide praise and encouragement. Also, conferencing enables the learner to benefit from the experience of others, which can shorten the learning process. On the other hand, self-determined feedback allows learners to proceed at their own paces and consumes less of the instructor's time. Also, sensitive learners can perfect their performance before they are judged by others.

In order for self-determined feedback to be appropriate, the learners must:

1. Be capable of objectivity interpreting information relative to themselves.
2. Be in command of necessary background information to adequately interpret the evaluation data.
3. Not be personally threatened by the information.

If these conditions are not present, the information is likely to be misinterpreted and feedback will be inadequate. Therefore, conferencing should be used. For example, if the behavior to be taught is "cooperate with co-workers," the person may think she or he is cooperating but may not actually be cooperating. This tends to occur because the learner is unable to analyze his own behavior honestly without the aid of another individual. The person may be seeing himself differently than he really is based on self-perception rather than on reality. The instructor should identify those situations in which people may need an outside objective observer to provide feedback and arrange for conferencing.

Another situation in which conferences should be used is when the learner does not have a sufficient background to interpret the evaluation results. For example, a person learning to be a computer programmer may make an error that results in the computer doing something she has never seen before. Therefore, the person would have no way of interpreting what has happened. On the other hand, an experienced instructor may be able to readily interpret the result and indicate what error has been made.

A third situation in which conferences should be used is when the instructor wants to be certain that the learner is accurately informed about the learning progress. In some cases, it is not possible to allow learners to judge whether or not they have learned the behavior. Failure to learn the behavior may cause safety hazards, or it may be costly in other ways. Therefore, the instructor needs to ensure that the learning has actually taken place. Conferencing is also required when the instructor has a legal obligation to provide feedback, even though the three criteria above have been met, for example, in the case of a safety violation in which the learner realizes the error but the instructor is legally responsible, or in which the instructor may need to enforce disciplinary proceedings even though the learner realizes what has been done.

Types of Feedback

Besides selecting the method for providing feedback (e.g., choosing between a conference and self-determined feedback), the instructional designer must determine the type of feedback that will be provided to learners. Two types will be discussed here:

1. Natural versus artificial feedback
2. Positive versus neutral versus negative feedback

Natural versus Artificial Feedback. *Natural feedback* is feedback which is apparent to the learner during the performance of a behavior. It can be interpreted directly by the learner without additional evaluation instruments (e.g., something works or it does not work). *Artificial feedback* is feedback from a source that would not typically be present in the real world (e.g., a written test interpreted by an instructor).

If possible, it is better to arrange for natural feedback than to arrange for artificial feedback. The motivation that occurs from a learner being able to immediately perceive if a real-world problem has been solved or has not been solved has great value. If a learner has not solved a problem adequately, it is very apparent, because something does not work. For example, if a person is asked to write a computer program to add a series of numbers, it is very apparent to the learner if the program results in the correct or the incorrect total.

Although natural feedback is desirable, there are many circumstances where it is not possible. For example, if an instructor is to evaluate a person's knowledge of complex electronics principles, it would be difficult to do so without creating written tests that diagnostically evaluate the learner's understanding of those principles. Such tests would not occur in the real world, and therefore, an instructor's interpretation of those tests, or the learner's interpretation of those tests, would be considered artificial feedback. That is not to say that it would be theoretically impossible to construct a series of practical applications of the content that would provide natural feedback and also test for all possible errors of perception of the principles and their applications. However, such applications would not be feasible in most instructional settings.

Positive versus Neutral versus Negative Feedback. A second method of classifying types of feedback is positive versus neutral versus negative feedback. *Positive feedback* is feedback that conveys acceptance of a learning result and encouragement. It may or may not be accompanied by a reward for performing correctly (e.g., praise or an opportunity to do something one desires). *Neutral feedback* is feedback in the form of nonevaluative comments. For example, acknowledgment of the learner during the learning process is neutral regarding successful learning. Neutral feedback is important in that it allows for an interaction between the instructor and the learner without evaluative comments regarding the learner. *Negative feedback* is feedback that conveys criticism that demeans and/or discourages the learner. It may or may not be accompanied by a punishment for performing incorrectly (e.g., being criticized or denied a desirable opportunity). Feedback is classified as positive or negative based on the manner in which it is presented and how it is perceived by the learner, and not on whether the learner has performed correctly or incorrectly. It is possible to provide positive feedback regarding an incorrect performance, and negative feedback regarding a correct performance.

If possible, neutral or positive feedback should be selected over negative feedback. Comments of encouragement or positive statements regarding an individual's performance have motivational value which enhance further learning. Negative feedback in the form of aggressive criticism or punishment has the result of inhibiting future learning. For example, suppose someone is

TABLE 10.4 Lesson Structure

PSYCHOMOTOR OBJECTIVE

Givens
A car with a flat tire, tools, and a replacement tire

Behavior
Change a tire.

Standard
The replacement tire is mounted on the car, the lugs are tight, and the tools and replacement tire are stored.

LESSON STAGE	CONTENT TO BE TAUGHT, PRACTICED, OR EVALUATED	METHODS/MEDIA (CONSISTENT WITH MODULARIZED FORMAT)
RATIONALE	*a.* Consequences of trying to drive on a flat tire *b.* Consequences of being stranded *c.* Money savings	Lecture/videotape; tutorial questioning/ instructor
NEED-TO-KNOW INFORMATION	*a.* The step-by-step procedure for changing a tire *b.* Safety precautions *c.* Lifting heavy objects	Reading/information sheet, textbook; self-questioning/self-check; self-determined/learner
DEMONSTRATION	Procedure for changing a tire	Demonstration/videotape
GUIDED PRACTICE	Procedure for changing a tire	Practice/assignment sheet; tutorial observation/instructor
UNGUIDED PRACTICE	Procedure for changing a tire	Practice/procedure sheet; conference/ instructor
EVALUATION	*a.* Knowledge base presented above *b.* Procedure for changing a tire	*a.* Test/written *b.* Product test/ checklist
FEEDBACK	*a.* Knowledge base presented above *b.* Procedure for changing a tire	Conference/instructor, tests

TABLE 10.5 Lesson Structure

COGNITIVE OBJECTIVE

Givens
A part requiring a wrench for removal and a variety of wrenches

Behavior
Decide which wrench to use.

Standard
A verbal description of the decision process is consistent with that specified on the instructor checklist.

LESSON STAGE	CONTENT TO BE TAUGHT, PRACTICED, OR EVALUATED	METHODS/MEDIA (CONSISTENT WITH TRADITIONAL FORMAT)
RATIONALE	*a.* Consequences of using the wrong wrench *b.* Time savings	Lecture/instructor, transparencies
NEED-TO-KNOW INFORMATION	*a.* Types of wrenches and their functions *b.* Procedure for making the decision	*a.* Reading/textbook *b.* Discussion/instructor
DEMONSTRATION	Procedure for making the decision	Demonstration/film; tutorial questioning/instructor
GUIDED PRACTICE	Procedure for making the decision	Practice/assignment sheet; tutorial observation/instructor
UNGUIDED PRACTICE	Procedure for making the decision	Practice/procedure sheet
EVALUATION	*a.* Knowledge base presented above *b.* Procedure for making the decision	*a.* Test/oral *b.* Performance test/checklist
FEEDBACK	*a.* Knowledge base presented above *b.* Procedure for making the decision	Conference/instructor, tests

TABLE 10.6 Lesson Structure

AFFECTIVE OBJECTIVE

Givens
A co-worker and a situation requiring cooperation

Behavior
Cooperate with co-workers.

Standard
Actions depicting cooperative activity are consistent with those specified on the instructor checklist.

LESSON STAGE	CONTENT TO BE TAUGHT, PRACTICED, OR EVALUATED	METHODS/MEDIA (CONSISTENT WITH TRADITIONAL FORMAT)
RATIONALE	The benefits of cooperation	Lecture/instructor
NEED-TO-KNOW INFORMATION	*a.* Types of actions that convey cooperation versus noncooperation *b.* Differences between assisting and taking over	Reading/textbook; tutorial questioning/instructor
DEMONSTRATION	Cooperative actions	Demonstration/videotape
GUIDED PRACTICE	Cooperative actions	Role playing/script; tutorial observation/instructor
UNGUIDED PRACTICE	Cooperative actions	Role playing/script; observation/another student; conference/other student
EVALUATION	*a.* Knowledge base presented above *b.* Cooperative actions	*a.* Test/written *b.* Performance test/rating scale
FEEDBACK	*a.* Knowledge base presented above *b.* Cooperative actions	Conference/instructor, tests

learning how to operate a word processing program using a microcomputer. Neutral feedback would occur if the instructor walked by and asked the learner how she or he was doing. There is no evaluation occurring, but there is communication between the instructor and the learner. This type of comment "opens the door" for further conversation if it is necessary. It also shows that the instructor is concerned about the learner. Positive feedback would occur if the instructor walked by and saw an error on the computer screen and said: "You are doing very well; the layout of the letter and the basic structure looks fine. I see that you have a typing error on line two that you may want to correct." Notice that positive feedback allows the evaluator to make comments about errors, but they are placed in a positive setting so the learner does not view them as personally threatening. Not only are the errors pointed out, but the learner is provided a way of correcting them without losing face.

Negative feedback would occur if the instructor walked by and viewed the screen and said: "I see you made another typing error on line two; if you continue doing that, you will never get a job in this field." In this case, the learner is placed on the defensive and is made to feel very negatively toward the instructor. In addition, the learner may begin to question his or her ability relative to the desired goal of entering the field of word processing.

In summary, it is not necessary for all feedback between an instructor and learner to be evaluative. Some feedback can be neutral. It is also possible within a generally positive instructional context to indicate that learners have made errors. Errors as well as ways in which they may be corrected can be indicated, and individuals can be left feeling good about themselves and their progress.

Entering Feedback Selections in the Lesson Structure

Tables 10.4 through 10.6 present sample lesson structures with the feedback procedure selections indicated; also indicated are the instructional resources that will be needed to implement those procedures. Notice that the feedback procedure selections are again presented in the same format as the methods and media. The feedback procedures are considered as methods, and the supporting resources are considered as media. For example, during the presentation of the need-to-know information for the lesson presented in Table 10.4, the learner would be expected to receive self-determined feedback from himself or herself, presumably based upon the self-check. During the feedback stage of the lesson, feedback would be provided through a conference with the instructor using the tests as a base of information. It is generally assumed that feedback will occur from the tutor to the learner during tutorial questioning or observation. Therefore, that does not have to be explicitly stated. Specifying feedback procedures in the lesson structure allows the instructional designer to clearly communicate the feedback procedures to be used and the support materials that will be used to provide that feedback. See Appendices B and C for additional examples of evaluation and feedback procedures selections.

SUMMARY

Evaluation and feedback perform related functions Evaluation is used to obtain information on the learning progress of a learner and the quality of instruction. Feedback is used to communicate interpreted evaluation results and encouragement to learners, and information about the quality of instruction to instructors.

Evaluation procedures are selected based on the expected formality of the evaluation and the type of content to be evaluated. Feedback procedures are selected based on who will provide the feedback, whether it will be natural or artificial, and/or whether it will be positive, neutral, or negative. The selection of evaluation and feedback procedures completes the structuring of a lesson. These selections provide the instructional designer with an indication of how learners will be evaluated and how the results of those evaluations will be fed back to learners.

ACTIVITIES AND EVALUATION

1. Develop or obtain a lesson structure that has been completed to the point of selecting instructional methods and media. Select evaluation and feedback procedures for that lesson. Include both evaluation and feedback methods and media.

2. Indicate why you have selected each evaluation and feedback procedure based on how it will facilitate learning.

REFERENCE

Pucel, D. J., *Performance-Based Instructional Design,* Performance Training Systems, St. Paul, MN, 1986.

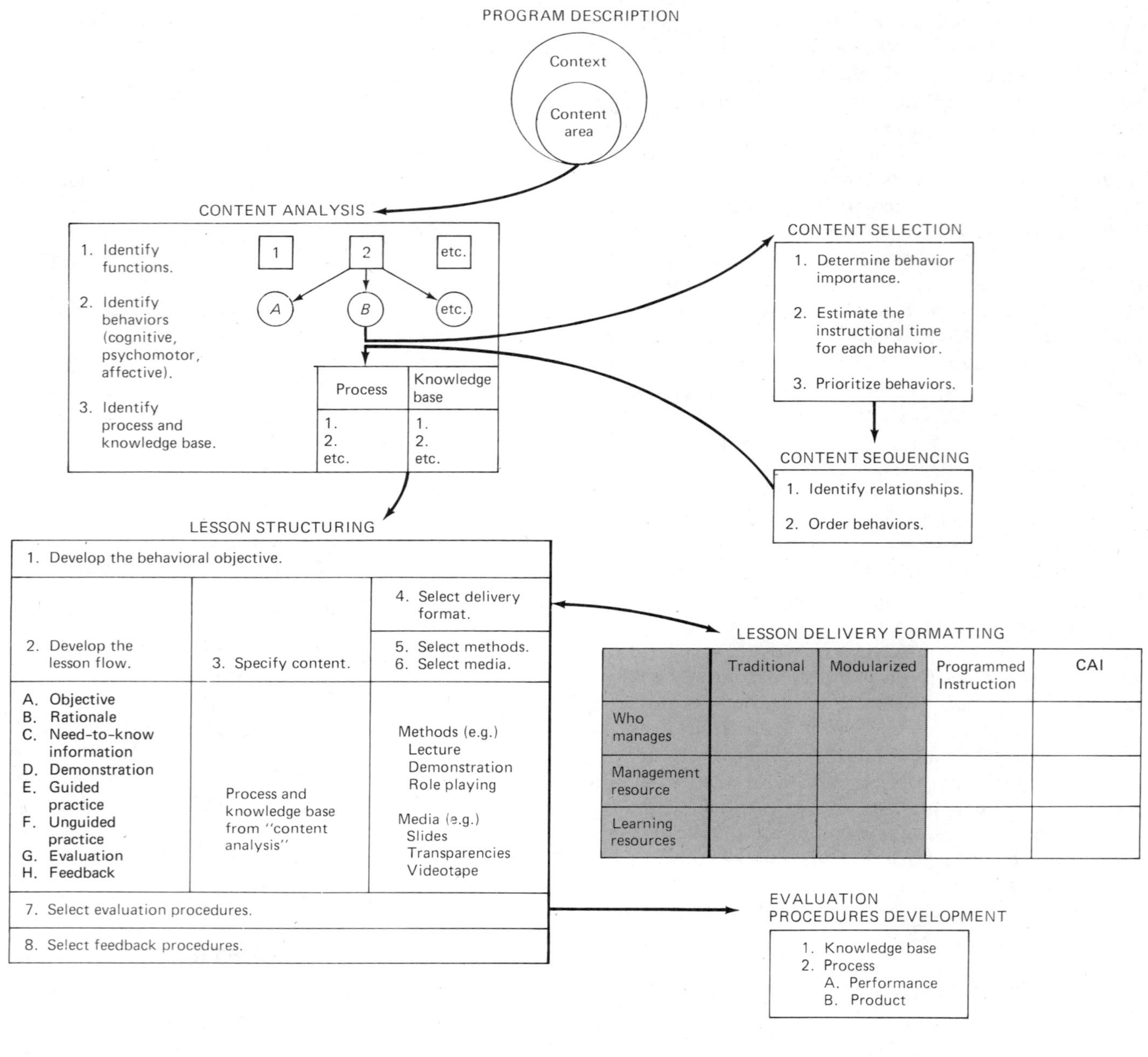

PROGRAM DESCRIPTION
Context
Content area
CONTENT ANALYSIS
1. Identify functions.
2. Identify behaviors (cognitive, psychomotor, affective).
3. Identify process and knowledge base.
1
2
etc.
A
B
etc.
Process
Knowledge base
1.
2.
etc.
1.
2.
etc.
CONTENT SELECTION
1. Determine behavior importance.
2. Estimate the instructional time for each behavior.
3. Prioritize behaviors.
CONTENT SEQUENCING
1. Identify relationships.
2. Order behaviors.
LESSON STRUCTURING
1. Develop the behavioral objective.
2. Develop the lesson flow.
3. Specify content.
4. Select delivery format.
5. Select methods.
6. Select media.
A. Objective
B. Rationale
C. Need-to-know information
D. Demonstration
E. Guided practice
F. Unguided practice
G. Evaluation
H. Feedback
Process and knowledge base from "content analysis"
Methods (e.g.)
Lecture
Demonstration
Role playing
Media (e.g.)
Slides
Transparencies
Videotape
7. Select evaluation procedures.
8. Select feedback procedures.
LESSON DELIVERY FORMATTING
Traditional
Modularized
Programmed Instruction
CAI
Who manages
Management resource
Learning resources
EVALUATION PROCEDURES DEVELOPMENT
1. Knowledge base
2. Process
A. Performance
B. Product

Formatting Traditional and Modularized Instruction, and Creating Multiple-Lesson Units

CHAPTER OBJECTIVE

Givens

Structured lessons which include the objective, lesson flow, content for each stage of the lesson flow, and selected methods and media

Behavior

Format a lesson delivery unit using the traditional or modularized format, and create multiple-lesson units.

Standard

Selection of lesson management and learning resources must be consistent with the format selected and the type of content to be taught. Development of multiple-lesson units must be based on behavior dependency.

OVERVIEW

This chapter presents an introduction to the process of lesson delivery formatting and a detailed discussion of how to format traditional and modularized instruction. Formatting of programmed and computer-assisted instruction are presented in Chapters 12 and 13.

Once a lesson has been structured, it must be formatted for delivery to learners. During the formatting process, many of the decisions made previously about the presentation of a particular lesson are synthesized. *Lesson delivery formatting* is the process of planning how a structured lesson will actually be implemented as it is presented to learners and evaluated. It provides answers to questions such as: Who will manage the instruction during delivery? What form will the management vehicle take (e.g., a lesson plan or a learning guide)? What specific learning resources will be used?

A *lesson delivery format* is an instructional management system used to manage the interaction of learners and learning resources throughout a lesson to bring about and evaluate learning. It is the detailed plan for how the structured lesson will be implemented. Typical formats are traditional, modularized, computer-assisted, and programmed instruction.

Before proceeding, the reader should review the introductory pages of Chapter 8 to refresh his or her understanding of the unique roles played by lesson structuring and lesson delivery formatting during the instructional design process. Since PBID is a generic system for planning instruction for any delivery format, lesson structuring techniques described in Chapters 8 through 10 apply equally to all formats. In fact, it is possible to present a particular structured lesson through more than one format. The different lesson delivery formats represent alternative ways of delivering structured lessons to learners.

The reader should also review the discussion of selecting a lesson delivery format presented in Chapter 9. This discussion presents: (1) the components of a lesson delivery format, (2) a detailed description of each format, and (3) criteria for deciding when to select and use each format.

Table 11.1 presents a summary of the major differences between the typical delivery formats and the types of lesson plans used with each. It is essentially the same as Table 9.1 and is presented again for ready reference. Types of lesson plans are discussed later in this chapter.

As you proceed, also keep in mind that a *lesson* is defined as a unit of instruction that contains *all* of the instruction and evaluation necessary to teach a behavior and to verify performance capability. A lesson is not defined in terms of a particular amount of instructional time (e.g., an hour or a day) or a particular learning activity (e.g., an exercise, a lecture, or a reading).

FORMATS VERSUS LEARNING RESOURCES

During formatting, it is important to distinguish between a lesson delivery format and a learning resource. A *lesson delivery format* is an instructional management system used to manage the interaction of learners and learning resources throughout a lesson to bring about and evaluate learning. Delivery formats differ primarily on the basis of who will manage the instruction, what type of lesson plan will be used, and what types of learning resources will typically be managed. A *learning resource* is a medium (e.g., a transparency, a videotape, or a textbook) used to accomplish a particular portion of a lesson. In order to implement most lessons, the utilization of a number of learning resources is required. These learning resources are orchestrated, or managed, through a delivery format.

For example, using the CAI delivery format, the computer provides lesson management instructions to learners regarding how they are to proceed through the lesson. The management directions to the learner could refer to learning materials within the computer itself or to external learning resources such as a textbook or a role-playing assignment. That portion of the actual instruction that is presented by the computer itself would be considered to be a learning resource. That part of the computer program that is aimed at managing the movement of learners through the learning resources would be considered to be the CAI lesson delivery format management.

An example of the use of the traditional format would be an instructor using and managing a lesson plan. Directions to the learner about what to do next are provided by the instructor; they are based on what is written in the lesson plan. The instructor may be required to utilize multiple learning resources, including herself

TABLE 11.1 Management and Typical Learning Resources Associated with Delivery Formats

	LESSON DELIVERY FORMATS			
	TRADITIONAL (Instructor-Directed)	MODULARIZED (Learner-Directed)	PROGRAMMED INSTRUCTION	COMPUTER-ASSISTED INSTRUCTION (CAI)
WHO MANAGES	Instructor	Learner	Learner	Learner
MANAGEMENT RESOURCE	Lesson plan (lesson plan explicit)	Learning guide (lesson plan explicit)	Programmed text (lesson plan implicit)	Computer program (lesson plan implicit)
TYPICAL LEARNING RESOURCES	Instructor as the primary resource with support materials	Independent study material with the instructor and other people as resources	Programmed "text"	Computer "program" and computer-controlled devices

or himself, a CAI program, transparencies, or a textbook. Management of learner interaction with the resources is provided by the instructor using the lesson plan.

The PBID system uses commonly accepted terminology regarding lesson delivery formats. A brief explanation of how each format is labeled will be presented to provide a context for the rest of the discussion. Traditional instruction is labeled *traditional* because it is the format which has traditionally been used in the past. Most instruction traditionally has been delivered by an instructor using a lesson plan to manage learning resources. Modularized instruction is labeled *modularized* because most instruction delivered by individual learners following a lesson plan under their own direction has been broken down into *modules,* or small, self-contained units of instruction. Programmed instruction is instruction characterized by breaking the content to be taught into very small portions, called *frames,* that are presented and evaluated through printed text. Its name is based upon the process used to develop such material, called *programming.* Computer-assisted instruction (CAI) is so named because a computer is used to provide and to manage the instruction.

EXPLICIT AND IMPLICIT LESSON PLANS

A *lesson plan* is a list of teaching steps developed to teach a lesson delivery unit and the learning resources that will be used at each step. As was explained in Chapter 8, a lesson delivery unit contains one or more behaviors that are taught together in the same lesson plan. At times, it makes sense to teach related behaviors together as one lesson delivery unit even though the separate lessons for each behavior should be structured separately. The teaching of related behaviors together facilitates learning by highlighting the relatedness of the behaviors; at times, it also increases teaching efficiency. In this chapter, the formatting of single-behavior lesson delivery units will be presented first. Later, the development of multiple-lesson lesson delivery units will be discussed.

The teaching steps in a lesson plan are developed in essentially the same manner as the process steps used in the behavior analysis portion of this book. They indicate the process that will be used to teach the lesson: what will be done first, what will be done second, and so on. The teaching steps of the lesson plan follow and implement the lesson structure developed earlier.

Although the designer must *always* develop a lesson plan, lesson plans take different forms, depending upon the delivery format used. They may be explicit, in which case the person implementing the lesson during delivery can actually see them, or implicit, in which case the person implementing the lesson during delivery cannot see them. If they are explicit, they are used directly by either the instructor or the learner.

With delivery of traditional instruction, the lesson plan is usually printed, or explicit. It lists the teaching steps in the form of a set of actions the instructor is to follow while delivering the lesson; it also lists the resources needed for the instructor to carry out those actions. With delivery of modularized instruction, the lesson plan is usually printed, or explicit. The teaching steps are presented as a list of learning steps to be followed by the learner as he or she proceeds through the listed learning resources.

With delivery of programmed or computer-assisted instruction, the lesson plan is not explicitly visible to the learner; it is implicit. The instruction is managed through a series of directions to the learner which are presented as needed to control instruction. The learner sees only one direction at a time when it is needed.

The lesson plan for programmed instruction usually takes the form of a flowchart of the frames to be included in the program. That flowchart is used during development by the instructional designer and is not usually seen by the instructor or learner.

The lesson plan for CAI is very similar to that used with programmed instruction. The computer is programmed to allow the learner to exercise only those options which the designer has built into the computer. The lesson plan for CAI usually takes the form of a flowchart of the screens to be included in the program. That flowchart is again used by the instructional designer during development, but it is usually not seen by the instructor or learner. The learner only sees one direction at a time, as needed.

FORMATTING TRADITIONAL INSTRUCTION

Instruction delivered with the traditional format is managed by an instructor who uses an explicit, written lesson plan. This format can be used to teach all types of content with a variety of learning resources. Although it can be used as the basis for individual tutoring, all learners are usually presented the content in essentially the same order and at the same pace. The instructor is the medium through which learners are directed to interact with learning resources. The instructor is also the primary medium for delivering the instruction. The lesson plan is written as a list of actions to be taken by the instructor to deliver the lesson. The actions represent how the instructor will orchestrate learning activities to teach the content within the lesson flow using the methods and media identified during lesson structuring. It is important that the steps be organized to implement the "lesson flow" so that a complete performance-based lesson is delivered. If any of the stages of the lesson flow are left out, learners may not be able to perform adequately.

Table 11.2 presents a sample lesson plan to teach how to change a tire using the traditional format. Notice that it is called an *instructor-oriented lesson plan* because the plan is aimed at directing the actions of the instructor as the lesson is orchestrated. The lesson plan parallels the lesson structure presented in Table 9.5. Also, notice that the objective has been numbered. All learning resources specific to teaching this lesson have also been identified using the same number as the prefix, followed by a unique number which identifies that resource. The sample lesson plan presents objective 133. The first resource is a transparency which is numbered 133-1. Although this numbering procedure is not essential, it helps keep track of the resources needed to teach each lesson and allows for systematic filing and storage of learning materials.

TABLE 11.2 Sample Instructor-Oriented Lesson Plan

OBJECTIVE 133

Givens
A car with a flat tire, tools, and a replacement tire

Behavior
Change a tire.

Standard
The replacement tire is mounted on the car, and the tools and the replacement tire are stored.

Instructor Actions	Resources
1. Present lecture on: *a.* Consequences of driving on a flat tire *b.* Consequences of being stranded *c.* Money savings *Sample question:* What happens to a tire if you drive on it when it is flat?	1. Overhead transparencies *a.* 133-1 *b.* 133-2
2. Review "safety precautions" and "lifting heavy objects" in the text and "procedure" on the information sheet. *Sample question:* Why is it important to block the tires before raising the car off the ground?	2. Textbook, information sheet 133-3
3. Present the demonstration using the information sheet as a guide.	3. Information sheet 133-4, tools, replacement tire
4. Have learners complete the quiz and provide feedback.	4. Quiz 133-5
5. Give learners the practice assignment.	5. Assignment sheet 133-6 (Make sure that tools and equipment are ready.)
6. Administer the knowledge-base test	6. Written test 133
7. Allow time for additional practice.	
8. As learners feel they are ready to demonstrate their skills, be ready to check out their performance.	8. Performance test 133-7

FORMATTING MODULARIZED INSTRUCTION

The modularized delivery format is managed by learners following a written, explicit lesson plan in the form of a *learning guide.* The format is used with a variety of self-instructional resources. When using this format, the instructor is also considered to be a resource. The learning guide presents learning steps to be followed by the learner during the completion of the lesson, and lists learning resources which are to be used at each step. Usually, learning is individualized and self-paced so that learners can proceed at their own pace.

TABLE 11.3 Sample Learning Guide (Learner-Oriented Lesson Plan)

OBJECTIVE 133

Givens
A car with a flat tire, tools, and a replacement tire

Behavior
Change a tire.

Standard
The replacement tire is mounted on the car, and the tools and replacement tire are stored.

Learning Step	Resources
1. View the videotape to determine the consequences of driving on a flat tire or of being stranded, and the implications for money savings.	1. Videotape 133-1
2. Read the information sheet to review the step-by-step procedure for changing a tire, and read the text for "safety precautions" and "how to lift heavy objects."	2. Information sheet 133-2, text pp. 23–31
3. Complete the self-check to determine your knowledge, and compare your answers with the model answers provided.	3. Self-check 133-3, model answers
4. View the videotape presentation to see how a tire is changed, and review information sheet 133-2.	4. Videotape presentation 133-4, information sheet 133-2
5. Read and complete the assignment sheet to practice changing a tire. *Caution:* The instructor must be with you before you start changing the tire.	5. Assignment sheet 133-5
6. Take the knowledge-base test on changing a tire.	6. Written test 133-6
7. Practice changing a tire to perfect your skill. Ask the instructor to evaluate your performance when you feel you have mastered the process.	7. Performance test 133-7
8. After the instructor has approved your performance, go on with objective 134.	

Table 11.3 presents a sample learning guide for the lesson "change a tire." It follows the lesson structure presented in Table 10.4. Notice that it is an alternative for presenting the traditional lesson contained in Table 11.2. The basic differences are that learning steps are written for direct use by the learner instead of listed as instructor actions, and the learning resources are selected for direct use by the learner rather than by the instructor. The learning guide is called a *learner-oriented lesson plan* because it is developed for use by the learner while he or she implements the lesson.

Learning steps are written as directives, or directions, to the learner. Each learning step has three parts:

1. A verb that indicates the type of action to be taken
2. The resources to use while taking that action
3. A rationale that indicates why the action is to be taken.

Table 11.4 presents some sample learning steps. As indicated earlier, the actions in each learning step should parallel and implement the lesson structure previously developed. Specification of each action is based on the verb selected (e.g., *read, view, practice, take,* and *review*). Selection of the resources is based on the types of media available within the institution and from commercial publishers. In addition, selection of resources must be based upon the instructional method being implemented and on whether learners will complete the learning step alone or with others. For example, if a demonstration is to be presented, a videotape of the activity might be appropriate, but a verbal presentation through a lecture would not. If it is assumed that the learner will perform with others, role playing might be appropriate, but reading alone would not.

The rationale for why the learner should complete a learning step should indicate the instructional intent of that particular step. This rationale is an important element in motivating learners and in making learning meaningful.

COMBINING SEPARATE BEHAVIORS INTO LARGER UNITS

As was pointed out earlier, at times behaviors are performed together in the real world because they are dependent upon one another. They might actually occur simultaneously or in proximity to one another. Therefore, it may make sense to teach them together even though lessons for each behavior should be structured separately. It may also make sense to teach behaviors together if the content for the behaviors is very similar. There are a variety of ways of combining individual behaviors into larger teaching units that may increase teaching and learning efficiency. Two will be presented:

TABLE 11.4 Sample Learning Steps

Verb	Resource	Why
Read	the information sheet	to review the procedure
View	the videotape	to see how the procedure is performed
Practice	with the assignment sheet	to apply the procedure with another person

developing multiple-behavior delivery units, and developing learning packages. Table 11.5 presents the relationship between lessons, delivery units, and learning packages. In addition to these methods of combining lessons into larger units, the teaching of lessons near one another without combining them into one unit will be discussed.

Developing Multiple-Behavior Delivery Units

As indicated earlier, a lesson plan is a list of steps developed to teach learners to perform a behavior or the group of behaviors contained in a lesson delivery unit. A lesson delivery unit may contain one or more behaviors and their associated lessons. The lesson plan for a lesson delivery unit unites the separate lessons for the behaviors to be taught together in one lesson plan. Lesson delivery units are identified through the sequencing procedures described in Chapter 6.

If behaviors have very similar content, they can be combined together in one lesson delivery unit. For example, the behaviors "change spark plugs" and "clean and gap spark plugs" might be taught in the same lesson delivery unit because they both relate to servicing the spark plugs of a car and because the content of both behaviors is highly interrelated. If behaviors are combined, a name for the lesson delivery unit must be developed that would relate to all of the behaviors contained in the unit. In this case, the name might be "service spark plugs."

If these two behaviors are included in one lesson delivery unit, the lesson structures for these behaviors must be combined. This is done by folding them together like decks of cards into one lesson structure and then presenting this combined lesson structure in one lesson plan. Figure 11.1 graphically presents this process. Notice that the structure for each of the separate lessons is still maintained in the same order. In other words, the lesson flow for each behavior in the lesson delivery unit should maintain the same order it had in the separate lesson structure for that behavior. This is done to ensure that a complete performance-based lesson is still taught for each behavior. Stages 1, 2, and 3 for behavior 1 are still in the same order, and stages 1, 2, and 3 for behavior 2 are still in the same order. This

TABLE 11.5 Combining Separate Behaviors for Instructional Delivery

Lesson ——→	Delivery Unit ——→	Learning Package
A unit of instruction which contains all of the instruction and evaluation necessary to teach a behavior and to verify performance capability.	One or more lessons united and taught using one lesson plan.	One or more separate delivery units which are presented to learners as one instructional unit.

FIGURE 11.1 Joining Lesson Structures in a Lesson Delivery Unit

	BEHAVIOR 1 STRUCTURE	BEHAVIOR 2 STRUCTURE	COMBINATION
	* * *	! ! !	! * * ! * !
	* * *	! ! !	! * * ! * !
	* * *	! ! !	! * * ! * !
	* * *	! ! !	! * * ! * !
	* * *	! ! !	! * * ! * !
	* * *	! ! !	! * * ! * !
Stages:	1 2 3	1 2 3	1 1 2 2 3 3

is true even though the stages for one behavior are inserted between the stages for the other behavior.

It is also appropriate to combine the same stage of the various behaviors. For example, the rationale stage for both behaviors could be combined so the learner could see why it is important to change and/or clean and gap spark plugs. This may be more efficient than having separate rationale stages for the two different behaviors included in the lesson.

Developing Learning Packages

A *learning package* includes the lesson plans and related learning resources associated with one or more lesson delivery units which are presented to learners as one instructional unit. It is most often associated with modularized instruction.

A learning package includes one or more learning guides and their associated learning resources. If more than one lesson delivery unit is included in the package, the composite of the separate learning guides is called a *package learning guide.*

Learning packages are created by using criteria similar to those used in the combining of behaviors into one lesson delivery unit, which was discussed previously. The lessons included must be dependent in some way, and someone must judge them to be more efficient to teach together in one package than in separate packages. For example, a learning package might include the separate learning guides for the behaviors, "greet a customer," "determine customer needs," "describe product features," and "close a sale." These behaviors would be included in one learning package because they are usually performed together, or in close proximity to one another, as a total action. One way to tell if it is reasonable to combine the learning guides into one learning package is to determine if the combination would result in a rationally titled program. In this case, a reasonable title for the package would be "Make a Sale." This title would apply to all of the individual behaviors to be taught within the package and would be meaningful within a marketing education program. If the only way to define the learning package is to list all of the component behaviors contained in the package, then one should question whether they should be combined or be in separate packages which are taught near one another.

In addition to the separate learning guides for the separate lessons and a composite title, each learning package should have a cover page. That cover page should include:

1. The overall title of the package
2. A list of each of the separate lessons included
3. A combined rationale which explains why people should learn what is contained in the package

Table 11.6 presents a sample cover page for the learning package "Make a Sale."

Although the content in learning packages may be evaluated using the separate evaluation instruments developed for each lesson, it is sometimes also desirable to evaluate together all of the behaviors included in a package at the end of the package.

In summary, a learning package includes:

1. A cover page
2. The lesson plans (learning guides) for the separate lesson delivery units included in the package
3. An overall evaluation (optional)

Teaching Lessons Near One Another

At times, instructional efficiency and effectiveness can be increased by teaching behaviors near one another, even though they should not be included in the same lesson delivery unit or learning package. For example, the behaviors "cooperate with co-workers" and "remove a car engine" might be appropriate to teach near one another. However, it is doubtful that they should be included in the same lesson delivery unit or in one learning package. The removal of a car engine requires the cooperation of a number of people, and both of these behaviors need to be taught in the program. The teaching of the two behaviors near one another would allow for the teaching of cooperation in association with a behavior that requires people to cooperate with one another. See Appendices B and C for additional examples of formatting traditional and modularized instruction.

TABLE 11.6 Sample Learning Package Cover Page

PACKAGE TITLE: MAKE A SALE

LESSONS INCLUDED

1. Greet a customer.
2. Determine customer needs.
3. Describe product features.
4. Close a sale.

RATIONALE

The ultimate goal of people involved in marketing is to finally sell products to customers. Purchasing products, advertising, display, and other marketing activities culminate in the actual sale. This package presents the major ingredients in actually making the sale to a customer.

SUMMARY

Lesson delivery formatting is the process of planning how a structured lesson will actually be implemented as it is presented to learners and evaluated. It provides answers to questions such as: Who will manage the instruction during delivery? What form will the management vehicle take (e.g., a lesson plan or a learning guide)? What specific learning resources will be used?

Lesson structuring techniques apply equally to all formats. However, each lesson delivery format represents an alternative way of delivering a structured lesson to learners. Therefore, although the formats have components in common, each one has unique characteristics of its own.

The four delivery formats most often used with performance-based instruction are: (1) the traditional format, (2) modularized instruction, (3) programmed instruction, and (4) computer-assisted instruction (CAI).

At times behaviors are dependent upon one another; therefore, it may be appropriate to teach them in larger units. It may also be appropriate to teach them in larger units because the content base for the behaviors overlaps substantially. Two ways of combining behaviors into larger units are developing multiple-behavior delivery units, and developing learning packages. Related behaviors can also be taught near one another without combining them into one unit.

ACTIVITIES AND EVALUATION

1. Obtain a completed lesson structure. Select either a traditional or a modularized lesson delivery format to teach that lesson. Explain why you selected that format based on: (1) lesson management, (2) the types of content to be taught, (3) the types of learning resources to be used, and (4) the need for assurance of uniformity of instruction and performance.
2. Develop a lesson plan or learning guide for that lesson (modify the methods or learning resources if necessary).
3. Indicate whether the behavior in that lesson should be taught with other behaviors in a multiple-behavior lesson delivery unit, within a learning package with other lessons, separately but with other behaviors, or totally independently. If appropriate, indicate which behaviors should be taught together.

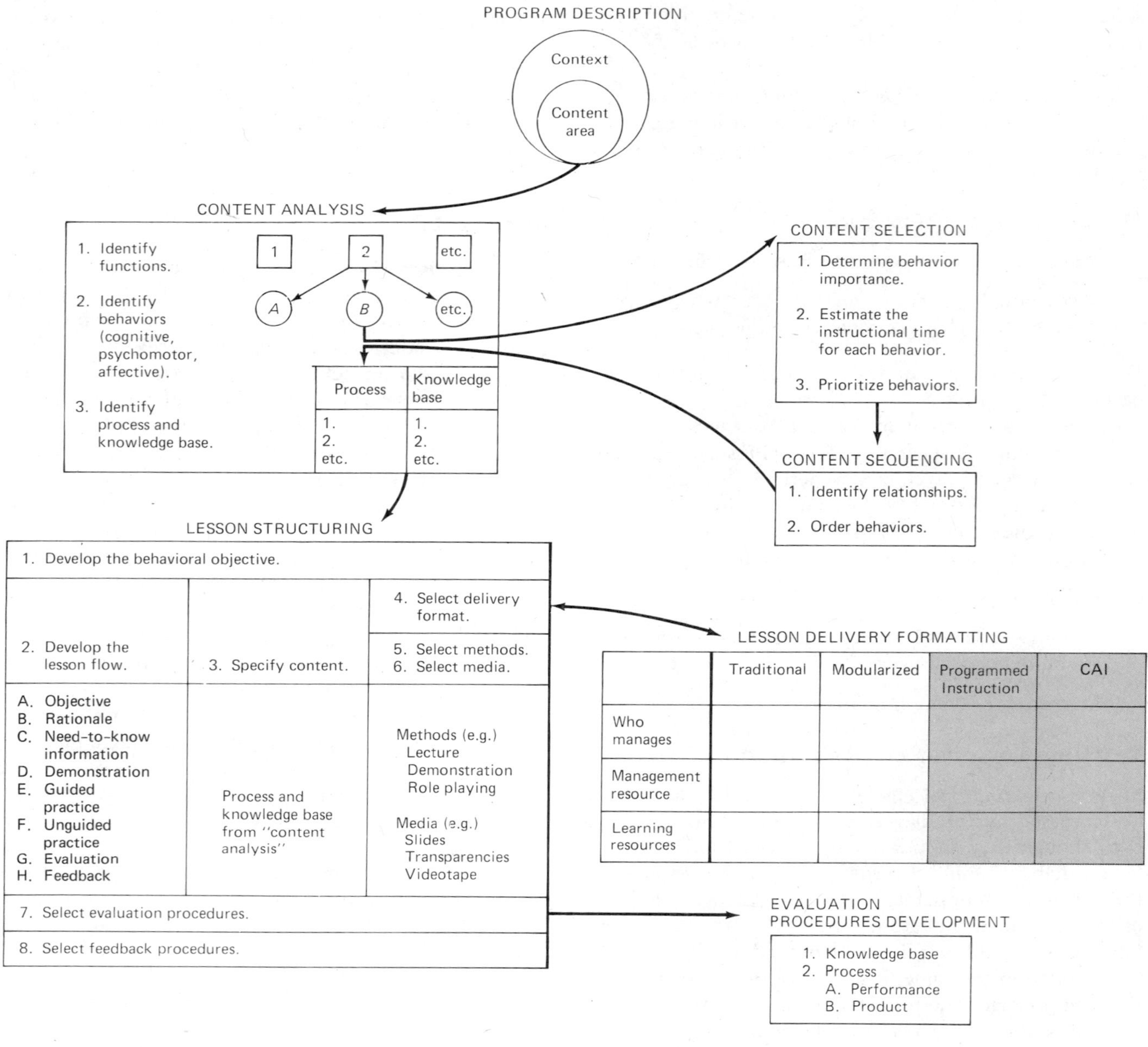
PROGRAM DESCRIPTION
Context
Content area
CONTENT ANALYSIS
1. Identify functions.
2. Identify behaviors (cognitive, psychomotor, affective).
3. Identify process and knowledge base.
1
2
etc.
A
B
etc.
Process
Knowledge base
1.
2.
etc.
1.
2.
etc.
CONTENT SELECTION
1. Determine behavior importance.
2. Estimate the instructional time for each behavior.
3. Prioritize behaviors.
CONTENT SEQUENCING
1. Identify relationships.
2. Order behaviors.
LESSON STRUCTURING
1. Develop the behavioral objective.
2. Develop the lesson flow.
3. Specify content.
4. Select delivery format.
5. Select methods.
6. Select media.
A. Objective
B. Rationale
C. Need-to-know information
D. Demonstration
E. Guided practice
F. Unguided practice
G. Evaluation
H. Feedback
Process and knowledge base from "content analysis"
Methods (e.g.)
Lecture
Demonstration
Role playing
Media (e.g.)
Slides
Transparencies
Videotape
7. Select evaluation procedures.
8. Select feedback procedures.
LESSON DELIVERY FORMATTING
Traditional
Modularized
Programmed Instruction
CAI
Who manages
Management resource
Learning resources
EVALUATION PROCEDURES DEVELOPMENT
1. Knowledge base
2. Process
A. Performance
B. Product

Formatting Programmed and Computer-Assisted Instruction

CHAPTER OBJECTIVE

Givens

A structured lesson which includes the objective, lesson flow, content for each stage of the lesson flow, and the decision to use the programmed or computer-assisted instruction delivery format

Behavior

Format a lesson for delivery using a programmmed and/or computer-assisted instruction delivery format.

Standard

Lesson management and learning resources must be consistent with the format selected and the type of content to be taught.

OVERVIEW

This chapter focuses on the formatting of programmed instruction (PI) and computer-assisted instruction (CAI). Although the techniques can also be used to develop PI and CAI learning resources to be used with other instructional formats, the development of such learning resources is not the specific focus of this chapter. This chapter has been developed with the assumption that people have already studied Chapter 11, which pertains to the selection of an instructional delivery format and the basic characteristics of each format.

When lessons for PI or CAI are formatted, learning materials should be orchestrated so that they can assume the role of a tutor. Learners often use these types of instruction without other people present. Therefore, the human aspects of instruction need to be compensated for so that learners obtain feedback and are motivated. The material should not only present content to be learned and to be used for evaluating learning, but it should also convey a friendly, positive, and accepting attitude toward the learner.

With the advent of PI and CAI and their potential, the role of the instructor has had to be reevaluated. It is generally accepted that a "real instructor" is still absolutely essential. These formats are not really intended as a total substitute for the instructor; they are most effective when used in conjunction with assistance from an instructor. For example, within a CAI program learners could be instructed to have products reviewed by the instructor, and the instructor could be available to answer questions. Only an instructor can understand each learner's needs, confusions, and other obstacles to the learning process (Scanland and Slattery, 1983).

During the formatting of both PI and CAI, there is a lesson plan. However, the plan is used by the instructional designer during development and is not explicitly seen by the instructor or the learner during the delivery of instruction. The lesson is presented to learners in a predetermined order, based on a frame or screen sequence, and detailed directions are given to the learner as the frames or screens are presented. Detailed instructor actions or learning steps, however, are not presented in the form of a written plan as in traditional or modularized instruction.

In the case of PI, the lesson plan is a frame sequence. The content of the lesson is broken down into small segments, called *frames.* The frames are presented in a written, printed text. Each frame contains information as well as directions which indicate what the learner is to do with the information. The designer must develop a frame sequence which indicates both the content to be included in each frame and the order in which the frames will be presented. The management of the program is determined by the sequence of the frames and by directions that indicate the next frame to which the learner is to proceed based on evaluation results.

With the CAI format, the plan is a screen sequence. In CAI, the content is presented primarily through a computer monitor. Each full picture of information is called a *screen.* A screen is a basic unit of information provided by a computer with a single activation of the computer. Each screen may provide a visual picture of information and/or information conveyed through computer-controlled devices (e.g., a videotape presentation or a sound recording).

The CAI designer develops a screen sequence to determine what will be included in each screen and the order in which the screens will be presented. At times, learners are also referred to learning resources not under the direct control of the computer (e.g., texts, films, or manuals). The management of the CAI program is determined by the sequence of the screens and by directions that indicate, based on evaluation results, the next screen to which the learner is to proceed. At times, the program itself is programmed to make decisions, based on evaluation results, about what the learner will be presented next. Both screen and frame sequences are developed from the lesson structure, as are instructor-oriented lesson plans and learning guides.

The primary differences between a lesson plan for traditional or modularized instruction and one for PI or CAI are:

1. In traditional or modularized instruction, the lesson plan is used to manage a number of learning resources external to the lesson plan itself. The management resource and the learning resources are separate entities even though some of the printed materials are at times attached to the modularized instruction lesson plan (learning guide).

2. In PI and CAI, the management resource and the primary learning resources are integrated into one medium (e.g., a text or a computer program). Management directions are provided as the lesson is presented through the primary learning resource.

At times, learners are referred to external resources.

Because the development of PI and CAI require an integrated management and learning resource, the level of detail in planning and producing them is much higher than in traditional or modularized instruction. The detail must be sufficient so that not only a plan to manage learning resources can be developed, but the learning resource itself (e.g., a programmed text or a computer program) can also be developed.

FORMATTING PROGRAMMED INSTRUCTION

The PI delivery format is used primarily to teach cognitive behaviors for which performance capability can be demonstrated through written responses. The written responses may include words, symbols, diagrams, or any other type of information that can be written. Programmed instruction can also be used to teach the knowledge base associated with psychomotor or affective behaviors; however, it is rarely used as the delivery format for lessons associated with psychomotor or affective behaviors. That is because the practice and evaluation stages associated with those lessons require psychomotor activity not possible using only a text. For example, PI could be used to present the need-to-know information as part of a modularized instruction lesson on how to change a tire. However, it would not be possible to provide the demonstration, practice, or performance evaluation using PI. In this case, a programmed text is used as a learning resource managed through another delivery format.

PI is usually delivered through a text. First, a frame sequence is developed. The term *frame* came from early experimentation with PI in which only one increment of information was presented at a time. That increment was literally "framed" like a window by a physical device so the learner could see only the amount of information contained in the frame. Modern PI texts usually no longer have just one piece of information visible at a time. A frame "has come to denote that amount of information which can, or should be, presented to the learner before requiring some sort of response by which learning can be assessed" (Friesen, 1973).

The incremental portions of information used to teach a behavior through PI are called *teaching points.* They are derived though content analysis. Figure 12.1 graphically presents the process.

The first level of analysis is to state the behavioral objective. Second, the content is broken down into the process used to perform the behavior and the related knowledge base. Chapter 7, which pertains to content analysis, presents procedures on how to complete these first two steps. To develop the PI learning resource to actually teach the process and knowledge base associated with a behavior, one must detail them even further.

FIGURE 12.1 Analyzing Content for Programmed Instruction

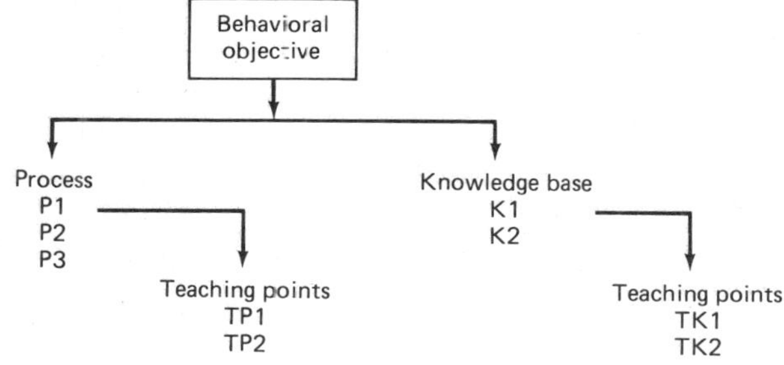

They must be detailed into teaching points. Each teaching point contains one piece of information to be learned (e.g., a fact, a relationship, or a concept).

Process steps requiring further analysis are detailed into subprocess steps, or subactions, until single teaching points are identified. The knowledge base is further detailed into facts, relationships, concepts, and so on, until single teaching points are identified. This extensive analysis is very costly and time-consuming, and it is a primary reason why PI is not more widely utilized. The costs can only be justified when a high degree of instructional precision is required, or when large numbers of people will use the programs individually and the costs can be widely distributed, eventually making the instruction cost-effective.

A frame presents one or more teaching points and an evaluation item or items focused on verifying that the learner has learned the teaching points. If what the learner is expected to do with the information is not apparent, explicit directions concerning what to do are also presented. The frame sequence is constructed which is consistent with the content analysis and the lesson structure for the lesson to be formatted. Table 12.1 presents a sample frame. First, the information to be learned (e.g., one or more teaching points) is presented. Then, an evaluation item is presented which requires the learner to actively react to the information to demonstrate that the information has been learned. In this example, the teaching point being taught is that cooperation increases productivity.

The following are some characteristics of "good" programmed instruction. These should be kept in mind when developing a program. They are adapted from *Designing Instruction: A Systematic or "Systems" Approach Using Programmed Instruction as a Model* by Paul A. Friesen (1973).

TABLE 12.1 Sample Frame

Information (teaching point): When a number of people are required to complete a job, cooperation yields more productivity than individual work efforts. Evaluation item: Cooperation increases ____________. (productivity)

1. Since PI is designed for learners to study independently, the population of learners who will use the program must be clearly defined. If the material does not fit the learners, it will not be effective.

2. The material should be designed to actively involve learners by presenting the information in small increments which can be mastered. At the end of each increment, a self-check is presented which allows learners to judge if they have learned the information. The self-check presents a question or problem which is to be answered either overtly, in writing, or covertly, by thinking out a response.

3. Immediately after the learner has completed the response, she or he is referred to a sample correct response so the adequacy of the response can be judged. This feedback provides immediate confirmation of results. If the learner has not obtained the correct response, he or she is asked to repeat the frames or is referred, or branched, to other learning frames which attempt to teach the same content in another way. The learner should not proceed to new material until mastery of the content has been verified.

4. As larger concepts or relationships begin to be developed through the learning of individual increments, or teaching points, frames are directed at an integration of the increments of information and how they aggregate to the larger concept or relationships.

Table 12.2 presents a page from a programmed text produced by IBM to teach computer programmers to use the FORTRAN language (IBM, 1963). As the learner proceeds through this program, the answers to the evaluation items listed down the right-hand side of the page are to be covered with a piece of paper. Upon answering the evaluation item, the appropriate answer is to be uncovered to provide immediate feedback concerning the correct answer. This program also refers learners to an accompanying problem book and illustrations.

Programmed texts can be organized as linear programs or branching programs. The programmed text material presented in Table 12.2 was programmed using linear programming. This is similar to linear sequencing, which has been discussed in Chapter 6 and presented in Figure 6.5. Linear programming requires the learner to follow only one (linear) path through the program. The programmer determines what that path will be and presents the frames in that order. Figure 12.2 presents an example of a linear program. The learner would proceed from frame 1 to frame 2, from frame 2 to frame 3, and so on. If the learner made an error and needed a review of the content, she or he would return to a previous frame which contains the needed information and then continue through the program.

Branching programming is similar to branching sequencing, discussed in Chapter 6 and presented in Figure 6.6. There are two ways of directing the learner to alternative learning frames: allow the learner to select among alternative paths, or direct the learner to alternative paths based on the nature of the evaluation re-

TABLE 12.2 Sample Programmed Text to Teach FORTRAN

1. A program is written for the purpose of "directing the computer" through the steps of the problem. For example, if the computer is going to perform arithmetic, it must be told each step of the operations. Q. A program is a detailed description of each __________ of the solution of a problem.	A. step
2. You will soon learn, for example, that the FORTRAN statement Y = A + B + C represents a "program" to find the sum of the three quantities A, B, and C and to set the value of Y equal to that sum. Q. The statement Y = A + B + C is actually a small computer __________.	A. program
3. A program language such as FORTRAN is like any language: it has both vocabulary and rules of grammar and punctuation. You will learn the rules and vocabulary of FORTRAN in this course. The FORTRAN language is particularly well adapted to mathematical problems. The way in which mathematical problems are programmed with FORTRAN closely resembles ordinary algebraic notation. Q. FORTRAN is particularly adapted to the programming of __________ problems.	A. mathematical

FIGURE 12.2 Sample Linear Programming Frame Sequence

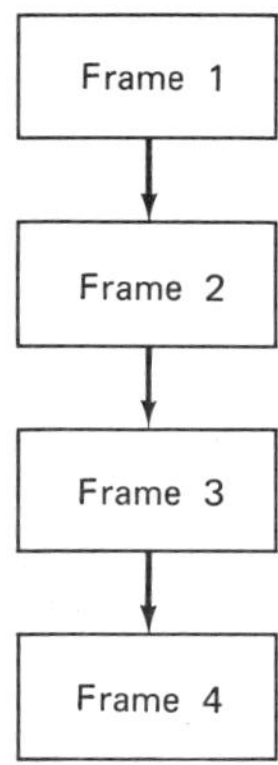

sponse. In both cases, there are alternative paths or branches within the learning resource. All learners would not be required to take the same frame sequence, and/or remediation could take place by receiving instruction that is different from that originally presented to the learner and which is based on evaluation results. One advantage of branching programming is that it presents the learner with the content in alternative ways, which may bring about new insights. Studying the same material again, upon missing an evaluation item, may not lead to increased learning. The difficulty with understanding the material the first time may still persist with repeated studying of the same material, but it may be relieved by studying the material using an alternative approach. Another advantage is that branching programming can be used to allow people who have already mastered information to discontinue studying it. They can be branched to new content.

Table 12.3 presents a sample frame from a branching program (Friesen, 1973). The learner would review the teaching point and respond to the evaluation item. Depending upon the answer to the evaluation item, the learner would be branched to different pages which contain learning materials aimed at the same teaching point but which address it in a different way. The information the learner next encounters would be different, depending upon the response to the evaluation item.

TABLE 12.3 Sample Branching Program Frame

Information (teaching point):

One meaning of the word *integral* is "necessary to the completeness of a whole." For example, we would say that a steering wheel is an integral part of an automobile because the automobile would not be complete if it did not have a steering wheel. However, there are degrees of completeness, so a person must be careful. If an automobile did not have a horn, it would be complete in the sense that it would function. Therefore, a horn is not integral to the automobile.

Evaluation item:

Which of the following best illustrates this definition of *integral?*

A—Salt is an integral part of bread. (Turn to page X.)

B—The earth is an integral part of the solar system as we know it. (Turn to page Y.)

C—Clothing is an integral part of the man. (Turn to page Z.)

In the evaluation items in Table 12.3, you could have bread without salt in it, so answer A is not correct. You could not have the solar system as we know it without earth, so answer B is the correct one. You could have a man without clothing, so answer C is also incorrect. Each of the pages (X, Y, or Z) would verify if the answer were correct and would provide information to reinforce the teaching point. If, after presenting the reinforcing information, the answer were incorrect, another evaluation item would be presented.

Figure 12.3 presents a sample branching-frame sequence chart. Notice that the designer must determine the next frame for each of the alternative answers to the evaluation items. The evaluation items in Figure 12.3 would result in two possible answers: yes, or correct; and no, or incorrect. Depending upon whether the answer were correct or incorrect, learners would be referred to different frames. If learners gave a correct answer to the evaluation item for frame 1, they would proceed to frame 2; if an incorrect answer were given, they would proceed to frame 1*a*; if they gave a correct answer to frame 1*a*, they would proceed to frame 2; if they gave an incorrect answer to frame 1*a*, they would proceed to frame 1*b*; and so on. It can readily be seen that the complexity of developing branching programs is much greater than that of developing linear programs.

Once the teaching points have been identified and the evaluation items and frame sequence have been developed, the frames are assembled into a programmed text. If illustrations and/or evaluation problems are large, and if they may interfere with the flow of the material in the text, they can be separated into supplementary documents. The supplementary documents are

FIGURE 12.3 Sample Branching Program Frame Sequence

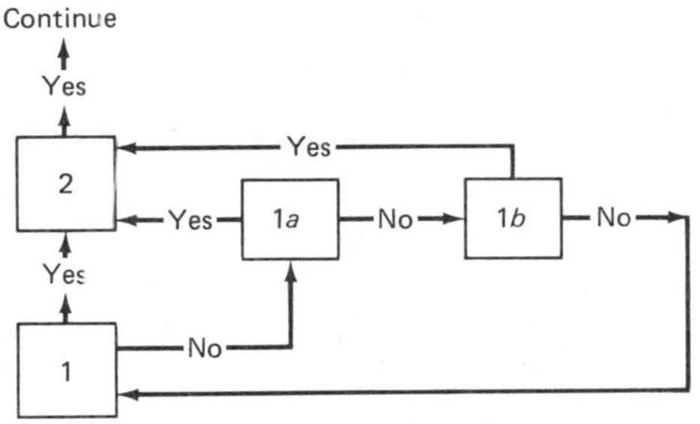

Each box represents a frame. Learners are directed to "yes" paths for correct answers and to "no" paths for incorrect answers.

used as references as learners proceed through the program.

INTRODUCTION TO COMPUTER-ASSISTED INSTRUCTION PROGRAMS

Computer-assisted instruction (CAI), generically, is instruction which uses a computer as the medium through which content is presented to learners, practiced, and/or evaluated. The computer is the device with which the learner interacts during instruction. CAI is often differentiated from computer-managed instruction (CMI), which is instruction managed through a computer (e.g., keeping data records on the progress of learners in order to manage their learning, or directing learners to content resources). In this book, the computer-assisted instructional delivery format combines CAI and CMI into a lesson delivery format which uses the computer as a management vehicle and as the primary instructional medium to present the content.

Again, it is important to differentiate between a lesson delivery format and a learning resource. A *lesson delivery format* is an instructional management system used to manage the interaction of learners and resources throughout a lesson to bring about and evaluate learning. Examples are traditional instruction, modularized instruction, PI, and CAI. A *learning resource* is a medium (e.g., a transparency, a videotape, or a textbook) used to accomplish a particular portion of a lesson. If the computer is used to accomplish only a particular portion of a lesson managed through another format, it is a learning resource to that lesson. If the computer is used to manage the interaction of the learners throughout the lesson, in addition to being the primary learning resource, then the CAI instructional delivery format is being used.

This chapter focuses on the development of instruction using the CAI delivery format through which lessons are managed and primarily delivered by a computer. In the event that only components of a lesson managed by another delivery format are to be taught with a computer, the techniques presented can also be easily generalized to the development of such single-purpose learning resources.

Alessi and Trollip (1985) present a way of classifying computer-based instructional programs. They suggest that most CAI is composed of combinations of one or more of the following five types of computer-based programs:

1. *Tutorials.* Programs that teach by carrying on a dialogue with the learner. They present information; ask the learner questions; and make decisions, based on the learner's comprehension, as to whether to move on to new information or to engage in review and remediation.
2. *Drills.* Programs that teach by presenting a selection of questions or problems repeatedly (e.g., arithmetic problems or vocabulary development) until the learner answers or solves them all at some predetermined level of proficiency.
3. *Simulations.* Programs that imitate a phenomenon in order to teach the learner about it. A subset of simulations is the demonstration program which simply shows the learner how to do something.
4. *Instructional games.* Programs which may or may not simulate reality but which are characterized by providing the learner with entertaining challenges while teaching an instructional component.
5. *Tests.* Programs designed to assess learning.

Alessi and Trollip (1985) further suggest that the instructional process can be divided into four phases, and that each type of computer instructional program is most useful at certain phases. The four phases are:

1. *Presenting information.* Information, including examples and demonstrations, is presented to the learner.
2. *Guiding the learner.* The learner does something under the guidance of the instructor. The instructor observes the learner and corrects errors.
3. *Practice.* The learner practices in order to be able to retain information and to become fluent, including being able to perform quickly with few or no errors.
4. *Assessing learning.* Information is obtained about the level of learning, the quality of teaching, and future instructional needs.

Figure 12.4 presents a summary of the instructional phases of Alessi and Trollip and the types of instructional computer programs they recommend be used with each phase. In addition, the phases and programs are shown in relation to the PBID lesson-flow stages. Notice that the phases correspond nicely with the PBID lesson-flow stages. The basic difference is that the PBID lesson stages present a more refined breakdown of the instructional process than the phases suggested by Alessi and Trollip.

The first three PBID lesson stages (rationale, need-to-know information, and demonstration) are included in the "presenting information" phase. It is recommended that tutorial and demonstration programs be used for this phase. The fourth lesson stage, guided practice, and the fifth lesson stage, practice for perfection, are equivalent to the "guiding the learner" and the "practice" phases. It is recommended that drills, instructional games, and simulations be used for these phases. The sixth and seventh stages, evaluation and feedback, are included in the "assessing learning" phase. Test programs are recommended for this phase. Simulation programs can be used with any of the phases. They can be used for presentation, practice, and evaluation.

FIGURE 12.4 Relationships Between the PBID Lesson Stages, Phases of Instruction, and Types of Computer Instructional Programs

ALESSI AND TROLLIP

PBID Lesson Stage	Phase of Instruction	Type of Computer Program	
RATIONALE	Presenting information	Tutorial	Simulation (could be used at any phase)
NEED-TO-KNOW INFORMATION			
DEMONSTRATION			
GUIDED PRACTICE	Guiding the learner	Drills and instructional games	
PRACTICE FOR PERFECTION	Practice		
EVALUATION	Assessing learning	Tests	
FEEDBACK			

It is apparent from this discussion that instruction delivered through the CAI lesson delivery format will usually be composed of one or more types of instructional computer programs. The first stages of a lesson would be accomplished with tutorials and simulations; the practice stages, with simulations, drills, and games; and the last stages, with tests and simulations.

FORMATTING COMPUTER-ASSISTED INSTRUCTION (CAI)

The major difference between PI and CAI is the learning resource. In PI, the primary learning resource is a text, while in CAI the primary learning resource is a computer and computer-controlled devices. In both cases, the lesson plan is implicit and learners are presented frames or screens along with directions. The advantage of using CAI over PI is the ability of the computer to more effectively manage complex instruction and to deliver instruction in innovative ways. CAI is not limited by the amount of material that can be placed on paper, the problems of turning pages, and the difficulty of finding material spread out within a text, which can become major deterrents to effective learning. For example, computers can produce animated graphics, quickly access alternative learning branches, control audiovisual devices, and display the output of a variety of devices on the same screen that is used to present text material. They can present tests and store the results, which can be used as a basis for decisions concerning future learning. Computers have opened doors to innovative instruction not available before.

This discussion of the development of CAI-formatted instruction builds on the previous discussion of PI, from which many of the CAI techniques have evolved. Therefore, portions of the developmental process which the two have in common will not be presented again.

Computers are controlled through computer programs. A computer program is a series of instructions that tells a computer what to do. The physical computer and devices attached to it are called *hardware*. Computer programs, including CAI programs, are called *software*. The software tells the hardware what to do in order to accomplish a purpose. Because computers are "dumb" and, unlike people, cannot generalize or make decisions based on past experience, every single decision and action they are to take must be written into the program. The process of writing the program is called *programming*.

The following nine steps would be used with the PBID system to develop a CAI program to present a CAI-formatted lesson. It must be recognized that a CAI program to deliver an entire lesson usually contains separate subprograms (e.g., tutorials, or simulations), to present various portions of the lesson, as was shown in Figure 12.4. These nine steps would be used to develop the total program for a lesson.

1. Structure the lesson.
2. Analyze the content to be taught and detail it into teaching points.
3. Develop a tentative linear flowchart of the content to be presented, practiced, and/or evaluated throughout the lesson.
4. Decide which type of subprogram will be used for each lesson stage, and which materials external to the computer or to computer-controlled devices (e.g., reference manuals) will be used.
5. Develop a tentative storyboard for each subprogram which indicates the content to be presented, practiced, and/or evaluated.
6. Revise the flowchart of the content for each subprogram, if necessary.
7. Develop a screen storyboard and screen sequence which indicate the content to be presented, practiced, and/or evaluated in each screen, and the branches and decision points for each subprogram.
8. Review the entire formatted lesson to make sure that all of the subprograms are adequately coordinated and all components of the lesson are presented.
9. Program the screens to implement the instructional lesson program.

Step 1, lesson structuring, was addressed in Chapters 8 through 10. Table 12.4 presents a sample lesson structure for a CAI-formatted lesson for the first major por-

TABLE 12.4 Lesson Structure

OBJECTIVE

Givens
A needs assessment that identifies the need for an instructional program

Behavior
Develop a program description.

Standard
All of the components of the program description are clearly stated and meet the criteria presented in this lesson.

LESSON STAGE	CONTENT TO BE TAUGHT, PRACTICED, OR EVALUATED	METHODS/MEDIA (CONSISTENT WITH CAI FORMAT)
RATIONALE	*a.* Importance of a program description *b.* Consequences of starting development without a program description	Tutorial
NEED-TO-KNOW INFORMATION	*a.* Components and definitions *b.* The step-by-step procedure for developing a program description	Test/self-check
DEMONSTRATION	Procedure for developing a program description	Simulation
GUIDED PRACTICE	Procedure for developing a program description	Simulation/learner-controlled
PRACTICE FOR PERFECTION	Procedure for developing a program description	Practice/manual (external reference)
EVALUATION	*a.* Knowledge base presented above *b.* Procedure for developing a program description	*a.* Test, written *b.* Test, simulation
FEEDBACK	*a.* Knowledge base presented above *b.* Procedure for developing a program description	*a.* Self-determined/computer-reported results *b.* What to do next

tion of the PBID system presented in this book: "develop a program description." Table 12.5 presents another sample CAI-formatted lesson structure for the lesson "balance an account." In these lesson structures the "methods/media" columns indicate the types of instructional computer programs used at each lesson stage. The computer is assumed to be the medium. However, if additional computer-controlled devices or other learning resources are to be used, they should be indicated as additional media. As with the structuring of any lesson, the methods and media decisions are tentative at this point.

Step 2 is to analyze the content to be taught throughout the lesson and to detail it into teaching points. That process was presented during the discussion of Figure 12.1 and the development of PI.

Step 3 is to develop a tentative linear flowchart of the sequence in which the teaching points will be presented, practiced, and/or evaluated throughout the lesson. Flowcharting is the process of developing a graphic chart that presents the flow of the lesson, or portion of a lesson, to be included in a program. Flowcharting is done at a variety of levels of increasing precision during CAI programming. The first level is to develop a flowchart of the general flow of the content of the program. The second level is to develop a screen sequence, which is a flowchart of the actual screens to be included in the program. If an authoring system is used to develop the program, flowcharting can usually stop at this point. However, if the program is to be programmed in a computer language such as PASCAL or COBOL, a third-level flowchart is also needed which depicts all of the detail needed to write such programs. Flowcharting of computer programs which are written in computer languages such as PASCAL or COBOL is done with a set of standard symbols (Alessi and Trollip, 1985). Sample symbols are presented in Figure 12.5.

Screen sequences are usually flowcharted using symbols which represent the types of screens to be included in the program. A typical set of symbols used in developing screen sequences has been developed by McGraw-Hill to facilitate the development of educational programs using the McGraw-Hill Interactive Authoring System (1984). A copy of a template of those symbols is presented in Figure 12.6. The application of these symbols is presented later in Figure 12.9.

The first-level flowchart should be a linear flowchart of the major flow of the program. It should provide a

TABLE 12.5 Lesson Structure

OBJECTIVE

Givens
A tally sheet indicating the previous account

Behavior
Balance an account.

Standard
The current balance equals the previous balance, plus the credit minus the debits.

LESSON STAGE	CONTENT TO BE TAUGHT, PRACTICED, OR EVALUATED	METHODS/MEDIA (CONSISTENT WITH CAI FORMAT)
RATIONALE	*a.* Importance of a balanced account *b.* Legal consequences of an unbalanced account	Tutorial
NEED-TO-KNOW INFORMATION	*a.* Definitions *b.* The step-by-step procedure for balancing an account	Test/self-check
DEMONSTRATION	Procedure for balancing an account	Simulation
GUIDED PRACTICE	Procedure for balancing an account	Simulation/learner-controlled
PRACTICE FOR PERFECTION	Procedure for balancing an account	Practice/supplemental problem booklet (external reference)
EVALUATION	*a.* Knowledge base presented above *b.* Procedure for balancing an account	*a.* Test, written *b.* Test, simulation
FEEDBACK	*a.* Knowledge base presented above *b.* Procedure for balancing an account	*a.* Self-determined/computer-reported results *b.* What to do next

general picture of how the content will be expected to come together. It should not include all of the decisions or branches. Figure 12.7 presents a first-level flowchart of a tutorial for the first two stages of the lesson "develop a program description." Figure 12.8 presents a first-level flowchart of a tutorial for the first two stages of the lesson "balance an account."

Step 4 in formatting a CAI lesson is to decide which type of subprogram will be used for each lesson stage and which materials external to the computer or computer-controlled devices will be used. The selection of the instructional computer program should follow the logic presented in Figure 12.4. Different types of programs will be needed for different stages of the lesson.

Step 5 is to develop a tentative storyboard for each subprogram. A storyboard presents the written text and anticipated graphics that will be used to present the content. The term *storyboard* comes from the procedure that is used to develop it. Usually the text is written with separate major teaching points on separate sheets. Those sheets are placed on a bulletin board. Tentative ideas for graphics are placed between the sheets of written text. Eventually, the basic message, or story, to be conveyed, and the order in which it will be conveyed, is worked out on the bulletin board. The graphics may eventually be produced as computer-generated graphics or they may be incorporated through computer-controlled devices (e.g., videodisks). If computer-

FIGURE 12.5 Standard Flowcharting Symbols

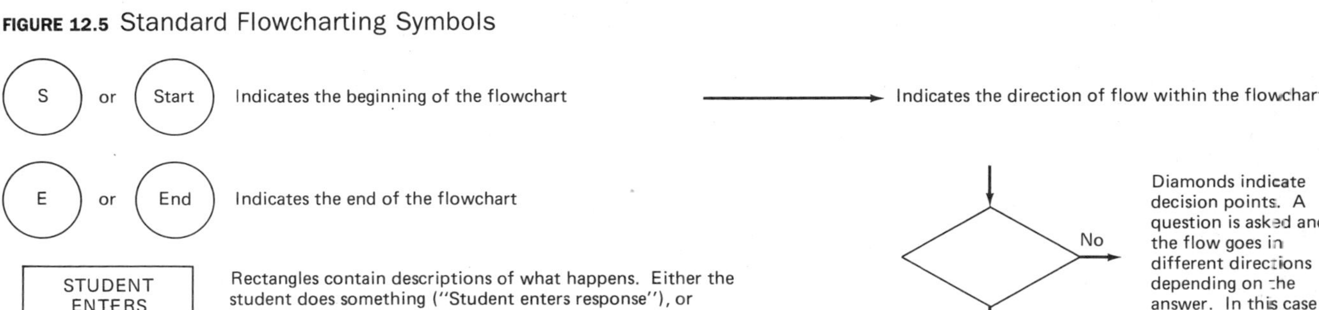

FIGURE 12.6 Screen Sequencing Symbols

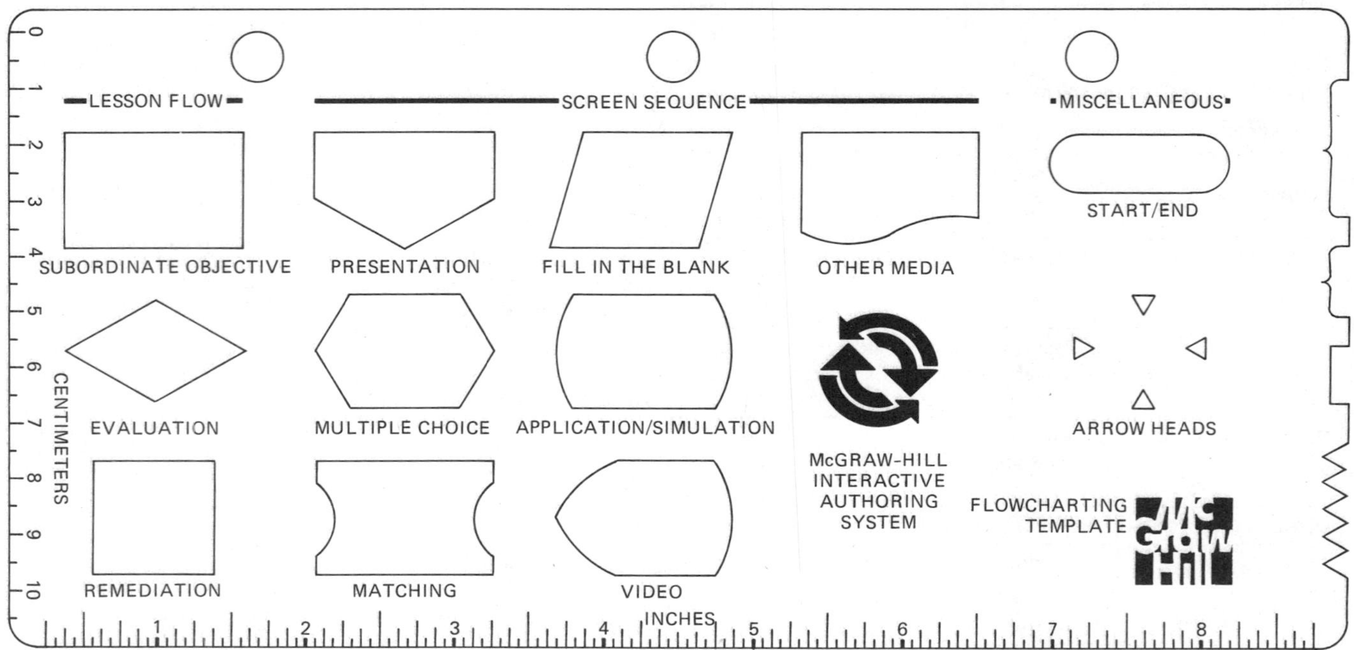

controlled devices are used, it is also possible to utilize audiovisual presentations. The storyboard follows the first-level flowchart.

Step 6 is to revise the flowchart, if necessary. If the telling of the "story" and the flowchart disagree, the flowchart is adjusted in light of the practical limitations of telling the story.

Step 7 is to develop a screen storyboard and screen

FIGURE 12.7 First-Level Flowchart: Develop a Program Description

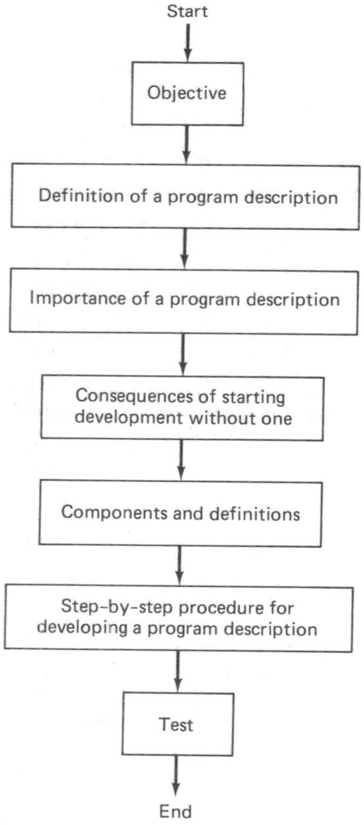

Start
Objective
Definition of a program description
Importance of a program description
Consequences of starting development without one
Components and definitions
Step-by-step procedure for developing a program description
Test
End

FIGURE 12.8 First-Level Flowchart: Balance an Account

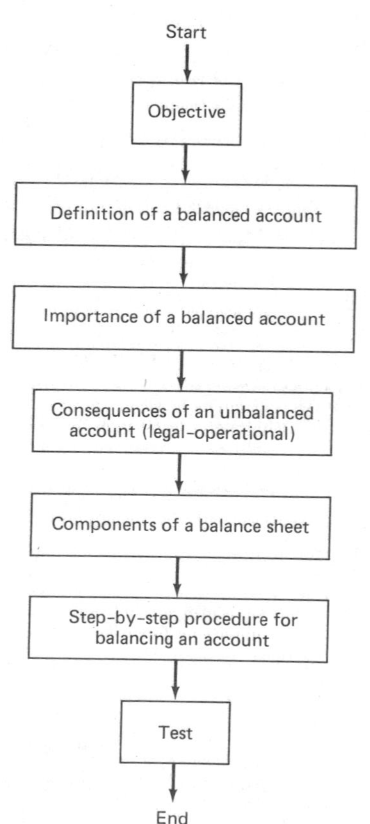

sequence which indicate the content to be presented, practiced, and/or evaluated in each screen and the decision points for each subprogram. After the general storyboard is developed, it is refined into a screen storyboard, and the flowchart is refined into a screen sequence. When developing a screen storyboard, the content to be included in each screen must be identified. Paragraphs of information that would be appropriate for presentation in a written text must be broken down into logical portions that can be presented on a video screen. Screens that indicate decision points on how the program will proceed between sections of screens must be inserted. Alternative remediation branches and branches which accommodate alternative learning styles must be developed. When material from external devices will be used, evaluation points and learner choice options must be inserted. Directions to learners as to how to proceed as they use the program must also be inserted.

Table 12.6 presents the storyboard of screens for a tutorial developed for the first two stages of the lesson "develop a program description." The screens were taken from the CAI program which parallels this book, entitled *Performance-Based Instructional Design* (Pucel, 1986). Notice that each of the screens is coded. This is extremely important during the development of a lengthy program. As the number of screens begins to increase, keeping track of them becomes a substantial developmental problem. Also, the coding allows for the screens to be easily referenced in the flowchart. The coding systems vary between developers. There is no standard. The following system was developed by the author while programming the CAI program mentioned previously. That program included over 700 screens developed over a one-year time period. With this system, the letter indicates the type of content to be presented in the screen. The first digit indicates the program, and the digits after the decimal point indicate the order of that screen in the program. Table 12.7 indicates the code letters for the types of screens and presents a sample screen code. The screen storyboard is accompanied by a flowchart of the screens, called a *screen sequence.* The screen sequence refers to each screen presented in the screen storyboard by code. Figure 12.9 presents such a screen sequence for the screen storyboard presented in Table 12.6. At this point, the elements to be included in the program and subprograms have been identified.

Step 8 in formatting a CAI lesson is to review the entire formatted lesson to make sure that all of the subprograms are adequately coordinated and that all components of the lesson are presented.

Step 9, the last step, is to program the screens to implement the instructional program. All of the information on the screen storyboards, decision points, evaluation items, and management directions must be programmed. It is the program that will communicate to the computer and to the learner instructions needed to

TABLE 12.6 Screen Storyboard: Develop a Program Description

Code	Content
P1.1	The objective of this lesson is to develop a program description.
P1.2	A program description defines the intent of an instructional program.
P1.3	A program description sets the target for program development. It gives the designer a clear definition of the expectations for the program.
P1.4	Just as a hunter would not know where to shoot without a definition of the target, the designer does not know how to focus the program development without a well-developed program description.
G1.5	*Note:* Develop a graphic of a hunter aiming at a target bull's-eye and a designer focusing on the program description.
P1.6	A program description should include: 1. The content area to be taught in the program (e.g., an occupation, a job, and/or basic skills). 2. The context within which the program will be delivered.
P1.7 P1.8 P1.9 P1.10	(Four screens to define program description components along with examples)
A1.11	Sample Program Description CONTENT AREA Basic math skills CONTEXT Program level: Secondary Expected length: One month, 80 hours Program focus: Remediation Institutional setting: Traditional format, in school Relationships to other programs: Basic skills for accounting program Special learner characteristics: Tested math skills below seventh-grade level
D1.12	Depress "F10" is you wish to evaluate your progress → To E1.13 Depress "F8" to complete an exercise → To S1.16 Depress "F1" to continue to the next section → To P2.1 Depress "F9" to return to the main menu → To M

TABLE 12.7 Screen Codes

P = text presentation		*Sample:* D1.12
G = graphic		This screen would be a decision screen in lesson 1. It is the twelfth screen in the lesson.
D = decision		
E = evaluation		
S = simulation		
M = menu		
A = application/example		

FIGURE 12.9 Screen Sequence for "Develop a Program Description"

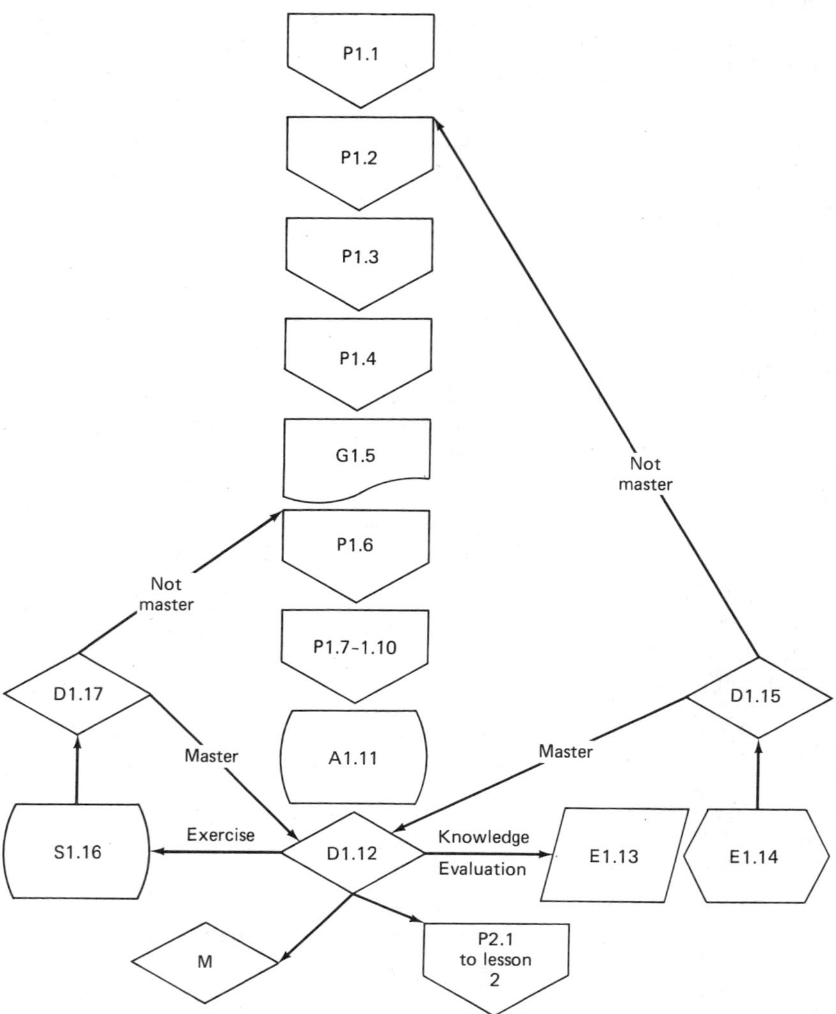

actually implement the instructional program. Chapter 13 presents "Programming Computer-Based Instructional Programs."

SUMMARY

The PI and CAI lesson delivery formats differ from the traditional and modularized formats in that the lesson plans are implicit rather than explicit. With both formats, the lesson delivery format and the primary learning resource are presented through the same medium. In PI, they are presented through a printed text. In CAI, they are presented through a computer. This limits the flexibility of these formats to deliver a variety of types of content. They are most useful in delivering cognitive content associated with cognitive behaviors, or the knowledge base associated with other types of behaviors. They are least useful in the development of psychomotor behaviors, unless the psychomotor behaviors are related to skills in placing responses on paper or to the use of computer devices. The organization of lessons for delivery through PI and CAI requires much greater precision than that needed for traditional instruction or modularized instruction. That is because PI and CAI require not only the development of lesson management and the selection of learning resources, but the detailed development of the learning resource (e.g., a programmed text or a computer program). Although lessons presented through the PI and CAI format are effective in presenting instruction, they do not replace the need for the assistance of an experienced instructor. Materials delivered through these formats can only present instruction in ways in which the original designer developed them. The materials have no ability to adjust themselves to the unanticipated needs of individual learners. An instructor is required to meet these needs.

ACTIVITIES AND EVALUATION

1. Obtain or develop a behavior-detailing sheet for a cognitive behavior which lists the process and knowledge base. Also obtain or develop a lesson

structure for that behavior with the objective and the content to be taught at each stage of the lesson flow specified.

2. Detail the process and/or knowledge base into teaching points using the procedure depicted in Figure 12.1.
3. Develop part of a programmed text with at least six frames which is designed to teach the teaching points identified in activity 2 above.
4. Determine which types of instructional computer programs you would use to teach each stage of the lesson flow.
5. Develop a screen storyboard and screen sequence for one of the programs identified in activity 4 above which includes at least 10 screens and one decision point.

REFERENCES

Alessi, S. M., and S. R. Trollip, *Computer-Based Instruction: Methods and Development,* Prentice-Hall, Englewood Cliffs, NJ, 1985.

Friesen, P. A., *Designing Instruction: A Systematic or "Systems" Approach Using Programmed Instruction as a Model,* Miller Publishing, Santa Monica, CA, 1973.

IBM Programmed Instruction Course: FORTRAN, International Business Machines Corp., IBM Education Center, Endicott, NY, 1963.

McGraw-Hill Interactive Authoring System, McGraw-Hill, New York, 1984.

Pucel, D. J., *Performance-Based Instructional Design,* Performance Training Systems, Inc., St. Paul, MN, 1986.

Scanland, W., and D. Slattery, "The Impact of Computer-Based Instruction upon Teachers," *Educational Technology,* vol. 11, 1983, pp. 32–39.

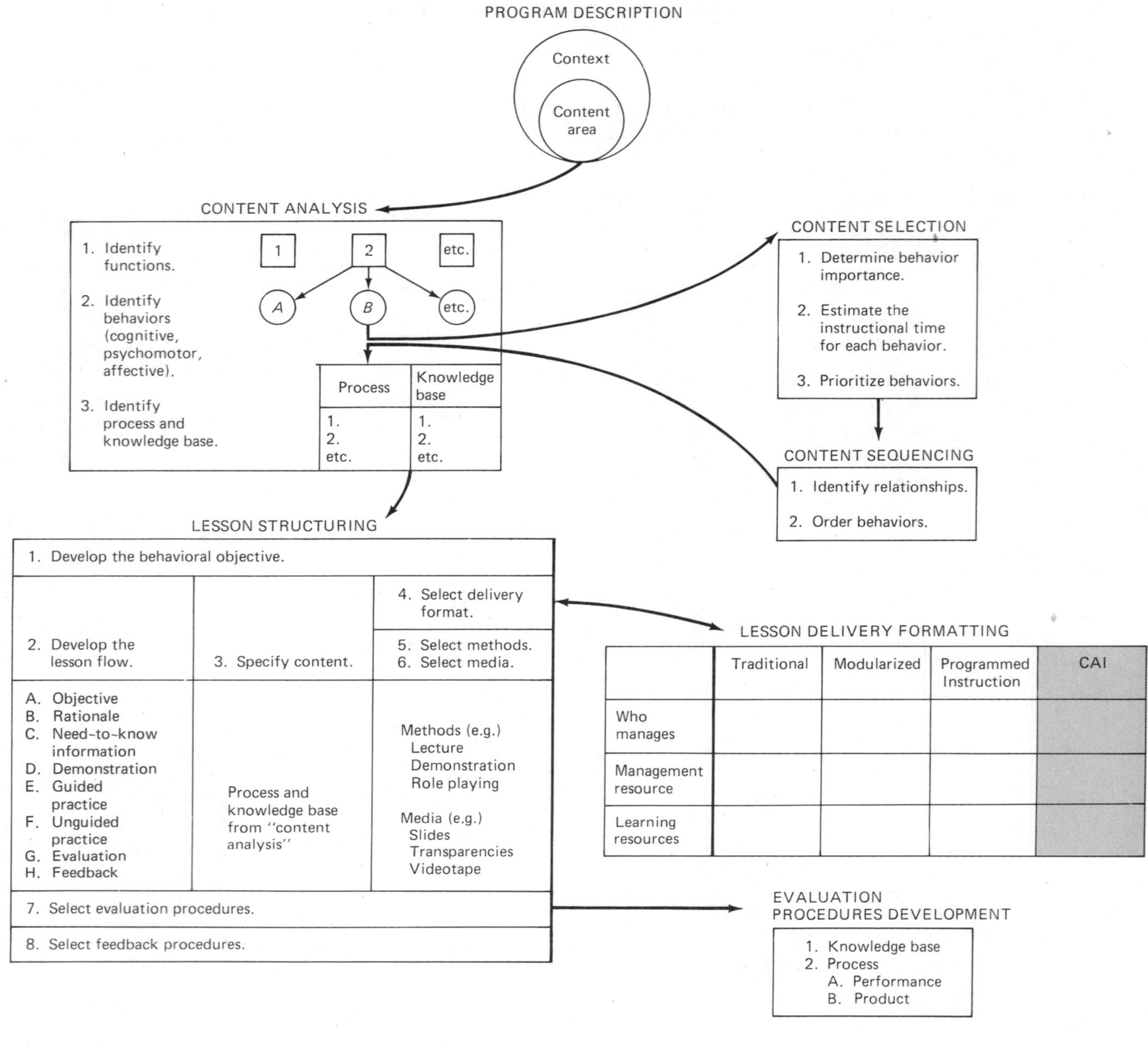

PROGRAM DESCRIPTION
Context
Content area
CONTENT ANALYSIS
1. Identify functions.
2. Identify behaviors (cognitive, psychomotor, affective).
3. Identify process and knowledge base.
1
2
etc.
A
B
etc.
Process
Knowledge base
1.
2.
etc.
1.
2.
etc.
CONTENT SELECTION
1. Determine behavior importance.
2. Estimate the instructional time for each behavior.
3. Prioritize behaviors.
CONTENT SEQUENCING
1. Identify relationships.
2. Order behaviors.
LESSON STRUCTURING
1. Develop the behavioral objective.
2. Develop the lesson flow.
3. Specify content.
4. Select delivery format.
5. Select methods.
6. Select media.
A. Objective
B. Rationale
C. Need-to-know information
D. Demonstration
E. Guided practice
F. Unguided practice
G. Evaluation
H. Feedback
Process and knowledge base from "content analysis"
Methods (e.g.)
Lecture
Demonstration
Role playing
Media (e.g.)
Slides
Transparencies
Videotape
7. Select evaluation procedures.
8. Select feedback procedures.
LESSON DELIVERY FORMATTING
Traditional
Modularized
Programmed Instruction
CAI
Who manages
Management resource
Learning resources
EVALUATION PROCEDURES DEVELOPMENT
1. Knowledge base
2. Process
A. Performance
B. Product

Programming CAI

CHAPTER OBJECTIVE

Given

A screen storyboard and screen sequence for a lesson

Behavior

Select a programming method and hardware, and develop screens.

Standard

The programming method and hardware selected and screen features must be consistent with criteria presented in this chapter.

OVERVIEW

A *program* is a series of instructions to a computer that tell it to execute operations to accomplish a purpose. In the case of CAI, the purpose is to teach people something. Chapter 12 addressed how to format a CAI lesson, how to select subprograms, and how to design those programs. This chapter is an introduction to the selection of a method of programming the computer and the development of the screens. The goal of this chapter is to introduce an instructional designer to elements which need to be considered when deciding to develop and to use an instructional computer program.

COMMUNICATING WITH THE COMPUTER

The computer programs that contain instructions which control a computer are called *software.* All of the physical devices associated with a computer are called *hardware.* The computer itself is considered to be the *central processor,* and all other devices attached to it are called *peripheral devices.* Communication with a computer is accomplished through input and output peripheral devices. *Input devices* are used to communicate information to a computer. *Output devices* are used to receive communication from the computer. The person who utilizes a computer to accomplish a purpose is called a *user.* Figure 13.1 presents a typical microcomputer configuration.

Today most computer users use microcomputers such as the IBM PC series, the Radio Shack TRS-80 series, the COMPAQ PC series, the Zenith series, or the Apple series. These computers can sit on a person's desk and are quite portable. Their small size and portability allow users ready access to actually operate the computers and to engage in interactive communication. In other words, users can communicate directly with the computer through input devices, and the computer communicates directly back to them through output devices. Typical input devices are keyboards, cassette tapes, disks, joysticks, and the mouse. Less typical are tapes, graphic pads, light pens, and videodisks (see the glossary for definitions). Each of these devices has been developed to facilitate the interactive capacity of computers and is small enough to accompany the computer on a standard desk. These devices allow the user to directly input information to the computer in a number of different ways and require relatively little expertise to operate.

Output devices are used to obtain information, or output, from a computer. Typical output devices used for immediate visual output are monitors (television screens), printers, and, to some extent, graphic plotters. Long-term storage of information is output onto disks, tapes, and, to some extent, punched cards. Sound is also possible through a speaker built into the computer.

Besides interactive input-output devices, computer-controlled devices are available that allow for the presentation of other images through the monitor. The output of videotape and videodisk units can be controlled by the computer and displayed on the monitor. This allows for access to both still and motion pictures of real objects as well as the presentation of large, complex, animated graphics.

In addition, microcomputers can be used as terminals to communicate with mainframe computers. A mainframe computer is a large-capacity computer, usually housed at a central location. Its main advantage is speed and storage capacity. When using a microcomputer as a terminal, a user can interact directly with a mainframe in much the same way as he or she can interact with the microcomputer itself. One of the best-known instructional computer systems that uses a mainframe and terminals is the PLATO system, operated by Control Data Corporation.

This brief discussion of computers and alternative input-output devices demonstrates the large array of hardware options open to the instructional designer and computer programmer. The question is: Which should be chosen for a particular instructional application? Although this question can only be answered in conjunction with considering the type of software the computer and its peripherals will be expected to implement, there are some general considerations that should be taken into account when selecting hardware.

SELECTING HARDWARE FOR INSTRUCTIONAL PROGRAMS

The selection of computer hardware for instructional purposes is dependent upon a large number of factors. They include, but are not limited to, the following:

1. Program speed requirements
2. The number of people who will be using the program simultaneously, and their location
3. Memory requirements

FIGURE 13.1 Typical Microcomputer Configuration

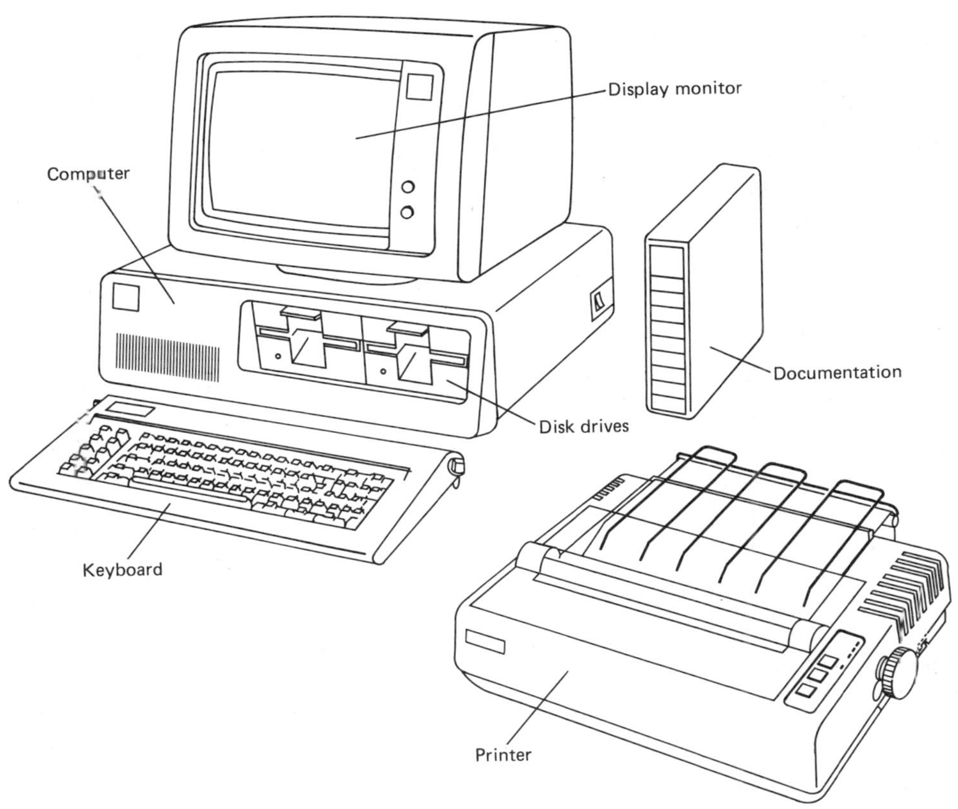

4. The need for interactive video
5. Existing equipment available
6. Type of output required (e.g., color screens and/or printed text)
7. Expertise of potential programmers
8. Budget

It is beyond the scope of this book to discuss all of the types of hardware variations and how they compare on the basis of these factors. The hardware available changes very rapidly, and what is not possible today becomes totally possible within six months. For example, in the early 1980s a 20-megabyte hard disk for a personal computer was as large as a typewriter and very expensive. By the mid-1980s, it was small enough to be placed within a person computer on an expansion card at a price of about one-fourth the original cost. It is recommended that designers consider each of the items presented above and present that information to hardware vendors, or to specialists in the field of instructional computer program development, at the time they are ready to develop a program. This will ensure that the hardware selected is from that which is currently available. Periodicals such as *PC World, A+, inCider,* and *BYTE* are also excellent resources to determine what is currently available. They often provide comparisons of hardware characteristics to accomplish specific purposes.

ALTERNATIVE METHODS OF AUTHORING SOFTWARE

The computer programs that control a computer are called *software.* Programs contain instructions to the computer hardware. Some of the instructions are contained in software, called *operating systems,* which computer manufacturers adopt to control the general operation of their computer hardware. The operating system used with a microcomputer is called a disk operating system (DOS). Examples are MS DOS (used with IBM PCs and compatibles), Apple DOS, and Pro DOS (used with Apple computers). Other software, called *application programs,* contain instructions written by programmers to get the computer to apply itself to a specific purpose or application.

Examples of application software are Lotus 1-2-3, WordStar, WordPerfect, dBASE III, and Performance-Based Instructional Design. Lotus 1-2-3 is designed for accounting applications that require a spreadsheet. WordStar and WordPerfect are designed for word-processing applications. The dBase III software is designed for developing and manipulating data files. Performance-

Based Instructional Design is designed to teach people about instructional design.

Each of these programs is designed for a particular application. However, in order for each of these application programs to operate on a particular computer, it must operate within the parameters of the operating system programs adopted by the manufacturer of that computer. Instructional software, therefore, is written as application programs within the parameters of the operating systems utilized by the hardware manufacturers through which the software will be delivered. Software can rarely be used without modification with a computer that uses a different operating system.

Production of instructional software is quite different from production of other instructional materials. What the programmer writes and enters into the computer often has little, if any, resemblance to the resulting computer output. For example, when writing a paragraph or drawing a diagram, what a person writes on the paper is also the end product. With a computer, the spacing and configuration of a paragraph and the production of a diagram requires the input of code so the computer can produce the paragraph or diagram. Figure 13.2 presents a message for an IBM PC, which appears on the monitor for approximately five seconds, and the corresponding computer code. The code has little resemblance to the way the message appears on the monitor.

Programming Languages

Programming languages are used to communicate with computers. They are very similar to spoken languages (e.g., English or Spanish). Each has its own set of words, symbols, and grammatical rules which have specific meanings. In order to communicate with a computer

FIGURE 13.2 Sample Message and Corresponding BASIC Code

Message: (Approximately five-second duration)

This program is licensed for use by St. Cloud AVTI, St. Cloud, MN. by PERFORMANCE TRAINING SYSTEMS, INC.

BASIC code:

```
1 CLS
10 SCREEN 1
20 LOCATE 10,12
30 PRINT TAB(3);"This program is licensed for use by"
35 PRINT TAB(5);"St. Cloud AVTI, St. Cloud, MN."
40 PRINT
50 PRINT TAB(19);"by"
60 PRINT
70 PRINT TAB(3);"PERFORMANCE TRAINING SYSTEMS,
INC."
100 FOR X=1 TO 3000:NEXT X
200 CLS
500 SYSTEM
```

using a language, the programmer must understand those rules and meanings.

Each computer has its own language, called *assembly code* or *machine language*. It is highly specific to that computer, and it communicates instructions to the hardware. Each language allows a programmer to maximize the flexibility of that computer, but such languages are complex and unique. Therefore, more general programming languages written in a form that more closely resembles English have evolved that can be used with a variety of computers. Common programming languages are PASCAL, COBOL, FORTRAN, BASIC, and PILOT.

In order for the computer to operate, however, directions written in these languages must be translated into the computer's machine language. This translation to machine language is done using specific programs, called *compilers*. Compilers are similar to foreign language translators. For example, a special compiler is needed to convert BASIC to IBM PC machine language.

Authoring Systems

Authoring systems have been developed to further simplify the programming of instructional software. They are even easier to use than programming languages. They vary in the extent to which the material that appears on the screen during programming agrees with what the computer will actually output. The most sophisticated authoring systems are used much like word processing programs. What is produced on the screen during production is what the learner will see when using the program.

An example of such an authoring system is the McGraw-Hill Interactive Authoring System, or MHIAS (McGraw-Hill, 1984). Figure 13.3 presents a screen developed with MHIAS. It has appeared exactly the same during programming with the authoring system.

The authoring system not only has allowed the information to be entered as it would with a standard word processing program, it also has allowed for limited graphics and the selection of colors. Different portions of the text can be different colors on the same screen, and portions of the screen can be flooded with different background colors. For example, the lines making up the box can be red, and the text can be black. The words *content* and *context* actually can be printed in white letters on a black background for emphasis, although they are capitalized here for emphasis.

Because using authoring systems is comparatively easier than using programming languages and machine languages, the question can be asked: Why not always use authoring systems? The reason is that as the ease of authoring increases, the programming flexibility decreases. Also, the more conversions of instructions needed to eventually arrive at machine language instructions, the longer the time it takes for the computer to respond to the instructions. Machine language pro-

FIGURE 13.3 Sample Authoring System Screen

A PROGRAM DESCRIPTION SHOULD INCLUDE
1. The CONTENT area to be taught in the program (e.g., occupation job, basic skills).
2. The CONTEXT within which the program will be delivered.

gramming allows the programmer to ask the computer to do anything the computer has been manufactured to do. It provides maximum flexibility. Other programming languages are each written to facilitate certain kinds of computer applications. In order to maximize one kind of application, a language becomes less efficient in executing other applications. For example, FORTRAN was written primarily to facilitate scientific and statistical applications. COBOL was written primarily to facilitate the processing of business information. PILOT was written to facilitate the development of instructional materials. If COBOL were used to produce scientific or statistical software, it would lead to less efficient programming than if FORTRAN were used.

Most authoring systems are even more specific in purpose. Each authoring system is designed to author a particular type of program. In the case of MHIAS, the system has been designed to develop instructional software. An examination of the screen flowcharting template presented in Figure 12.6 shows the limited types of computer screens that the system has been designed to present. Although they are sufficient to author instructional software aimed at cognitive development, they would not be sufficient to author other types of software, such as that needed to teach architectural drafting. A system for authoring computer-assisted drafting (CAD) instructional material would be more appropriate.

Programs produced with authoring systems tend to be slower than those produced with programming languages. That is because most of them are written in a programming language. For example, MHIAS is written in PASCAL. This requires the software produced with the system to first be stored in PASCAL-compatible formats, and to then be converted from PASCAL to machine language. Such multiple conversions of the programming to arrive at the machine language slow down programs.

SELECTING THE METHOD OF AUTHORING SOFTWARE

In the final analysis, the decision to use a particular method of authoring must be made on the basis of a cost-benefit analysis. The major costs are reflected in personnel time, the cost of the programming software (e.g., the cost of an authoring system or a language compiler), and the cost of operating, or running, the program after it is produced. The benefits are the speed of the final program, the flexibility with which innovative ideas can be programmed and later modified, and the compatibility of the program with a variety of computers. Table 13.1 presents these cost-benefit considerations in selecting authoring methods and shows how each of the three methods of authoring relates to each of the considerations.

Programming in machine language is most costly. The primary cost is that of hiring a programmer who is trained in machine language. Few instructional designers are willing to develop the expertise needed to use machine language. The capability of the computer to be programmed in machine language comes with the purchase of the computer, and there is no need to buy additional languages or authoring systems. Machine language programs provide great flexibility in implementing innovative ideas, and they run very fast. Therefore, the cost of operating the program once it is produced is relatively low. However, machine languages are limited to running on the type of machine for which they were developed, and program modifications are very difficult and usually need to be made by the original programmer.

Programs produced with other programming languages are the next most expensive. Most instructional

TABLE 13.1 Selecting an Authoring Method

	AUTHORING METHODS		
	Machine Language	Other Programming Language	Authoring System
Programming expertise required	Extensive	Substantial	Minimal
Flexibility for different types of applications	Very flexible	Most effective with selected applications	Limited to specific applications
Speed of final program	Fast	Moderate	Slow
Intercomputer compatibility	Little	Substantial	Limited
Program modification	Difficult	Moderate	Easy
Overall production cost	High	Moderate	Low

designers are not likely to develop sufficient expertise to program in these other languages, but many are willing to learn enough about them to understand programming concerns relative to instructional design. Although programming expertise tends to be more available than machine language expertise, it is expensive to hire programmers. An additional, but minimal, cost is that of purchasing the compiler to translate the language selected. The use of programming languages produces the next most flexible programs in terms of possible innovations. However, each language has been designed to optimize certain types of programming, and the appropriate language must be selected for a particular application. The programs run moderately fast; they can be run on many different computers so long as they have compilers which can translate that language. Program modifications are moderately difficult and need to be made by experienced programmers.

Programming produced with authoring systems is the least costly. Although authoring systems are more expensive to purchase than programming languages, and although the cost of operating the programs in terms of computer time is high, the personnel costs involved with producing the programs is usually much less because of their ease of operation. Instructional designers can easily develop the expertise to produce programs with authoring systems. They are no more difficult to operate than word processing programs. Therefore, it is less likely that a separate computer programmer would have to be hired. However, the programming of innovative ideas with authoring systems is limited. Each authoring system is designed to produce instructional programs of a particular type, and the screen options available have been developed with that type of program in mind. Intercomputer compatibility of programs produced with an authoring system is limited. The computer operating systems must be the same. In other words, programs produced for the IBM PC will not run on Apple computers. The speed at which the programs operate is relatively slow. Programs are relatively easy to modify.

DEVELOPING SCREENS

The purpose of any method of authoring instructional software is to produce screens that teach effectively. The various types of programming methods discussed in the preceding paragraphs are only alternative ways of generating screens and procedures for managing them during instruction. This section on developing screens is not intended to allow instructional designers to develop expert skills in screen development and management. It is intended to provide an understanding of basic considerations in designing screens so that their instructional effectiveness can be maximized. This understanding is important so that CAI lessons can be effectively designed and formatted. People interested in further detailed programming techniques for the development and management of screens should consult other sources such as *Computer-Based Instruction: Methods and Development* (Alessi and Trollip, 1985), *Tutorial Instruction on a Computer* (Dennis, 1979), *Screen Design Strategies for Computer-Assisted Instruction* (Heines, 1984), *Designing Instructional Computing Materials* (MECC, 1981), and *Microcomputer/Videodisc Courseware Design* (DeBloois, 1982). In addition, each of the major authoring systems available have manuals which address the development of the types of screen which can be produced and managed with that system.

Major screen design considerations can be categorized into the following eight items:

1. Content organization
2. Text writing
3. Scrolling
4. Graphics
5. Density
6. Highlighting
7. Interactive video segments
8. Conventions

Content Organization

The purpose of a screen is to effectively present content to learners so that they can accomplish an instructional objective. Therefore, the content organization within a screen is just as important as the content organization within a program and a lesson. In general, the content should be presented in a functional manner. It should build from the top down, and from the left-hand side to the right-hand side, just as it would if it were on the printed page of a text. The learner should first encounter information that clearly identifies the screen content. In other words, it should answer the questions: "What is the point of viewing this screen?" "What does it contain?" This can be done through techniques such as using a heading or highlighting the key words in the text to focus the learner on the main point of the screen. The example presented in Figure 13.3 uses both techniques. The screen has a heading presented in a box, and key words which identify each component of a program description are highlighted with capital letters.

Graphics, such as diagrams or caricatures, should be placed in logical reference to the text. In other words, at times a text description should be followed by a graphic example because a graphic is an example of what has been presented in the text. At other times, a graphic should be followed by explanatory text because text explains the graphic example. Determination of the order of the graphic and text should be based on the logical presentation of the material; it should not be left to chance. This same type of relationship is important if interactive video presentations are used. Video presentations need to be placed in logical relation to the accompanying text.

Text Writing

The writing of text for CAI screens is very different from the writing of text for a manuscript, book, or letter. To maintain learner interest and focus, the screen text should be written in a telegraphic style; in other words, information should be written more like a telegram to a friend than a letter. A screen has only limited space; however, in order for learners to easily grasp a teaching point the entire teaching point should be presented on one screen. In a book, readers can easily look up and down the page to review how the material they are reading relates to other portions of the page and to other ideas. Once a screen has been read and the learner moves on, referring to that screen again becomes relatively difficult. If a major point is separated onto multiple screens, the likelihood of the learner effectively grasping the teaching point is reduced. If a teaching point cannot be placed within one screen, then it should be broken down into a number of logical units which can each be placed on a separate screen. These separate screens should be preceded by a screen which indicates the relationship among the parts of the teaching point that will be covered in the next screens. The screen presented in Figure 13.3 demonstrates this technique. It is not possible to discuss the components of a program description adequately in one screen; therefore, each of the components should be identified first and subsequent screens should then present more in-depth discussions of these components.

Scrolling

Designers try to bypass the problem of rewriting text for CAI into telegraphic style by using scrolling. Scrolling means adding new text lines to the bottom line of the screen and moving everything else up. The effect is that of a window moving down the page of a book and allowing the viewer to see only what is in the window. Most people find it difficult to physically read scrolling text, and it is very difficult to differentiate teaching points from one another. Rather than use scrolling text within CAI, the designer is advised to use standard printed text material.

Graphics

Graphics refer to nontext material which is pictorial. The pictorial information might be in the form of caricatures, graphs, charts, or graphic pictures. Graphics usually appear on the screen with accompanying text. They are used to increase teaching effectiveness. Graphics should be used to highlight the point to which the learner should be attending. They should not be used as entertainment which detracts from attending to the material to be learned. Flemming and Levie (1978) point out that graphics have the capacity to attract attention more than text. If graphics complement what is being presented in the text, they are an aid; if they do not, they detract from the instructional goal. In general, the simpler the form of graphic that makes the instructional point, the better.

Density

Density refers to how much of the screen is covered with text or graphics. The screen should be pleasing and easy to look at. Text should not be squeezed into one part of the screen with other parts totally vacant. Spacing should be attractive; text should be readable; and the major points to be learned should be apparent. Although there are no widely accepted rules for determining screen density, the author has found that a screen is most effective if no more than 50 percent of it is covered with text. Blank space can include margins and double spacing between major points. This ratio for the total screen density can change if graphics are used. The space available for text should still be only 50 percent filled, but the spacing of the graphic should be based on what is pleasing to the eye. The overriding consideration in determining screen density is whether the screen is pleasing to the eye.

Highlighting

Highlighting refers to techniques used to call attention to particular portions of the text or graphics. Highlighting can be done in a variety of ways. The most common are accomplished through using a variety of type fonts, underlining, boxes, color, and blinking. It is generally recommended that text be presented in a type font similar to that used in standard books and that one type font be used throughout a program. Examples, or the text surrounding graphics, might use different fonts for emphasis. Upper- and lowercase letters should be used, not all capital letters, since people are used to reading such text. Underlining, boxes, color, and blinking should be used only where emphasis is required. If they are used indiscriminately, their value is reduced: learners will not be able to differentiate what is important from what is not. The exception is the use of colors as conventions for screen borders. For example, in the performance-based instructional design program referred to earlier, all of the presentation screens were surrounded with a purple border, all evaluation screens were surrounded by a red border, and all of the menus were presented with white letters on a black background. This allows learners to identify the types of screens by the color of the borders.

Interactive Video Segments

Interactive video segments of a program are accomplished through screens which can activate a computer-controlled video device such as a videotape recorder or a videodisk player. Such screens should present information that orients learners to video segments and should provide them with directions concerning how to activate the segments. At times, the orientation may include multiple screens that precede the activation of the video device. Videoscreens activate video devices by instructing the computer to access marked sections on a tape or disk to be played back through the monitor.

It is important to use only video segments that are integral to the lesson being presented. At times, designers mistakenly use video to make programs more appealing and entertaining. Care must be taken not to become so concerned about the entertainment value of the video that the educational goal becomes clouded. Video should be used when learners can benefit from observing real-life situations and real objects, or when graphics are very complex and lengthy and standard computer memory devices cannot efficiently produce them. For example, animated graphics are possible on a microcomputer, but they take a lot of memory storage. The use of a videodisk to play back a recorded animated graphic may be more efficient.

Conventions

Conventions refer to programming practices that are common throughout a program. Learners tend to be more comfortable, and they can learn to use programs more quickly and effectively, if things are done in the same way throughout a program. The following is a list of items contained in programs for which adopting conventions is recommended:

1. The location of directions (e.g., along the bottom of the screens)
2. The types of responses that the learner will typically have to make (e.g., depress the space bar to continue; depress "B" to back up)
3. The way new topics or teaching points are introduced (e.g., in capital letters, with the same color, and/or in a box)
4. The use of consistent paragraph structures, centering, and margins
5. The use of standard colors for borders on the same types of screens (e.g., purple for presentation screens and red for evaluation screens)

SUMMARY

The programming of subprograms used with the CAI delivery format requires unique skills and expertise in both hardware selection and the actual programming of screens. Both hardware and programming methods vary substantially in terms of cost and the expertise needed to operate them. Therefore, an instructional designer must conduct a cost-benefit analysis of both hardware and programming methods before undertaking the development and programming of CAI.

Regardless which hardware and programming methods are selected, a person must always keep in mind the major purpose of developing a program. That purpose is to develop screens that lead to effective instruction focused on an instructional objective. The purpose of each subprogram should be clearly specified during lesson structuring. Screens must be designed and developed to clearly communicate the instructional message. In order to accomplish this goal for each screen, the eight categories of screen development factors presented must be considered.

ACTIVITIES AND EVALUATION

1. Obtain or develop a screen storyboard and screen sequence for a CAI subprogram which is based on the planning techniques presented in Chapter 12. They should include at least 10 screens and one decision point.
2. Select the hardware with which the program will be developed and used. Justify the hardware selection based on the hardware selection factors presented in this chapter.
3. Select a programming method and justify your selection based on the considerations presented in Table 13.1.
4. Lay out two screens which present or evaluate information and one decision screen. Describe how each layout (e.g., the organization of the content within the screen and/or highlighting) is intended to accomplish your instructional goal.
5. Indicate whether a graphic or interactive video segment would, or would not, enhance the presentation. If one would enhance the presentation, what would be included and how would the presentation be enhanced?

REFERENCES

Alessi, S. M., and S. R. Trollip, *Computer-Based Instruction: Methods and Development,* Prentice-Hall, Englewood Cliffs, NJ, 1985.

DeBloois, M., *Microcomputer/Videodisc Courseware Design,* Educational Technology Publications, Englewood Cliffs, NJ, 1982.

Dennis, R. J., *Tutorial Instruction on a Computer,* report no. 6e, Department of Secondary Education, University of Illinois, Urbana, 1979.

Fleming, M., and W. H. Levie, *Instructional Message Design: Principles From the Behavioral Sciences,* Educational Technology Publications, Englewood Cliffs, NJ, 1978.

Heines, J. M., *Screen Design Strategies for Computer-Assisted Instruction,* Digital Press, Bedford, MA, 1984.

McGraw-Hill Interactive Authoring System, McGraw-Hill, New York, 1984.

MECC, *Designing Instructional Computing Materials,* Minnesota Educational Computing Consortium, St. Paul, 1981.

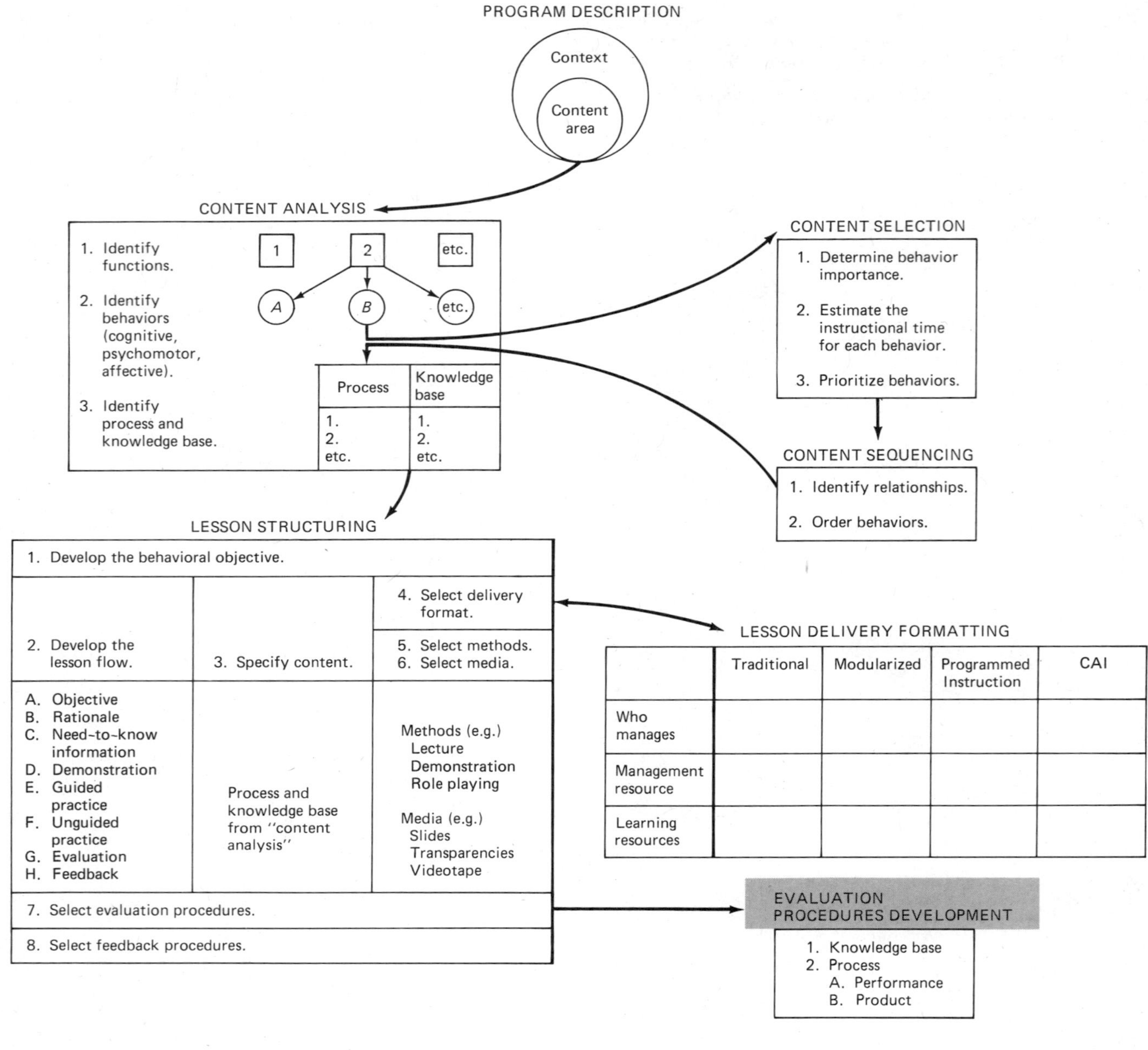

PROGRAM DESCRIPTION
Context
Content area
CONTENT ANALYSIS
1. Identify functions.
2. Identify behaviors (cognitive, psychomotor, affective).
3. Identify process and knowledge base.
1
2
etc.
A
B
etc.
Process
Knowledge base
1.
2.
etc.
1.
2.
etc.
CONTENT SELECTION
1. Determine behavior importance.
2. Estimate the instructional time for each behavior.
3. Prioritize behaviors.
CONTENT SEQUENCING
1. Identify relationships.
2. Order behaviors.
LESSON STRUCTURING
1. Develop the behavioral objective.
2. Develop the lesson flow.
3. Specify content.
4. Select delivery format.
5. Select methods.
6. Select media.
A. Objective
B. Rationale
C. Need-to-know information
D. Demonstration
E. Guided practice
F. Unguided practice
G. Evaluation
H. Feedback
Process and knowledge base from "content analysis"
Methods (e.g.)
Lecture
Demonstration
Role playing
Media (e.g.)
Slides
Transparencies
Videotape
7. Select evaluation procedures.
8. Select feedback procedures.
LESSON DELIVERY FORMATTING
Traditional
Modularized
Programmed Instruction
CAI
Who manages
Management resource
Learning resources
EVALUATION PROCEDURES DEVELOPMENT
1. Knowledge base
2. Process
A. Performance
B. Product

Introduction to Evaluation Procedures Development

CHAPTER OBJECTIVES

Given

The need to develop evaluations of learning

Behavior

Recall when and why to evaluate the dangers of evaluation error, and the characteristics of good evaluation.

Standard

Evaluation error and the characteristics of good evaluation must be related to the purposes of evaluation.

OVERVIEW

Before beginning to develop evaluation instruments, it is important to clearly understand why and when to evaluate learning, possible sources of evaluation error, and the characteristics of good evaluation instruments. These concepts are important in the development of all evaluations and apply equally to the evaluation of cognitive, affective, and psychomotor behavior.

OVERALL GOAL OF EVALUATION

The overall goal of educational evaluation has changed as the role of education in society has changed. Prior to the 1960s, the primary goal of evaluation was selection. That goal was based on the philosophy that only the "best" learners should continue to pursue an education in a particular content area and that society needed relatively few well-educated people. People with minimal educations were assumed to be able to become productive citizens, based on the composition of society and jobs available. Consistent with this belief, learners were judged using "norm-referenced" procedures and learning was "graded" based on what was known as the "curve." The curve was used to compare the performance of individuals in a class against the performance of others in the class. Those individuals who did "best" received an *A*, and those who did "worst" received in *F*. Those who received an *F* were essentially selected out of an opportunity for further education in that particular content area. The responsibility for learning was placed almost solely on the learner. Tests were considered to be selection devices.

Since the 1960s, the philosophy toward education has changed, and with it, the primary goal of evaluation. People now believe that individuals should be helped to learn to their full potentials and that the responsibility for learning is not only on the learner, but also on the instructor. In light of this philosophy, the primary focus of evaluation has become diagnostic. Students are taught, evaluations are administered, and the results are judged against a desired performance standard. Results become input for determining the direction of further instruction. If learners do not accomplish an educational objective, the instructor is expected to help them to meet that objective.

It is virtually impossible to examine evaluation instruments to determine which of these philosophies (selection or diagnostic) the instrument is attempting to implement. Well-constructed evaluation instruments look the same. What philosophy an instructor has, however, is crucial to how the instruments are used during the evaluation process. Throughout this book, the discussion of evaluation procedures is founded on the concept that they should be used as diagnostic tools during the learning process in order to facilitate learning.

THE TIMING AND INTENT OF EVALUATION

Educational evaluation can be conducted at various times for a variety of intents. Figure 14.1 indicates when a person should evaluate for a given intent.

Pretesting

Pretests are instruments that are administered to learners prior to their taking part in instruction. They are used to determine how much learners know about the content associated with an instructional objective prior to instruction. If the curriculum allows for it, learners who have "mastered the content" associated with an objective (both the knowledge base and the process) should be allowed to skip ahead to another objective. For example, learners who demonstrate mastery of how to change a tire on a pretest should be allowed to move on to instruction on another aspect of car repair without having to receive instruction on how to change a tire.

If learners do not demonstrate mastery, the instructor can use the pretest information to diagnose where in-

FIGURE 14.1 The Timing and Intent of Evaluation

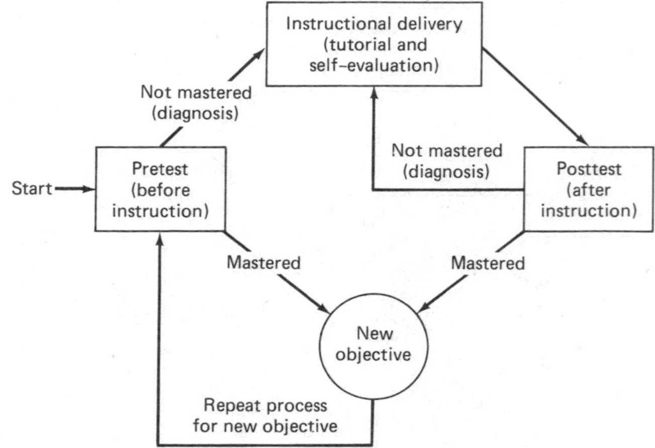

struction should begin for each of them. Maybe a learner has already mastered a portion of the content, and all of the instruction regarding changing a tire is not necessary. Although the chart does not show it, the instructor could also find that the learner needs more instruction than was planned for in the lesson. The learner may not possess the prerequisite information necessary to meaningfully enter the lesson on changing a tire. Therefore, remediation may be necessary before the learner enters instruction.

Testing During Instructional Delivery

The main purpose of evaluation during the delivery of instruction is to obtain information that is useful in adjusting instruction as learners are guided toward mastery. Evaluation during this period can be formal and/or informal. A detailed discussion of the types of instruments that are used to gather information during the instructional process, and how to select them, is presented in Chapter 10. The reader should review Table 10.1 to be reminded of the different types of instruments and when they should be used.

Posttesting

Posttests take place after the instruction regarding an objective has been assumed to be completed. They are used to determine the extent to which learners have mastered the process and knowledge base associated with the behavior; they are also used as a basis for recording progress. Posttests are also called *criterion examinations* or *competency certification examinations* because they are used to judge the extent to which a person has met the predetermined standards for mastery.

If learners have mastered the content, they are allowed to proceed to instruction on another objective. If learners have not mastered the content, they are usually allowed to take part in additional instruction in order to master the content. If this happens, the posttest is used in the same way as an evaluation conducted during instructional delivery: as a basis for diagnosing and adjusting the learning process.

EVALUATING VERSUS MEASURING

In order to effectively evaluate learner progress, vocational educators and trainers in business and industry must differentiate measuring from evaluating. *Measuring* is the process of determining the dimensions, capacity, or amount of something. It is usually accomplished with relatively precise instruments and devices which have relatively little error. For example, the diameter of a piece of steel can be measured with a micrometer. The volume of a liquid can be measured with a measuring cup. Voltage can be measured with a voltmeter. In each case, if the measuring device is not damaged or if the quantity or size of that which is being measured has not been destroyed, one can measure repeatedly and arrive at essentially the same measurement. This is because the facet of the object or substance to be measured is well defined and is usually singular (e.g., diameter, volume, or voltage), and the measuring instrument is relatively precise (e.g., a micrometer, a cup, or a voltmeter).

Evaluation is the process of determining the significance or worth of something by careful appraisal and study. The concept of evaluation is used when determining learner progress. It is usually characterized by instruments (e.g., tests, checklists, and rating scales) which are not as precise as those used to measure physical phenomena. It is also characterized by the need to gather and synthesize more than one type of data to arrive at a determination of the extent of learning (e.g., data on process as well as knowledge-base mastery). Therefore, some of the perspectives which people have when measuring need to be changed when evaluating learners. Although the two concepts are similar, they also have important differences.

For example, when measuring the diameter of a piece of steel, one would be sensible to record the measurement in thousandths of an inch. However, when recording a written test score, one would not be sensible to record the score to the third decimal place. Also, if the performance of learners is being compared, a 1-point difference between learners is usually not very significant. Tests do not produce results to that level of precision. Evaluation of learning progress also differs from measurement in the need to combine different types of information to determine if a person has mastered the content (e.g., information on process mastery from performance and product evaluations and information from written and oral tests). This is in contrast to measuring one facet of an object to determine its length.

It is important to remember that evaluation of learning is complex in that it usually requires the gathering of multiple pieces of information to make judgments about the adequacy of learning, and that the instruments used to gather the data are not as precise as devices used when measuring. Care needs to be taken in interpreting and using scores obtained from educational evaluation instruments. The reason the evaluation instruments are not as accurate as devices used during measuring is because of error.

EVALUATION ERROR

The term *error,* when used in the context of educational evaluation, refers to differences in scores on evaluation instruments that are due to factors other than differences in amount of learning. For example, if two learners have learned exactly the same amount but receive different test scores because one was sick while taking the test, the difference in scores is due to error caused by being sick rather than to a difference in the amount of learning. If the two learners have learned the same amount, and if no factors have contributed to error, one would assume that they would both achieve the same score.

All evaluations have some error, regardless of how precise they are intended to be. Designers must control that error as much as possible. In order to do so, they must be aware of the types of error that might affect evaluations. Error can arise from four major sources: (1) the learner, (2) the instrument, (3) the scorer, and (4) guessing.

Learner Error

Learner error refers to evaluation error caused by the learner which is not related to level of content mastery. For example, a learner might not read a test item carefully and, therefore, he might respond with the wrong answer. Another learner might put the answer in the wrong place because she skipped a previous item. Another learner might miss a word while reading a question. This type of error is difficult to control. An instructor can try to minimize it by trying to eliminate the factors which contribute to it. For example, the instructor can: (1) caution learners to check their answers before turning the test in, (2) motivate learners to do their best, (3) make sure the test is administered in a comfortable environment (e.g., with good lighting, heating, and seating, and little noise), and/or (4) administer the evaluations when learners are more likely to be rested (e.g., early in the class period rather than at the end). Even though an instructor addresses these issues, however, he or she cannot control factors such as the emotional condition of the learner or the amount of sleep the learner had the night before.

Instrument Error

Instrument error is due to failure of an evaluation instrument to produce the same results from learners who perform the same. The most obvious example is if all learners are tested on the same piece of equipment and it wears out during the testing process. The first learner would be tested on a new piece of equipment, and the last learner would be tested on a worn piece of equipment. Even though both learners might perform the same, they would not obtain the same test result because of the wear on the equipment.

Instrument error is also possible when written tests are used. Items may be written in such a way that the careful learner might misinterpret them and put down the wrong answers. Instrument error, in this case, is usually due to inability on the part of the designer to communicate with the learner through the evaluation instrument items. Learners might read the items and not understand them, or they might get the impression that they should do something other than what is intended. A primary source of this type of error is the difference between the vocabulary of the learners and the designers. For example, instructors may use specialized terminology while developing their evaluation instruments without considering that those terms may not have been taught yet. Since most beginning learners would not understand these terms, test items that include them might make no sense and the learners might guess at or misunderstand them. This type of error is not due to guessing or carelessness; it is due to the instrument.

Scorer Error

Scorer error occurs when evaluation responses are judged inconsistently. In other words, learners actually give the same responses but are judged differently. This type of error often occurs because the person who designed the instrument did not adequately indicate how a scorer should judge the extent to which a response is correct. Since the scorer (usually the instructor) does not know exactly what the correct answer should be, a great deal of unfocused judgment must be used to determine learning progress. The problem is not that the instructor has exercised judgment, but that such judgment rarely can be applied uniformly to all learners. The instructor may try to be very objective and free of personal bias, but without adequate guidance, his or her judgments will be influenced by many irrelevant factors. For example, if the learner is very similar to the scorer, the scorer tends to judge higher; or if the grammar and neatness of the answer are good, the scorer tends to judge higher. These factors do not relate to how well the learner has mastered the content, but they relate to other factors which the scorer cannot separate from his or her judgments. Therefore, adequate criteria which scorers can use to judge the evaluation responses are important. Without them, the evaluator will apply her or his personal standards of performance. If another instructor judges the same person's responses, different results are likely to occur.

Guessing Error

Guessing error refers to error caused by people not knowing an answer and guessing it. Guessing causes a learner's score on an instrument to vary from one time to another, even though his or her knowledge does not vary. If a learner took a test yesterday and happened to have guessed some items correctly, the score will tend to be higher than the actual level of learning. The score will be equal to the amount of the learner's knowledge, reflected by those items he or she has answered correctly because of knowing the content, plus the items answered correctly because of correct guessing. If the learner takes the same test tomorrow and no new learning has taken place, the new score will be equal to the score she or he gets because of knowing the content, plus the score on those that will be guessed correctly. If during the second administration of the test she or he guesses fewer items correctly, the score will be lower than the first score. Therefore, during both test administrations the part that the learner actually knew would result in the same score, but total scores would vary based on the difference in how well he or she guessed the first time and how well she or he guessed the second time.

In summary, there are many sources of error that can affect a test score. All of them contribute to inaccurate judgments of learning progress. Therefore, they must be controlled as much as possible during the development of evaluation procedures and instruments. Failure to do so will minimize the effectiveness and usefulness of evaluations.

NEED FOR MULTIPLE EVALUATIONS

The error associated with any one assessment can be minimized by conducting a number of different assessments and averaging their results. For example, even when machinists want an accurate measurement of the diameter of a steel cylinder, they measure the diameter a number of times at different places with a micrometer and average the readings to obtain an average reading. The average reading is correct more often than any of the separate readings. When determining a person's blood count, medical laboratory personnel test a number of samples and calculate an average to obtain a more accurate evaluation. If multiple measurements are used as a basis for accuracy in such exact situations as micrometer reading and blood counting, the need for multiple assessments in education to arrive at an evaluation of learning progress should be apparent.

Multiple assessments need not always mean multiple instruments. It is also possible to conduct multiple assessments within one instrument by having a number of items which assess the same thing. For example, in a written test it is possible to write a number of items on each major knowledge-base objective with each item being an assessment of that objective. Therefore, within the one test, each knowledge-base objective would have been assessed multiple times.

CHARACTERISTICS OF GOOD EVALUATION

Evaluation procedures are designed to assess the extent to which learners have mastered content that has been or is to be taught. In order to ensure that evaluation procedures adequately do this, the instructional designer must design them with a set of characteristics. He or she should become thoroughly familiar with these characteristics since they are critical to the reduction of evaluation error. They will be continually referred to during later discussions of constructing evaluation instruments. Each of these characteristics is presented along with examples.

Validity

The most important characteristic of an evaluation instrument is *validity.* Validity refers to whether an instrument measures what you want it to measure. For example, an instrument designed to assess whether a learner can disassemble and assemble a two-barrel carburetor should provide information which will allow someone to judge the extent to which learners have mastered that behavior. Validity is considered to be the most important characteristic because if an instrument possesses validity, it also possesses each of the other characteristics of a good instrument. However, if an instrument does not possess each of the characteristics discussed below, it will not be valid. This will become more clear as the discussion progresses.

Comprehensiveness

Evaluation instruments should be *comprehensive.* A comprehensive instrument is one that reflects all of the content to be assessed by the instrument. This characteristic ensures that the instrument is measuring the right content. A comprehensive instrument need not include all possible items that could be written, but the items that are included should sample all of the content to be assessed.

For example, if we want to assess a person's competence on a behavior with five knowledge-base objectives, the instrument must be designed to assess proficiency on all five objectives. If it does, it will be a comprehensive evaluation of that knowledge base. If, however, the evaluation instrument includes items which assess only four of the five knowledge-base objectives, the instrument will not comprehensively assess the knowledge base for that behavior. Comprehensiveness applies not only to knowledge-base evaluation, but also to process evaluation. All of the important process steps or actions must be reflected in a performance or product evaluation, or it will not be comprehensive.

As an evaluation instrument is designed, comprehensiveness must be conscientiously considered. It is very easy to construct items only on those knowledge-base objectives which lend themselves most readily to evaluation. If an instrument is not comprehensive, it cannot be valid because it does not reflect all of the content the designer wants to assess. Content mastery cannot be validly judged based on an assessment of only a portion of the content.

Discrimination

In order for an instrument to be valid, it must also discriminate. *Discrimination* refers to whether an instrument is capable of separating those who have learned the content being assessed from those who have not. Just because learners attain different scores on an instrument does not necessarily mean that they have actually learned different amounts of the content. Instruments can be poorly constructed; items may not address the basic factors which differentiate those who have mastered the content from those who have not. Some items may pertain to relatively insignificant facts, or pieces of information, which are not truly related to whether a person has mastered the desired behavior. Therefore, although different learners may attain different scores, the scores may not reflect the extent to which they have mastered the behavior.

Only items that are directly related to whether a person has mastered the behavior should be included in an instrument. For example, if a designer is interested in determining if a person possesses the knowledge base for the behavior "change a tire," the test items should address the knowledge-base objectives for that behavior. If the designer includes items on the historical evolution of tires, differences in scores may be due to knowledge of that history rather than to the extent of mastery of the desired knowledge base.

In order to ensure that an instrument will discriminate, a designer should review the instrument after it has been developed to detect items that obviously measure irrelevant content, and develop the instrument with constant focus on the content to be taught. [The content should have been identified during content analysis (see Chapter 7) and further defined relative to specific evaluations during lesson structuring (see Chapter 10)].

Since the goal of evaluation is to separate those who have mastered the content from those who have not, an instrument that does not discriminate is not valid.

Objectivity

An *objective instrument* is one that can be scored consistently. Different individuals scoring an objective instrument will arrive at the same score for the same person. Earlier, scoring error was discussed. If an instrument is truly objective, scoring error is eliminated.

The opposite of an objective instrument is a *subjective instrument.* A subjective instrument is one which calls for scorer judgment during the scoring process. Because different scorers exercise judgment in different ways, the scores which they assign to the same individual using a subjective instrument will tend to be different. Throughout our discussions concerning instrument development the need to develop instruments which are as objective as possible will be stressed. Since the goal of evaluation is to assess a person's actual proficiency regarding the content, an instrument which is not objective does not allow us to measure what we want to measure. Therefore, an instrument which lacks objectivity also lacks validity.

Reliability

Reliability refers to the ability of an instrument to produce consistent results. It is a reflection of the total amount of error in an evaluation. If an evaluation has one or more sources of error, the results will not be consistent, and therefore, it will not be reliable. For example, if Mary and Joe have developed exactly the same amount of knowledge relating to types of robots, they should both obtain the same score on a test designed to measure that knowledge. If they have the same amount of knowledge but do not obtain the same score, the test is not producing consistent results and is not reliable. Another example of inconsistent results is Mary taking the same test twice (without additional learning between them) and getting a different score each time. In this case, Mary has the same knowledge, but the test score obtained from the instrument changes. Such a test would be unreliable. An unreliable test is not valid.

Just because a test is reliable, however, does not mean that it is valid. It is possible to have a reliable test which produces consistent results but which measures the wrong content. For example, a highly reliable test developed for a machine shop course would be of little value to someone teaching practical nursing. It would be reliable because it produces highly consistent results, but it would not be valid because it does not measure the content you want it to measure. In order for a test to be valid, it must be comprehensive, objective, discriminate, and reliable.

From the discussion above, it is apparent that the primary desired characteristic of any evaluation is validity. There are many possible sources of error that can make an evaluation invalid. Each of the other characteristics discussed relate to various sources of error and, therefore, invalidity. A critical review of each instrument in light of these characteristics should increase a designer's assurance that it will be valid.

SUMMARY

The overall goal of evaluation within PBID is to diagnostically assess the extent of learning as a basis for guiding further instruction, and to provide a basis for recording and reporting extent of content mastery. Evaluation typically has one of three intents during the total instructional process. It can be used as a pretest prior to instruction, during the delivery of instruction, or as a posttest after instruction has been completed. A variety of evaluation procedures can be used. (See Table 10.1.) When using those evaluation procedures it is important to recognize that they are not as precise as measures of physical phenomenon. They have sources of error that must be controlled by the designer during the process of development. Primary sources of that error are the learner, the instrument, the scorer, and guessing. That error must be taken into account when developing evaluation instruments and interpreting evaluation results. The designer can minimize error by taking steps to ensure that all evaluation procedures are objective and reliable so differences in evaluation scores actually differentiate people based on extent of content mastery.

ACTIVITIES AND EVALUATION

1. Draw the flowchart presented at the beginning of Chapter 14 and label each evaluation point, including the lines indicating the flow from one point to another. Explain the purpose of evaluation at each point in the chart.
2. Define each source of educational evaluation error. Give an example of each.
3. Describe the characteristics of good evaluation, and explain how each affects the utility of an evaluation procedure.

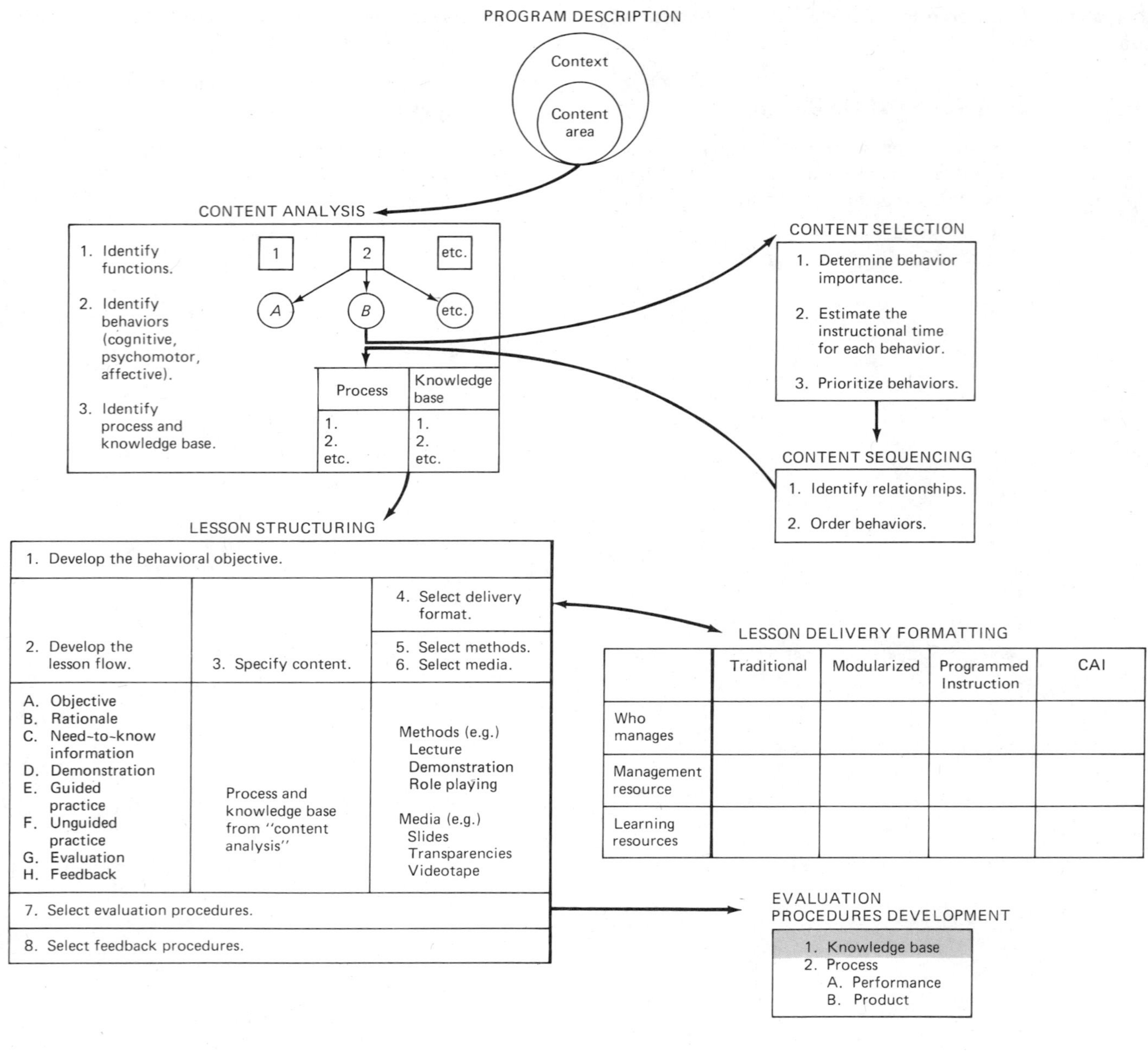

PROGRAM DESCRIPTION
Context
Content area
CONTENT ANALYSIS
1. Identify functions.
2. Identify behaviors (cognitive, psychomotor, affective).
3. Identify process and knowledge base.
1
2
etc.
A
B
etc.
Process
Knowledge base
1.
2.
etc.
1.
2.
etc.
CONTENT SELECTION
1. Determine behavior importance.
2. Estimate the instructional time for each behavior.
3. Prioritize behaviors.
CONTENT SEQUENCING
1. Identify relationships.
2. Order behaviors.
LESSON STRUCTURING
1. Develop the behavioral objective.
2. Develop the lesson flow.
3. Specify content.
4. Select delivery format.
5. Select methods.
6. Select media.
A. Objective
B. Rationale
C. Need-to-know information
D. Demonstration
E. Guided practice
F. Unguided practice
G. Evaluation
H. Feedback
Process and knowledge base from "content analysis"
Methods (e.g.)
Lecture
Demonstration
Role playing
Media (e.g.)
Slides
Transparencies
Videotape
7. Select evaluation procedures.
8. Select feedback procedures.
LESSON DELIVERY FORMATTING
Traditional
Modularized
Programmed Instruction
CAI
Who manages
Management resource
Learning resources
EVALUATION PROCEDURES DEVELOPMENT
1. Knowledge base
2. Process
A. Performance
B. Product

Chapter 15

Developing Knowledge-Base Evaluation Instruments

CHAPTER OBJECTIVE

Givens

A knowledge base to be evaluated

Behavior

Develop a test-construction blueprint and a knowledge-base evaluation instrument.

Standard

The test blueprint, test items, and assembled evaluation instrument must be focused on the behaviors to be taught and meet the criteria presented in this chapter.

OVERVIEW

The purpose of knowledge-base evaluations is to determine the extent to which learners have mastered a defined knowledge base. The knowledge base is defined during content analysis and lesson structuring (see Chapters 7 and 8) as a set of knowledge-base objectives. This chapter presents procedures for developing knowledge-base evaluation instruments that possess the characteristics of good evaluation which were presented in Chapter 14. They have been adapted from *Individualizing Vocational and Technical Instruction* (Pucel and Knaak, 1975). They apply equally to cognitive, affective, and psychomotor behavior. Samples of written tests that incorporate the techniques discussed in this chapter are presented in Appendices D and E.

Oral tests should also be developed using these procedures. The primary difference between a formal written test and a formal oral test is who reads the items. In the case of a written test, the learner reads the items and responds. In the case of an oral test, someone other than the learner reads the items to the learner and the learner responds. However, both types of tests must be constructed with the same level of precision.

Self-checks used to facilitate self-questioning are also constructed using procedures for developing knowledge-base evaluation instruments. Self-checks are evaluations that are administered by learners in order to self-diagnose their learning progress. For learners to accomplish this goal, self-checks must be precisely developed.

Table 10.1 shows the knowledge-base evaluation instruments from which a designer might select. With the exception of informal tutorial questioning, the development of evaluation instruments calls for the formal techniques presented in this chapter. Informal tutorial questioning is done as the need arises by the instructor while the learner is in the process of learning. Such questioning is usually spontaneous and, therefore, does not lend itself to detailed preplanning. Procedures for the development of informal questioning evaluation will be presented in Chapter 18.

LEVELS OF TEST ITEMS

Many designers and instructors are critical of written tests. They feel that written test results seem to have little relationship to how well a person can actually apply a behavior. A well-constructed test should overcome this criticism. Although the evaluation of knowledge base and process measure different things, they should both relate to ultimate performance of the behavior being taught.

The Taxonomy of Educational Objectives (Bloom, 1956) describes six different levels of educational objectives. Properly constructed test items can evaluate the mastery of objectives at any level. Although all six are meaningful, the first three (knowledge level, comprehension level, and application level) will be discussed here because they appear to be most useful in developing an understanding of why some knowledge-base tests appear to be related to performance while others do not.

Knowledge-Level Items

A test developed at the "knowledge level" is designed to measure the ability to repeat facts. (Care should be taken to clearly differentiate Bloom's use of the word *knowledge* from common usage or from a *knowledge base.*) It does not attempt to assess whether a person understands the facts or can apply the facts; it only attempts to assess whether a person can repeat the facts. Table 15.1 shows an example of an item written at the knowledge level regarding a principle of electricity called *Ohm's law*. If learners can answer this question, we know that they can repeat the formula for Ohm's law. We do not know whether they understand the formula or whether they can apply the formula.

Comprehension-Level Items

Items written at the comprehension level are designed to determine if learners can use certain knowledge when told to do to so in situations such as those they were taught, or if they can translate the knowledge into their own words. For example, assume that an instructor has taught people how to calculate the resistance in a circuit using Ohm's law when amperage and voltage are given. Question *A* in Table 15.2 shows an appropriate comprehension-level item.

If learners can arrive at the correct answer to this item, we know that they can do what they were taught. We still do not know whether they can apply Ohm's law in a setting where a unique problem is encountered or when they are not told that Ohm's law is the prin-

TABLE 15.1 Sample Knowledge-Level Item

What is the formula for Ohm's law? (*Answer:* $E = IR$)

TABLE 15.2 Sample Comprehension-Level Items

A. Using Ohm's law, calculate the resistance in a circuit that draws 3 amperes of current at 120 volts.

$$(\textit{Answer: } \frac{120}{3} = 40 \text{ ohms})$$

B. Describe in your own words the relationships between voltage, amperage, and resistance as presented in the Ohm's law formula. (*Answer:* Voltage is equal to the current, in amperes, times the resistance, in ohms.)

ciple that should be used in obtaining a solution. However, we do know that they have more of a command of Ohm's law than just knowing the formula. Another example of a comprehensive-level item related to the Ohm's law formula is question *B* in Table 15.2.

If the learners can internalize the information taught and repeat the information back in their own words, then they have comprehended. In this example, the key to whether or not an item is a comprehension-level item, as contrasted with a knowledge-level item, is whether learners are asked to present the relationship in their own words. If they are asked to describe the relationship in the exact words they were taught, the item would be a knowledge-level item.

Application-Level Items

The third level at which test items can be written that appears to be useful to instructors is the application level. Application-level items are used to determine if learners can apply knowledge in new, untaught situations. In other words, given a situation where knowledge should be applied, can learners apply it, even though they never encountered that particular situation before? Most designers would like learners eventually to be able to apply knowledge whenever appropriate, and not only in those specific instances or cases that were discussed during instruction. This type of testing usually requires the presentation of a real-life problem that learners are asked to solve, or to which they are expected to react. If information concerning Ohm's law were taught as indicated above, Table 15.3 would be an appropriate application-level item. Unlike comprehension items, application items require learners to use the information learned in a new situation without direction about the principle or principles to be applied.

It is important not to confuse application-level items used to test a knowledge base and process evaluation techniques. Application-level items focus on the ability to apply the knowledge base, and process evaluation techniques focus on whether a person can perform a behavior.

Let us look at another series of examples relative to computer software usage in accounting. Assume that the goal is to teach learners to "differentiate when to use word processing, database management, and spreadsheet software." Further, assume that this behavior will be taught through a PBID lesson.

TABLE 15.3 Sample Application-Level Item

What size fuse would be needed to operate a hair dryer which has 80 ohms resistance on a 120-volt circuit?

$$(\textit{Answer: } \frac{120}{80} = 1.5 \text{ amperes})$$

Knowledge-level items would be directed at definitions of the purposes of each type of software and recalling selection criteria (e.g., "What is the definition of a spreadsheet?"). Comprehension-level items would present samples of each type of application, and learners would be asked to determine which type of program would be appropriate. Since these items would be presented in the context of teaching the behavior, learners would realize that they were to choose among the alternatives presented in the lesson.

Application-level items would occur when real-life situations, independent of those taught, were presented throughout future instruction when learners would have to select software. Notice that the application situations would occur in the future. If problem situations were presented during the lesson on differentiating when to use the software, learners automatically would know which knowledge to apply. Even though the situation might be new to them, the context would tell them to apply particular principles. Therefore, in this later situation, the items would be at the comprehension level rather than at the application level.

As you can see, designers can obtain more information about the ability of learners to actually utilize information if they design their test items to measure at the comprehension and application levels instead of at the knowledge level.

There are times, however, when items written at the knowledge level are appropriate. During the teaching of any material. instructors must first introduce basic definitions, formulas, and principles upon which additional instruction can be built. During the initial introduction of the material, it might be very appropriate to test a person's mastery of basic facts. One should have the basic formula for Ohm's law thoroughly in mind before attempting to apply the formula. Therefore, knowledge-level items are typically used when first introducing information. Most instructors then move on to applying facts to a series of examples. These examples are used to show learners how to apply the information. Learners are then tested with comprehension-level items to determine if they can apply the knowledge in situations such as those they were taught. Later, learners are asked to apply and integrate many types of knowledge to new situations which they have never seen before. In most content areas, when learners have arrived at this level of understanding, they are ready to effectively apply a content area. At this stage, application-level items would be appropriate; results from them would tend to be closely related to a learner's ability to perform a behavior.

Designers must consciously determine which levels of items to include in any given test. The levels of the items should be consistent with the stage or stages of the lesson within which the evaluation will be conducted. Remember that the tests should be diagnostic and should indicate the extent to which mastery of the content has been attained. Therefore, if the goal is to assess comprehension, the test should also include some knowledge-level items. This allows for a diagnostic assessment to determine if a person at least knows the facts, if he or she cannot demonstrate comprehension. Similarly, if the goal is to assess at the application level, the test should include some knowledge and comprehension-level items.

TEST-CONSTRUCTION BLUEPRINT

The first step in the development of any evaluation instrument is to clearly specify the content to be evaluated. When developing a knowledge-base test, this is done through a test-construction blueprint. A test-construction blueprint is a worksheet that allows a designer to indicate which test items measure which knowledge-base objectives. Table 15.4 presents a sample test-construction blueprint for the behavior "change a tire." Test-construction blueprints for the behaviors "identify and apply for a job" and "communicate with others" can be found in Appendices D and E.

A test-construction blueprint indicates the behavior to be taught in the form of a learning objective. It indicates the knowledge-base objectives to be evaluated along the left-hand side. It also indicates the number of each item on the test that measures each knowledge-base objective. For example, item 3 on the test for "change a tire" measures the objective "recall safety procedures." Item 16 pertains to lifting heavy objects. The test for this sample behavior includes a total of 16 items.

The test-construction blueprint performs five major functions for the designer. First, it allows the designer to ensure that the test is focused on the important content. If a test item cannot be related to one of the knowledge-base objectives, it should not be included in the test. For example, a test item on the history of tires would not be appropriate for inclusion in the test for "change a tire." It could not be matched directly with any of the knowledge-base objectives.

Second, the blueprint allows the designer to ensure that the test will be comprehensive. The test will be comprehensive if it includes a sample of items related to each of the knowledge-base objectives. If one objective has no items, the test is not comprehensive. For example, if there were no items on safety, the test would not measure all of the objectives and would not be comprehensive.

Third, the blueprint allows the designer to determine the amount of weight each objective has in the test. This determination is based on the number of items

TABLE 15.4 Sample Test-Construction Blueprint

OBJECTIVE

Given
A car with a flat tire at the side of the road

Behavior
Change a tire.

Standard
The replacement tire is mounted on the car, the lugs are tight, and the tools and replacement tire are stored.

Knowledge-Base Objectives	Test-Item Numbers
1. Explain the procedure for changing a tire.	1, 5, 8, 12, 15
2. Identify the tools needed to change a tire.	4, 7, 10, 13
3. Recall the principles for lifting heavy objects.	2, 9, 14, 16
4. Recall safety procedures.	3, 6, 11

written on each objective. For example, the most important objective in the sample presented in Table 15.4 is objective 1: "explain the procedure for changing a tire." More items are written for that objective than for any of the others. Therefore, that objective will have the most weight in the results from the test. If objective 1 is not the most important objective, it should not have the most items. The weight of each objective in a test can be controlled by the relative number of items written on each objective.

Fourth, the blueprint allows for ready diagnoses of where learners are having difficulty learning. One can score the test for each of the separate objectives and determine with which particular objective a learner is having difficulty. For example, if a learner did not answer items 4, 7, 10, and 13 correctly, you could diagnose that the person was having difficulty with identifying the tools. Such diagnostic scoring is becoming more feasible as tests are being administered through computers and are being scored by computers. The computers can quickly provide scoring by separate objective.

Fifth, the blueprint is useful in revising a test as the instructional program is revised. If the designer is clear about which items measure which knowledge-base objectives, when it comes time to revise the material related to a particular objective, the related test items can be quickly identified and revised. For example, if the procedure for lifting heavy objects changed, items 2, 9, 14, and 16 would need to be reviewed and possibly changed.

CONSTRUCTING TEST ITEMS

Next, the major types of test items will be presented along with some hints concerning how to write them. Procedures regarding assembling the items into an actual test will be discussed later.

Remember, each test item should be written in reference to a test-construction blueprint similar to that presented in Table 15.4. Also, the level of each item should be consistent with your evaluation intent. Notice that throughout this discussion the word *item* has been used, not the word *question*. That is because not all requests for responses from learners are questions. Some are statements. Although questions are items, all items are not questions.

Objective Items

True-false items, multiple-choice items, and matching items are all forms of *objective test items*. Objective test items can be stored consistently. They all require the learner to select the correct answer from among a number of possible answers. Once a scoring key is developed which indicates the correct choices, anyone can score the test using that key and arrive at the same score for a particular learner. Each of the types of objective test items will be presented with guidelines for their development. Subjective test items, which require judgment during scoring, will be presented later in this chapter.

True-False Items. *True-false items* can be divided into regular true-false items, modified true-false items, and cluster true-false items. A *regular* true-false item presents learners with a statement which must be judged to be true or false. For example,

_F_ 1. A magnet will attract *glass*.

Since this statement is false, the learner should indicate that the statement is false. The learner could indicate this in a variety of ways, depending upon the directions which are given. Table 15.5 presents a sample set of directions:

TABLE 15.5 Regular True-False Directions

The following statements are either true or false. If the statement is true, place a *T* in the numbered blank space on your answer sheet. If the statement is false, place an *F* in the blank. The first item is answered as an example.

The same test item presented above could also be written as a *modified* true-false item. A modified true-false item requires the learner to indicate if the statement is true or false; if it is false, the learner is asked to do something else. For example, a learner could be presented the above item and told that if the item were false, a word should be written in the blank space on the answer sheet that changes the underlined word and makes the statement true. If this statement were added to the directions given above, the answer on the answer sheet would appear as follows:

_F_ 1. *iron*

There are a large number of possible modifications that can be used. Any of them are acceptable so long as the directions clearly indicate exactly what the learner is supposed to do.

At times, a designer may wish to write a number of regular true-false items that all pertain to the same principle, as presented in Table 15.6. In such cases, it would be possible to combine such a set of regular true-false items into a *cluster* true-false set to conserve space on the test and to save item-writing time. A cluster true-false set is composed of a *root statement*, followed by a number of incomplete statements that will complete the root statement, resulting in either true or false statements. Table 15.6 shows the sample related true-false items as a cluster true-false set.

Each possible completion of the root statement is considered to be an item because it calls for a response from the learner. All of the items that relate to the same root statement are called a *set*. Table 15.7 presents sample directions for a cluster true-false set. Notice that they are different from those used with regular true-false items. Cluster true-false items are written using the same general guidelines as those used when writing any true-false item. However, they are generally written only if there are at least three items in the set. If there are only two possible items, they should be written as regular true-false items. Table 15.8 presents a list of guidelines for writing true-false items.

The major advantage of true-false items is that they are easy to construct and score. The major disadvantage is that a learner has a 50 percent chance of guessing each item correctly. Therefore, a test containing only true-false items must contain a large number of items in order to provide a valid assessment of a person's mastery of a knowledge base.

Multiple-Choice Items. *Multiple-choice items* are characterized by a statement or question followed by

TABLE 15.6 Related True-False Items in an Alternative True-False Cluster

Related True-False Items	True-False Cluster
	A magnet will attract
T F 1. A magnet will attract iron.	T F 1. iron.
T F 2. A magnet will attract glass.	T F 2. glass.
T F 3. A magnet will attract aluminum.	T F 3. aluminum
T F 4. A magnet will attract steel.	T F 4. steel.

TABLE 15.7 Directions for a Cluster True-False Set

Each of the incomplete sentences presented below is followed by a number of words or phrases which complete the sentence and make it true or false. If a word or phrase completes a true statement, circle the *T* before the word or phrase. If it completes a false statement, circle the *F.* The first item is answered as an example.

TABLE 15.8 Guidelines for Writing True-False Items

1. Make approximately half of the items true and half of the items false.
2. Make sure that the true statements are not consistently longer than the false statements. (There is a tendency for true statements to be longer than false statements because true statements generally must include qualifying information to ensure that the statement is true. Few things are true in all situations.)
3. Avoid using absolute terms such as *always* and *never.* (Few things are always true or never true. Therefore, statements including these terms are usually false.)

at least four alternative choices, one of which is correct. The learner is asked to select the correct choice. There are two basic formats for multiple-choice items: the question format and the completion format. These formats can be used interchangeably, depending upon personal preference. Table 15.9 shows four examples of multiple-choice items. Question 1 is a knowledge-level item asked in a question format. It is a knowledge-level item because it asks for a fact.

Question 2 also uses the question format. However, it presents a problem which must be solved. Depending

TABLE 15.9 Sample Multiple-Choice Items

_____ 1. Where should the blocks be placed when changing a tire at the side of the road?
   A. in front and back of all tires
   B. in front of all tires
   C. in back of all tires
   D. in front and back of those tires not to be changed

_____ 2. What ampere fuse would be required in a 120-volt circuit operating a 60-ohm iron?
   A. 0.2 ampere
   B. 1 ampere
   C. 2 amperes
   D. 3 amperes

_____ 3. When changing a tire at the side of the road, you should place the blocks in
   A. front and back of all tires.
   B. front of all tires.
   C. back of all tires.
   D. front and back of those tires not to be changed.

_____ 4. A 60-ohm iron operating in a 120-volt circuit would require a _____-ampere fuse.
   A. 1
   B. 2
   C. 3
   D. 4

TABLE 15.10 Sample Multiple-Choice Directions

Directions: Each of the following questions or incomplete statements is followed by several words or phrases, or a series of numbers. Choose the one which best answers the question or completes the statement correctly. Place the letter associated with that choice (A, B, C, or D) in the numbered blank space on your answer sheet. The first item is answered as an example.

upon the context of this item, it could be at the comprehension or the application level.

Question 3 is written as a completion item. It presents an incomplete sentence which the learner is to complete correctly.

Completion items can also be written with blanks at or near the end of the sentence. For example, see question 4 in Table 15.9.

Table 15.10 shows a typical set of multiple-choice item directions, and Table 15.11 presents guidelines for writing multiple-choice items.

At times, multiple-choice items are also used with

TABLE 15.11 Guidelines for Writing Multiple-Choice Items

1. Each item should have at least four possible choices. (This reduces the chance of guessing the correct answer. The chance of guessing the answer to an item can be calculated by dividing 100 percent by the number of possible choices (e.g., 100 × 4 = 25 percent). If three choices are used, the chance of guessing increases to 33⅓ percent (100 × 3 = 33⅓ percent).
2. Make sure that all of the possible choices would be reasonable to someone who does not know the content. (An obviously wrong choice is the same as no choice at all.)
3. Choices should be called for at or near the end of a sentence rather than at the beginning or in the middle. (See the discussion of completion items later in this chapter.)
4. If choices are a series of numbers, they should be placed in ascending or descending order (e.g., 10, 15, 20, 25, or 25, 20, 15, 10). The purpose of having an item is to determine if a learner understands which is the correct answer and not whether he or she can sort out a series of numbers.
5. List each choice on a separate line. (It is much easier for a learner to see and review the separate choices if they are placed on separate lines going down the page than if they are placed across the page. See the sample items presented earlier.)
6. Use capital letters to indicate each choice. (Capital letters are easier to distinguish from the rest of the printing on a page.)
7. Punctuate items just as you would punctuate a sentence. (If the choices are complete sentences, they should begin with a capital letter and end with a period. If they are not complete sentences, they should not begin with capitals or end with periods. If an item is a question, it should be followed by a question mark.)
8. If choices such as "A and B above," "none of the above," or "all of the above" are used, sometimes they should be the correct answer and sometimes they should be the incorrect answer. They should not be used only when they are the correct answers or only as filler because other incorrect answers cannot be developed.

TABLE 15.12 Test Items Related to Characteristics of a Good Test

1. A test which measures what you want it to measure is
   A. objective.
   B. valid.
   C. reliable.
   D. comprehensive.
2. A test which measures consistently is
   A. objective.
   B. valid.
   C. reliable.
   D. comprehensive.
3. A test which can be scored consistently by different people so they will all arrive at the same score for the same learner is
   A. objective.
   B. valid.
   C. reliable.
   D. comprehensive.

charts, graphs, or pictures. Portions of each chart, graph, or picture are identified by letters A, B, C, and so on, and the learner is asked to respond to the item by making a choice. If this type of item is used, the directions must be very clear so the learner knows exactly what is expected. As photocopying equipment has gotten more sophisticated, the use of this type of item has increased.

The multiple-choice item is the most widely used type of test item. It has the advantages of being an objective-type item with no scoring error, as well as having relatively low guessing error. It is also flexible in that it can be written in a variety of forms.

Matching Items. A matching set contains a group of items related to a common topic. All of the items in the set are answered by selecting a choice from a common pool, or group of choices. Often, a matching set is viewed as a method of simplifying the writing of a series of separate multiple-choice items relating to a topic. For example, we could write the test items in Table 15.12 as multiple-choice items. All of these items deal with a common topic: characteristics of a good test. Therefore, they could be combined into the matching set in Table 15.13. This matching set would allow us to assess the same things as we did with the multiple-choice items, but it would allow us to do it more efficiently.

The relationships between the words or phrases to be matched can be stated in many ways. The directions for each matching set included in a test must point out the basis upon which the items and the choices are to be matched. Table 15.13 contains directions to match terms and definitions. Table 15.14 presents guidelines for writing matching items.

Subjective Items

Subjective test items require judgment during scoring. They also require learners to select an answer from all of the knowledge they possess, because alternative choices are not provided. A major difficulty in constructing these items is the development of scoring criteria. These criteria allow one scorer to judge different learners on the same basis, or different scorers to judge the same learner on the same basis. This requires the creation of a scoring guide that specifies criteria for the expected answers. Even though a scoring guide is created, however, the actual responses by the learner are often not exactly like the ones expected, and the scorer must make judgments.

Subjective items should be used only when objective-test items would not be effective. They are recommended for limited situations: when you want learners to synthesize knowledge and apply it to the solution of a problem and when you want learners to be able to recall an answer versus recognizing which is the correct answer from among those presented. For example, learners might be asked to synthesize and list a procedure for solving a problem that has not been specifically taught. The learner would have to synthesize a body of related knowledge and arrive at a new, unique solution. Each type of subjective item will be presented along with guidelines for its development.

Completion Items. A *completion item* is a sentence containing one or more blanks which the learner fills

TABLE 15.13 Matching Set of Items Related to Characteristics of a Good Set

Directions: Match the definitions of characteristics of a good test in the left column with the correct terms in the right column and place the answer in the corresponding blank before each definition. The first item is answered as an example.

Definitions		Terms
__D__	X. A test which samples all of the content you wish to assess is	A. objective.
_____	1. A test which measures what you want it to measure is	B. valid.
		C. reliable.
		D. comprehensive.
_____	2. A test which measures consistently is	E. subjective.
		F. discriminating.
_____	3. A test which can be scored consistently by different people so they will all arrive at the same score for the same learner is	G. random.

TABLE 15.14 Guidelines for Writing Matching Items

1. Matching sets usually include at least three, but not more than ten, items to be matched. (If there are only two items, it is more efficient to write two multiple-choice items. If there are more than ten, the items might be broken down into two sets.)
2. Include at least three more choices than there are things to match. If answers can be used more than once, a minimum of four choices can be used. However, this must be made explicit in the directions. (To reduce guessing, the last choice made should be made from at least four choices.)
3. Use only related materials in the same set. (This allows one set of directions to apply to all items in the matching set and allows all of the choices to be reasonable answers to each item.)
4. Place the column containing the longer statements on the left side of the page. (People tend to read an item on the left side of the page and then scan the choices on the right side. Since the items on the left are only read once and the choices on the right are scanned many times, the long statements should be on the left.)
5. Make sure that all of the possible choices would be reasonable to someone who does not know the content. (An obviously wrong choice is the same as no choice at all.)
6. If choices are a series of numbers, they should be placed in ascending or descending order (e.g., 10, 15, 20, 25, or 25, 20, 15, 10).
7. List each choice on a separate line. (It is much easier for a learner to see and review the separate choices if they are placed on separate lines going down the page than if they are placed across the page. See the sample items presented earlier.)
8. Use capital letters to indicate each choice. (Capital letters are easier to distinguish from the rest of the printing on a page.)
9. Punctuate items just as you would punctuate a sentence. (If the choices are complete sentences, they should begin with a capital letter and end with a period. If they are not complete sentences, they should not begin with capitals or end with periods.)

in to make a true statement. (See Table 15.15 for an example.)

Directions for completion items typically are stated as in Table 15.16.

Completion items are easy to construct, but they are difficult to score. The problem is to determine, without being arbitrary, which answers are reasonable and which are not. In Table 15.15 the instructor anticipated that the correct answer was *gasoline.* What should the instructor do if learners respond with *V-6, metal, noisy,* or *Japanese*? Would those answers also be considered correct? Why or why not?

In this case, the instructor anticipated one answer and got a wide variety of answers, many of which were not anticipated. This requires judgment in scoring. If completion items are used, the instructor should accept

TABLE 15.15 Sample Completion Item

gasoline	1. Most American automobiles have __________ engines.

TABLE 15.16 Directions for Completion Items

Each of the statements below contains a blank or blanks at or near the end of the statement. You are to place the word or words which correctly fill the blanks in the spaces provided to the left of each statement. The first item is answered as an example.

all reasonable answers and, over time, expand the scoring guide for each item, or refine the item to try to minimize the range of reasonable responses.

The problem relating to the example in Table 15.15 demonstrates that subjective items must be scored by someone who is proficient in the content area. They should not be scored by people who are not competent to make necessary judgments. Table 15.17 presents guidelines for writing completion items.

Listing Items. *Listing item sets* calls for the learner to list a specific number of things. They are a way of simplifying a large number of completion items, as a matching set is a way of simplifying a large number of multiple-choice items. Each item in a listing set could be written as a separate completion item. There are no general directions for listing items, since each listing item set has its own specific directions. There are two general forms of listing sets. One form asks the learner to list a number of objects or things, but does not require that they be listed in order. The other form asks the learner to list a number of things in order. This latter type is usually used when testing knowledge of procedural steps.

Table 15.18 is an example of a listing set in which order is not an important factor. Each response is considered an item. This set asks the learner to list four different types of test items, but it does not call for any order in the listing. An example is given, although examples are not always required with listing items.

TABLE 15.17 Guidelines for Writing Completion Items

1. Place the blank or blanks at or near the end of the sentence. (The learner should have all of the information needed to fill in a blank before encountering the blank. If the blank is near the beginning of a sentence, the learner must read the entire sentence once and then return to the beginning to try to determine what should go into the blank.)
2. Rarely include more than two blanks.
3. Develop a scoring guide of possible correct responses. The more complete the list is, the less subjectivity will have to be exercised in judging if an answer is correct. (During the scoring process, the list may need to be expanded to accommodate unanticipated correct answers.)
4. Completion items should not be created by simply taking statements from textbooks available to the learners and eliminating one word from each. Important statements should be paraphrased so learners cannot simply memorize the sentences during studying.
5. Make sure that the scorer is proficient in the content being assessed.

TABLE 15.18 Sample Listing Set in Which Order is Not Important

List four different types of test items. The first item is answered as an example.

	Scoring guide:
X. true-false	modified true-false
1. ________	cluster true-false
2. ________	multiple-choice
3. ________	matching
4. ________	completion

Table 15.19 is an example of a set which requires the learner to list things in order. In this case, order is important, and the learner is informed that the strokes must be listed in order.

As with completion items, listing items are difficult to score. The designer should identify all possible correct answers and create a scoring guide. If the items are to be listed in a particular order, the designer must also determine how the items will be scored if one item is out of order, or if all of the items are out of order. Table 15.20 contains a few helpful hints which may be useful when developing listing items.

Essay Items. An *essay item* requests the learner to give a narrative written response such as a description or an explanation. Essay-type items allow the designer to determine if the learner can synthesize information. *Synthesis* means drawing together a variety of information in order to apply it in meaningful ways that are new to the learner. Table 15.21 is an example of an essay item that requires such synthesis (if one assumes that this relationship has not been explicitely taught during instruction). In order to answer this item, the learner

TABLE 15.19 Sample Listing Set in Order

List the four strokes of a four-cycle gasoline engine in order.

	Scoring guide:
1. ________	intake
2. ________	compression
3. ________	power
4. ________	exhaust

TABLE 15.20 Guidelines for Writing Listing Items

1. If an example is used, the first response to be listed in the first listing set should be used as an example and should be indicated by an *X*.
2. Generally, not more than 10 things are listed within one listing set.
3. If the listing must be in order, this must be indicated in the directions.
4. Develop a scoring guide of as many possible answers to the listing items as you can before administering them to learners. Be ready to accept additional legitimate answers provided by learners.
5. Make sure that the scorer is proficient in the content being assessed.

TABLE 15.21 Essay Item Requiring Synthesis

Explain the relationship between validity and reliability.

would have to draw together, or synthesize, information on both validity and reliability to arrive at the explanation of the relationship.

Essay items begin with words that direct the learner to provide answers requiring synthesis. Such words are *describe, explain, how, why,* and *what.*

Compared with other types of items, essay items are very difficult to score. Not only are learners being asked for information, but they are asked to arrive at explanations of relationships which can be correctly viewed from many different perspectives. This requires the scorer to be very clear about which explanations are correct and which are incorrect. Such judgments require that the scorer understand the content well.

If learners are expected to structure their responses in certain ways, the essay item should indicate that structure. For example, learners could be asked to specifically address the relationship between validity and reliability in terms of similarities and differences. This would further focus the learner and the scorer.

Scoring objectivity can be increased by creating a scoring guide which lists the specific things that learners should be expected to include within the essay answer. The item can then be scored by judging how many of those things were actually included. Rules should also be established for granting credit if certain relationships are brought out in the explanation and others are not. For example, how many points will be awarded for each concept? How should points be awarded if the concepts are discussed but are in the wrong order? Table 15.22 presents guidelines for writing problem items.

Problems. *Problems* are test items that require learners to respond with a numerical or symbolic solution. For example, Table 15.23 is a problem because it is answered by a numerical solution.

Problems are also solved with symbolic solutions

TABLE 15.22 Guidelines for Writing Essay Items

1. Begin each essay item with a word that requires learners to synthesize information.
2. Use essay items only if you wish learners to synthesize information to arrive at a narrative explanation or description. If you wish learners to provide a listing, use a listing-type item.
3. Identify the specific concepts or ideas you wish to have included in the answers.
4. Identify any expected relationships between the concepts or ideas.
5. Develop definite rules for granting credit while evaluating each essay item response. Be ready to accept alternative reasonable explanations as possible correct answers.
6. Make sure that the scorer is proficient in the content being assessed.

TABLE 15.23 Sample Problem

What size fuse would be needed to operate a hair dryer which has 80 ohms resistance on a 120-volt circuit?

(*Answer:* $\frac{120}{80}$ = 1.5 amperes)

---

such as graphs and computer programming code. The following problem would be solved with computer programming code:

Develop a FORTRAN program to arrive at the average sales price for products sold.

Table 15.24 presents guidelines for writing problem items.

Object Identification Items. *Object identification items* are used when the designer wants learners to be able to correctly label objects. For example, you may want people to be able to label the major parts of a machine. Item numbers would be attached to each of the major parts of the machine with tape, and learners would be asked to write the name of each part in the blanks next to the same numbers on an answer sheet. Instead of using the real object, one could also use a picture of the object.

ASSEMBLING A TEST

A set of guidelines for assembling a test will be presented. They facilitate test taking, administration, and scoring. They address the ordering of items, the development of test headings, the insertion of directions, the numbering of the items, and the provision of space for responses. Samples of complete, assembled knowledge-base tests are presented in Appendices D and E.

Item Order

Tests are generally assembled so that learners encounter the easiest type of item to respond to first, and the most difficult type of item to respond to last. Many educators feel that this organizational pattern produces less psychological strain on the learner than if the test were organized in a reverse pattern. The following is the preferred order for presenting items on a test:

1. True-false
2. Modified true-false
3. Cluster true-false
4. Multiple-choice
5. Matching
6. Completion
7. Listing
8. Essay or problem (in either order)

This order is not in terms of which items will be easiest for a given individual. It is not possible to judge which items a particular person will find most difficult. However, it is much easier to respond to a true-false item than to an essay-type item. Therefore, true-false items should be placed on a test before essay items.

The following discussion of how to organize a test will assume that the designer wants to include all types of items in the test. However, all item types need not be included in every test. It is possible to construct a test of any combination of one or more item types. If only some of the item types are to be included in a test, they should be presented in the relative order presented above.

TABLE 15.24 Guidelines for Writing Problem Items

---

1. Clearly indicate the type of symbolic solution expected (e.g., a drawing or a programming code number).
2. Use problems only if you want learners to synthesize information to arrive at symbolic or numerical solutions. If you want learners to provide a listing, use a listing-type item.
3. Identify the specific dimensions of the problem that need to be considered in the solution.
4. Identify any expected ordering of the dimensions of the problem solution.
5. Develop definite rules for granting credit while evaluating each problem response. Be ready to accept alternative solutions as correct.
6. Make sure that the scorer is proficient in the content being assessed.

Test Heading

A test should begin with a clear heading. The heading should fulfill at least two functions: (1) It should identify the (program) course in which the test is to be used, and (2) it should identify the specific content the test will assess. For example, if the test is on automatic transmissions as part of the general auto mechanics course, the name of the course and the content covered by the test (automatic transmissions) should be indicated. Sometimes the date the test was developed is also included so the instructor can tell the difference between one version of a test on that content and another version. Other optional pieces of information included in the heading are the instructor's name, the institution name, and/or the test form.

Directions

Some people place a set of general directions immediately following the heading. The general directions are used primarily for administrative purposes. They inform the learner about what should be done after the test is completed, or about any general announcements of which the learner should be aware during the time she or he is taking the test. After the general directions, the items are placed on the test; appropriate directions precede each item type. Each set of directions should include the following four pieces of information:

1. The type of item
2. The type of response expected (e.g., T, F, A, B, or fill in the blank)
3. Where to place the response (e.g., on the test or on the answer sheet).
4. An example response

At times, some designers also indicate the amount of points that will be awarded for each type of item.

Item Numbering

Items should be numbered consecutively from the beginning to the end of a test. If the test calls for a total of 50 different responses, the items should be numbered from 1 to 50. On a test, there should only be one number 1, one number 2, one number 3, and so on. Renumbering should not be begun for each type of item. The example for each type of item should be indicated with an *X*. This makes the examples easily distinguished from the other items. It also does not confuse the numbering system, particularly if computerized answer sheets are used.

Space For Responses

If an answer sheet is used, the blank spaces should be numbered in the same way as the items on the test. Answers to the examples can be placed on the test or on the answer sheet when one is used. The blanks on the answer sheet should be large enough for learners to respond adequately to an item. If learners are to respond on the test itself, the blanks are usually placed in front of the item numbers (e.g., _____ 1.).

SUMMARY

The purpose of knowledge-base evaluations is to determine the extent to which learners have mastered a defined knowledge base. These evaluations are developed around the knowledge-base objectives identified during content analysis, and they use a test-construction blueprint. Test items can be developed to assess different levels of understanding (e.g., knowledge, comprehension, and/or application). They can also be written as a variety of types. Some types are objective, and some are subjective.

Once the items have been written, they are assembled into a test. That test can be a written or an oral one, or it can be a self-check. The designer must consider item ordering, test headings, directions, item numbering, and space for responses as the test is assembled.

ACTIVITIES AND EVALUATION

1. Select a behavior for which the knowledge-base objectives have been identified. Develop a test-construction blueprint for that behavior.
2. Develop one of each type of test item for that behavior, and indicate which items measure which knowledge-base objectives on the blueprint.
3. Assemble those items into a test which includes a heading, general directions, and directions for each item type. Develop an answer sheet, if one is required.

REFERENCES

Bloom, B. S., *Taxonomy of Educational Objectives: The Classification of Educational Goals, Handbook, I: Cognitive Domain,* David McKay, New York, 1956.

Pucel, D. J., and W. C. Knaak, *Individualizing Vocational and Technical Instruction,* Charles E. Merrill, Columbus, OH, 1975.

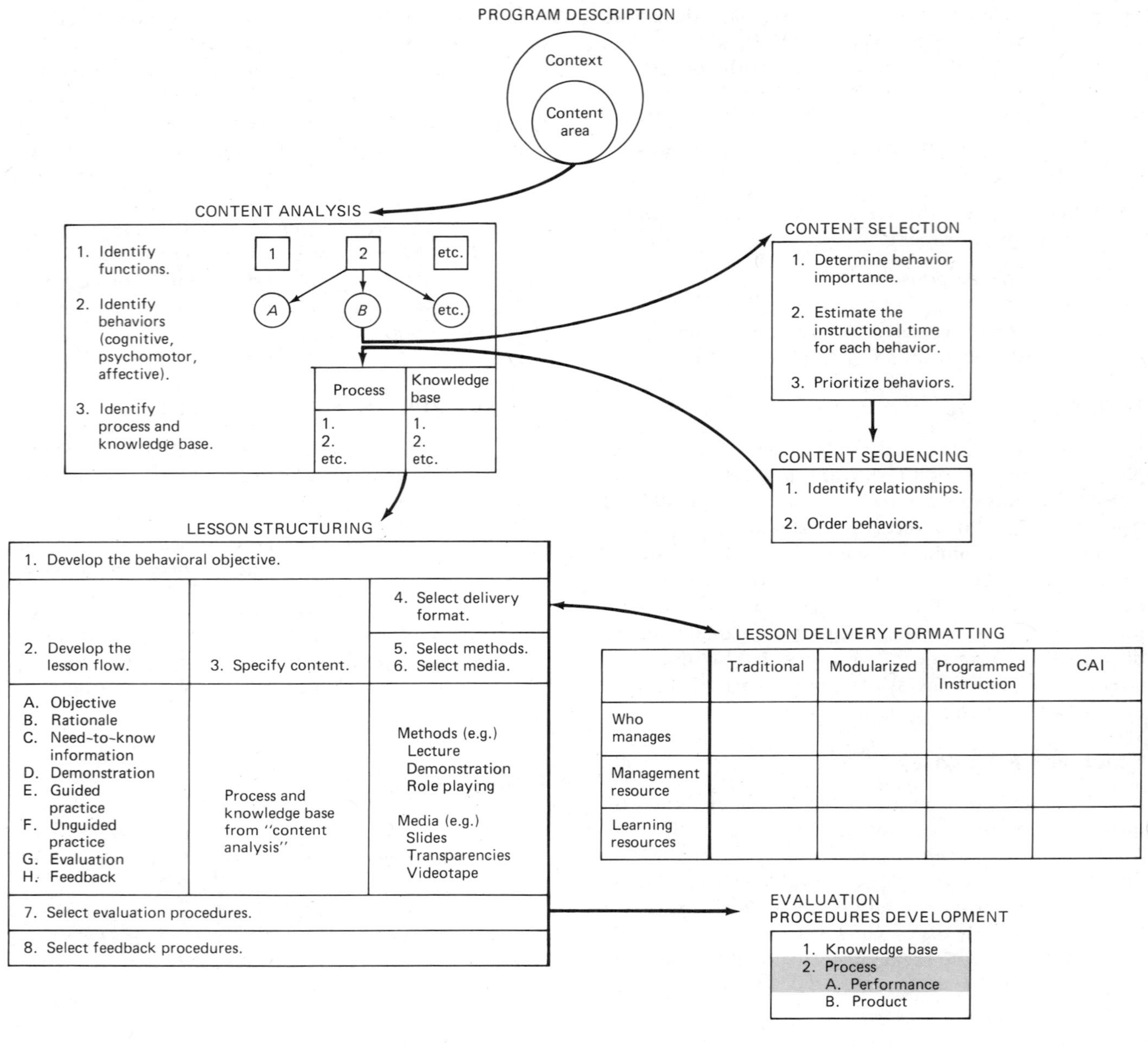

PROGRAM DESCRIPTION
Context
Content area
CONTENT ANALYSIS
1. Identify functions.
2. Identify behaviors (cognitive, psychomotor, affective).
3. Identify process and knowledge base.
1
2
etc.
A
B
etc.
Process
Knowledge base
1.
2.
etc.
1.
2.
etc.
CONTENT SELECTION
1. Determine behavior importance.
2. Estimate the instructional time for each behavior.
3. Prioritize behaviors.
CONTENT SEQUENCING
1. Identify relationships.
2. Order behaviors.
LESSON STRUCTURING
1. Develop the behavioral objective.
2. Develop the lesson flow.
3. Specify content.
4. Select delivery format.
5. Select methods.
6. Select media.
A. Objective
B. Rationale
C. Need-to-know information
D. Demonstration
E. Guided practice
F. Unguided practice
G. Evaluation
H. Feedback
Process and knowledge base from "content analysis"
Methods (e.g.)
Lecture
Demonstration
Role playing
Media (e.g.)
Slides
Transparencies
Videotape
7. Select evaluation procedures.
8. Select feedback procedures.
LESSON DELIVERY FORMATTING
Traditional
Modularized
Programmed Instruction
CAI
Who manages
Management resource
Learning resources
EVALUATION PROCEDURES DEVELOPMENT
1. Knowledge base
2. Process
A. Performance
B. Product

Developing Performance Tests

CHAPTER OBJECTIVE

Givens

A process to be evaluated

Behavior

Develop a psychomotor, cognitive, or affective performance test.

Standard

The test must be developed to assess a specific process and must include an evaluation instrument and assignment.

OVERVIEW

The goal of process evaluation is to determine if learners can *perform* a desired behavior. The behavior could be cognitive, affective, or psychomotor. The process to be evaluated is defined during behavior detailing (see Chapter 7) and lesson structuring (see Chapter 10). This chapter presents procedures for developing process evaluation instruments that meet the characteristics of good evaluation presented in Chapter 14.

You will notice that terminology in this chapter differs somewhat from that presented in many other books which discuss performance evaluation (Butler, 1972; Pucel and Knaak, 1975). That is because the terminology has been expanded to cover the evaluation of cognitive and affective processes as well as psychomotor processes. Terminology in the past has focused primarily on psychomotor performance. Consider the terminology carefully as you proceed. The procedures presented in this chapter have been adapted from those presented in *Individualizing Vocational and Technical Instruction* (Pucel and Knaak, 1975).

Process can be evaluated by observing a learner perform the process, or by evaluating the resulting product. For example, if a behavior to be evaluated is "make a cake," one could evaluate a learner while making the cake (performance evaluation), or one could evaluate the finished cake (product evaluation). At times, performance evaluations can also be expanded to include recipient reaction evaluation. When evaluating performance of behaviors which directly impact other people, one can also ask those people to evaluate that impact. For example, it is possible not only to observe a person performing the process of "cooperate with co-workers," but to ask the co-workers if they felt that cooperation was being exhibited.

The instruments used to conduct these two major types of process evaluation are performance tests, which are focused on the process of performing, and product tests, which are focused on the product of performing. As was discussed in Chapter 10, process evaluations can be either formal or informal. If they are formal, they are used to gather information to prove or disprove that a person has mastered the process of performing a behavior. Therefore, they are considered to be tests, just as formal knowledge-base evaluations are tests. Because they are tests, they must be constructed with the same level of precision as formal knowledge-base evaluations if the learner's progress is to be evaluated effectively.

As was pointed out during the discussion of knowledge-base evaluations, although self-checks are not formal evaluation instruments aimed at recording the progress of learners, they must also be constructed with precision. Learners must be able to determine their progress against an expected standard of performance. Therefore, even though the process evaluation self-checks are self-administered, they must meet the criteria for process evaluation that will be presented here.

If one examines Table 10.1, all of the process evaluation procedures described should follow the techniques presented in this chapter with the exception of informal tutorial observation, which is done as the need arises and while the learner is in the process of learning how to perform. Such observation is usually spontaneous and, therefore, does not lend itself to detailed preplanning. Procedures for developing that type of evaluation will be presented in Chapter 18.

The selection of whether to evaluate the process of performing or the product of performing was discussed in Chapter 10. Table 10.3 presents a list of advantages of each type of evaluation. The designer's decision as to which to evaluate should be made carefully.

Process evaluations are usually developed in one of two formats: checklists or rating scales. The procedures for developing each differ only in the way criteria are specified and scoring is done. A checklist is developed so the evaluator can make a judgment between two categories (e.g., satisfactory versus unsatisfactory). A rating scale is developed so the evaluator is required to make judgments between more than two categories (e.g., above average, average, and below average). Checklists are used most often because they are easier to construct and use. This chapter focuses on performance test development in the form of checklists. Product test development and the development of rating scales is presented in Chapter 17.

PERFORMANCE TEST DEVELOPMENT PROCEDURES

A *performance test* is an instrument designed to evaluate a learner's ability to perform a desired process. It is focused on the process of performing. Performance tests are constructed in two parts: the instrument that will be used to evaluate the performance, and the assignment that will be given to the learner to actually perform so the performance can be evaluated. The development of the instrument is accomplished using the following seven steps:

1. State the objective (behavior) to be evaluated.
2. Specify the process steps.
3. Specify the criteria for judging the steps.
4. Indicate critical processes.
5. Specify the scoring procedure.
6. Specify the performance time.
7. Determine the minimum acceptable score (if needed).

Alternative methods for determining the adequacy of overall performance based on the score obtained on a performance test are presented in Chapter 19.

Psychomotor Performance Tests

Each of the steps in the development of a performance test will first be presented using psychomotor examples. Performance test development techniques will then be applied to cognitive and affective performance tests.

Objective. The objective should be stated as a three-part behavioral objective, which was described in Chapter 8. It should include the *givens* needed by the learner to perform the behavior (e.g., tools, materials, environment, or other individuals), the *behavior* to be evaluated, and the *standard* against which performance of the behavior will be judged.

It is critical that all three parts of a behavioral objective be clearly specified before the development of the performance test begins. The behavioral objective is the focal point of the performance test.

The first two parts of the behavioral objective are relatively easy to specify. As was pointed out in Chapter 8, the standard at times is complex and has many criteria. In these cases, the behavioral objective may need to refer to another document in which the standard is more fully specified. Specifying it fully in the objective itself may make the objective too lengthy for effective use in other stages of instructional design.

In Table 16.1, the standard is easily contained in the objective of the performance test. (Remember, the focus of a performance test is on the process of performing; therefore, the standard is specified in order to judge the adequacy of the process used, not the quality of the completed product.)

If the process is more complex, however, such as making a pot of coffee with an electric percolator or replacing a carburetor on a car, specifying all of the process steps to be judged in the standard would make the objective extremely long and would reduce its effectiveness. Therefore, one could refer to another document which would clearly specify the standard.

In the case of making a pot of coffee, the document could be a recipe, operating instructions for the electric percolator, or an instructor checklist which lists the criteria that will be used to evaluate performance. In the case of replacing the carburetor, the document could be a repair manual or an instructor checklist in which the designer lists the expected procedure.

The designer may also face situations in which instruction is being designed and evaluated for a process that has not been published in existing literature but which the instructor will be expected to evaluate. In that case, the designer may have to create a reference document that clearly specifies the expected process standard. It could take the form of the process portion of the behavior-detailing analysis discussed earlier, or it could take the form of an instructor checklist.

In Table 16.2 the standard is not easily described and refers to a document in which the complex standard is more fully detailed: an instructor checklist.

As was indicated in Chapter 8, it is not sufficient to indicate that the standard is "to industry standards." That statement does not allow the designer to focus the design of the instruction or the evaluation, nor does it clearly specify what is expected of the learner. "Industry standards" must be clearly specified in the behavioral objective standard or be defined in a reference source where the standards are clearly specified. The standards must be published in some form. The objective to prepare a full pot of coffee with an electric percolator will be used as the basis for developing a sample performance test throughout the rest of this discussion.

Process Steps. After stating the objective, the designer must specify the process that the learner will be expected to perform. This is done during the behavior-detailing stage of content analysis, as indicated in Chap-

TABLE 16.1 Sample Objective with an Easily Contained Standard

Given
A sewing needle and thread

Behavior
Thread a sewing needle.

Standard
A single strand of thread is inserted through the eye of the needle.

TABLE 16.2 Objective with a Complex Standard Detailed Elsewhere

Givens
A clean electric percolator, percolator cord, coffee, filter, water, tablespoon, electricity

Behavior
Prepare a full pot of coffee.

Standard
The procedure specified in the instructor checklist

ter 7. Examples of how to identify the process steps for psychomotor, cognitive, and affective behaviors are presented in Tables 7.5 through 7.7. Those examples and the discussion concerning how to identify the process steps should be reviewed at this point. Notice that process steps can be specified as procedural steps or actions.

Review Table 16.3 and identify the process, or procedural steps, and the objective for the behavior "prepare a full pot of coffee with an electric percolator." They are created as the first steps in the development of a performance checklist. Notice that the process steps follow the three major considerations for detailing a process which were discussed in Chapter 7:

1. Begin each step with a verb.
2. List all major steps.
3. Include only one major activity in each step.

Criteria. Stating the objective and the procedural steps are the first two stages of developing a performance test. However, they do not allow one to judge the quality of the performance or to obtain a score that is useful in providing feedback and reporting learners' progress. Just like a written test should have an answer key so than one can judge whether a learner has provided the correct response, a performance test must specify criteria useful in judging whether a procedural step has been completed correctly. *Criteria* are the bases for judging whether a learner has performed each process step correctly.

Table 16.3 presents criteria for judging whether learners perform each step to the expected level of performance. The criteria should be clear enough to allow an instructor to judge the same performance consistently. They should also be clear enough to allow different instructors to judge the same performance consistently. In other words, the goal is to make the scoring "objective." If different instructors are going to use the same performance checklist, it is important that they develop the checklist jointly so they can agree upon the criteria. That will ensure that the criteria are understood by those who will be using the checklist and that the criteria will be applied uniformly.

TABLE 16.3 Sample Psychomotor Performance Checklist

OBJECTIVE

Givens
A clean electric percolator, a percolator cord, coffee, a filter, water, a tablespoon, and electricity

Behavior
Prepare a full pot of coffee with an electric percolator.

Standard
The procedure specified in the instructor checklist must be completed in the order listed within 10 minutes.

CRITICAL	PROCESS (PROCEDURAL STEPS)	SAT.	UNSAT.	CRITERIA
	1. Assemble the materials.	1	0	Givens assembled
	2. Disassemble the percolator.	1	0	Major parts separated
*	3. Select cold water.	1	0	Cold to touch
	4. Fill the percolator with water.	1	0	To full line
	5. Place the basket on the stem.	1	0	Basket on stem
	6. Place the basket and stem assembly into the percolator.	1	0	Assembly inserted, stem in base hole
	7. Place the filter into the basket.	1	0	Filter inside basket, firmly around outside
*	8. Measure the coffee.	2	0	One tablespoon per cup
	9. Place the measured coffee in the basket.	1	0	Measured coffee in basket
	10. Place the cover on the basket.	1	0	Cover over basket
	11. Place the cover on the percolator.	1	0	Cover on percolator
	12. Plug the cord into the percolator.	1	0	Cord in percolator
	13. Plug the cord into the electric receptacle.	1	0	Cord into receptacle

Total score ________

Starting time ________
Ending time ________
Minimum acceptable score = 14

When writing criteria, avoid certain terms such as *accurately, correctly, appropriately,* and *properly.* These terms do not convey sufficient precision. Criteria should clearly indicate what is accurate, correct, precise, and so on.

Critical Steps. The next step in the development of a performance test is to determine if there are any critical steps. A critical step is one that must be performed with 100 percent accuracy because the liability of allowing a learner to continue without performing that step correctly would be too great. A critical step usually involves safety, cost of material, cost of time, and/or other resources. On a performance checklist, critical steps are indicated by asterisks (*) to the left of steps or actions. When a performance test is administered, the evaluation would be stopped if a learner did not perform a critical step or action correctly. Table 16.3 has critical steps identified in the column at the far left.

In this table, it has been determined that one must select cold water and measure the coffee based on the criteria in order for the coffee to be adequately produced. If these two steps are not adequately performed, then the coffee would have to be discarded. Rather than allowing the learner to complete the process after inadequately performing these steps and waste coffee, the performance test would be stopped. In this case, identification of critical steps has been based on cost of materials.

Performing a critical step is treated in the same way as going through a stop sign is treated on a driver's test. If a person goes through a stop sign without stopping during a driver's test, that is viewed as a significantly dangerous act; therefore, rather than just taking off points from the driver's test score, the tester stops the driver's test and the learner is required to return at a later time to retake the test.

Scoring Procedures. When a checklist is used, scoring is done on the basis of satisfactory versus unsatisfactory performance. The criterion for determining whether or not each procedural step is done satisfactorily or unsatisfactorily is specified in the criteria section of the checklist. If a procedural step meets the criterion, it is scored as satisfactory and the learner earns a certain number of points. If a procedural step does not meet the criterion, it is scored as unsatisfactory and the learner earns no points. When the performance is completed, all points earned are added together to arrive at a total score. That total score is then used as a basis for determining the extent of mastery of the behavior. If one is judging performance based on mastery versus nonmastery of material, a score reflecting mastery must also be specified. In many cases, *mastery* is defined as "performing the behavior 100 percent correctly." In other cases, some procedural steps might be performed incorrectly with the total process still being judged satisfactory. In those cases, the mastery-level score would be based on what would be considered to be adequate mastery performance. Judging overall performance based on the total score is discussed further in Chapter 19.

The number of points awarded for correctly performing each procedural step should be based on the importance of that step within the total performance of the behavior. For example, if measuring coffee is considered to be twice as important as the other steps in preparing a pot of coffee, it should be awarded 2 points and the other steps should each be awarded 1. Review Table 16.3 for how it is to be scored.

Performance Time. At times, it is not only important that a person complete a performance correctly, but that performance must be completed within certain time limitations. Time limits can be specified in two different ways. First, the maximum time allowed for the completion of the behavior can be specified. For example, the "standard" for the objective presented in Table 16.3 indicates that the performance must be completed within 10 minutes. In this case, the learner would have to repeat the test if it were not successfully completed within 10 minutes. Specifying time in this manner makes time a critical item. Learners either complete the performance within the specified time, or they do not. Monitoring performance time would be accomplished by entering the starting time on the checklist when the performance starts, entering the ending time when it is completed, and subtracting the two times. Notice that Table 16.3 has spaces to enter these times.

Second, the amount of time can be specified through a rating scale which awards a different number of points for completing the performance in different amounts of time. For example, a person may be given 3 points if a performance is completed within 5 to 7 minutes, 2 points if the performance if completed within 8 to 10 minutes, and 0 points if the performance takes longer than 10 minutes. If this latter approach were used, the total performance test score and the total amount of points for the time it took to complete the performance would be added together to arrive at a total score.

Minimum Acceptable Score. The minimum acceptable score is then calculated, which includes both the score on the test of performance and the score for the amount of time; or a separate minimum performance test score can be assigned to the amount of points obtained on completing the procedure, and another minimum acceptable score can be set for the amount of time. In other words, it would be possible to have one minimum acceptable score on the performance itself equal to 14 points, and another minimum acceptable score for time equal to 2 points.

Table 16.4 presents another sample performance checklist for the behavior "change a tire." Notice that no time requirement is indicated.

TABLE 16.4 Sample Psychomotor Performance Checklist

OBJECTIVE

Givens
A car with a flat tire, tools, and a replacement tire

Behavior
Change a tire.

Standard
Satisfactory performance on the performance checklist

CRITICAL	PROCEDURE	SAT.	UNSAT.	CRITERIA
*	1. Block the tires.	1	0	Blocks in front and back of tires not to be raised
	2. Position the jack.	1	0	Under jack-point as in manual
	3. Remove the hubcap.	1	0	Hubcap pried off
	4. Loosen the lug nuts.	1	0	Lug nuts loosened by one-quarter turn
	5. Etc.			

Total score ________

Minimum acceptable score = (e.g., 12)

Cognitive Performance Tests

The previous examples presented the development of performance tests for psychomotor behaviors. The procedures are equally applicable to cognitive and affective behaviors; however, each has unique components. The major uniqueness of cognitive performance evaluation is that the process to be evaluated is often not directly visible. It is occurring in the form of information processing within a person's mind. Therefore, checkpoints must be created to monitor the process as it is occurring. Checkpoints are analogous to those used when analyzing electronic circuits or in computer programs.

As the process takes place, certain things are assumed to be happening. However, for the evaluator to be sure that they are, stimuli must be produced which are capable of being seen, heard, smelled, and so on. Some of these stimuli may eventually be visible in a final product, but often they are not.

The basic logic for the development of cognitive performance tests has been used by mathematics instructors for many years when they have asked learners to show their calculations while solving a problem. They have not only been concerned with the end result, but with the process for getting there.

Table 16.5 presents a cognitive performance test for the behavior "decide which wrench to use." The process is again identified during behavior detailing. In this example, it is not possible to determine if a person has located the correct object without having her or him do something (e.g., point to it). It is also not possible to determine if a person has classified it correctly without having him or her do something (e.g., say the name).

Therefore, during the development of cognitive performance tests another component is added for each process step: the type of action expected. When selecting a type of action, one must take care to minimize the interruption of the learner. Types of actions are usually physical, verbal, or written. The rest of the process for developing a cognitive performance test is essentially the same as that used to develop psychomotor performance tests.

Affective Performance Tests

The purpose of affective process evaluation is to determine if learners can convey emotional tones that are associated with an affective behavior. Emotional tones are communicated through the actual words chosen, the way in which words are communicated, and body language, which includes posture and gestures.

Affective behaviors are communicated while performing the psychomotor or cognitive behaviors needed to carry out a function; therefore, affective behaviors are observed while a person is performing either a cognitive or psychomotor behavior. They rarely occur alone. One exhibits an affective behavior while in the process of doing something else. For example, to evaluate the behavior "cooperate with co-workers," the person being evaluated must be doing something requiring cooperation, such as carrying a table with another person.

The procedure for the development of an affective performance test is very similar to that for developing a psychomotor performance test. An affective performance test is developed using the first five steps presented earlier for the development of psychomotor performance tests:

TABLE 16.5 Sample Cognitive Performance Checklist

OBJECTIVE

Givens
A part requiring a wrench for removal and a variety of wrenches.

Behavior
Decide which wrench to use.

Standard
According to the instructor checklist

PROCESS (PROCEDURAL STEPS)	SAT.	UNSAT.	TYPE OF ACTION	CRITERIA
1. Identify the location of the object.	1	0	Point	Points to object
2. Determine the type of object (e.g., a bolt or a stud).	1	0	Label	Names the object
3. Match the functions of types of wrenches with the object.	1	0	Point	Points to wrench designed for object
4. Determine the size of the object.	1	0	Measure	Measures by trying various sizes
5. Select the wrench designed to remove the object.	1	0	Apply	Uses a wrench that fits the object tightly

Total score ________

Minimum acceptable score = 5

1. State the objective, or the behavior, that is to be evaluated.
2. Specify the process, or actions.
3. Specify the criteria for judging the actions.
4. Specify the scoring procedure.
5. Determine the minimum acceptable score, if needed.

A key difference between the development of a psychomotor or a cognitive performance test and the development of an affective performance test is that the process to be evaluated is listed as a set of actions rather than as procedural steps. The rationale for this distinction and for how the tests are developed is presented in Chapter 7. Table 16.6 is a sample completed affective checklist. It will be referred to throughout the following discussion.

The behavioral objective for an affective performance test should be written in three parts. The actions to be observed should convey emotional tones through actual words chosen, the way in which words, are communicated, and body language. Table 16.6 presents a partial list of such actions for the affective behavior "cooperate with co-workers."

Criteria for judging actions are specified in terms of what one would see if a person performed each of the actions correctly. For example, what would one see if a person actually listened to co-workers? One would see the person accurately repeating what others have said and incorporating what was said into his or her own conversation. This would verify that the person really did listen. Notice that the criteria in Table 16.6 are *not* specified in terms of the psychomotor or cognitive behavior which is being performed that requires the cooperation. In other words, if two people were cooperating while carrying a table, the observer would not focus on the process of carrying the table, but on the cooperative interaction between the two people as they carried the table.

The development of the scoring procedure for affective performance tests is the same as that used with psychomotor and cognitive behaviors.

The sample affective process evaluation presented in Table 16.6 uses relatively large, complex actions to define the expected affective behavior. This is possible if one can assume that people comprehend the concepts of assisting, compromising, communicating, and so on. However, at times one is faced with the need to teach much more precise actions which convey emotional tones. That is the case in the example of "accept a customer as an individual" presented in Table 16.7. In this example, the goal is to teach people how to convey that they accept customers as individuals so that the customers feel comfortable during the selling process. In this case, the psychomotor or cognitive behavior would be selling. The affective behavior to be demon-

TABLE 16.6 Sample Affective Performance Checklist

OBJECTIVE

Givens
Co-workers and a situation requiring cooperation

Behavior
Cooperate with co-workers.

Standard
Satisfactory score on the affective checklist

ACTIONS	SAT.	UNSAT.	CRITERIA
1. Listen to co-workers.	1	0	*a.* Repeats what others say
	1	0	*b.* Incorporates what others say in own conversation
2. Communicate with co-workers.	1	0	*a.* Talks to others
	1	0	*b.* Uses terms which others comprehend
	1	0	*c.* Ask others if they understand
3. Assist others when asked.	1	0	When others ask for assistance, the person assists
4. Compromise.	1	0	*a.* Changes mind to agree with the majority if there is more than one correct way to do the behavior
	1	0	*b.* Searches for a solution which most can support

Total score ________

Minimum mastery level = (e.g., 14)

strated would be "accept the customer as an individual." Notice that the actions in this example are much more precise. The criteria are also more precise.

In the affective examples presented, there is a recipient of the performance. Therefore, it would also be possible to evaluate the performance based on a recipient reaction. This can be done by asking recipients for their global reactions to the performance (e.g., "Did you feel accepted?") or by having them complete a checklist.

PERFORMANCE TEST ASSIGNMENTS

The second part of administering a formal performance test is to give an assignment to the learner. The learner must be directed to perform a behavior so the performance can be observed and evaluated. The assignment can be given to the learner either orally or in writing. Without an assignment, the learner will not know what he or she is expected to perform.

Psychomotor or Cognitive Performance Test Assignment

Table 16.8 presents the assignment format for a psychomotor behavior. The assignment should begin with a clear statement of the behavioral objective that the learner is expected to demonstrate. It should include the givens, which specify what the learner will need to complete the behavior. The amount of givens specified should allow the learner to clearly comprehend the behavior expected. However, care must be taken not to provide answers to part of the performance test. For example, if part of the test is to determine if people can select the correct tools and equipment, the tools and equipment should not be listed in the givens on the assignment sheet. The objective should also specify the behavior that the learner is expected to demonstrate, and the standard against which the learner will be judged. If the standard is complex, reference should be made to the checklist or to some other document within which the standard is published. Again, as with the givens, care needs to be taken not to provide answers to part of the performance test.

The second item in the assignment indicates where the performance should take place. Usually the performance will take place in a laboratory or a classroom, but at times it may take place at another location. For example, if a person is in a health occupations program, the performance might take place in a clinical setting such as a hospital.

The third part of the assignment is specifications relating to the expected performance. For example, if the performance is expected to produce a product, specifications might include the types, sizes, and/or color of material, or a blueprint of the product to be produced. If a person is asked to drill a hole with a drill press, one might specify the type of material to be drilled and the size of the hole.

If time to complete the performance is of concern,

TABLE 16.7 Sample Affective Performance Checklist

OBJECTIVE

Givens
A situation in which a person is selling something to a customer, and a customer

Behavior
Accept the customer as an individual.

Standard
Satisfactory score on the affective checklist

ACTIONS	SAT.	UNSAT.	CRITERIA
1. Smile.	1	0	Standard smile as indicated on reference chart 1
2. Control voice volume.	1	0	Normal conversational volume, similar to that used by customer
3. Select words.	1	0	Approximately ninth-grade level, as indicated in reference list
4. Compromise.	1	0	Changes mind to agree with the customer if the customer's views are also correct
5. Position body.	1	0	*a.* Face the customer at least 90 percent of the time
	1	0	*b.* Stand or sit erect
6. Maintain eye contact.		0	Look customer in the eye at least 80 percent of the time

Total score ________

Minimum acceptable score = 6

the time allotted to complete the performance is also indicated. This informs the learner of the total amount of time available to complete the performance test.

In the assignment for a cognitive objective, it is also important to indicate when a visible action should be made and what type of visible action should be made. For example, when selecting the wrench associated with Table 16.5, learners must be informed that they are supposed to point to the object, and that they are to name the type of object. Otherwise, these steps would be invisible to the evaluator.

In addition to the five items already mentioned, there may be other directions needed by the learner to complete a performance. For example, some performances must be completed with the help of others. In those cases, the procedure for identifying someone to help or assist with the performance would be indicated.

TABLE 16.8 Psychomotor or Cognitive Performance Test Assignment Format

The assignment should include:

1. The behavioral objective
2. Where the performance should take place
3. Specifications (e.g., sizes, blueprint, material, and color)
4. Time allotted
5. Types of visible actions expected, and when (cognitive only)
6. Other directions needed by the learner

Table 16.9 presents a sample psychomotor performance assignment for the behavior "change a tire."

Affective Performance Test Assignment

The format for an affective performance test assignment is slightly different than that used with psychomotor and cognitive behaviors. Table 16.10 presents the components of the assignment format for an affective performance test. It includes the behavioral objective, where the performance should take place, performance specifications, the time allotted, and other directions as needed. The primary difference between the assignment format for affective performance tests and other forms

TABLE 16.9 Psychomotor Performance Test Assignment

Givens
A car with a flat tire, tools, and a replacement tire

Behavior
Change a tire.

Standard
Satisfactory score on the performance checklist

1. Change a tire.
2. The car is at the side of the road.
3. The tire should be the rear right one.
4. The tire should be changed within 15 minutes.
5. Before starting to change the tire, ask the instructor to come and observe the process you use to change the tire.

TABLE 16.10 Affective Assignment Format

The assignment should include:

1. The behavioral objective
2. Where the performance should take place
3. Performance specifications (e.g., scenarios):
   a. Setting
   b. Players
   c. Players' roles
   d. Equipment or materials
4. Time allotted
5. Other directions needed by the learner

of performance tests is in the performance specifications. The performance specifications can include the setting, players that are involved, roles each player is expected to play, any equipment and materials that are needed, and any other details needed. Part of the definition of the setting includes a description of the cognitive or psychomotor behavior that should be taking place while the affective behavior is to be evaluated (e.g., "carry a table" or "sell something"). If the behavior to be evaluated does not involve other people (e.g., "care for equipment"), specifications related to other people are not needed.

Affective behaviors are evaluated during real-life situations or during role-playing simulations. It is suggested that if one is not familiar with role playing as an instructional method, one should obtain references and review how that method is implemented.

The performance specifications must be clearly stated. If role playing is used, they are usually stated as a scenario which define the situation within which the performance is to take place. Players may receive either the same scenario or differing scenarios. Therefore, there may need to be a somewhat different assignment sheet for each player. This is to simulate the real-life situations in which different people have different perspectives of what is happening in a given situation and they have to arrive at a solution which is acceptable to all. Each scenario presents a context within which a player is to view the performance that is to take place. It must define the setting, the various players, the roles of the players, and any equipment or materials that will be needed from the perspective from which a particular player is to perceive the situation.

If each person is to receive a different scenario, it is important that each one not see the scenarios of the other people. For example, if the behavior "cooperate with co-workers" is to be evaluated, each person must be provided with a scenario that sets the stage for the interaction and clearly defines the role she or he is to play. One person may be the lead worker, with the other people to follow. One person may be instructed through the scenario to be disruptive; one uncooperative; and one apathetic. The person being evaluated would then be judged in terms of the ability to be cooperative in light of these types of people and circumstances.

TABLE 16.11 Affective Performance Test Assignment

Givens
Co-workers and a situation requiring cooperation

Behavior
Cooperate with co-workers.

Standard
Satisfactory score on the affective checklist.

1. The performance should take place within the machine-shop lab.
2. Performance specifications:
   a. The setting is three people who are to plan which of five components of a product each will produce.
   b. The players are yourself and two other learners who have a background in machine shop.
   c. You must help the group arrive at a solution which is acceptable to all of you.
   d. The materials required are a production schedule for the production of the product, blueprints for each of the separate components, and a scenario for you and each of the other learners.
4. The plan is to be complete in 20 minutes.
5. After you complete the assignment, turn in a production schedule which indicates who will produce each component.

Table 16.11 presents a sample affective performance test assignment for the affective behavior "cooperate with co-workers." In this case, the scenario for all people in the performance is the same, so the same assignment sheet can be given to all of them.

SUMMARY

The ability of a learner to perform the process associated with a behavior can be evaluated through either a performance test or a product test. A performance test focuses on the process of performing, and a product test focuses on the characteristics of a finished product as the result of performing.

Performance tests usually take the form of checklists that require the evaluator to judge between two categories such as satisfactory versus unsatisfactory. However, if finer distinctions are needed in the quality of performance, rating scales can be developed which allow the evaluator to judge between more quality categories and, therefore, differentiate performance more precisely.

A performance test is composed of two parts. The first is the instrument, such as a performance checklist, which will be used by an evaluator to judge the adequacy of the performance. The second is the assignment that will be given to learners so they will know which behavior to perform.

Performance tests can be used with psychomotor, cognitive, and affective behaviors. Affective performance tests concentrate on the emotional tones communicated by an individual performing a cognitive or a psychomotor behavior. During the development and administration of an affective performance test it is important to separate the emotional tones being communicated from the actual procedures performing the psychomotor or cognitive behavior.

EVALUATION AND ACTIVITIES

1. Select a psychomotor, a cognitive, and an affective behavior for which you would like to develop a performance test. Identify, using the behavior-detailing procedures presented in Chapter 7, the process that a person would follow in completing those behaviors.

2. Develop a performance test for each behavior using the formats for performance tests presented in this chapter.
   a. State the objective be evaluated.
   b. Specify the procedural steps or actions. (Also enter the types of visible actions expected on the cognitive performance test.)
   c. Specify criteria for judging the steps or actions.
   d. Indicate the critical steps or actions (if any).
   e. Determine how many points will be awarded for each step or action, and enter that number in the column labeled "satisfactory."
   f. Specify the performance time (if needed).
   g. Determine the minimum acceptable score (if needed).

3. Develop an assignment sheet for each behavior.

REFERENCES

Butler, F. C., *Instructional Systems Development for Vocational and Technical Training,* Educational Technology Publications, Englewood Cliffs, NJ, 1972.

Pucel, D. J., and W. C. Knaak, *Individualizing Vocational and Technical Instruction,* Charles E. Merrill, Columbus, OH, 1975.

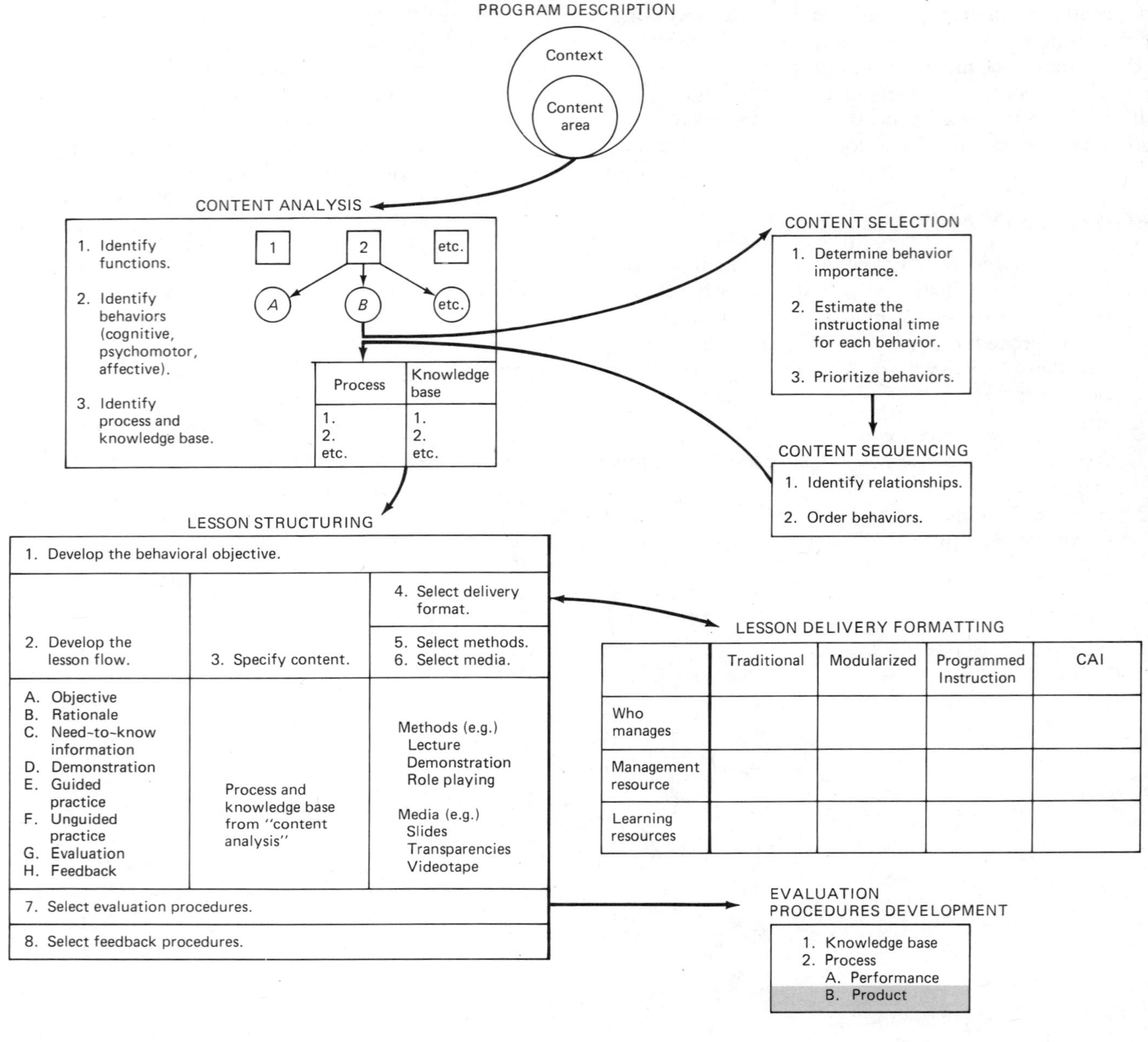
PROGRAM DESCRIPTION
Context
Content area
CONTENT ANALYSIS
1. Identify functions.
2. Identify behaviors (cognitive, psychomotor, affective).
3. Identify process and knowledge base.
1
2
etc.
A
B
etc.
Process
Knowledge base
1.
2.
etc.
1.
2.
etc.
CONTENT SELECTION
1. Determine behavior importance.
2. Estimate the instructional time for each behavior.
3. Prioritize behaviors.
CONTENT SEQUENCING
1. Identify relationships.
2. Order behaviors.
LESSON STRUCTURING
1. Develop the behavioral objective.
2. Develop the lesson flow.
3. Specify content.
4. Select delivery format.
5. Select methods.
6. Select media.
A. Objective
B. Rationale
C. Need-to-know information
D. Demonstration
E. Guided practice
F. Unguided practice
G. Evaluation
H. Feedback
Process and knowledge base from "content analysis"
Methods (e.g.)
Lecture
Demonstration
Role playing
Media (e.g.)
Slides
Transparencies
Videotape
7. Select evaluation procedures.
8. Select feedback procedures.
LESSON DELIVERY FORMATTING
Traditional
Modularized
Programmed Instruction
CAI
Who manages
Management resource
Learning resources
EVALUATION PROCEDURES DEVELOPMENT
1. Knowledge base
2. Process
A. Performance
B. Product

Developing Product Tests

CHAPTER OBJECTIVE

Givens

A process to be evaluated which produces a product

Behavior

Develop a product test.

Standard

The test must be developed to evaluate the characteristics of a specific product and must include an evaluation instrument and assignment.

OVERVIEW

This chapter builds on the general overview of process evaluation and the detailed discussion of performance test development presented in Chapter 16. It concentrates on the unique aspects of product evaluation. The difference between performance evaluation and product evaluation can be reviewed in Chapter 16. The procedures presented in this chapter have been adapted from those presented in *Individualizing Vocational and Technical Instruction* (Pucel and Knaak, 1975).

A product test is one type of process evaluation. It focuses on the evaluation of the product of a performance. Although all processes can be evaluated with a performance test, only some processes can be evaluated with a product test. Product tests can only be conducted in those situations in which a physical change that can be attributed to a performance remains after completion of the performance. Product tests can be used with psychomotor, cognitive, and affective behaviors. For example, the psychomotor behavior "change a tire" will result in a changed tire; the cognitive behavior "allocate salary increases" will result in a distribution of salary increase money; and the affective behavior "cooperate with co-workers to allocate projects" will result in a list of projects being allocated to co-workers that contains each of the co-worker's signatures, which indicates that they agree to the allocation. In each of these cases, a physical change remains after completion of the performance which can be attributed to the performance. A new part is in place, or a blank sheet of paper has something written on it.

Some performances have no products. For example, if a person dives into a swimming pool, the quality of the dive cannot be evaluated after it is completed because after the process is completed there is no physical change remaining that reflects the quality of the dive. The fact that the swimmer may be dry before starting the dive and wet after completing the dive does not reflect on the quality of the dive. Likewise, in evaluating the behavior "put on a sterile gown" when preparing an operating room, someone must observe a person putting on a gown to determine whether or not it was done using sterile procedures. If someone only observes the individual after the gown has been put on, it is not possible to determine that sterile procedures have been used. The gown may have been dropped on the floor without it getting dirty, and it then may have been put on.

The basic difference between a performance test and a product test is that a performance test concentrates on the process of performing, and a product test concentrates on the characteristics of the finished product of performing. As with a performance test, a product test has two parts: the evaluation instrument to be used by the evaluator, and the assignment that is given to the learner.

PRODUCT TEST DEVELOPMENT

The development of a product evaluation instrument is accomplished using the following five-step process:

1. State the objective to be evaluated.
2. Specify the product characteristics to be observed.
3. Specify the criteria for judging the quality of each characteristic.
4. Specify the scoring procedure.
5. Specify the performance time.
6. Determine the minimum acceptable score (if needed).

Objective

The first step in the development of a product test is to state the behavioral objective to be evaluated and to identify the product of performing a behavior. (See Table 17.1.)

Notice that the standard in this case is stated in terms of observable characteristics of the product of performing, in other words, what can be seen after the performance has been completed. The process for inserting the thread through the needle is not the focus of this objective. The focus is on what would be seen after the thread has been inserted. One would see "a single stand of thread through the eye of the needle."

Again, as in stating the behavioral objective for a performance test, if the standard is complex and therefore cannot be reasonably listed in the objective itself, it is appropriate to state it in terms of a satisfactory

TABLE 17.1 Behavioral Objective Stated as the Basis for the Development of a Product Test

Given
A sewing needle and thread

Behavior
Thread a sewing needle.

Standard
A single strand of thread is through the eye of the needle.

score on the product checklist or in reference to other published material. That material then clearly states the standard.

In the following objective for a product test for the behavior "change a tire," the standard is complex. If all of the expected characteristics were listed in the objective, it would become extremely long and would not be functional for other portions of the instructional design process. Therefore, reference is made to another document in which the standard is more completely stated (e.g., the product checklist). (See Table 17.2.) The product of this performance is obviously a changed tire.

Product Characteristics

After the behavioral objective has been stated and the product that will result has been identified, the expected characteristics of the completed product must be identified. These characteristics should be capable of distinguishing a satisfactory product from an unsatisfactory one. Examine Table 17.2 for product characteristics for the behavior "change a tire." Notice that the basic format of a product test is very similar to that of a performance test. However, the standard is in reference to the product, and instead of procedural steps being listed, characteristics of the product are listed along the left-hand side.

Criteria

After the objective of the product test and the characteristics of the product to be observed have been identified, the next step is to state the criteria that will be used to determine whether or not each of the characteristics of the completed product is of sufficient quality. In this case, criteria are the bases for judging if a characteristic of a product meets quality standards. Notice that in Table 17.2 a criterion is presented for each characteristic. The criteria should be clear enough to allow an evaluator to consistently judge the same product characteristic. They should also be clear enough to allow different evaluators to consistently judge the same characteristic.

Scoring Procedure

The next step in the development of a product checklist is to determine how it will be scored. Point values are assigned to the satisfactory attainment of quality for each characteristic. More-important characteristics should be weighted more heavily and assigned more points than less-important ones.

Unsatisfactory performance should be awarded no points. After the point values for each characteristic are established, they must be entered on the product checklist and totalled.

Performance Time

As with a performance test, it is possible to evaluate the time needed to complete the product. Time can be evaluated either in terms of an absolute limit (e.g., "complete in 10 minutes or one must repeat the evaluation") or on a rating scale similar to that presented during the discussion of the development of a performance checklist. Quality and time scores are added together to obtain the total score.

TABLE 17.2 Sample Product Checklist

OBJECTIVE

Givens
A car with a flat tire, tools, and a replacement tire

Behavior
Change a tire.

Standard
Satisfactory score on the product checklist within 10 minutes

CHARACTERISTICS	SAT.	UNSAT.	CRITERIA
1. A replacement tire has been mounted.	1	0	Tire that is on the car is not the one that was to be replaced.
2. Lugs are tight.	1	0	Torqued to foot-pounds in the manual
3. Tools are replaced.	1	0	Tools are returned to where they were before the test.
4. The replaced tire is stored.	1	0	Replaced tire is secure in the spare-tire compartment.

Total score ______

Minimum acceptable score = 4

TABLE 17.3 Product Test Assignment

Givens
A car with a flat tire, tools, and a replacement tire

Behavior
Change a tire.

Standard
Satisfactory score on the product checklist

1. Change a tire.
2. The car is at the side of the road.
3. The tire should be the right rear tire.
4. The tire should be changed within 15 minutes.
5. After changing the tire, ask the instructor to come and observe what you have done before moving the car.

Minimum Acceptable Score

If a minimum acceptable score is expected, it must be specified. (See Table 17.2.)

PRODUCT TEST ASSIGNMENT

The assignment is the vehicle through which the instructor tells the learner to produce something to be evaluated. The assignment can be given either orally or in writing. The assignment format is identical to that used with a performance test with the exception that the learner must be informed about how the product will be presented for evaluation (e.g., "present it to the instructor" or "ask the instructor to come and observe"). This enables the final product to be evaluated. Table 17.3 presents a sample product test assignment. Notice that item 5 indicates what should be done after the product is completed. In this case, after changing the tire, the learner would ask the instructor to come and observe what has been done before moving the car.

INSTRUCTOR CHECKPOINTS

At times, a person may be willing to infer that portions of a process have been performed correctly if certain evidence is provided. This is done when it is not reasonable to invest the time it would take to observe the total performance yet a product is not produced, or when the product would not provide sufficient information about the actual process used to create it.

In such cases, instructor checkpoints can be used to direct the learner to stop the performance and to inform the instructor. The instructor can then come and evaluate the outcome of the performance to those points. An instructor checkpoint is indicated as a box in the left-hand column of the product test. After an instructor has completed the evaluation of the items related to the checkpoint, he or she places a checkmark in the box to indicate that the related procedural steps or characteristics have been evaluated.

Table 17.4 presents a sample checklist with instructor checkpoints for the behavior "prepare a full pot of coffee with an electric percolator." In this case, we assume that a simple taste test would be too subjective, and a full performance test would be too time-consuming. Two instructor checkpoints are presented. The first indicates that before placing the cover on the percolator, the learner is to call the instructor. This would allow the instructor to evaluate items 1 through 8 before the performance continues. At that point, it would be possible to determine if all the materials have been assembled, whether the water in the percolator is cold, whether the percolator has been filled to the full line, and so on. If the performance were totally completed and an instructor checkpoint were not used, these items would not all be observable. The second instructor checkpoint takes place after the percolator has stopped brewing. At this point it is possible to determine if procedural steps 9 through 13 have been completed adequately and whether or not the coffee has been brewed. Again, if the performance were totally completed and only the product (in this case, the coffee) evaluated, these steps would not have been capable of being evaluated.

Instructor checkpoints can also be used to periodically stop a performance to observe the next steps in the performance. For example, if one were evaluating "change a tire," one could have an instructor checkpoint prior to the jacking of the car. In that case, steps completed earlier (e.g., tires were blocked and jack was positioned correctly) could be evaluated. However, in addition, one could be present to observe and evaluate the performance of jacking the car to ensure that safety precautions were adequately followed.

Instructor checkpoints can also be used to periodically stop product development to evaluate its stages. For example, when evaluating "replace the power supply in a microcomputer," it would make sense to stop the performance and evaluate the quality of the installation of the power supply before the computer is completely reassembled. Otherwise, one would have to disassemble the computer to evaluate the installation of the power supply. After the computer is complete reassembled, it could again be evaluated to judge the quality of the reassembly.

Instructors will find that it is most practical to use instructor checkpoints when judging lengthy performances or complex products with portions no longer visible after completion. In the case of lengthy performances, the instructor can be called to directly observe only critical performance steps. In the case of complex products, the instructor can inspect portions before the product is completed; for example, a carburetor for a car could be inspected before the cover is placed on it and before it is placed on the car engine. Otherwise the carburetor, or product, would have to be taken from the car and opened to judge if it were assembled correctly.

TABLE 17.4 Performance Test with Instructor Checkpoints

OBJECTIVE

Givens
A clean electric percolator, a percolator cord, coffee, filter, water, a tablespoon, and electricity

Behavior
Prepare a full pot of coffee with an electric percolator.

Standard
The procedure specified in the instructor checklist

CRITICAL CHECKPOINT	PROCESS OR CHARACTERISTICS	SAT.	UNSAT.	CRITERIA
	1. Assembled the materials	1	0	Givens assembled
*	2. Selected cold water	1	0	Cold to touch
	3. Filled the percolator with water	1	0	To full line
	4. Placed basket on the stem	1	0	Basket on stem
	5. Placed the basket and stem assembly into the percolator	1	0	Assembly inserted, stem into base hole
	6. Placed the filter into the basket	1	0	Filter inside basket, firmly around outside
*	7. Measured the coffee	2	0	One tablespoon per cup
	8. Placed the measured coffee in the basket	1	0	Measured coffee in basket
☐	Before placing the cover on the percolator, call the instructor.			
	9. Placed the cover on the basket	1	0	Cover over basket
	10. Placed cover on percolator	1	0	Cover on percolator
	11. Plugged the cord into percolator	1	0	Cord in percolator
	12. Plugged the cord into receptacle	1	0	Cord into receptacle
*	13. Coffee brewed	3	0	Coffee hot, percolator stopped perking
☐	After the coffee has been brewed, call the instructor.			

Total score ________

Minimum acceptable score = 14

If instructor checkpoints are used, the assignment format must also include those instructor checkpoints. This is necessary because without the checkpoints indicated, the learner would not know when to stop to ask the instructor to evaluate the performance or product.

RATING SCALES

The discussions of the development of performance tests and product tests in Chapter 16 and this chapter have centered on the development of checklists. The checklist is an instrument used to judge performance on a two-category scale such as satisfactory versus unsatisfactory, good versus bad, or yes versus no. At times, one may want to make finer distinctions about performance or product quality. In these cases, rather than developing a checklist, that person would develop a rating scale. The basic difference between a checklist and a rating scale is in the way in which the criteria are specified. Whereas a checklist allows a person to make judgments between two categories, a rating scale allows an evaluator to make judgments among more than two categories, for example, above average, average, and below average.

Rating scales need more criteria than checklists, since judgments are classified into more categories. One criterion allows a decision between two categories (e.g., satisfactory versus unsatisfactory). Two criteria allow classification into three categories (e.g., above average, average, and below average). There is always one less criterion than categories of judgments. In the example of averages, one must specify a criterion to separate average from above average, and another criterion to separate below average from average. Or one could define a criterion for defining above average and another criterion for defining average; if neither criteria were met, the performance would be below average.

Table 17.5 presents a sample performance rating scale for the behavior "change a tire." Notice that in this case criteria are developed for above average and average.

TABLE 17.5 Sample Performance Rating Scale

OBJECTIVE

Givens
A car with a flat tire, tools, and a replacement tire

Behavior
Change a tire.

Standard
Satisfactory performance on the performance rating scale

PROCEDURE	ABOVE AVERAGE (3)	AVERAGE(2)	BELOW AVERAGE (1)
1. Block the tires.	Blocks in front and back of all tires not to be jacked	Blocks in front and back of two not to be jacked	Does not meet criterion for average
2. Position jack.	Jack is directly below jack point	Jack is within 1 inch of being below jack point	Does not meet criterion for average
3. Etc.			

Total score ________

Minimum acceptable score = (30)

Below average is defined as not meeting one of the other two criteria. The total score is obtained by adding the point values for each of the criterion levels obtained for each procedural step or characteristic. In this example, above average is assigned 3 points, average 2 points, and below average 1 point.

SUMMARY

Product tests focus on the product that results after performing a process. They include an evaluation instrument and an assignment sheet. Product tests are developed around characteristics of a product and are used to judge the quality of those characteristics.

Instructor checkpoints are used to stop a performance so performance steps or product characteristics completed earlier can be evaluated, or they can be used to observe performance steps which are about to occur. They can increase the efficiency of process evaluation by eliminating the necessity for an evaluator continually being present as the performance is taking place. They can also increase efficiency by allowing for the examination of product development before portions of the product are no longer visible (e.g., before they become covered up by further assembly of the product).

Rating scales are used in place of checklists to increase the precision of quality judgments about performance or products. They increase the number of categories within which judgment of quality can be categorized.

ACTIVITIES AND EVALUATION

1. Select a behavior for which you would like to develop a product test. Make sure that a product is produced.
2. Develop a product checklist for that behavior.
   a. Specify the objective.
   b. Specify the product characteristics to be observed.
   c. Specify the criteria for each characteristic.
   d. Specify the scoring procedure.
   e. Specify performance time, if needed.
   f. Determine the minimum acceptable score, if needed.
3. Develop an assignment sheet for the product test.
4. Convert one set of criteria to judge one characteristic into a rating scale.
5. Indicate how you might adapt the product test to incorporate instructor checkpoints.

REFERENCE

Pucel, D. J., and W. C. Knaak, *Individualizing Vocational and Technical Instruction,* Charles E. Merrill, Columbus, OH, 1975.

Informal Evaluation

CHAPTER OBJECTIVE

Givens

A structured lesson

Behavior

Develop informal knowledge-base and process evaluations.

Standard

The evaluations must address the key information and process points associated with mastering a specific behavior.

OVERVIEW

Previous chapters have discussed the formal evaluation of learner progress toward stated objectives. The aims of such evaluation include formal recordkeeping and certification of the extent of mastery, reporting of progress, and providing of feedback. In contrast, the goal of informal evaluation is only to assess learning progress as a basis for adjusting instruction and providing feedback to learners during the process of instruction. The goal of informal evaluation is *not* to obtain information to record a learner's progress or to report that progress to others. Although formal evaluation usually takes place after learners have had sufficient instruction to be able to adequately demonstrate the extent of content mastery, informal evaluation takes place continually throughout the learning process. Table 10.1 shows that there are three major forms of informal evaluation procedures. They are self-checks, oral tutorial questioning, and tutorial observations. A more detailed discussion of the differences between formal and informal evaluation procedures is presented in Chapter 10.

Informal evaluations take place throughout the teaching and learning process so that the instructor and learner can assess how learning is proceeding. The results of that assessment are then used to adjust the teaching-learning process. In Chapter 10, the learner was likened to a rocket in flight that needs continuous feedback in order to adjust its course as winds and other conditions change. Learners need feedback in order to adjust the course of their learning and their perceptions of the adequacy of their skill. That feedback must be diagnostic, not just evaluative. In other words, it is not sufficient to just tell a learner that something has been done incorrectly. Information must also be provided that will allow the learner to adjust toward the desired behavior.

DEVELOPING INFORMAL EVALUATION PROCEDURES

Informal evaluation procedures may result in actual instruments which have the same form as formal knowledge-base or process tests (self-checks), or they may take the form of a list of questions to be asked or key points to be observed by the instructor during the learning process. In any case, they must be planned. They must focus on the major goals of the instruction taking place at the time.

Self-Checks

A self-check is an evaluation conducted by the learner to determine his or her learning progress. As was pointed out in Chapters 15 through 17, although self-checks are informal evaluation devices, they should be developed with the same precision as formal evaluation instruments so the learner can obtain diagnostic feedback to adjust accordingly. Such self-checks take the form of written tests and performance or product tests. The basic difference between self-checks and formal evaluation instruments is in their purpose and in who carries them out. Self-checks are not used to formally record progress; they are administered by the learners themselves.

Self-checks are planned to occur whenever the information or procedures learned become prerequisite to learning the next information or procedures. For example, suppose that to learn how to operate a word processing program the learner needs to use four major procedural steps, each of which requires the learner to master a previous step; the learner should complete a self-check after each step before proceeding to the next. The self-check would allow the learner to determine whether he or she has mastered the step sufficiently to move on to the next step. If the instructional materials were developed without the self-checks, the learner might attempt to learn all four steps, and he or she might not master any of them because of incorrect mastery of the first step. Although, through the use of the formal evaluation instruments, the instructor would still be able to determine whether or not learners had mastered the process by the end of the lesson, self-checks save time and frustration by redirecting learning before errors are compounded.

Self-checks can also guide the mastery of knowledge bases that are taught incrementally. In such cases, a self-check is appropriate after each increment to ensure that learners master the first increments before proceeding.

Tutorial Questioning and Observation

Oral tutorial questioning is the process of asking learners questions during the learning process to determine the extent of their mastery of the knowledge base related to a behavior. Tutorial observation is the process of observing learners during the learning process to determine the extent of their mastery of the process of performing a behavior. Both tutorial questioning and observation usually occur spontaneously as an instructor is interacting with and observing a learner during the learning process. Although they occur spontaneously, the instructor should clearly have in mind the knowledge-base objectives associated with the lesson and the process which the learner is to learn.

For example, if a person is learning to operate a word processing program with a microcomputer, the instructor should identify the key concepts and procedures to be learned. Then questions should be developed which can be asked of learners during the learning process. Also, the basic steps of procedure or actions to be learned should be identified so they can be observed. Based on the answers to the questions and on the observations of the basic procedural steps or actions, the instructor can determine if the learners are progressing satisfactorily or if adjustments are needed.

In other words, when a lesson is planned, the instructor or designer should identify key questions to be asked and process steps or actions to be observed which can be used as a basis for diagnosing if learners are having difficulty. The instructor should try to anticipate the nature of the problems that learners might have; therefore, she or he should plan to make sure that learners are questioned about or observed during those critical points. Also, the instructor should plan possible corrective action so that if a problem is identified, a solution can be presented. Although it is recognized that the teaching/learning process is fluid and must be spontaneous, during the planning of a lesson informal evaluation and feedback need to be anticipated to the extent possible. Informal evaluation should not, however, be limited to that which is planned.

The instrument used with oral tutorial questioning and observation takes the form of a list of questions or points to be observed. The list is used to remind the instructor to evaluate key points. Table 18.1 presents a sample list of questions concerning key knowledge-base information and key process points to be observed in our word processing example. Some instructors place these questions and the list of points on a notecard which they carry during instruction. Such a list is also useful if someone other than the instructional designer is going to work with the learners.

Table 18.2 summarizes the five major considerations for preparing and conducting informal tutorial questioning and observation. First, questions and observations should be focused on the knowledge base and process identified during planning. Second, if learners do not appear to understand the knowledge base or process, the questioning should be diagnostic. The goal is to determine where the learner is having difficulty and to help correct that difficulty. This is usually done by determining where the learner began to "go wrong." In other words, at what point was the learner's knowledge no longer correct, or at which point did the process become incorrect? That is the point at which remediation will need to begin.

TABLE 18.1 Sample List of Tutorial Questions and Points to Be Observed

Knowledge-Base Questions	Process Observation Points
1. What is the function of a word processing program? 2. What does INSERT mean? 3. Why must you SAVE the file you are working on? (etc.)	1. Insert a line into an existing paragraph. 2. Set margins. 3. Save a file. 4. Load a file. (etc.)

Third, the questioning and feedback should be done in a conversational style. The goal is to help adjust learning in a nonthreatening manner. The evaluation and feedback should be considered to be helpful, not threatening. This can be accomplished most easily by treating the evaluation and feedback as a conversation. If the conversation reveals that learning is not progressing satisfactorily, the conversation should turn to mutual diagnostic questioning with the goal of determining where learning has taken a wrong turn. The solution should also be considered in terms of a shared accomplishment.

Fourth, the conversation should be conducted using vocabulary and terminology that is understandable to the learner. In other words, the conversation must be at the level of the individual learner's understanding. Communication does not take place if each person in the conversation cannot understand the words the other is using.

Fifth, the learner should be clearly given the perception that the conversation is aimed at "helping," rather than at "criticizing." The perception of criticizing would have the effect of making the learner defensive. If the learner considers the conversation to be aimed at helping, he or she will be much more receptive to a continued, open interaction with the instructor during the instructional process.

TABLE 18.2 Considerations for Preparing and Conducting Informal Tutorial Questioning and Observation

1. Focus on major concepts and points.
2. Question diagnostically if the learner does not seem to understand a knowledge base or process. As a starting point, identify what the learner does know. Begin asking questions from that point to where the learner is incorrect. This will be useful in determining what remediation is necessary.
3. Use a conversational style.
4. Communicate at the learner's level. The vocabulary and terminology used should be understandable by the learner.
5. Put the learner at ease. She or he should not be made to feel defensive.

SUMMARY

The goal of informal evaluation is to assess learning progress as a basis for adjusting instruction and providing feedback to learners during the process of instruction. It takes place through self-checks, tutorial questioning, and tutorial observation. These are aimed at identifying learning difficulties during the learning process, and helping the learner correct those difficulties. Self-checks are self-administered instruments which allow learners to judge their own learning progress. Informal tutorial questioning and observation are conducted by the instructor. Informal tutorial questioning focuses on the knowledge base associated with a behavior. Informal tutorial observation focuses on the process of performing a behavior. If a person has not mastered either knowledge base or performance, the goal should be to identify what problems exist and to help the learner modify the learning process so that correct learning takes place.

ACTIVITIES AND EVALUATION

1. Select a behavior for which you would like to conduct informal tutorial questioning and observation. Identify at least three key knowledge-base questions which you feel each learner should be able to answer.
2. Identify at least three key process points associated with that behavior which you would observe during interaction with individual learners.
3. Place the questions and points into a table similar to Table 18.1.
4. Identify where in the lesson you would use a self-check. Explain why you would use it there.

Summarizing and Reporting Learner Progress

CHAPTER OBJECTIVE

Given

Learner evaluation data

Behavior

Summarize and report learner progress during and after instruction.

Standard

The evaluation data obtained during the instructional program must be summarized using criterion-referenced procedures for each behavior or for a reporting period. Postinstruction data must focus on the original intent of the program as specified in the program description.

OVERVIEW

Learner progress can be summarized and reported both during and after an instructional program. Although this chapter focuses primarily on summarizing and reporting progress during the program, a brief introduction to assessing postinstruction progress is presented at the end of the chapter. The primary purposes of summarizing and reporting learner progress during the program are to determine the extent to which learners have mastered program content, to report learner progress, and to provide diagnostic feedback useful in adjusting instruction. The primary purpose of postinstruction progress assessment is to determine the extent to which people who have completed the instructional program have attained the goal (e.g., increased productivity or jobs). It also provides diagnostic information which can be used to adjust the program in the future.

Data gathered through formal evaluation procedures during an instructional program are used to monitor learner progress during the program. They must be summarized and judged against standards in order for learner progress to be reported. As was pointed out in Chapter 10, learner progress can be judged against a norm-referenced standard (a learner's progress is judged by comparing it to the performance of other learners) or a criterion-referenced standard (a learner's progress is judged by comparing it against a predetermined performance standard called a *criterion*). Performance-based instruction uses criterion-referenced standards which are based on performance expectations. This allows progress to be reported as the extent to which a person has mastered content.

Although there are a variety of ways of expressing scores which represent the extent to which a learner has mastered content, the two most frequently used are raw scores and percentage scores. A *raw score* is the score obtained by counting the number of points earned on an instrument. A *percentage score* expresses a raw score as a percentage of the total possible raw-score points. For example, assume that a performance test has a total of 40 points and that a learner earns 30. The person's raw score would be 30. The person's percentage score would be 30/40 = 75 percent. The examples presented in this chapter will utilize percentage scores because they are more easily interpreted.

Although percentage scores are widely used, they do have theoretical limitations which designers must consider. First, the combining and averaging of percentage scores is frowned upon by mathematicians. They point out that 50 percent of 40 is not the same as 50 percent of 100. Second, the relationship between a person's percentage score and the amount of actual mastery of a behavior is not linear. In other words, it is not possible to say that a person who achieves a score of 50 percent on a test has mastered half as much of a behavior as a person who achieves a score of 100 percent. Typically it is more difficult to attain a 10 percentage point gain between 90 percent and 100 percent than it is to gain it between 20 percent and 30 percent. Although these theoretical concerns are real, most people consider them to be overshadowed by the practicality and usefulness of percentage scores as a basis for reporting mastery.

ALTERNATIVE TYPES OF REPORTING

Three approaches to reporting criterion-referenced progress will be presented: (1) mastery approach, (2) multiple-criterion approach, and (3) time-period approach.

Mastery Approach

The *mastery approach* to reporting learner progress is most compatible with the philosophy of performance-based instruction. The mastery approach is used to report whether a person has met the performance expectation for each behavior included in a program. A mastery-level score is set at the minimum achievement level needed to adequately perform the behavior.

Progress is reported as a list of behaviors that have been mastered. This approach to reporting progress is closely associated with individualized, self-paced instruction procedures. An assumption is made that learners will have an opportunity to continue to study a behavior until it is mastered. At that time, mastery will be recorded on the list. Table 19.1 presents a partial mastery report for an auto mechanics program. In the example, Mary Doe has mastered four of the behaviors presented and has not mastered three.

With this approach, mastery of a behavior is achieved when a learner has *mastered each of the separate formal evaluations* associated with that behavior. For example, assume that a behavior has a knowledge-base test, a product test, and a performance test associated with it. In order to master that behavior, a learner would

TABLE 19.1 Sampling Listing of Behaviors Mastered

Mary Doe *January 19XX*
Auto Mechanics Program Behaviors Mastered:

Behaviors	Mastery
Change a tire.	______
Check and add oil.	M
Drain coolant.	M
Decide which system needs maintenance.	M
Decide which tool to use.	______
Care for tools.	M
Cooperate with co-workers.	______

M = Mastered

have to achieve a mastery score on each of the three separate tests.

Mastery on each test is determined by whether or not a learner has achieved at least the mastery-level score. For example, if the mastery-level score on the knowledge-base test were 80 percent, on the performance test, 100 percent, and on the product test, 90 percent, a learner would have to achieve each of these scores in order to master that behavior. A score of 90 percent on the knowledge-base test would not compensate for a score of 80 percent on the product test.

The establishment of each mastery-level score requires judgment. There is no very precise way to establish such scores. How they are usually set is based on common sense and experience. However, a number of guidelines are available for establishing and validating mastery-level scores. The procedures presented were adapted from those presented by Pucel and Knaak (1975).

The process of establishing a mastery-level score is similar to the process of calibrating a measuring instrument. Most fields have instruments that require calibrating. For example, if we make a new ruler in a machine shop, we must in some way compare the new ruler with an old ruler or with another measuring device. This will allow us to calibrate the new ruler and put the markings on it that will allow us to measure in inches. If we buy a new syringe for giving injections that is not marked or calibrated, we must have some way of calibrating that syringe so that we know how much fluid is being injected. If we buy a new voltmeter, we must calibrate that new voltmeter by comparing the readings obtained from it with the readings obtained from another instrument that we know can accurately measure volts.

The same problem exists when constructing assessment instruments. We would like the instruments to be able to help us separate those people who have mastered a behavior from those who have not. However, the test instrument will only produce a series of numbers which, in and of themselves, are not meaningful. The problem facing the designer is to calibrate those numbers against something that is known so that the numbers become meaningful and a mastery-level score can be established.

The solution to the calibration problem is simple if the learner is expected to perform everything totally correctly or to get a 100 percent score. If this is the case, the learner either gets everything correct or she or he is judged to have not mastered the behavior. The problem becomes quite complex if the learner is not required to get everything correct in order to be judged as having mastered the behavior. The question becomes: What score must a person attain in order to be judged as having mastered the behavior?

At this point, designers often set mastery-level scores arbitrarily, for example, at 80 percent. This may be necessary at first because of time constraints in getting a program to be operational. However, if it is not possible to set the score more precisely at first, at some point the adequacy of the mastery-level scores should be assessed. Mastery scores set too low will result in inadequately prepared learners, and scores set too high can lead to a waste of time and other resources.

One way of arriving at or of validating an appropriate mastery-level score is to calibrate the scores against people who are satisfactorily performing in a role (e.g., people in an occupation). People who are satisfactorily performing are selected, and they are administered the assessment instrument. The scores they obtain on the instrument are then used to calibrate the instrument. Another method is to use expert judgment. Experts are asked to judge the performance of learners, and then the learners actually take the instrument. The scores on the instrument are then compared with the expert judgment and a mastery-level score is assigned.

Both of these procedures have inherent problems. The first procedure is difficult because it requires the identification of people who are performing satisfactorily in a role, and it requires that these people be available for assessment. The second procedure relies heavily on the judgment of experts. The judgments are only as good as the quality of the experts and their knowledge of a particular behavior.

Mastery Scores Based on People Practicing Successfully. Let us assume that we must establish some way of certifying mastery of the behavior "perform a vertical weld on mild steel." Instruments are first constructed to measure the process and knowledge base associated with the behavior. If one assumes that the instruments are well-constructed, the next concern would be to determine how to judge the results or the scores obtained from the instruments. If we use the procedure of assessing workers on the job, we would identify a group of welders who are judged as being able to perform a vertical weld on mild steel satisfactorily and who are judged to have a sufficient amount of knowledge of how to perform the behavior. Assume that we are able to identify 30 welders who are judged as having at least entry-level job skills related to performing a vertical weld on mild steel. We would administer our assessment instruments to the welders and determine their scores.

The scores on each instrument would then be placed in separate frequency distributions, such as the one presented in Table 19.2. A frequency distribution summarizes the number of people who have attained a certain score on an instrument. Let us assume that our 30 welders have achieved the scores on the knowledge-base test indicated in the frequency distribution presented in Table 19.2. One welder has attained a score of 90, five have attained a score of 82, none has attained a score of 78, and so on.

The mastery-level score would be determined by reviewing the frequency distribution and looking for natural breaks in the scores near the low end of the distribution. A natural break is a point in the distribution that seems to separate one group of scores from another group. In our example, a natural break appears near the bottom of the sample distribution between the scores of 79 and 76. One group had scores of 79 and above and another group had scores of 76 and below, separated by a break in the scores. Therefore, it would be logical to set the mastery-level score between 76 and 79 (e.g., at 78). If there is no natural break in the distribution, the mastery-level score is established at the lowest score above which most people performing satisfactorily in the role fall. The lowest score is not always selected because at times there are members of a group who perform far below the majority. Since these people are considered to be not typical of the group, the mastery-level score is established above their scores just following the bulk of the scores of the group.

We must assume that our sample of workers represents a typical group of workers. If the 30 welders that were selected were people who had ability far above that of typical welders to perform a vertical weld, the mastery-level scores established would not be appropriate for welders in general. The same would be true if the group selected consisted of very poor welders. If we can assume that the group of welders selected represents the range of successful welders, the mastery-level score established by this method will be quite accurate.

TABLE 19.2 Frequency Distribution for the Knowledge-Base Test

Score	Frequency	
90	1	
89	0	
88	0	
87	3	
86	2	
85	2	
84	3	
83	4	
82	5	
81	3	
80	2	
79	2	(Natural break
78	0	"mastery level")
77	0	
76	1	
75	2	
	$N = 30$	

Mastery Scores Based on Expert Judgment. Another method of establishing mastery-level scores used by designers is the expert judgment method. It relies primarily upon the judgment of the instructor or other knowledgeable people in the field. This procedure requires people to first review the instrument and judge which score would be necessary in order to be reasonably sure that a person has mastered a behavior. That score is later adjusted based upon information gathered on learners as they actually progress through instruction. It is adjusted by answering the question: Does the mastery-level score that was originally set actually separate those learners who have mastered the behavior from those who did not? In order to answer this question, the instructor must obtain some judgment of the proficiency of the learners on the behavior, and also assessment instrument scores. After these two pieces of information have been gathered for a sufficient number of people, the mastery-level score can be checked for reasonableness by observing how many learners who were judged to have mastered the behavior actually achieved scores above the mastery level, and how many learners who were judged as not having mastered the behavior achieved scores below the mastery level.

Using this procedure with our welding example, we would do the following: The instructor would construct the assessment instruments and select a mastery-level score for each which was based upon her or his judgment or upon the judgment of an advisory committee or another group of knowledgeable experts in the field. A separate mastery score would be assigned for each instrument associated with the behavior. The instructor, or other individuals, would select the score for each instrument which they felt would reflect a sufficient level of proficiency to perform satisfactorily at entry level in the role. Let us assume that the mastery-level score for the knowledge-base test has been established at 80 or above. The instructor would then begin to use the test and that mastery score as learners progress through instruction on the behavior.

The two pieces of information necessary to judge the adequacy of that mastery score would be obtained as follows: When a learner wished to be certified as having mastered the behavior, the instructor would administer the knowledge-base test. Before the instructor saw the test score, he or she would judge whether the learner had developed sufficient proficiency to perform at entry level. It is important that the instructor make this judgment prior to seeing the test score. The objective of checking the scores against the ratings is to determine the satisfactoriness of the mastery score. If the instructor views the assessment instrument scores before making the judgments, knowledge of the assessment instrument scores might affect the judgments.

The judgments and the scores for individuals are placed in a table such as that presented in Table 19.3. In some cases, learners will achieve scores above the mastery score and others will achieve scores below the mastery score. If a learner does not attain the mastery score the first time and retakes the instrument later, the score from only the first attempt is recorded. Actual mastery records for the group are based on the originally established mastery score. If that score is adjusted using this procedure, the adjusted score is used only with future groups.

Table 19.3 presents a summary of a group of learners' first attempts at completing the knowledge-base test for the behavior "perform a vertical weld on mild steel." Each learner's score is accompanied by a prior rating of the learner's proficiency level, which was based on a judgment of the instructor or another expert in the behavior being assessed. As one can see by examining Table 19.3, Paul was rated as having unsatisfactory performance, but he obtained a score of 87, which was relatively high. Warren was judged as having satisfactory performance, but he obtained a score of 70, which was relatively low. There does, however, appear to be a meaningful separation of those judged to be satisfactory from those judged to be unsatisfactory between a score of 78 and 74. This does not agree with the originally established mastery-level score of 81 or above. Therefore, the mastery score would be adjusted to "78 or above" for the future.

This technique relies heavily upon the judgment of the instructor or upon other experts in the field. The extent to which their judgments are accurate will determine the extent to which the mastery-level score will be accurate. The procedure should be repeated whenever it appears that the mastery-level score is no longer appropriate.

The methods of determining the adequacy of the established mastery-level scores discussed above relate to separate assessment instruments. It is also possible to obtain an overall indication of the adequacy of the mastery levels which have been set for an entire program. What would happen if all of the mastery-level scores are set consistently too high or too low? Follow-up studies of people who complete the program can provide answers to this question. If learners completing the program are found to not have developed enough skill to perform adequately in the role, the mastery-level score(s) may have been set too low. It is more difficult to determine if the scores are set too high, unless they are set extremely high. If the scores are set much too high, the learners will be overtrained for the role. When this happens, many will leave that role for a more-challenging one. In both cases, continued placement and retention in roles related to the training program will be low. In addition, as indicated earlier, if mastery-level scores are set too high, the efficiency of the instructional program is reduced. Overtraining may be an inefficient use of time and resources.

TABLE 19.3 Example Summary of Instructor's Judgments and Instrument Scores

Students' Names	KNOWLEDGE BASE Judgment	Score	
John	S	90	
Sam	S	90	
Pete	S	89	
Mary	S	88	
Paul	U	87	
Ken	S	85	
Sally	S	85	
Jim	S	84	
Bill	S	82	Original
Steve	S	81	mastery level
Jerry	U	79	
Howard	S	79	
Dave	S	79	New
Bob	S	78	mastery level
Ray	U	74	
Jack	U	74	
Lyle	U	72	
Don	U	71	
Warren	S	70	
Stan	U	70	

S = Satisfactory
U = Unsatisfactory

Multiple-Criterion Approach

At times there is a need to report the extent of mastery, and not only mastery versus nonmastery. Typical means of reporting levels of mastery are the use of letter grades and ratings (e.g., *A, B, C,* or 1, 2, 3). This requires the establishment of multiple criteria which allow for the determination of differences between each of the various levels of mastery. For example, one must determine a score range which differentiates an *A* from a *B*, a *B* from a *C*, and a *C* from a *D*. As with the establishment of a mastery-level score using the mastery approach, there is no precise way of determining these multiple criteria. Establishment must be based on a rationale and on common sense. A set of typical criteria are presented in Table 19.4.

Notice that each grade or rating has a verbal criterion associated with it that conceptually defines that grade relative to a person's ability to perform a behavior. One begins the process of assigning grades based on multiple criteria by first developing such a conceptual differentiation between the grades. Next, score ranges which correspond to these conceptual differentiations are developed which are similar to the mastery-level score. Typical multiple-criterion score ranges are 100–91 = *A*, 90–81 = *B*, 80–71 = *C*, 70–61 = *D*, 60 and below = *F*; or 100–94 = *A*, 93–88 = *B*, 87–80 = *C*, 79–75 = *D*, and 74 or below = *F*.

The simplest method of using this approach would

TABLE 19.4 Typical Criteria for Assigning Grades or Ratings

Score Range	Grade	Rating	Criteria
______ – ______	*A*	5	Performs behaviors with exceptional ability
______ – ______	*B*	4	Performs behavior above job-entry level
______ – ______	*C*	3	Performs behavior at job-entry level
______ – ______	*D*	2	Performs behavior with periodic assistance
______ – ______	*F*	1	Cannot perform the behavior satisfactorily with assistance

be to report a separate letter grade or rating for each test associated with each behavior. However, that is usually not acceptable. Learners and others generally want one summary grade or rating of the extent of mastery of a total behavior. This requires the combining of information regarding the mastery of the separate tests related to a behavior in order to arrive at one composite score.

The development of a composite score based on raw scores is very difficult. Therefore, it is recommended that all scores to be combined first be converted to percentages. Once the scores have been converted, the weight that each test should have in the composite score should be decided. This step is very important because it determines the extent to which each test will influence the report of behavior mastery. For example, if the extent of mastery of performance is more important relative to a given behavior than mastery of the knowledge base, it should have more weight.

Table 19.5 presents an example of how weighting is done for a behavior that has three tests associated with it: a knowledge-base test, a performance test, and a product test. Let us assume that we want the performance test to influence the grade twice as much as either of the other two tests, and that the other two tests should have equal weight. The weights that would be assigned to each type of test are presented in Table 19.5.

Given these weights, the knowledge-base test would account for 1/4 = 25 percent of the influence on the composite score for the behavior; the performance test, 2/4 = 50 percent; and the product test, 1/4 = 25 percent.

Once the raw scores on component tests have been converted to percentages and weights are assigned to each test, the scores are combined as follows:

1. The percentage score for each test is multiplied by its associated weight.
2. The products of these multiplications are added together.
3. An average percentage score is calculated by dividing the total by the total number of weights.
4. A person's grade, or rating, is assigned by comparing his or her average percentage score with the criterion score ranges.

TABLE 19.5 Sample Weights

Tests	Weight
Knowledge-base	1
Performance	2
Product	1
Total	4

For example, let us assume that a learner has attained a knowledge-base test score of 80 percent, a performance test score of 90 percent, and a product test score of 70 percent, and that each test is weighted as indicated in Table 19.5. The learner's composite score would be calculated as presented in Table 19.6. If the multiple-criterion scale which defines an *A* as being equal to 100 to 91, *B* as being equal to 90 to 81, and so on, were being used with this program, the learner would be assigned a *B* on that behavior. Table 19.7 summarizes the steps in implementing this multiple-criterion approach.

Time-Period Approach

Although PBID is most compatible with reporting progress by behavior, at times it may be desirable or necessary to report progress for a time period within which multiple behaviors are learned. For instance, many secondary schools issue report cards quarterly. This requires combining progress information across multiple behaviors.

In order to do this, the techniques discussed in the multiple-criterion approach are used. The only difference is that instead of combining data on only one behavior, data on all tests for all behaviors accomplished during a reporting period are combined. This further complicates the process of weighting each test because one must not only be concerned about the weighting of tests for each behavior, but also the relative weighting between the behaviors. For example, if progress on two behaviors is to be combined within a time period (e.g., a quarter or six weeks), and one behavior is three times more important than the other, the total of the weights for the tests for the first behavior should be three times larger than those for the second behavior. Table 19.8 presents the weights that would be assigned for this example. In this example, the tests for behavior 1 have a total weight of 9, and those for behavior 2, a weight

TABLE 19.6 Calculating the Multiple-Criterion Grade for One Behavior

Tests	Weight	Score	Weight × Score
Knowledge-base	1	80	80
Performance	2	90	180
Product	1	70	70
Totals	4		330

Average percentage score $= \frac{330}{4} = 82.5$

TABLE 19.7 Steps in Implementing the Multiple-Criterion Approach

1. Identify the tests which will enter the grade or rating.
2. Determine the emphasis that should be given each test in the grade and assign weights to reflect those emphases.
3. Administer each test and obtain scores.
4. Convert the scores on all tests to percentages.
5. Multiply each percentage score by its corresponding weight and add the weighted totals for all of the tests to arrive at a grand total.
6. Add the total of all weights that were used in multiplying the percentages.
7. Divide the grand total by the sum of all weights to arrive at an average percentage.
8. Assign grades or ratings based on the average percentage using a multiple-criterion–based scale which reflects the expected levels of behavior mastery.

of 3. If grades were assigned using these weights, nine-twelfths, or 75 percent, of the grade for the period would be based on behavior 1, and three-twelfths, or 25 percent, would be based on behavior 2. Again, it can be seen that the assignment of weights is important so that the composite score and the progress report will accurately reflect the relative importance of each test related to each behavior.

We will now proceed through a complete example of how grades would be assigned to a group of people for a time period using the multiple-criterion approach. Let us assume that we have four learners who each have taken two knowledge-base tests and two performance tests during the time period for which grades are to be assigned. Each learner has attained the scores presented in Table 19.9. The highest raw score possible on the first knowledge-base test (KB1) was 60; on the second knowledge-base test (KB2), 100; on the first performance test (P1), 30; and on the second performance test (P2), 40.

TABLE 19.8 Weighting Multiple Behaviors to Be Included Within One Progress Report

	TITLE?		
	Behavior 1 Weight	Behavior 2 Weight	Total for Period
Knowledge-base test	3	1	4
Performance test	6	2	8
	9	3	12

TABLE 19.9 Sample Test Scores for a Time Period

	TESTS			
Learner	KB1	KB2	P1	P2
John	55	80	25	38
Mary	50	95	28	27
Pete	60	75	20	35
Sally	52	85	30	30
Highest raw score possible	60	100	30	40

Table 19.10 indicates how each of the raw scores (RS) for each learner would be converted to percentage scores (%).

Table 19.11 presents how each of the percentage scores would be multiplied by the appropriate weight, how the multiplied percentages would be totaled for each learner, and how the average percentage score for each learner would be calculated. We will assume that the weight for KB1 equals 1, for KB2 equals 2, for P1 equals 5, and for P2 equals 2. The total amount of weights used is 10.

Averages are calculated by summing the multiplied percentages and dividing by the sum of the weights.

Example:

$$\frac{92 + 160 + 415 + 190}{1 + 2 + 5 + 2} = \frac{857}{10} = 85.7 \text{ Avg. \%}$$

Grades would then be assigned by comparing the average percentages with a multiple-criterion scale. Two are indicated in Table 19.12.

The actual report of progress using the time-period approach is similar to the typical report card used in schools. For example, if the program is nine months long and progress is reported every six weeks, one composite progress report would be entered for each six-week period. Progress would be reported as a rating or a letter grade.

POSTINSTRUCTION PROGRESS

Learner progress, besides being described in relation to success in the instructional program, can be judged in terms of postinstructional progress. Some people refer to this as *summative evaluation.* The assumption is

TABLE 19.10 Example of Conversion of Raw Scores to Percentages

Learner	TESTS			
	KB1	KB2	P1	P2
	RS : %†	RS : %	RS : %	RS : %
John	55 (92)	80(80)	25 (83)	38 (95)
Mary	50 (83)	95(95)	28 (93)	27 (68)
Pete	60 (100)	75(75)	20 (67)	35 (88)
Sally	52 (87)	85(85)	30 (100)	30 (75)
Highest score possible	60	100	30	40

†Percentage $= \frac{\text{learner score}}{\text{highest raw score possible}}$,

e.g., $\frac{55}{60} = 91.7 = 92\%$

made that people engage in instructional programs in order to accomplish goals. In performance-based instruction the goal is to develop the capability, or to increase the capability, to perform adequately in a given role. Judging of postinstruction progress is, therefore, based on the extent to which people who have participated in an instructional program have acquired the capability to perform in a role. The overall goal of the program should have been described in a program description, and it is assumed that people who enter the program are striving for that goal. However, this is not always true. Individuals may also have separate, unique goals.

The primary assessment vehicle for determining posttraining success is the follow-up study. Whereas the knowledge-base and process assessments conducted during the instructional program focus on the extent to which learners have mastered content, follow-up studies focus primarily on the extent to which people have attained the desired goal based on successfully completing an instructional program. For example, if an instructional program has been designed to prepare computer programmers, what success have graduates of the program had in obtaining jobs as computer programmers and maintaining those jobs? If a program has been designed to increase the productivity of people assembling television sets, has productivity increased? If the program has been designed to decrease the error rate in data handling, has the error rate decreased? In the final analysis, if people complete an instructional program without attaining the goal for which the program has been established, the program is unsuccessful.

In addition to determining the success of people who have completed the program in terms of the original goal, such follow-up evaluations typically gather data which might be used to diagnose the reasons for the success or failure of a program. For example, evaluations try to answer the question: If people have not been accomplishing the goal, why not?

Data for such follow-up studies are often gathered from program completers, people who are affected by program completers performing in the role (e.g., employers, other workers, or family members), or production records. At times, data are also gathered from people who did not complete the program to determine why they did not.

A discussion of detailed techniques for the development and implementation of such studies is beyond the scope of this book. However, the reader can refer to *The Minnesota Vocational Follow-up System: Rationale and Methods* (Pucel, 1972) for a discussion of such follow-up studies in vocational education, or to issues of the *Journal of Performance Instruction* for discussions of posttraining assessment procedures used in business and industry.

TABLE 19.11 Example of Applying Weights and Calculating Average Percentages

Learner	TESTS				Total: Average	
	KB1	KB2	P1	P2		
	% × wgt.	% × wgt.	% × wgt.	% × wgt.		
John	92 × 1 = 92	80 × 2 = 160	83 × 5 = 415	95 × 2 = 190	857	85.7
Mary	83 × 1 = 83	95 × 2 = 190	93 × 5 = 465	68 × 2 = 136	874	87.4
Pete	100 × 1 = 100	75 × 2 = 150	67 × 5 = 335	88 × 2 = 176	761	76.1
Sally	87 × 1 = 87	85 × 2 = 170	100 × 5 = 500	75 × 2 = 150	907	90.7

TABLE 19.12 Assigning Grades Based on Average Percentages

Learner	ACCORDING TO CRITERIA			SAMPLE CRITERIA	
	Avg.	One	Two	One	Two
John	85.7	*B*	*C*	*A* = 100–91	*A* = 100–94
Mary	87.4	*B*	*C*	*B* = 90–81	*B* = 93–88
Pete	76.1	*C*	*D*	*C* = 80–71	*C* = 87–80
Sally	90.7	*A*	*B*	*D* = 70–61	*D* = 79–75
				F = 60 or less	*F* = 74 or less

SUMMARY

Learner progress can be summarized and reported both during and after an instructional program. The primary purposes of summarizing and reporting learner progress during the program are to determine the extent to which learners have mastered program content, to report learner progress, and to provide diagnostic feedback to the learner and the instructor which is useful in adjusting instruction. The approach to summarizing and reporting learner progress during a program which is most consistent with the PBID system is the mastery approach. It is designed to assure that learners reach mastery level on each of the separate behaviors. However, at times the extent of mastery must be reported (multiple-criterion approach) or progress must be reported over a time period (time-period approach). Each of these requires the weighting and combining of multiple scores over one or more behaviors, and the establishment of multiple criteria for determining the extent of mastery differences between various grades or ratings.

The primary purpose of the postinstruction progress assessment is to determine the extent to which people who have completed the instructional program have attained the goal of the program (e.g., increased productivity and jobs). It also provides diagnostic information which can be used to adjust the program in the future.

ACTIVITIES AND EVALUATION

1. Assume that you have taught a behavior which has been evaluated using two tests. The first test has a mastery score of 85 percent and the second has a mastery score of 90 percent. A learner has received a score on the first test of 100 percent and a score on the second of 86 percent. Has the learner mastered the behavior? Why or why not?

2. Given the example data for four learners and the worksheet presented in Table 19.13, determine the grade you would assign to each using the multiple-criterion approach. Use the following multiple criteria in assigning the grades: 100–91 = *A*, 90–81 = *B*, 80–71 = *C*, 70–61 = *D*, 60 and below = *F*. Test KB1 has a relative weight of 3 and Test P1 has a relative weight of 7.

Learner	TEST DATA	
	KB1	P1
Rudy	52	80
Bonnie	57	95
Jack	49	75
Susan	51	85
Highest raw score possible	60	95

3. Assume that you have been offering an instructional program to prepare practical nurses. You have been asked to develop a postinstruction assessment of the people who have completed the program. What types of data might you gather and from whom?

TABLE 19.13 Worksheet for Activity 2

WORKSHEET									
Learner	TESTS						Total	Avg.	Grade
	KB1			P1					
	RS	% × wgt.	=	RS	% × wgt.	=			
		×			×				
		×			×				
		×			×				
		×			×				
	Weights = 3			7					

REFERENCES

Pucel, D. J., *The Minnesota Vocational Follow-up System: Rationale and Methods,* Department of Industrial Education, University of Minnesota, St. Paul, 1972.

Pucel, D. J., and W. C. Knaak, *Individualizing Vocational and Technical Instruction,* Charles E. Merrill, Columbus, OH, 1975.

*National College Verb List: The Functional, Forceful Four Hundred Fifty-Five**

* Calvin K. Claus, *National College Verb List,* Paper presented at a meeting of the National Council on Measurement in Education, Chicago, IL, February 1968.

"CREATIVE" BEHAVIORS			
Alter	Predict	Reorder	Revise
Ask	Question	Reorganize	Rewrite
Change	Rearrange	Rephrase	Simplify
Design	Recombine	Restate	Synthesize
Generalize	Reconstruct	Restructure	Systematize
Modify	Regroup	Retell	Vary
Paraphrase	Rename		

COMPLEX, LOGICAL, JUDGMENTAL BEHAVIORS			
Analyze	Contrast	Discover	Infer
Appraise	Criticize	Evaluate	Plan
Assess	Deduce	Formulate	Structure
Combine	Defend	Generate	Suggest
Compare	Designate	Induce	Substitute
Conclude	Determine		

GENERAL DISCRIMINATIVE BEHAVIORS			
Choose	Differentiate	Isolate	Pick
Collect	Discriminate	List	Place
Define	Distinguish	Match	Point
Describe	Identify	Omit	Select
Detect	Indicate	Order	Separate

SOCIAL BEHAVIORS			
Accept	Contribute	Help	Praise
Admit	Cooperate	Interact	React
Agree	Dance	Invite	Reply
Aid	Disagree	Join	Smile
Allow	Discuss	Laugh	Talk
Answer	Excuse	Meet	Thank
Argue	Forgive	Participate	Visit
Communicate	Greet	Permit	Volunteer
Compliment			

LANGUAGE BEHAVIORS			
Abbreviate	Hyphenate	Recite	Syllabicate
Accent	Indent	Say	Tell
Alphabetize	Outline	Sign	Translate
Articulate	Print	Speak	Verbalize
Call	Pronounce	Spell	Whisper
Capitalize	Punctuate	State	Write
Edit	Read	Summarize	

"STUDY" BEHAVIORS			
Arrange	Copy	Locate	Quote
Categorize	Diagram	Look	Record
Chart	Find	Map	Reproduce
Cite	Follow	Mark	Search
Circle	Gather	Name	Sort
Classify	Itemize	Note	Underline
Compile	Label	Organize	

MUSIC BEHAVIORS			
Blow	Finger	Play	Strum
Bow	Harmonize	Pluck	Tap
Clap	Hum	Practice	Whistle
Compose	Mute	Sing	

PHYSICAL BEHAVIORS			
Arch	Grab	March	Stand
Bat	Grasp	Pitch	Step
Bend	Grip	Pull	Stretch
Carry	Hit	Push	Swim
Catch	Hop	Run	Swing
Chase	Jump	Skate	Throw
Climb	Kick	Ski	Toss
Face	Knock	Skip	Walk
Float	Lift	Somersault	

ARTS BEHAVIORS			
Assemble	Fold	Paint	Shake
Blend	Form	Paste	Sketch
Brush	Frame	Pat	Smooth
Build	Hammer	Polish	Stamp
Carve	Handle	Pour	Stick
Color	Heat	Press	Stir
Construct	Hold	Roll	Trace
Cut	Illustrate	Rub	Trim
Dab	Melt	Sand	Varnish
Dot	Mix	Saw	Wipe
Draw	Nail	Sculpt	Wrap
Drill			

DRAMA BEHAVIORS			
Act	Emit	Leave	Proceed
Clasp	Enter	Move	Respond
Cross	Exit	Pantomime	Show
Direct	Express	Pass	Sit
Display	Imitate	Perform	Turn

* Calvin K. Claus, *National College Verb List,* Paper presented at a meeting of the National Council on Measurement in Education, Chicago, IL, February 1968.

*Legal Office Procedures PBID Sample Components**

* Edited with permission from materials prepared by Sharon R. Anderson.

Contents

		Page
Table B.1	Program Description	192
Table B.2	Functions	192
Table B.3	Partial Content Analysis	192
Table B.4	Priority Chart	193
Table B.5	Stating the Objective (Psychomotor)	193
Table B.6	Behavior Detailing (Psychomotor)	193
Table B.7	Lesson Structuring (Psychomotor)	194
Table B.8	Learner-Oriented Lesson Plan (Psychomotor)	195
Table B.9	Stating the Objective (Cognitive)	195
Table B.10	Behavior Detailing (Cognitive)	195
Table B.11	Lesson Structuring (Cognitive)	196
Table B.12	Instructor-Oriented Lesson Plan (Cognitive)	197
Table B.13	Stating the Objective (Affective)	197
Table B.14	Behavior Detailing (Affective)	197
Table B.15	Lesson Structuring (Affective)	198
Table B.16	Instructor-Oriented Lesson Plan (Affective)	199
Table B.17	Sample Sequence Chart	200

TABLE B.1 Legal Office Procedures: Program Description

CONTENT AREA

Legal office procedures

CONTEXT

Level of the program:	Postsecondary
Expected length of the program:	50 hours
Program focus:	Initial preparation
Institutional setting:	Performance-based, self-paced school
Relationships with other programs:	Standalone program
Special learner characteristics:	High school graduate or equivalent
Other	

TABLE B.2 Legal Office Procedures: Functions

CONTENT AREA

Legal office procedures

SAMPLE FUNCTIONS

1. Communicate with clients.
2. Bill clients.
3. Maintain a diary system of appointments and due dates.
4. Maintain a record of court matters.
5. File and retrieve client information.

TABLE B.3 Legal Office Procedures: Partial Content Analysis

	FUNCTIONS				
BEHAVIORS	1. Communicate with clients.	2. Bill clients.	3. Maintain diary system.	4. Maintain record of court matters.	5. File and retrieve client information.
1. Maintain a cordial relationship by phone.	X				
2. Maintain a cordial relationship in person.	X				
3. Maintain a professional attitude.	X				
4. Answer customers' questions.	X				
5. Select fee classifications.		X			
6. Record lawyer's time.		X			
7. Prepare a bill.		X			
8. Prepare a diary.			X		
9. Prepare a docket calendar.				X	
10. Calculate due dates.				X	
11. Open a new file.					X
12. Close a file.					X

TABLE B.4 Legal Office Procedures: Priority Chart

BEHAVIOR LIST	1. Importance rating (from 1 to 5)	2. Estimated instructional time, hours	3. Priority (in rank order)
1. Select fee classifications.	4	2	12
2. Maintain a cordial relationship in person.	5	6	1
3. Maintain a cordial relationship by phone.	5	6	2
4. Record lawyer's time.	3	4	8
5. Prepare a bill.	3	4	9
6. Prepare a diary.	2	4	10
7. Prepare a docket calendar.	2	3	11
8. Open a new file.	3	2	5
9. Close a file.	3	2	6
10. Maintain a professional attitude.	5	6	3
11. Answers customers' questions.	5	4	4
12. Calculate due dates	5	4	7

TABLE B.5 Legal Office Procedures: Stating the Objective

PSYCHOMOTOR OBJECTIVE 004

Givens
A new client questionnaire, a typewriter, an index card, a label, and an unused legal-size folder

Behavior
Open a new file.

Standard
According to the process indicated on the instructor's checklist

TABLE B.6 Legal Office Procedures: Behavior Detailing

PSYCHOMOTOR OBJECTIVE 004

Givens
A new client questionnaire, a typewriter, an index card, a label, and an unused legal-size folder

Behavior
Open a new file.

Standard
According to the process indicated on the instructor's checklist

Process	Knowledge Base
1. Review client questionnaire. 2. Obtain file number. 3. Type index card. 4. Type label. 5. Assemble a file.	1. Recall typing procedures. 2. Recall file classifications. 3. Recall file opening procedures.

TABLE B.7 Legal Office Procedures: Lesson Structuring

PSYCHOMOTOR OBJECTIVE 004

Givens
A new client questionnaire, a typewriter, an index card, a label, and an unused legal size folder

Behavior
Open a new file.

Standard
According to the process indicated on the instructor's checklist

LESSON STAGE	CONTENT TO BE TAUGHT, PRACTICED, OR EVALUATED	METHODS/MEDIA (CONSISTENT WITH MODULARIZED FORMAT)
RATIONALE	Need for organization of client materials	Lecture/videotape
NEED-TO-KNOW INFORMATION	*a.* Typing procedures *b.* File classifications *c.* File opening procedures	Reading/textbook, information sheets
DEMONSTRATION	Process for opening a new file	Demonstration/videotape
GUIDED PRACTICE	Process for opening a new file	Practice/assignment sheet; tutorial observation
PRACTICE FOR PERFECTION	Process for opening a new file	Practice/assignment sheet
EVALUATION	*a.* Knowledge base presented above *b.* Process for opening a new file	*a.* Test/written *b.* Performance test/checklist
FEEDBACK	*a.* Knowledge base presented above *b.* Process for opening a new file	Conference/instructor; test instruments

TABLE B.8 Legal Office Procedures: Learner-Oriented Lesson Plan

PSYCHOMOTOR OBJECTIVE 004

Givens
A new client questionnaire, a typewriter, an index card, a label, and an unused legal-size folder

Behavior
Open a new file.

Standard
According to the process indicated on the instructor's checklist

Learning Steps	Resources
1. View videotape 706-004-01 to identify the need for organization of client materials.	1. Videotape 706-004-01
2. Read Chapter 3 of "Type Right 75" to review procedures for typing labels and index cards	2. Chapter 3, "Type Right 75"
3. Read information sheet 706-004-02 to identify classifications of new files.	3. Information sheet 706-004-02
4. Read information sheet 706-004-03 to identify the procedures for opening a new file.	4. Information sheet 706-004-03
5. View videotape 706-004-04 to observe the procedures for opening a new file.	5. Videotape 706-004-04
6. Open a new file while being observed by the instructor using assignment sheet 706-004-05.	6. Assignment sheet 706-004-05
7. Open a new file using assignment sheet 706-004-06.	7. Assignment sheet 706-004-06
8. Contact your instructor when you feel you are ready to complete the written criterion exam.	
9. Ask the instructor to observe your performance after you have satisfactorily completed the written criterion exam.	
10. After the instructor has approved your performance, go on to behavior 706-005.	

TABLE B.9 Legal Office Procedures: Stating the Objective

COGNITIVE OBJECTIVE 003

Givens
A service requiring billing

Behavior
Select the fee classification.

Standard
Fee agrees with type of client, funding source, and type of service rendered.

TABLE B.10 Legal Office Procedures: Behavior Detailing

COGNITIVE OBJECTIVE 003

Givens
A service requiring billing

Behavior
Select the fee classification.

Standard
Fee agrees with type of client, funding source, and type of service rendered.

Process	Knowledge Base
1. Determine the service rendered.	1. Recall types of service.
2. Determine the type of client.	2. Recall types of clients.
3. Determine the funding source.	3. Recall types of funding sources.
4. Determine the corresponding fee.	

TABLE B.11 Legal Office Procedures: Lesson Structuring

COGNITIVE OBJECTIVE 003

Givens
A service requiring billing

Behavior
Select the fee classification.

Standard
Fee agrees with type of client, funding source, and type of service rendered.

LESSON STAGE	CONTENT TO BE TAUGHT, PRACTICED, OR EVALUATED	METHODS/MEDIA (CONSISTENT WITH TRADITIONAL FORMAT)
RATIONALE	*a.* Why different fees are charged for different services *b.* Importance to lawyer	Lecture/instructor, transparencies
NEED-TO-KNOW INFORMATION	*a.* Types of services *b.* Types of clients *c.* Types of funding sources	Reading/fee manual, information sheet; tutorial questioning
DEMONSTRATION	Process for selecting fee classifications	Demonstration/ live instructor, information sheet
GUIDED PRACTICE	Process for selecting fee classifications	Practice/assignment sheet; tutorial observation
PRACTICE FOR PERFECTION	Process for selecting fee classifications	Practice/assignment sheet
EVALUATION	Knowledge base presented above Process for selecting fee classifications	Test/written Performance test/ checklist
FEEDBACK	Knowledge base presented above Process for selecting fee classifications	Conference/instructor; test instruments

TABLE B.12 Legal Office Procedures: Instructor-Oriented Lesson Plan

COGNITIVE OBJECTIVE 003

Givens
A service requiring billing

Behavior
Select the fee classification.

Standard
Fee agrees with type of client, funding source, and type of service rendered.

Instructor Actions	Resources
1. Present lecture on why there are different fees for different services.	1. Overhead transparencies 706-003-01
2. Review the fee manual for types of services, clients, and funding sources. *Sample question:* What is the organizational structure of a fee manual?	2. Fee manual
3. Present the demonstration, using information sheet 706-003-02 as a guide.	3. Information sheet 706-003-02
4. Have students practice using assignment sheet 706-003-03 with observation.	4. Assignment sheet 706-003-03
5. Have students practice using assignment sheet 706-003-04.	5. Assignment sheet 706-003-04
6. Administer tests on choosing fees.	6. *a.* Written criterion exam 706-003-05 *b.* Performance checklist 706-003-06
7. Provide feedback through individual conferences.	7. Test information

TABLE B.13 Legal Office Procedures: Stating the Objective

AFFECTIVE OBJECTIVE 005

Givens
A client and a situation requiring interaction with the client

Behavior
Maintain a cordial relationship with a client in person.

Standard
Display actions according to the instructor's checklist.

TABLE B.14 Legal Office Procedures: Behavior Detailing

AFFECTIVE OBJECTIVE 005

Givens
A client and a situation requiring interaction with the client

Behavior
Maintain a cordial relationship with a client in person.

Standard
Display actions according to the instructor's checklist.

Process	Knowledge Base
1. Control voice quality.	1. Recall methods of changing tone of voice.
2. Adjust speed of communication and directiveness to client's temperament.	2. Recall methods of achieving tactful and diplomatic attitudes.
3. Refer questions outside of your responsibility level.	3. Differentiate between secretarial and attorney responsibilities to clients.
4. Allow client to complete his or her agenda.	

TABLE B.15 Legal Office Procedures: Lesson Structuring

AFFECTIVE OBJECTIVE 005

Givens
A client and a situation requiring interaction with a client

Behavior
Maintain a cordial relationship with a client in person.

Standard
Display actions according to the instructor's checklist.

LESSON STAGE	CONTENT TO BE TAUGHT, PRACTICED, OR EVALUATED	METHODS/MEDIA (CONSISTENT WITH TRADITIONAL FORMAT)
RATIONALE	Importance of secretarial contacts with clients	Lecture/instructor; tutorial questions
NEED-TO-KNOW INFORMATION	*a.* Methods of changing tone of voice *b.* Methods of achieving a tactful and diplomatic attitude *c.* Methods of differentiating between secretarial and attorney response to clients	Reading/textbook, information sheets; discussion/instructor
DEMONSTRATION	Process for maintaining cordial relationships with clients	Demonstration/videotape; field trip/law office; discussions/lawyer and/or secretary
GUIDED PRACTICE	Process for maintaining cordial relationships with clients	Role playing/script; tutorial observation
PRACTICE FOR PERFECTION	Process for maintaining cordial relationships with clients	Role playing/script; tutorial observation/another student
EVALUATION	*a.* Knowledge base presented above *b.* Process for maintaining cordial relationships with clients	*a.* Test/written *b.* Performance test (role-play)/checklist
FEEDBACK	*a.* Knowledge base presented above *b.* Process for maintaining cordial relationships with clients	Conference/instructor; test instruments

TABLE B.16 Legal Office Procedures: Instructor-Oriented Lesson Plan

AFFECTIVE OBJECTIVE

Givens
A client and a situation requiring interaction with a client

Behavior
Maintain a cordial relationship with a client in person.

Standard
Display actions according to the instructor's checklist.

Instructor Actions	Resources
1. Present lecture on importance of secretarial contacts with clients. *a.* First impressions. *b.* Potential clients. *c.* Frequency of contact. *Sample question:* Can you give me an example of a first impression you have had in an office, e.g., a doctor's office?	1. Overhead transparencies 706-005-01
2. Review the information contained in Chapter 2 of *Office Procedures.* *Sample question:* Would you demonstrate for me a friendly tone of voice? How about a rude one?	2. Chapter 2 of *Office Procedures*
3. Review information sheet 706-005-02. Conduct a discussion around the questions: What would be a tactful way of handling a client who came into the office without an appointment? How would you handle a client who asked you for legal advice?	3. Information sheet 706-005-02
4. Have students view videotape demonstration 706-005-03.	4. Videotape 706-005-03
5. Visit Olson, Olson, & Olson Law Firm to observe client contacts. Discuss tone of voice, tactfulness, diplomacy, and attorney and secretarial responsibilities with secretaries and lawyers, if available.	5. Field trip to Olson, Olson, & Olson
6. Participate in role playing with student using script 706-005-04.	6. Script 706-005-04
7. Have student participate in role playing with another student using script 706-005-05.	7. Script 706-005-05
8. When student feels competent, administer written test.	8. Written criterion exam 706-005-06
9. Observe performance during role-play with student using script 706-005-07.	9. Script 706-005-07; performance checklist 706-005-08
10. Provide feedback through individual conferences.	10. Test information

TABLE B.17 Sample Sequence Chart

This sequence chart presents only the behavior that would be taught immediately before and after the sample behaviors for which lessons have been developed and the rationale for why.

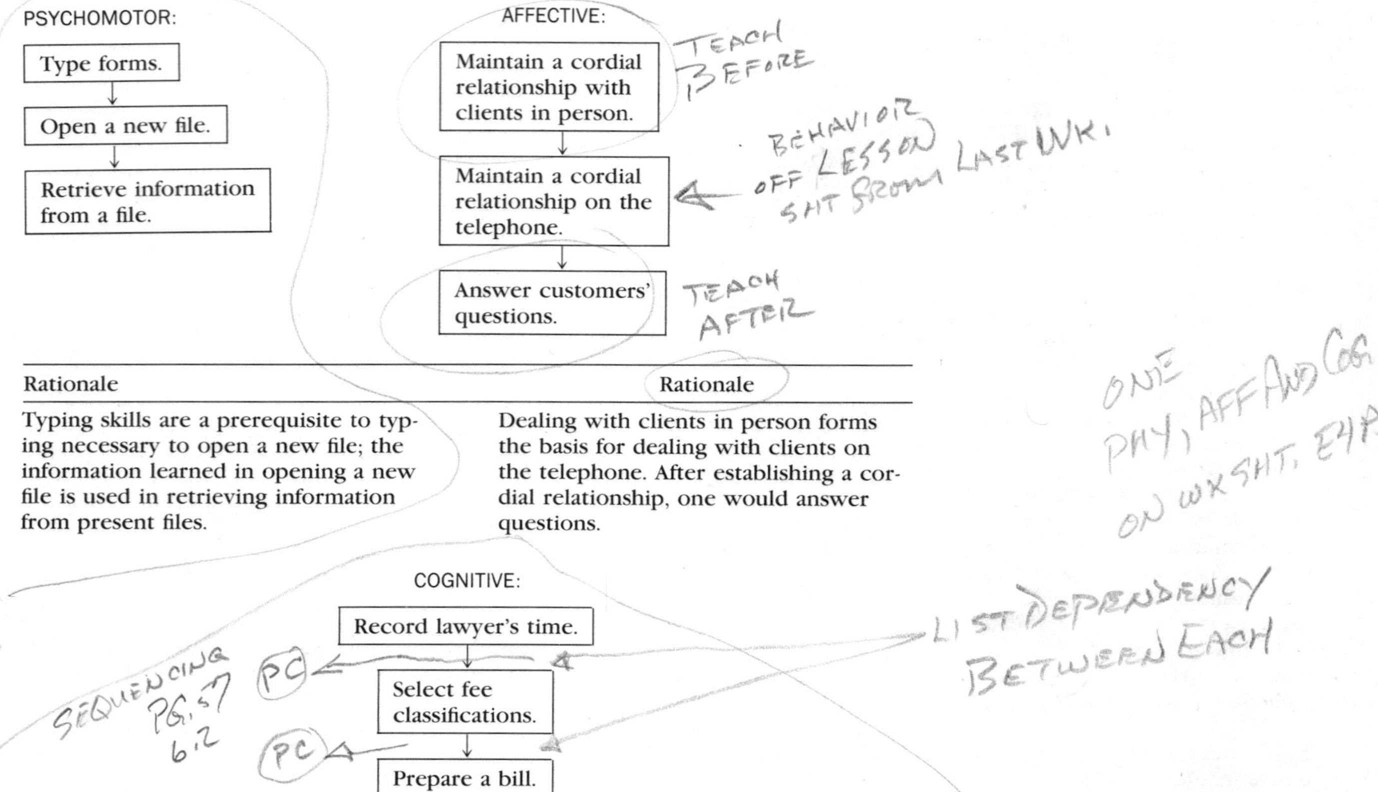

Rationale	Rationale
Typing skills are a prerequisite to typing necessary to open a new file; the information learned in opening a new file is used in retrieving information from present files.	Dealing with clients in person forms the basis for dealing with clients on the telephone. After establishing a cordial relationship, one would answer questions.

Rationale
Somebody must be able to record a lawyer's time in order to classify the type of service rendered. This allows for the selection of a fee classification which is necessary to prepare a bill.

APPENDIX C

*Introduction to (IBM) Microcomputer Systems PBID Sample Components**

* Edited with permission from materials prepared by Gene Zuck.

Contents

		Page
Table C.1	Program Description	203
Table C.2	Functions	203
Table C.3	Content Analysis	204
Table C.4	Partial Priority Chart	205
Table C.5	Stating the Objective (Psychomotor)	205
Table C.6	Behavior Detailing (Psychomotor)	205
Table C.7	Lesson Structuring (Psychomotor)	206
Table C.8	Learner-Oriented Lesson Plan (Psychomotor)	207
Table C.9	Stating the Objective (Cognitive)	207
Table C.10	Behavior Detailing (Cognitive)	207
Table C.11	Lesson Structuring (Cognitive)	208
Table C.12	Instructor-Oriented Lesson Plan (Cognitive)	209
Table C.13	Stating the Objective (Affective)	210
Table C.14	Behavior Detailing (Affective)	210
Table C.15	Lesson Structuring (Affective)	211
Table C.16	Instructor-Oriented Lesson Plan (Affective)	212

TABLE C.1 Introduction to Microcomputer Systems: Program Description

CONTENT AREA

Introduction to microcomputer systems

CONTEXT

Level of the program:	Adult training 7.3.
Expected length of the program:	21 hours: 3 hours per day, 1 day per week, for 7 weeks
Program focus:	Awareness: This program focuses on providing people with a basic understanding of microcomputer systems.
Istitutional setting:	Traditional school: This program will be taught in a traditional manner, with lectures and demonstrations within a school environment.
Relationships with other programs:	Standalone: This program is a standalone program with no prerequisites.
Special learner characteristics:	High school graduates with a need to understand basic terminology and usability aspects of a microcomputer system
Other	

TABLE C.2 Introduction to Microcomputer Systems: Functions

CONTENT AREA

Introduction to microcomputer (MC) systems

FUNCTIONS

1. Select MC software.
2. Select MC hardware.
3. Configure MC system.
4. Select MC system.
5. Install MC system.
6. Operate MC system.
7. Communicate with vendors/users.

TABLE C.3 Introduction to Microcomputer Systems: Content Analysis

BEHAVIORS	1. Select MC software.	2. Select MC hardware.	3. Configure MC system.	4. Select MC system.	5. Install MC system.	6. Operate MC system.	7. Communicate with vendors/users.
	FUNCTIONS						
1. Determine MC system needs.	X	X	X	X			X
2. Determine MC system limitations.	X	X	X	X			X
3. Compare MC system needs with limitations.	X	X	X	X			X
4. Formulate MC system requirements.	X	X	X	X			X
5. Compare word processing (WP) packages.	X					X	X
6. Compare spreadsheet (SS) packages.	X					X	X
7. Compare database (DB) management packages.	X					X	X
8. Compare standard CPU and memory options.		X					X
9. Compare monitors.		X					X
10. Compare printers.		X					X
11. Compare auxiliary storage devices.		X					X
12. Compare expansion capabilities.		X	X				X
13. Formulate different MC configurations.			X	X			X
14. Cooperate with computer dealer.				X			X
15. Cooperate with hardware manufacturers.				X		X	X
16. Cooperate with software developers.				X		X	X
17. Cooperate with end users.				X		X	X
18. Compare MC configuration prices.				X			X
19. Identify MC system components to install.					X		
20. Connect MC system hardware components.					X		
21. Load and execute installation programs.					X		
22. Load application software for initial setup.					X		
23. Execute software setup routines.					X		X
24. Boot the system.					X	X	
25. Treat a MC system with care.					X	X	
26. Identify end-user needs.							X
27. Select application software.						X	X
28. Formulate problem solution.						X	
29. Load and execute application software (WP, SS, and DB).						X	

TABLE C.4 Introduction to Microcomputer Systems: Partial Priority Chart

PSYCHOMOTOR BEHAVIORS	1. Importance rating (from 1 to 5)	2. Estimated time, hours	3. Priority (in rank order)
Boot the system.	5	.5	1
Load and execute application software (WP, SS, and DB).	5	.5	2
Execute software setup routines.	2	.5	9
COGNITIVE BEHAVIORS			
Compare WP packages.	4	2	4
Select application software.	4	2	5
Compare MC configuration prices.	4	1	6
AFFECTIVE BEHAVIORS			
Cooperate with end users.	3	1	7
Treat an MC system with care.	4	5	3
Cooperate with software developers.	3	1	8

TABLE C.5 Introduction to Microcomputer Systems: Stating the Objective

PSYCHOMOTOR OBJECTIVE 31

Givens
An installed two-floppy IBM MC system with DOS 3.2

Behavior
Boot the system.

Standard
The MC system is turned on, the DOS system diskette is inserted in drive A with the door closed, and the DOS system prompt is displayed on the monitor screen.

TABLE C.6 Introduction to Microcomputer Systems: Behavior Detailing

PSYCHOMOTOR OBJECTIVE 31

Givens
An installed two-floppy IBM MC system with DOS 3.2

Behavior
Boot the system.

Standard
The MC system is turned on, the DOS system diskette is inserted in drive A with the door closed, and the DOS system prompt is displayed on the monitor screen.

Process	Knowledge Base
1. Insert system (DOS) diskette.	1. Recall background information on PC processor and memory functions.
2. Turn on monitor and adjust settings.	2. Recall background information on DOS operating system.
3. Turn on printer, position paper, and adjust settings.	3. Recall MC hardware care precautions.
4. Position keyboard and turn on computer.	4. Recall procedures for inserting floppy diskettes.
5. Enter the date.	5. Recall monitor operating features.
6. Enter the time.	6. Recall printer operating features.
	7. Recall system booting and shutdown procedures.

TABLE C.7 Introduction to Microcomputer Systems: Lesson Structuring

PSYCHOMOTOR OBJECTIVE 31

Givens
An installed two-floppy IBM MC system with DOS 3.2

Behavior
Boot the system.

Standard
The MC system is turned on, the DOS system diskette is inserted in disk drive A with the door closed, and the DOS system prompt is displayed on the monitor screen.

LESSON STAGE	CONTENT TO BE TAUGHT, PRACTICED, OR EVALUATED	METHODS/MEDIA (CONSISTENT WITH MODULARIZED FORMAT)
RATIONALE	*a.* Basis for all computer operation and software usage *b.* Consequences of incorrect system initialization	Reading/textbook
NEED-TO-KNOW INFORMATION	*a.* PC processor/memory function *b.* DOS booting concepts *c.* Floppy disk/diskette features *d.* Monitor/printer features *e.* Booting and shutdown procedure *f.* MC hardware care precautions	Reading/textbook; lecture/videotape; self-check/written
DEMONSTRATION	Process for booting	Demonstration/videotape
GUIDED PRACTICE	Process for booting	Practice/procedure sheet, assignment sheet; tutorial observation/instructor
PRACTICE FOR PERFECTION	Process for booting	Practice/another person
EVALUATION	*a.* Knowledge base presented above *b.* Process for booting procedure	*a.* Self-check/written *b.* Performance test/checklist
FEEDBACK	*a.* Knowledge base presented above *b.* Process for booting	Conference/instructor, test information

TABLE C.8 Introduction to Microcomputer Systems: Learner-Oriented Lesson Plan

PSYCHOMOTOR OBJECTIVE 31

Givens
An installed two-floppy IBM MC system with DOS 3.2

Behavior
Boot the system.

Standard
The MC system is turned on, the DOS system diskette is inserted in disk drive A with the door closed, and the DOS system prompt is displayed on the monitor screen.

Learning Steps	Resources
1. Read textbook to determine why it is important to learn how to boot the system.	1. Textbook: section I
2. Read textbook on PC processor memory functions and DOS booting concepts to determine the relationship between DOS and the PC memory.	2. Textbook: section II
Complete self-check; if not completed satisfactorily, reread chapter.	Textbook: self-check 13-1
View videotape on floppy disk and monitor/printer features MC hardware care precautions to see how they are used.	Videotape: part I
Complete self-check; if not completed satisfactorily, review videotape lesson.	Textbook: self-check 31-3
3. View videotape to observe step-by-step procedure and care precautions for booting the system.	3. Videotape 31-2: part II
4. Read assignment 1 in the text and have instructor observe your performance.	4. Textbook: assignment 1; procedure sheet 31-4; instructor; MC system and DOS 3.2
5. Remove the performance test from the text and ask another person to observe and critique you as you practice.	5. Textbook: performance test 31-5, 31-6; another person; MC system and DOS 3.2
6. Complete the self-check; if completed satisfactorily, ask the instructor to observe your performance.	6. Textbook: self-check 31-6; instructor; MC system and DOS 3.2; performance checklist 31-7
7. Meet with the instructor to discuss your performance and receive the next assignment.	7. Instructor; performance checklist; self-check 31-6

TABLE C.9 Introduction to Microcomputer Systems: Stating the Objective

CCGNITIVE OBJECTIVE 34

Givens
An end user's problem definition requiring a software solution

Behavior
Select application software.

Standard
The learner's verbal description of the decision process is consistent with the series of instructor problem analysis worksheets.

TABLE C.10 Introduction to Microcomputer Systems: Behavior Detailing

COGNITIVE OBJECTIVE 34

Givens
An end user's problem definition requiring a software solution

Behavior
Select application software.

Standard
The learner's verbal description of the decision process is consistent with the series of instructor problem analysis worksheets.

Process	Knowledge Base
1. Determine available application packages.	1. Recall types and purpose of word processors, spreadsheets, and database managers.
2. Identify package features and benefits.	2. Recall features and benefits of word processor, spreadsheet, and database manager packages.
3. Match package features and benefits with end user's needs.	3. Differentiate between end user's needs and package features.

TABLE C.11 Introduction to Microcomputer Systems: Lesson Structuring

COGNITIVE OBJECTIVE 34

Givens
An end user's problem definition requiring a software solution

Behavior
Select application software.

Standard
The learner's verbal description of the decision process is consistent with the series of instructor problem analysis worksheets.

LESSON STAGE	CONTENT TO BE TAUGHT, PRACTICED, OR EVALUATED	METHODS/MEDIA (CONSISTENT WITH TRADITIONAL FORMAT)
RATIONALE	Selecting application software to solve problems and maximize productivity	Reading/handout; lecture/instructor
NEED-TO-KNOW INFORMATION	*a.* Features and benefits of word processors, spreadsheets and database managers. *b.* Applications for word processors, spreadsheets, and database managers *c.* Matching end user's needs with application and package features	Lecture/instructor; discussion/instructor
DEMONSTRATION	Process for selecting applications software	Case study/information sheets; tutorial questioning; discussion/instructor
GUIDED PRACTICE	Process for selecting applications software	Practice/case study worksheets; tutorial questioning
PRACTICE FOR PERFECTION	Process for selecting applications software	Case study/worksheets; performance test checklist/other student
EVALUATION	*a.* Knowledge base presented above *b.* Process for selecting applications software	*a.* Test/written *b.* Case study/print *c.* Worksheets
FEEDBACK	*a.* Knowledge base presented above *b.* Process for selecting applications software	Conference/instructor, case study

TABLE C.12 Introduction to Microcomputer Systems: Instructor-Oriented Lesson Plan

COGNITIVE OBJECTIVE 34

Givens
An end user's problem definition requiring a software solution

Behavior
Select application software.

Standard
The learner's verbal description of the decision process is consistent with the series of instructor problem analysis worksheets.

Instructor Actions	Resources
1. Lecture on why it is important to learn the behavior.	1. *a.* Lecture notes 34-1 on: 1. Productivity 2. Consequences of incorrect software selection *b.* Transparencies 34-2
2. Assign reading.	2. Handout on types of software 34-3
3. Lecture on need-to-know information.	3. *a.* Lecture notes 34-1 on: 1. Features and benefits of word processing, spreadsheet, and database management software 2. User applications of word processing, spreadsheet, and database management software 3. Matching end-user needs with applications and package features *b.* Transparencies 34-4
4. Lead a discussion of desirability of features, and matching end-user needs	4. Discussion notes 34-5
5. Demonstrate the selection of application software by reviewing three different case studies involving the use of word processing, spreadsheet, and database management software. Conduct informal questioning and discussion on case study subject matter.	5. *a.* Demonstration notes 34-6 on: 1. Case study 1 (WP) 2. Case study 2 (SS) 3. Case study 3 (DB) *b.* Case study examples 34-6 *c.* Discussion notes 34-6
6. Assign case studies to be completed with guidance. Conduct informal questioning and discussion on case study subject matter.	6. Case study worksheets.
7. Select teams consisting of two students. Assign case studies to be completed, critiqued by the other team members, and then submitted for review by the instructor.	7. *a.* Another student *b.* Case study worksheets 34-8 *c.* Performance checklist 34-9
8. Evaluate learner's performance of the behavior and understanding of all related knowledge.	8. *a.* A written test on the need-to-know information 34-10 *b.* Performance test 34-11
9. Provide the student with feedback and direction.	9. *a.* Test information *b.* Next assignment

TABLE C.13 Introduction to Microcomputer Systems: Stating the Objective

AFFECTIVE OBJECTIVE 43

Givens
An IBM (or compatible) MC system, and a situation requiring system care

Behavior
Treat an MC system with care.

Standard
Usage actions depicting care specified on the checklist have been performed to the level defined on that checklist.

TABLE C.14 Introduction to Microcomputer Systems: Behavior Detailing

AFFECTIVE OBJECTIVE 43

Givens
An IBM (or compatible) MC system, and a situation requiring system care

Behavior
Treat an MC system with care.

Standard
Usage actions depicting care specified on the checklist have been performed to the level defined on that checklist.

Process	Knowledge Base
1. Protect and store floppy disks. 2. Ensure paper flow and ribbon feeding. 3. Move components without jarring them. 4. Keep components clean.	1. Recall floppy disk handling procedures. 2. Differentiate between normal and abnormal printer equipment functioning. 3. Recall disk drive usage. 4. Recall moving procedures. 5. Clean equipment periodically.

TABLE C.15 Introduction to Microcomputer Systems: Lesson Structuring

AFFECTIVE OBJECTIVE 43

Givens
An IBM (or compatible) MC system, and a situation requiring system care

Behavior
Treat an MC system with care.

Standard
Usage actions depicting care activity specified on the checklist have been performed to the level defined on that checklist.

LESSON STAGE	CONTENT TO BE TAUGHT, PRACTICED, OR EVALUATED	METHODS/MEDIA (CONSISTENT WITH TRADITIONAL FORMAT)
RATIONALE	*a.* Consequences of incorrect usage of MC system equipment *b.* Benefits of careful usage of MC system equipment	Lecture/instructor, transparencies; reading/information sheet
NEED-TO-KNOW INFORMATION	*a.* Floppy disk handling procedures *b.* Differences between normal and abnormal equipment functioning *c.* Disk drive care *d.* Cleaning equipment *e.* Moving procedures	Reading/text; lecture/instructor, transparencies
DEMONSTRATION	Process for treating MC system with care	Demonstration/instructor; tutorial questioning; reading/information sheets
GUIDED PRACTICE	Process for treating MC system with care	Practice/equipment, assignment sheets; tutorial observation
PRACTICE FOR PERFECTION	Process for treating MC system with care	Practice/assignment sheets; tutorial observation/another student
EVALUATION	*a.* Knowledge base presented above *b.* Process for treating MC system with care	*a.* Test/written *b.* Performance test/checklist
FEEDBACK	*a.* Knowledge base presented above *b.* Equipment usage	Conference/test information

TABLE C.16 Introduction to Microcomputer Systems: Instructor-Oriented Lesson Plan

AFFECTIVE OBJECTIVE 43

Givens
An IBM (or compatible) MC system, and a situation requiring system care

Behavior
Treat an MC system with care.

Standard
Usage actions depicting care activity specified on the checklist have been performed to the level defined on that checklist.

Instructor Actions	Resources
1. Lecture on why it is important to treat an MC system with care.	1. *a.* Lecture notes 43-1 on: 1. Consequences of incorrect usage of MC system equipment 2. Benefits of careful usage of MC system equipment *b.* Transparencies 43-2
2. Lecture on need-to-know information.	2. *a.* Lecture notes 43-3 on: 1. Floppy diskette care: • surface care and handling • storage environment • inserting and retracting from disk drive 2. Benefits of careful diskette usage 3. Disk drive care: • opening and closing of doors • operating light 4. Printer care: • paper flow • ribbon feeding 5. Difference between normal and abnormal equipment usage 6. Cleaning and moving equipment 7. Normal/abnormal actions and benefits *b.* Transparencies 43-4
3. Demonstrate the normal/abnormal equipment usage actions, lead informal questioning, and discussions on demonstrated actions.	3. *a.* Demo notes 43-5 on: 1. Floppy diskette care 2. Disk drive care 3. Printer care *b.* Information sheets 43-5 *c.* MC system and DOS 3.2
4. Assign equipment usage exercises to be completed with guidance. Conduct informal questioning and discussions on exercises.	4. *a.* Assignment sheets 43-6 *b.* MC system and DOS 3.2
5. Allow the learners to practice to perfect this behavior.	5. *a.* Another student *b.* Assignment sheet 43-7
6. Evaluate the learner's performance of the behavior and understanding of all related knowledge.	6. *a.* Written test 43-8 *b.* Performance checklist 43-9
7. Provide the student with feedback and direction.	7. *a.* Test information *b.* Next assignment

*Sample Written Test: Apply for a Job**

* Edited with permission from materials prepared by Judy Oliverius.

TEST-CONSTRUCTION BLUEPRINT

Givens: A description of the type of job you seek
Behavior: Identify and apply for a job.
Standard: The job identified is consistent with your description, the application letter contains the basic components, and the resume has all items completed.

Knowledge-Base Objectives:

1. Identify key resources in selecting a job.	1, 9, 14, 20, 31, 32, 33, 34, 35
2. Recall job application procedures.	2, 8, 15
3. Identify basic information which should be included in a resume.	6, 19, 22, 23, 29
4. Identify the basic outline of a resume.	3, 17
5. Identify the content of a letter of application.	4, 11, 12, 13, 18, 30
6. Recall the response alternatives used in filling out an application form.	5, 7, 10, 16, 21, 24, 25, 26, 27, 28

Sales 5304 Selling Today
Instructor: Judy Oliverius

Identify and Apply for a Job

True-False Items

Directions: Some of the following statements are true and some are false. If the statement is true, place a T in the corresponding blank on your answer sheet. If the statement is false, place an F in the blank. The first item is answered as an example.

X. A private employment agency provides job placement for a fee.

1. The most common resource used in looking for a job is the newspaper want ads.

2. It is recommended that you should submit a resume to the employer without asking.

3. The first item on a resume should be the person's name.

4. The middle paragraph of an application letter should explain why you are interested in working for the employer.

5. An employer will judge you by your handwriting on your application form.

6. When writing your resume, there is no need to list special instruments or equipment that you have used.

7. When filling out an application form, it is alright to ask for a phone book to look up addresses.

8. The receptionist is the only person to whom you should return your completed application form.

9. Friends are not considered a resource when you are looking for a job.

10. If you have no answer for a question on an application form, you should draw a line in that space.

Cluster True-False Items

Directions: The following incomplete statement is followed by words which complete the statement and make it true or false. If the word completes a true statement, place a T in the corresponding blank on the answer sheet. If the completed statement is false, place an F in the blank. The first item is answered as an example.

A letter of application contains a ______________________ paragraph.

X. central

11. middle

12. beginning

13. closing

Multiple-Choice Items

Directions: Each of the questions or incomplete statements listed below is followed by several words or phrases. From these, you are to choose the one which answers the question or completes the statement correctly. Place the letter of that word or phrase (A, B, C, D, or E) in the numbered blank space on your answer sheet. The first item is answered as an example.

X. Which of these is *not* a primary purpose of a resume?

- A. to formulate in your mind what you have done
- B. to obtain an interview
- C. to serve as a sales tool within a prospective employer's company
- D. to develop an autobiography

14. Which source do you refer to if you use the direct calling method to look for a job?

- A. occupational handbook
- B. employment agency
- C. yellow pages
- D. want ads

15. Which of the following do you accomplish when you take a job application home to fill it out?

- A. You show sincere interest in the job.
- B. You can use your visit to return the application as a reminder that you are ready and able to come to work.
- C. You can work answers out on scrap paper, then neatly transfer them to the application.
- D. A and B
- E. all of the above

16. What is the best response to put down on an application form that asks for a desired starting wage?

- A. negotiable
- B. prevailing wage
- C. just put a slash through the answer area
- D. none of the above

17. Which two pieces of information come before extracurricular activities on a resume?

- A. personal data and education background
- B. personal data and honors/awards
- C. personal data and references
- D. experience and honors/awards

18. The opening paragraph in a letter of application contains

- A. the reason you are writing.
- B. the reason you feel you are qualified for the job.
- C. how you heard about the opening.
- D. A and C
- E. all of the above

19. Your personal data on a resume include all of the following except your

- A. birthdate.
- B. height and weight.
- C. marital status.
- D. honors/awards.

20. Which of the following is *not* listed as a resource when applying for a job?

- A. employment agency
- B. friends
- C. want ads
- D. company bulletin board

21. Which is considered the most appropriate answer when you are asked the reason for leaving your previous job?

    A. summer job
    B. did not like former boss
    C. too far to drive
    D. did not like work

22. Which of the following are the two ways you can organize your work history on a resume?

    A. by employer and by function
    B. by job and by employer
    C. by job and by function
    D. by employer and by location

23. Which statement about a resume is *incorrect?*

    A. Elaborate as much as possible.
    B. Avoid the "I" approach.
    C. Write an original letter, not a copy.
    D. Keep it short, and make sure you sign your letter.

Matching Items

Directions: The two columns below contain terms and definitions pertaining to job applications. Match each definition in the left column with the proper term in the right column. Place the identifying letter of the term in the blank space provided on the answer sheet. The first item is answered as an example.

Definitions	*Terms*
X. husband's or wife's name	A. dependents
	B. occupation
24. last place you lived before moving to where you live now	C. spouse
	D. temporary address
25. worker for a company	E. employer
	F. previous address
26. place where you are living for the time being	G. employee
	H. permanent address
27. people you support or help support	

Completion Items

Directions: Each of the statements below contains a blank near the end of the statement. You are to supply the missing word. Write your word in the large blank space on the answer sheet. The first item is answered as an example.

X. When you fill out an application form, be sure that your grammar, spelling, and ______________ are correct.

28. When you sign the blank on an application form, use your complete ______________ name.

29. The type of resume that lists information in reverse order is a ______________ resume.

30. When you write a letter of application, you should include your address and telephone number in the ______________ paragraph.

31-35. Listing Items

Directions: List in the blanks provided on the answer sheet the five people or places in a school where you can obtain information regarding jobs.

Sales 5304 Selling Today
Instructor: Judy Oliverius

Name ____________________

Date ____________________

IDENTIFY AND APPLY FOR A JOB
ANSWER SHEET

True-False

X. ___T___
1. ________
2. ________
3. ________
4. ________
5. ________
6. ________
7. ________
8. ________
9. ________
10. ________

Cluster True-False

X. ___F___
11. ________
12. ________
13. ________

Multiple-Choice

X. ___D___
14. ________
15. ________
16. ________
17. ________
18. ________
19. ________
20. ________
21. ________
22. ________
23. ________

Matching Items

X. ___C___
24. ________
25. ________
26. ________
27. ________

Completion Items

X. ___Punctuation___
28. ________________
29. ________________
30. ________________

Listing Items

31. ________________
32. ________________
33. ________________
34. ________________
35. ________________

*Sample Written Test: Communicate with Others**

* Edited with permission from materials prepared by JoAnn Kovach.

TEST-CONSTRUCTION BLUEPRINT

Givens: The need to effectively communicate on the job
Behavior: Communicate with others.
Standard: Communication demonstrates the elements of communication and takes into account personal communication styles.

Specific Objectives:

1. Identify and distinguish the elements of the communication process.	1, 5, 7, 8, 9, 14, 17, 30, 32
2. Identify the characteristics of the four personal communication styles.	3, 6, 11, 12, 13, 15, 19, 31
3. Identify the characteristics and uses of self-disclosure and feedback.	4, 16, 21, 24, 25, 26, 27, 28, 29, 33, 34, 35
4. Identify the ego states and transactions used in transactional analysis.	2, 10, 18, 20, 22, 23

Human Relations 12091
JoAnn Kovach

Communicate with Others

General Directions: Write your responses on the answer sheet. After you are finished with the exam, place your exam and the answer sheet on the front table.

I. True-False Items

Directions: Some of the following statements are true and some are false. If the statement is true, place a T in the corresponding blank on the answer sheet. If the statement is false, place an F in the blank. The first item is answered as an example.

__T__ X. Style flexing is adapting one's personal communication style to meet the needs of another person.

1. Effective communication takes place when the message is understood by both the initiator and the respondent.

2. An ulterior transaction occurs when the message says one thing but has another meaning.

3. People with a directive personal communication style are good listeners.

4. The sharing of one's reactions to another person's behavior is called feedback.

5. The nonverbal communication filters include emotions and role expectations.

6. People with the supportive personal communication style are low in sociability.

7. One way to become a better listener is to anticipate what the speaker is going to say next.

8. The responsibility of the receiver in the communication process is to understand what the initiator meant.

9. One example of a communication filter is semantics.

10. A person who has straight posture, a serious look, and a demanding tone of voice would most likely be in a Natural Child ego state.

II. Cluster True-False Items

Directions: The following incomplete statement is followed by phrases which complete the statement and make it true or false. If the phrase completes a true statement, place a T in the corresponding blank on the answer sheet. If the completed statement is false, place an F in the blank. The first item is answered as an example.

The emotive personal communication style is

__F__ X. impersonal.

11. high in sociability.

12. low in dominance.

13. action-oriented.

III. Multiple-Choice Items

Directions: Each of the questions or incomplete statements listed below is followed by several phrases. Choose the phrase which answers the question or completes the statement correctly. Place the letter of the correct phrase (A, B, C, or D) in the numbered blank space on the answer sheet. The first item is answered as an example.

D X. Attitudes are formed as a result of ________________.

A. reward and punishment received as a child
B. cultural influence
C. identification with role models
D. all of the above

14. Which of the following is *not* characteristic of information giving?

A. one-way communication
B. communication distributed via memos and bulletin boards
C. communication used to transmit facts and instructions
D. communication which provides for immediate feedback

15. Which personal communication style in the excess zone would not admit to being wrong?

A. supportive
B. emotive
C. directive
D. reflective

16. The Johari window is a model for ________________.

A. providing effective feedback
B. learning the secrets of other people
C. understanding the process of self-disclosure
D. enabling us to hide our feelings and attitudes

17. The communication process includes the ________________.

A. sender, filters, message, self-disclosure, and receiver
B. sender, filters, message, receiver, and feedback
C. sender, message, self-disclosure, receiver, and feedback
D. sender, filters, message, feedback, and self-disclosure

18. Which of the following could be described as an Adult response?

A. "Let's discuss the major options you have."
B. "Oh, boy, my pay raise came through!"
C. "Let me help you with those forms. You look tired."
D. "Young workers don't have what it takes to get the job done."

19. People high on the sociability continuum tend to ________________.

A. openly express their feelings
B. dominate others
C. be reserved and impersonal
D. seek control over others

20. Which of the following is *not* descriptive of transactional analysis?

A. theory of communication
B. based on the influence of one's subconscious mind
C. tool for understanding ourselves and achieving emotional control
D. study of the four basic ego states within everyone's personality

21. Which of the following is *not* a reward for the use of self-disclosure?

A. improvement in job status
B. increased self-awareness
C. reduction of stress
D. increased accuracy in communication

22. Which of the following is *not* characteristic of a complementary transaction?

   A. may take place between the same ego states
   B. produces an unexpected response to the message
   C. may take place between different ego states
   D. produces the predicted response to the message

23. Which of the following could be described as a Sympathetic Parent response?

   A. "You should have budgeted your time more carefully."
   B. "I need it soon. Let's set a new due date."
   C. "You really look upset. Is anything wrong?"
   D. "I told the committee you wouldn't have it on time."

Matching Items

Directions: The two columns below contain descriptions and terms pertaining to the Johari window. Match each description in the left-hand column with the proper term in the right-hand column. Place the letter of the proper term in the blank space provided on the answer sheet. The first item is answered as an example. Note: Responses in the right-hand column may be used more than once.

__B__ X.	reduced by encouraging others to give you feedback	A. open area
24.	information known to self but not to others	B. blind area
25.	least likely area to disappear	C. hidden area
26.	information known to self and to others	D. unknown area
27.	information not known to self or to others	
28.	making this area larger is the goal	
29.	information not known to self but to others	

V. Completion Items

Directions: Each of the statements below contains a blank at or near the end of the statement. You are to supply the missing word. Write the word in the large blank space provided on the answer sheet. The first item is answered as an example.

X. The study of personal space is called ____proxemics____.

30. The initiator of the communication process is called the ________________.

31. People who prefer an orderly work environment have a(n) ________________ personal communication style.

32. Beliefs based on emotions are known as ________________.

VI. Listing Items

Directions: List three guidelines for giving feedback to someone else. Place your answers on the corresponding blanks on the answer sheet. The first item is answered as an example.

X. focus on behavior rather than on the person

33. ________________________________

34. ________________________________

35. ________________________________

*Telemarketing Call Performance Checklist**

* Edited with permission from materials prepared by Gary Hager.

OBJECTIVE

Givens
Telephone, telephone numbers, script, product information, plain paper, pen, table, and chair

Behavior
Make a phone call, determine client's wants and needs, and make appointment for a sales representative.

Standard
According to the criteria presented on the performance checklist

CRITICAL	PROCESS (PROCEDURAL STEPS)	SAT.	UNSAT.	CRITERIA
	1. Assemble equipment.	1	0	Telephone, telephone numbers, script, product information, plain paper, pen, table, and chair
	2. Position telephone.	1	0	Within arms' length
	3. Choose telephone number.	1	0	Choose number from list.
	4. Dial telephone number.	1	0	Raise receiver and dial telephone number using the same sequence of digits.
	5. Wait for client to answer.	1	0	Listen for client to respond.
	6. Greet the client.	1	0	Use a tone of voice that is softer than a normal conversation voice.
	7. Read the greeting from the script.	1	0	Read the greeting with a smile on your face and with enthusiasm.
	8. Identify yourself and company to client.	1	0	State your name and the name of the company for which you work.
	9. Read the attention-getting statement from script.	1	0	Read statement with enthusiasm and a clear voice.
	10. Wait for client to respond.	1	0	Caller lets client make a statement.
	11. Ask client first question to determine needs and wants.	1	0	Ask client first question from script.
	12. Let client respond to individual questions.	1	0	Listen for information, writing down the information the client gives.
	13. Ask another question from the script.	1	0	Ask question that follows client's answer to determine specific want or need.
	14. Repeat steps 12 and 13.	1	0	Return to steps 12 and 13, questioning client to find two to four specific needs or wants.
	15. Begin to close telephone call.	1	0	Review the client's needs or wants that you have written on the piece of paper. Use a clear voice.
	16. Listen for the client to respond	1	0	Listen for the client to respond to make changes of specific wants or needs.
	17. Set appointment for client to meet with sales representative.	1	0	Set the appointment date, time, and place, and verify the name of client and name of sales representative.
	18. Thank client.	1	0	Use a "thank you" from the script. Use a clear and enthusiastic voice.
	19. Place receiver on phone.	1	0	Place receiver on phone cradle.
	20. Make note for sales representative.	1	0	Using a 5 × 7 card, write the specific two or four wants or needs information on the card plus the information of the appointment.

Total score ________

Minimum acceptable score = 19

*Separate from a Child Performance Checklist**

* Edited with permission from materials prepared by Jan MacKenthun.

OBJECTIVE

Givens
A parent, his or her child, and a playroom environment

Behavior
Separate from child.

Standard
A satisfactory score on the separation performance checklist

CRITICAL	PROCESS (PROCEDURAL STEPS)	SAT.	UNSAT.	CRITERIA
*	1. Approach child.	1	0	Parent is within 2 to 3 feet of child.
	2. Bend to the child's level.	1	0	Parent sits, kneels, or crouches near child.
	3. Establish eye contact.	1	0	Parent looks at child's face and gives the child full attention.
	4. Touch child.	1	0	Parent has hand(s) or arm(s) on or around child.
*	5. Tell child you are leaving.	1	0	Parent indicates that it is time to separate (e.g., "I'm leaving . . . .")
	6. Tell child where you are going.	1	0	Parent indicates verbally or points to where she or he will be.
	7. Tell child when you will return.	1	0	Parent indicates how long the separation will be.
	8. Tell child who will be there for him or her.	1	0	Parent draws the child's attention to the caretaker who will be there.
	9. Allow the child to respond.	1	0	Parent responds to child's questions or statements or waits a few seconds to be sure the child knows what will happen.
	10. Say parting words.	1	0	Parent says "good-bye," "see you later," "have fun," or similar words.
	11. Give parting touch.	1	0	Parent hugs, kisses, or pats child.
*	12. Leave.	1	0	Parent goes out the door.

Total score ________

Minimum acceptable score = 9

Glossary

Advisory committee A group of individuals which is assembled to advise people developing or operating an instructional program.

Affective behavior A behavior which involves visible actions which communicate emotional tones toward something (e.g., a person, an object, a thing, or a concept).

Apperception The process of perceiving and understanding something in terms of previous experience.

BASIC Acronym for "Beginners' All-purpose Symbolic Instruction Code," a high-level computer language invented by Kemeney and Kurtz at Dartmouth College in 1963.

Behavior A visible action of an individual which may or may not be the result of a visible process leading to that action.

Behavior analysis The process of identifying and classifying behaviors.

Behavior detailing The procedure of identifying the process and knowledge base that must be taught and that a learner must master in order to perform a behavior (process and knowledge-base identification).

Behavior format The format for writing a behavior which includes: (1) an action verb, (2) what is acted upon, and (3) modifying information.

Behavioral objective (learning objective) The goal of an instructional lesson containing: (1) givens, (2) the behavior, and (3) the expected standard of performance.

Branching sequence Behaviors sequenced so there is either more than one way to arrive at a particular behavior, or more than one behavior which can be the destination from a behavior (analogous to tree branches and trunk).

Case study A presentation to learners of a detailed real-life example which occurred in the past.

Checklist An instrument used to judge a performance or a product on scales with two categories (e.g., satisfactory versus unsatisfactory, good versus bad).

COBOL Acronym for "COmmon Business-Oriented Language." It is a high-level computer language developed in the early 1960s.

Cognitive behavior A behavior which involves primarily the manipulation of information resulting in visible action.

Common-element behaviors Behaviors which require common content to learn and apply (e.g., common process and/or common knowledge base).

Computer-assisted instruction (CAI) Instruction presented to learners through a computer.

Computer-assisted instruction (CAI) format A format in which the learner manages the delivery of a lesson by interacting with a computer program.

Conceptual sequence Instruction organized around a conceptual structure of a content area, as contrasted with concern for how the behaviors are utilized in the real world (e.g., geometry organized around theorems, postulates, and axioms). (Compare with *Empirical sequence.*)

Content analysis The process of identifying the specific content from a content area to be taught within a program. Content analysis has three stages: (1) function identification, (2) behavior identification, and (3) behavior detailing.

Content-dependent behaviors Behaviors that are related because of relationships between the content to be taught to learn them. Two types of content dependency are common-element dependency and prerequisite dependency.

Content selection The process of selecting the behaviors to be taught within a program from a total set of possible behaviors.

Content sequencing The process of arranging the behaviors to be taught in an instructional program into the order in which they will be taught.

Contingent behaviors Behaviors in which the output from performing one behavior becomes the input for the next behavior.

Criteria The bases for judging whether a learner has performed correctly.

Critical step A performance step that must be performed with 100 percent accuracy or the performance will be stopped.

Demonstration An accurate showing of the precise actions necessary to perform a behavior.

Dependent behaviors Behaviors that must be taught in a certain order because they build upon one another or because they are usually performed together.

Discussion An instructor-controlled process of people interacting and sharing information and experiences related to an objective.

Drill program A program that teaches by presenting a selection of questions or problems (e.g., arithmetic problems or vocabulary development) repeatedly until the learner answers or solves them at some predetermined level of proficiency.

Empirical sequence Organization of behaviors based on how phenomena occur in the real world (e.g., where they are actually used; actual relationships among things, events, and people). (Compare with *Conceptual sequence.*)

Error Differences in scores on evaluation instruments that are due to factors other than differences in the amount of learning.

Evaluation The process of obtaining information about the extent of learner mastery.

Evaluation procedures Procedures for determining learning progress.

Feedback The process of communicating interpreted results and encouragement to learners.

Field trip A visit to an actual location where learners can observe the real-world application of processes they are learning.

Fixed-paced instruction Instruction which requires learners to proceed at a given rate of speed. It is often associated with group instruction in which individuals proceed at the pace of the group.

Flowcharting The process of developing a graphic chart which presents the flow of instruction within a program.

Formal education Educational activity focused at accomplishing a specific educational goal.

FORTRAN Acronym for "FORmula TRANslation." It is a high-level computer language originally developed in 1956 for mathematical processing of scientific and engineering data.

Frame A unit of information in programmed instruction that contains the amount of information which can or should be presented to the learner before requiring some sort of response by which learning can be assessed.

Functions Major groupings of behaviors that are usually performed together. They represent major activity subdivisions within a content area.

Game program (instructional) A program, often computerized, which may or may not simulate reality but which is characterized by providing the learner with entertaining challenges while teaching an instructional component.

Givens Statement of what will be needed to perform a behavior in the role for which learners are being prepared (e.g., tools, equipment, and environment).

Graphic pad A device on which graphic images can be drawn and stored in a computer.

Hardware The physical devices associated with a computer.

Independent behaviors Behaviors which can be taught at any time during the program because they are not the basis for learning other behaviors in the program and/or because they are not performed with other behaviors.

Individualized instruction Instruction that is designed to meet the specific needs of each individual learner. Although it is often associated with modularized instruction, it can be a characteristic of any instructional format.

Informal education Educational activity through which a person might learn, but which is not focused on a specific educational goal.

Input devices Devices attached to a computer which communicate information to the computer.

Instructional media Software, hardware, and personnel which serve as modes of communication to convey content to learners (e.g., a videotape player, a computer, or a live instructor).

Instructional methods Instructional procedures or processes used to present content to learners (e.g., a lecture or a demonstration).

Joystick A computer input device, like the control lever of an airplane, which provides two-dimensional control information to a computer.

Knowledge-base identification The process of determining the information a person "needs to know" in order to meaningfully perform and/or apply a behavior.

Knowledge evaluations Procedures used to determine the information possessed by the learner (e.g., written tests, learner self-checks, or oral questioning).

Learning guide A list of the learning steps to be followed by the learner during the completion of a lesson and a list of the learning resources which are to be used at each step.

Learning package The lesson plans and learning resources associated with a lesson delivery unit which are presented to learners as one instructional unit.

Learning resource A medium used to accomplish a particular portion of a lesson (e.g., a transparency, a videotape, or a textbook).

Learning step A directive which indicates the action a learner is to take.

Lecture A verbal presentation of information.

Lesson A unit of instruction which contains all of the instruction and evaluation necessary to teach a behavior and to verify performance capability.

Lesson delivery format An instructional management system used to manage the interaction of learners and learning resources throughout a lesson to bring about learning (e.g., traditional instruction, CAI, modularized instruction, and programmed instruction).

Lesson delivery unit A combination of one or more

behaviors that are taught together using one composite lesson plan.

Lesson flow The sequence of stages within a lesson.

Lesson plan A list of steps developed to teach learners to perform one behavior, or the group of behaviors contained in a lesson delivery unit and the learning resources that will be used at each step. Lesson plans take different forms, depending upon the delivery format used.

Lesson structure The organization of a lesson, including lesson flow; content to be taught, practiced, or evaluated; and the methods and media that will be used to implement the lesson.

Lesson structuring The process of developing a general plan for how a lesson will be pedagogically organized for delivery to the learners and evaluated.

Light pen A computer input device that is used to provide information to computers by pointing to locations on a video display screen.

Linear sequencing Behaviors sequenced so a behavior can be arrived at from only one other behavior.

LOGO A computer language developed at the Massachusetts Institute of Technology by Papert in 1969 to teach children reasoning; it is based on Piaget's theory of learning.

Machine language A computer language that is machine specific and uses only numbers to express commands. It is the fastest class of computer languages to execute.

Management vehicle A mechanism for directing the presentation of resources to learners (e.g., print material and/or a computer).

Mastery The ability to perform a desired behavior to a specified standard.

Meaningful learning Learning in which people can see the relationships between the various behaviors taught, and how they add up to a logical, meaningful whole.

Model A miniature representation of something.

MODEM An acronym for a "MODulator-DEModulator," which is a computer hardware device that allows signals to be transmitted from one computer to another over communication networks.

Modularized instruction format A format in which the learner manages the delivery of the lesson by following a learning guide written as directions to the learner.

Module The directions and learning materials necessary to achieve a learning objective.

Monitor A device connected to a computer that displays output on a screen; similar to a television.

Mouse A computer input device that is used to position a cursor on a video display screen by moving a small box across a flat surface.

MS-DOS An acronym for "MicroSoft Disk Operating System". The system is used with IBM PCs and compatibles.

Need-to-know information Information which is essential to the meaningful completion of the process of performing a behavior.

Oral tutorial questioning The process of asking learners questions during the learning process to determine the extent of mastery of a knowledge base.

Output devices Devices attached to a computer that communicate information from the computer.

PASCAL A high-level computer language developed in 1971 at the University of California at San Diego which is well-suited to tasks involving graphics, numerical operations, and character manipulations.

Pedagogy The art, science, or profession of teaching.

Percentage score Expression of a raw score as a percentage of the total possible raw-score points.

Performance-based instructional design (PBID) system An integrated system for developing and evaluating instruction aimed at ensuring performance capability. The PBID system is organized into components that parallel the decision making of an instructional designer.

Performance test An instrument designed to evaluate a person's performance of a desired process.

Peripheral devices Devices which are separate from, but attached to, the central processing unit of a computer (e.g., a separate monitor or a printer).

PILOT Acronym for "Programmed Inquiry Learning Or Teaching," which is a computer language designed for interactive computer-assisted instruction.

Posttests Tests administered to learners after they have taken part in instruction.

Practice The planned learner application of what has been taught.

Prerequisite behavior A behavior which is required in order to perform a subsequent behavior, or a behavior which a learner is expected to have developed prior to entering an instructional program.

Pretests Tests administered to learners before they take part in instruction.

Process detailing The outlining of the procedural steps or actions necessary to perform a behavior.

Process evaluations Procedures used to determine if a person can perform a desired behavior (e.g., a performance test and a product test).

Product test An instrument designed to evaluate the quality of a product produced as the result of performing a process.

Program (computer) A series of instructions to a computer that tell it to execute operations to accomplish a purpose.

Program description A description of the intent of an instructional program. It defines the content area to be taught and the context within which that content is expected to be taught.

Programmed instruction format A format in which the learner manages the delivery of a lesson by completing a printed, programmed text that presents instruction in small steps with immediate feedback and freedom on the part of the learner to vary the rate of instruction.

Proximate behaviors Behaviors that occur together in the real world or in proximity to one another.

Psychomotor behavior A behavior which involves primarily visible physical manipulations.

Questioning The process of presenting learners with questions about what has been taught and having them present answers.

Rating scale An observation instrument used to judge a performance or product on a scale with more than two categories (e.g., above average, average, and below average).

Raw score The score obtained by counting the number of points earned on a testing instrument.

Reading An instructional method which directs learners to read written material directed at an instructional objective.

Role playing An instructional method for involving learners in interactions simulating real-life situations.

Rote-learning Learning through repetition without understanding.

Screen A full computer monitor picture of information. The basic unit of information provided by a computer with a single activation of the computer.

Screen sequence A flowchart of screens that accompanies a CAI screen storyboard.

Self-check An evaluation administered by the learner to self-diagnose learning progress.

Self-paced instruction Instruction through which individuals can proceed at their own pace.

Semiskilled workers Workers having or requiring less training than skilled labor and more than unskilled labor.

Simulation A realistic imitation of a real-world situation in a learning environment.

Skill The ability to use one's knowledge effectively and readily in execution and performance.

Skilled workers Workers or labor with skill and training in a particular occupation, craft, or trade.

Software (computer) The programs that contain instructions which control a computer.

Standard The basis for judging whether a behavior has been performed adequately.

Storyboard The written text and anticipated graphics that will be used to present content through a CAI program.

Structured education Education using content and procedures which are planned in advance.

System A regularly interacting or interdependent group of items forming a unified whole.

Task A piece of work assigned to be done.

Teaching point An incremental portion of information used to teach a behavior through programmed instruction or CAI.

Test A procedure used to prove or disprove that something has met a standard.

Test-construction blueprint A worksheet that allows a designer to indicate which test items measure which knowledge-base objectives.

Traditional instruction format A format in which the instructor manages the delivery of the lesson by following a lesson plan written as directions to the instructor.

Tutorial observation The process of observing learners during the learning process to determine the extent of their mastery of performing a behavior.

Tutorial program A CAI program that teaches by presenting information, presenting questions to the learner, and making decisions based on learner comprehension whether to move on to new information or to engage in review and remediation.

Tutorial questioning The process of asking learners questions during the learning process to determine the extent of mastery of a knowledge base.

Unskilled Not skilled in a specified branch of work: lacking technical training.

Unstructured education Education in which the content and procedures are not planned in advance.

User A person who utilizes a computer to accomplish a purpose.

Validation The process of verifying judgments.

Videodisk (laser disk) A computer memory device in the form of a movable platter on which video images, audio signals, and computer programs are stored.

Index

A+, 127
Action verb, 34–35, 63
Advanced organizer, 74
Advisory committee, 39, 46–47, 229
Affective behavior, 82, 229
  analysis of, 41–43
  considered in evolution of performance-based instruction, 9–12
  defined, 4, 34–36
  general application of PBID to teaching of, 4, 16, 18, 19, 22, 25
  lesson structuring for, 72, 76–77, 101
  performance tests to evaluate, 160–164
  process detailing for, 63–66
Alessi, S. M., 116–117, 130
Allen, Charles R., 7–8, 10
American Institute for Learning, 9
Analysis chart, 18–19, 40–43
Anderson, Sharon R., 190
Apperceptive mass, 7, 229
Application-level test items, 145–146
Application programs, 127–128
Apprenticeship, 5–6, 10
Artificial feedback, 98–99
Assembly code, 128–129
Audiovisual media, 89
Ausubel, D. P., 52, 73, 74
Authoring systems, 128–130
Auxiliary knowledge, 8

Bacon, Sir Francis, 6
BASIC, 128, 229
Behavior analysis, 17–19, 34, 38–42, 67, 229
Behavior detailing, 18–20, 34, 61–67
  determining how far to break down behaviors, 66–67
  knowledge-base identification, 19, 20, 62, 65–67, 144, 230
  process detailing, 19, 20, 62–65, 67
Behavior listing, 17, 19, 42–43
Behavior selection (*see* Content selection)
Behavior types, 4, 9, 34–35
    (*See also* Affective behavior; Cognitive behavior; Psychomotor behavior)
Behavioral objective, 9, 113
  development of, 22, 25, 71–73
  in evaluation, 156–164, 168–172
  statement of, 73–74
Bloom, Benjamin, 9, 35, 65, 144
Body language, 35–36
Branching programming, 114–115
Branching sequence, 58, 229
Brown, Elmer Ellsworth, 6
Butler, F. Coit, 9, 10, 54
BYTE, 127

CAI (*see* Computer-assisted instruction)
Carroll, John B., 10
Case study, 85, 229
CBVE (competency-based vocational education), 10–11
Central processor, 126
Chart, 87
Chase, W. G., 73
Checklist, 156, 164, 171, 229
Chi, M. T. H., 73
Claus, Calvin K., 187–189
CMI (computer-managed instruction), 116
COBOL, 118, 128–129, 229
Cognitive behavior, 39, 63, 82, 229
  analysis of, 42–43
  considered in evolution of performance-based instruction, 9, 10, 12
  defined, 4, 34, 35
  general application of PBID to teaching of, 4, 16, 18, 19, 22, 25
  lesson structuring for, 72, 76–77, 100, 113, 122
  performance tests to evaluate, 160, 162–163
  process detailing for, 63–65
Common content elements, 54
Common-element dependency, 55–58, 229
Competency-based instruction, 4, 10–12
Competency-based vocational educational (CBVE), 10–11
Compiler, 128
Completion items in tests, 150
Component skills, 37
Comprehension-level test items, 144–145
Comprehensiveness of evaluation instrument, 139
Computer-assisted instruction (CAI), 4, 12, 21, 23, 70, 91, 229
  formatting of, 24–25, 104–106, 109, 112–113, 117–122, 229
  introduction to, 116–117
  programming of, 116, 126–133
  and selection of lesson delivery format, 80–83
  types of, 116
Computer-managed instruction (CMI), 116
Conceptual systems of content sequencing, 53
Conference feedback procedure, 98
Content analysis, 16–19, 25, 33–43, 61–67, 229
  behavior analysis in, 17–19, 34, 38–42, 67, 229
  behavior detailing in, 18, 20, 34, 61–67
  behavior listing in , 17, 19, 42–43
  function identification in, 17–19, 34, 36–38, 67
  stating behaviors in, 34–35
  types of behavior, 35–36
Content area, 17, 28–29, 39
Content dependency, 55–59, 229
Content organization in screen design, 130–131
Content selection, 16, 19–20, 25, 45–49, 229
  costs and behavior selection, 49
  procedure for selecting behaviors, 46–48

Content selection *(continued)*
program prerequisites versus behaviors to be taught, 48–49
validating priority judgments, 48
Content sequencing, 16, 20–21, 25, 51–59
determining dependency among behaviors, 56–57
developing sequence charts, 58–59
efficiency and, 52–53, 58, 59
meaning and, 52–54, 59
sequencing behaviors, 57–58
sequencing procedures, 54–56
Content specification, 22, 23, 25, 70, 75–77
Context, instructional, 17, 29–31
Contingent dependency, 55–58, 229
Control Data Corporation, 126
Conventions in screen design, 131–132
Core course, 21, 52, 57
Criterion-referenced standard, 94–95, 178
Criterion tests, 9–10
Critical step, 157
Cutaway, 86

Decisions, type of, 37
Demonstration as instructional method, 74, 84, 229
Density in screen design, 130–131
Dependency matrix, 56–58
Dependent behaviors, 20–21, 54–58, 229
Developmental level, 54
Diagnostic evaluation, 5
Directive verb (*see* Action verb)
Discrimination of evaluation instrument, 139–140
Discussion as instructional method, 84, 229
Disk operating system (DOS), 127
Distributive education, 9
DOS (disk operating system), 127
Drill, 85, 116, 230
Duties, 34, 36

Educable mentally retarded (EMR), 30
Efficiency of instruction, 52–53, 58, 59, 107–109
Empirical sequence, 53–54, 230
EMR (educable mentally retarded), 30
Error in evaluation, 136–139, 140, 230
Essay items in tests, 151
Evaluation error, 137–139
Evaluation procedures, 4, 8, 16, 135–185, 229
characteristics of good, 139–140
evaluation error, 137–139
formality of, 94–95
goal of, 136
informal, 156, 173–176
introduction to development of, 135–141
knowledge-base, 24, 95–96, 143–153
need for multiple, 139
performance tests, 24, 72–73, 155–165
process evaluation, 24, 72–75, 95–97
product tests, 4, 70, 77, 83, 168–172
sample tests, 213–223
selection of, 22–25, 70, 94–98, 101
summarizing and reporting learner progress, 177–185
timing and intent of, 136–137

Experimentation, 6
Explicit lesson plan, 105–107
Exploration programs, 29, 30

Factory system, 6
Feedback, 5, 75, 230
artificial, 98–99
conference procedure, 98
in informal evaluation, 174–176
natural, 98–99
negative, 99, 101
neutral, 99, 101
positive, 99, 101
selection of procedures, 22, 24–25, 70, 98–101
self-determined procedure, 98, 144, 174, 176
tutorial questioning and observation, 174–175
types of, 98–101
Field trip, 85, 230
Fixed-paced instruction, 230
Florida, State of, Division of Vocational, Adult, and Community Education, 10–11
Flowchart, 87–88, 106, 117–121, 230
Formatting (*see* Lesson delivery format)
FORTRAN, 128–129, 230
Frame, 105, 106, 112–116, 230
Frequency of use criterion, 46, 47
Friesen, Paul A., 114, 115
Fryklund, Verne C., 8, 10
Function identification, 17–19, 34, 36–38, 67
Functions, 34, 36–39, 43, 230

Gagné, Robert M., 9
Game program (instructional), 116, 230
Givens, 71, 73, 157, 230
Graphic pad, 126, 230
Graphics:
as instructional medium, 87–88
in screen design, 130–131
Guessing error in evaluation, 138–139

Hager, Gary, 224–225
Hardware, 85, 90–91, 117, 126–127, 230
Herbart, Johann Friedrich, 7–8, 12, 21, 52, 73
Herbartian Lesson, 7–8, 12
Highlighting in screen design, 131

Implicit lesson plan, 105–106
InCider, 127
Independent behaviors, 20–21, 54–55, 230
Individualized instruction, 10, 230
Industrial age, 6–8, 11, 12
Industrial revolution, 6
Industrial schools, 6
Informal evaluation, 156, 173–176
development procedures, 174–175
goal of, 174
self-checks, 144, 174, 176
tutorial questioning and observation, 144, 174–176
Information age, 11–12

Information topics, 8
Initial preparation, 29
Input devices, 126, 230
Institutional setting, 17, 29, 30
Instructional content, 17, 28–29, 39
Instructional context, 17, 29–31
Instructional design, 4–5, 9, 11
Instructional media, 22, 23, 25, 83–91, 230
Instructional methods, 22, 23, 25, 83–91, 230
Instructional objective, 34
Instructional program, 4, 17
Instructional setting, 17, 29, 30
Instructional Systems Design (ISD), 9
Instructional time, 46, 47
Instrument error in evaluation, 137–138
Interactive video segments, 131–132
Introduction to (IBM) microcomputer systems: PBID sample components, 201–212
ISD (Instructional Systems Design), 9
Item order in tests, 150

Job analysis, 9
Job description, 38
Job elements, 8
Joystick, 126, 230

Karnes, M. Ray, 8
Knaak, W. C., 4, 10, 14, 144, 179
Knowledge-base evaluations, 24, 95–96, 143–153, 230
  assembling a test, 152–153
  constructing test items, 146–152
  levels of test items, 144–146
  test-construction blueprint, 146
Knowledge-base identification, 19, 20, 62, 65–67, 144, 230
Knowledge-level test items, 144
Kovach, JoAnn, 219–223

Laser disk, 232
Learner characteristics, 17, 29–31, 54
Learner error, 137
learner progress, summarizing and reporting, 177–185
  follow-up studies, 183–185
  mastery approach, 178–181, 185
  multiple-criterion approach, 181–182, 185
  based on expert judgment, 180–181
  based on people practicing successfully, 179–180
  postinstruction progress, 183–184
  purpose, 178, 185
  summative evaluation, 184
  time-period approach, 182–183, 185
Learning guide, 106–109, 230
Learning module, 10
Learning package, 10, 108–109, 230
Learning process, 54
Learning resource, 82–83, 104–105, 116, 230
Lecture, 84, 230
Legal office procedures: PBID sample components, 190–200
Length of program, 17, 29, 46, 47
Lesson, 70, 230
Lesson delivery format, 16, 24–25, 70, 103–133, 230
  combining separate behaviors into larger units, 107–109
Lesson delivery format *(continued)*
  explicit and implicit lesson plans, 105–106
  formatting computer-assisted instruction, 117–122
  formatting modularized instruction, 106
  formatting programmed instruction, 113–117
  formatting traditional instruction, 106
  learning resources and, 81–83, 104–105, 116
  lesson management, 81–82
  programming computer-assisted instruction, 126–133
  selection of, 21–23, 25, 70, 80–83
  uniformity of instruction and performance assurance, 81, 83
Lesson delivery unit, 21, 36, 105, 230
  learning packages, 108–109
  multiple-behavior, 108
Lesson flow, 22–23, 25, 70, 73–75, 106, 230
Lesson management, 81–82
Lesson plan, 105, 231
  differences in, 112–113
  explicit versus implicit, 105–106
  instructor-oriented, 106
  learner-oriented, 107
  learning guide, 106–107
Lesson structuring, 16, 21–25, 69–101
  developing behavioral objectives, 22, 25, 70–73
  developing lesson flow, 22–23, 25, 70, 73–75
  selection:
    of evaluation procedures, 22–25, 70, 94–98
    of feedback procedures, 22, 24–25, 70, 98–101
    of lesson delivery format, 21–23, 25, 70, 80–83
    of methods and media, 22, 23, 25, 70, 83–91
  specifying content to be taught, 22, 23, 25, 70, 75–77
Level of program, 17, 29
Light pen, 126, 131
Linear programming, 114–115
Linear sequence, 58–59
Listing items in tests, 150

McGraw-Hill Interactive Authoring System (MHIAS), 118, 120, 128–129
Machine language, 128–129, 231
MacKenthun, Jan, 226–227
Mainframe computer, 126
Management vehicle, 231
Mass labor, 6
Mass production, 6
Mastery learning, 10–11, 95, 178–181, 231
Matching items in tests, 149
Meaningful learning, 17, 21, 52–54, 231
Media, instructional, 83–91
Media purpose, 85–91
Memorization, 6, 7, 85
Methods, instructional, 23, 83–91
MHIAS (*see* McGraw-Hill Interactive Authoring System)
Micheels, William J., 8
Microcomputer, 126, 127
Mockup, 86
Model, 86, 231
MODEM, 231
Modularized instruction, 12, 21, 70, 91, 231
  formatting of, 24–25, 104–107, 109, 112–113
  and selection of lesson delivery format, 80–83

Module, 231
(*See also* Learning module; Modularized instruction)
Monitor, 126, 231
Motion as media element, 85, 87–88
Mouse, 126, 231
MS-DOS (MicroSoft Disk Operating System), 127, 231
Multiple-behavior lesson delivery units, 108
Multiple-choice items in tests, 147–149

National Center for Educational Statistics, 29
National College Verb List, 187–189
Natural feedback, 98–99
Need-to-know information, 19, 65–66, 74, 231
Needs assessment, 4, 28
Negative feedback, 99, 101
Neutral feedback, 99, 101
"Nice to know" information, 66
916 Area Vocational-Technical Institute, 10
Norm-referenced standard, 94–95, 178

Object identification items in tests, 151–152
Objective test items, 147–149
Objectivity of evaluation instrument, 139
Objects as media element, 85–89
Occupational competencies, 10–11
Occupational education, 5–13
Oliverius, Judy, 213–218
Operating systems, 127
Oral tutorial questioning, 144, 174–176, 231, 232
Output devices, 126, 231

Package learning guide, 108–109
PASCAL, 118, 128–129, 231
PBID (*see* Performance-based instructional design)
PC World, 127
Pedagogy, 12, 231
Percentage score, 178, 231
Performance-based instructional design (PBID):
behavior detailing in, 18–20, 61–67
components of, 4–5, 17–25
content analysis in, 16–19, 25, 33–43, 61–67, 229
content selection in, 16, 19–20, 25, 45–49, 229
content sequencing in, 16, 20–21, 25, 51–59
evaluation and feedback procedures in, 16, 25, 135–185
intent of, 16–17
lesson delivery format in, 16, 24–25, 70, 103–133
lesson structuring in, 16, 21–25, 69–101
program description in, 16, 17, 25, 27–32
as system, 16
Performance-based lesson flow, 22, 73–75
Performance capability, 4, 70, 77, 83, 167–172
Performance checklists, samples:
separate from a child, 226–227
telemarketing call, 224–225
Performance tests, 24, 72–73, 155–165, 231
affective, 160–164
assignments, 162–164
checklists in, 156, 164
cognitive, 160, 162–163
criteria in, 158–159
critical steps in, 159

Performance tests *(continued)*
development procedures, 156–162, 164
minimum acceptable score in, 159
objective in, 157–164
performance time in, 159
process steps in, 157–158
psychomotor, 157–159, 162–163
rating scales in, 156, 164
Peripheral devices, 126, 231
PI (*see* Programmed instruction)
Piaget, Jean, 54
Pie chart, 87
PILOT, 128–129, 231
PLATO, 126
Positive feedback, 99, 101
Posner, G. J., 53–54
Posttesting, 137, 231
Potential future need, 46
Practice of behavior, 74, 85, 231
Prerequisite behavior, 30, 31, 48–49, 54–58, 231
Prerequisite dependency, 55–58
Pretesting, 136–137, 231
Priority rankings of behaviors, 46–48
Problems:
functions organized around, 37
as test items, 151–152
Process detailing, 19, 20, 62–65, 67, 231
process-detailing approaches, 64–65
stating the process, 63–64
types of processes, 62–63
Process evaluation, 24, 72–75, 95–97, 156, 168, 231
(*See also* Performance tests; Product test)
Process steps, 63–64
Processes, types of, 62–63
Product test, 24, 72–73, 156, 167–172, 231
assignment, 170
criteria in, 169
development procedures, 168–170
instructor checkpoints, 170–171
minimum acceptable score in, 170
objective in, 168–172
performance time in, 168
product characteristics in, 169
rating scales in, 171–172
scoring procedure in, 169
Program description, 16, 17, 25, 27–32
components of, 28–31
content area, 17, 28–29
context, 17, 29–31
validation of, 31
Program focus, 17, 29–30
Program length, 17, 29, 46, 47
Programmed instruction, 4, 12, 21, 70, 91, 232
formatting of, 24–25, 104–106, 109, 112–117
and selection of lesson delivery format, 80–83
Programmed texts, 114–116
Programming computer-based instruction, 116, 126–133
communicating with the computer, 126
developing screens, 130–132
methods of authoring software, 127–130
selecting hardware, 126–127
Programming languages, 128–129
Proximate dependency, 55–58, 232

Psychomotor behavior, 63, 82, 232
  analysis of, 41–43
  considered in evolution of performance-based instruction, 8–12
  defined, 4, 34, 35
  general application of PBID to teaching of, 4, 16–19, 22, 25
  lesson structuring for, 71, 75, 77, 99, 122
  performance tests to evaluate, 157–159, 162–163
  process detailing for, 63–65
Pucel, D. J., 4, 10, 14, 121, 144, 179

Questioning as instructional method, 84, 232

Rating scale, 156, 164, 171–172, 232
Rationale for lesson, 73–74
Raw score, 178, 232
Reading as instructional method, 84, 232
Relationships to other programs, 17, 29, 30
Reliability of evaluation instrument, 140
Remediation, 29, 30
Retraining, 29–30
Role playing, 84–85, 232
Role-related affective behaviors, 41–42
Rote learning, 7, 52, 85, 232

Schematic drawing, 87–88
Scorer error in evaluation, 138
Screens, 112, 117, 118, 121, 130–132, 232
Scrolling, 131
Self-check (*see* Self-determined feedback procedure)
Self-determined feedback procedure, 98, 144, 174, 176, 232
Self-paced instruction, 232
Sequence chart, 58–59
Sequencing (*see* Content sequencing)
Service occupations, 11
Simulation, 232
  computer-based, 116
  as instructional method, 84
Software, 85, 90–91, 117, 126, 232
  for computer-assisted instruction, 126–132
  methods of authoring, 127–129
Sound as media element, 85, 87
Special learner characteristics, 17, 29–31
Standard for behavioral objective, 71–73, 157, 168, 232
Steam engine, 6
Storyboard, 117, 119–121, 232
Strassman, Paul, 11
Strike, K. A., 53–54
Structured education, 232
Subjective test items, 147–150
Subprogram, computer, 117–121
Systems, 37, 232
Systems approach, 8–9

Task analysis, 9–10, 17, 34
Task detailing, 34
Teaching points, 113, 115, 117, 118, 232
Test, 8, 232
  computer-based, 116
  (*see also* Evaluation procedures)
Test-construction blueprint, 146, 232
Text writing in screen design, 131
Trade analysis, 9
Traditional instruction. 4, 12, 21, 23, 70, 91, 232
  formatting of, 24, 104–106, 109, 112–113
  and selection of lesson delivery format, 80–83
Trollip, S. R., 116–117, 130
True-false items in tests, 147
Tutorial, computer-based, 116, 232
Tutorial questioning and observation, 144, 174–176, 232

Uniformity of instruction, 81, 83
Unit of instruction, 7
  (*See also* Lesson delivery unit)
U.S. Bureau of Labor Statistics, 11
U.S. Department of the Air Force, 9, 54, 55
U.S. Department of Labor, 29
Unstructured education, 232
Updating, 29, 30

Validation:
  of behaviors, 40
  of evaluation instruments, 138
  of priority judgments, 48
  of program description, 31
Vestibule schools, 6
Videodisk, 126, 232
Visual images as media elements, 85–89
Vocational education, 5–13

Words as media element, 85–86
Work sampling programs, 29, 30

Zuck, Gene, 201